The British at
INDIANAPOLIS

Ian Wagstaff

Other great books from Veloce –

Speedpro Series
4-cylinder Engine – How to Blueprint & Build a Short Block For High Performance (Hammill)
Alfa Romeo DOHC High-performance Manual (Kartalamakis)
Alfa Romeo V6 Engine High-performance Manual (Kartalamakis)
BMC 998cc A-series Engine – How to Power Tune (Hammill)
1275cc A-series High-performance Manual (Hammill)
Camshafts – How to Choose & Time Them For Maximum Power (Hammill)
Competition Car Datalogging Manual, The (Templeman)
Cylinder Heads – How to Build, Modify & Power Tune Updated & Revised Edition (Burgess & Gollan)
Distributor-type Ignition Systems – How to Build & Power Tune New 3rd Edition (Hammill)
Fast Road Car – How to Plan and Build Revised & Updated Colour New Edition (Stapleton)
Ford SOHC 'Pinto' & Sierra Cosworth DOHC Engines – How to Power Tune Updated & Enlarged Edition (Hammill)
Ford V8 – How to Power Tune Small Block Engines (Hammill)
Harley-Davidson Evolution Engines – How to Build & Power Tune (Hammill)
Holley Carburetors – How to Build & Power Tune Revised & Updated Edition (Hammill)
Honda Civic Type R, The – High-Performance Manual (Cowland & Clifford)
Jaguar XK Engines – How to Power Tune Revised & Updated Colour Edition (Hammill)
Land Rover Discovery, Defender & Range Rover – How to Modify Coil Sprung Models for High Performance & Off-Road Action (Hosier)
MG Midget & Austin-Healey Sprite – How to Power Tune New 3rd Edition (Stapleton)
MGB 4-cylinder Engine – How to Power Tune (Burgess)
MGB V8 Power – How to Give Your, Third Colour Edition (Williams)
MGB, MGC & MGB V8 – How to Improve New 2nd Edition (Williams)
Mini Engines – How to Power Tune On a Small Budget Colour Edition (Hammill)
Motorcycle-engined Racing Car – How to Build (Pashley)
Motorsport – Getting Started in (Collins)
Nissan GT-R High-performance Manual, The (Gorodji)
Nitrous Oxide High-performance Manual, The (Langfield)
Rover V8 Engines – How to Power Tune (Hammill)
Secrets of Speed – Today's techniques for 4-stroke engine blueprinting & tuning (Swager)
Sportscar & Kitcar Suspension & Brakes – How to Build & Modify Revised 3rd Edition (Hammill)
SU Carburettor High-performance Manual (Hammill)
Successful Low-Cost Rally Car, How to Build a (Young)
Suzuki 4x4 – How to Modify For Serious Off-road Action (Richardson)
Tiger Avon Sportscar – How to Build Your Own Updated & Revised 2nd Edition (Dudley)
TR2, 3 & TR4 – How to Improve (Williams)
TR5, 250 & TR6 – How to Improve (Williams)
TR7 & TR8 – How to Improve (Williams)
V8 Engine – How to Build a Short Block For High Performance (Hammill)
Volkswagen Beetle Suspension, Brakes & Chassis – How to Modify For High Performance (Hale)
Volkswagen Bus Suspension, Brakes & Chassis – How to Modify For High Performance (Hale)
Weber DCOE, & Dellorto DHLA Carburetors – How to Build & Power Tune 3rd Edition (Hammill)

Those Were The Days ... Series
Alpine Trials & Rallies 1910-1973 (Pfundner)
American 'Independent' Automakers – AMC to Willys 1945 to 1960 (Mort)
American Station Wagons – The Golden Era 1950-1975 (Mort)
American Trucks of the 1950s (Mort)
American Trucks of the 1960s (Mort)
American Woodies 1928-1953 (Mort)
Anglo-American Cars from the 1930s to the 1970s (Mort)
Austerity Motoring (Bobbitt)
Austins, The last real (Peck)
Brighton National Speed Trials (Gardiner)
British Lorries of the 1950s (Bobbitt)
British Lorries of the 1960s (Bobbitt)
British Touring Car Racing (Collins)
British Police Cars (Walker)
British Woodies (Peck)
Café Racer Phenomenon, The (Walker)
Drag Bike Racing in Britain – From the mid '60s to the mid '80s (Lee)
Dune Buggy Phenomenon, The (Hale)
Dune Buggy Phenomenon Volume 2, The (Hale)
Endurance Racing at Silverstone in the 1970s & 1980s (Parker)
Hot Rod & Stock Car Racing in Britain in the 1980s (Neil)
Last Real Austins 1946-1959, The (Peck)
MG's Abingdon Factory (Moylan)
Motor Racing at Brands Hatch in the Seventies (Parker)
Motor Racing at Brands Hatch in the Eighties (Parker)
Motor Racing at Crystal Palace (Collins)
Motor Racing at Goodwood in the Sixties (Gardiner)
Motor Racing at Nassau in the 1950s & 1960s (O'Neil)
Motor Racing at Oulton Park in the 1960s (McFadyen)
Motor Racing at Oulton Park in the 1970s (McFadyen)
Superprix – The Story of Birmingham Motor Race (Page & Collins)
Three Wheelers (Bobbitt)

Truckmakers
DAF Trucks since 1949 (Peck)

Enthusiast's Restoration Manual Series
Citroën 2CV, How to Restore (Porter)
Classic Car Bodywork, How to Restore (Thaddeus)
Classic British Car Electrical Systems (Astley)
Classic Car Electrics (Thaddeus)
Classic Cars, How to Paint (Thaddeus)
Reliant Regal, How to Restore (Payne)
Triumph TR2, 3, 3A, 4 & 4A, How to Restore (Williams)
Triumph TR5/250 & 6, How to Restore (Williams)
Triumph TR7/8, How to Restore (Williams)
Volkswagen Beetle, How to Restore (Tyler)
VW Bay Window Bus (Paxton)
Yamaha FS1-E, How to Restore (Watts)

Essential Buyer's Guide Series
Alfa GT (Booker)
Alfa Romeo Spider Giulia (Booker & Talbott)
Austin Seven (Barker)
BMW GS (Henshaw)
BSA Bantam (Henshaw)
BSA 500 & 650 Twins (Henshaw)
Citroën 2CV (Paxton)
Citroën ID & DS (Heilig)
Corvette C2 1963-1967 (Falconer)
Fiat 500 & 600 (Bobbitt)
Ford Capri (Paxton)
Harley-Davidson Big Twins (Henshaw)
Hinckley Triumph triples & fours 750, 900, 955, 1000, 1050, 1200 – 1991-2009 (Henshaw)
Honda CBR600 (Henshaw)
Honda FireBlade (Henshaw)
Honda SOHC fours 1969-1984 (Henshaw)
Jaguar E-type 3.8 & 4.2-litre (Crespin)
Jaguar E-type V12 5.3-litre (Crespin)
Jaguar XJ 1995-2003 (Crespin)
Jaguar/Daimler XJ6, XJ12 & Sovereign (Crespin)
Jaguar/Daimler XJ40 (Crespin)
Jaguar XJ-S (Crespin)
Land Rover Series I, II & IIA (Thurman)
MGB & MGB GT (Williams)
Mercedes-Benz 280SL-560DSL Roadsters (Bass)
Mercedes-Benz 'Pagoda' 230SL, 250SL & 280SL Roadsters & Coupés (Bass)
MG Midget & A-H Sprite (Horler)
MG TD, TF & TF1500 (Jones)
Mini (Paxton)
Morris Minor & 1000 (Newell)
Norton Commando (Henshaw)
Peugeot 205 GTi (Blackburn)
Porsche 911 (964) (Streather)
Porsche 911 (993) (Streather)
Porsche 911 (996) (Streather)
Porsche 911 SC (Streather)
Porsche 928 (Hemmings)
Rolls-Royce Silver Shadow & Bentley T-Series (Bobbitt)
Subaru Impreza (Hobbs)
Triumph Bonneville (Henshaw)
Triumph Spitfire & GT6 (Baugues)
Triumph Stag (Mort & Fox)
Triumph TR6 (Williams)
Triumph TR7 & TR8 (Williams)
Vespa Scooters – Classic 2-stroke models 1960-2008 (Paxton)
VW Beetle (Cservenka & Copping)
VW Bus (Cservenka & Copping)
VW Golf GTI (Cservenka & Copping)

Auto-Graphics Series
Fiat-based Abarths (Sparrow)
Jaguar MKI & II Saloons (Sparrow)
Lambretta Li Series Scooters (Sparrow)

Rally Giants Series
Audi Quattro (Robson)
Austin Healey 100-6 & 3000 (Robson)
Fiat 131 Abarth (Robson)
Ford Escort MkI (Robson)
Ford Escort RS Cosworth & World Rally Car (Robson)
Ford Escort RS1800 (Robson)
Lancia Delta 4WD/Integrale (Robson)
Lancia Stratos (Robson)
Mini Cooper/Mini Cooper S (Robson)
Peugeot 205 T16 (Robson)
Saab 96 & V4 (Robson)
Subaru Impreza (Robson)
Toyota Celica GT4 (Robson)

WSC Giants
Ferrari 312P & 312PB (Collins & McDonough)
Gulf-Mirage 1967 to 1982 (McDonough)
Matra Sports Cars – MS620, 630, 650, 660 & 670 – 1966 to 1974 (McDonough)

General
1½-litre GP Racing 1961-1965 (Whitelock)
AC Two-litre Saloons & Buckland Sportscars (Archibald)
Alfa Romeo Giulia Coupé GT & GTA (Tipler)
Alfa Romeo Montreal – The dream car that came true (Taylor)
Alfa Romeo Montreal – The Essential Companion (Taylor)
Alfa Tipo 33 (McDonough & Collins)
Alpine & Renault – The Development of the Revolutionary Turbo F1 Car 1968 to 1979 (Smith)
Alpine & Renault – The Sports Prototypes 1963 to 1969 (Smith)
Alpine & Renault – The Sports Prototypes 1973 to 1978 (Smith)
Anatomy of the Works Minis (Moylan)
André Lefebvre, and the cars he created at Voisin and Citroën (Beck)
Armstrong-Siddeley (Smith)
Art Deco and British Car Design (Down)
Autodrome (Collins & Ireland)
Autodrome 2 (Collins & Ireland)
Automotive A-Z, Lane's Dictionary of Automotive Terms (Lane)
Automotive Mascots (Kay & Springate)
Bahamas Speed Weeks, The (O'Neil)
Bentley Continental, Corniche and Azure (Bennett)
Bentley MkVI, Rolls-Royce Silver Wraith, Dawn & Cloud/Bentley R & S-Series (Nutland)
Bluebird CN7 (Stevens)
BMC Competitions Department Secrets (Turner, Chambers & Browning)
BMW 5-Series (Cranswick)
BMW Z-Cars (Taylor)
BMW Boxer Twins 1970-1995 Bible, The (Falloon)
Britains Farm Model Balers & Combines 1967-2007, Pocket Guide to (Pullen)
Britains Farm Model & Toy Tractors 1998-2008, Pocket Guide to (Pullen)
Britains Toy Models Catalogues 1970-1979 (Pullen)
British 250cc Racing Motorcycles (Pereira)
British at Indianapolis, The (Wagstaff)
British Cars, The Complete Catalogue of, 1895-1975 (Culshaw & Horrobin)
BRM – A Mechanic's Tale (Salmon)
BRM V16 (Ludvigsen)
BSA Bantam Bible, The (Henshaw)
Bugatti Type 40 (Price)
Bugatti 46/50 Updated Edition (Price & Arbey)
Bugatti T44 & T49 (Price & Arbey)
Bugatti 57 2nd Edition (Price)
Caravans, The Illustrated History 1919-1959 (Jenkinson)
Caravans, The Illustrated History From 1960 (Jenkinson)
Carrera Panamericana, La (Tipler)
Chrysler 300 – America's Most Powerful Car 2nd Edition (Ackerson)
Chrysler PT Cruiser (Ackerson)
Citroën DS (Bobbitt)
Classic British Car Electrical Systems (Astley)
Cliff Allison, The Official Biography of – From the Fells to Ferrari – (Gauld)
Cobra – The Real Thing! (Legate)
Concept Cars, How to illustrate and design (Dewey)
Cortina – Ford's Bestseller (Robson)
Coventry Climax Racing Engines (Hammill)
Daily Mirror 1970 World Cup Rally 40, The (Robson)
Daimler SP250 New Edition (Long)
Datsun Fairlady Roadster to 280ZX – The Z-Car Story (Long)
Diecast Toy Cars of the 1950s & 1960s (Ralston)
Dino – The V6 Ferrari (Long)
Dodge Challenger & Plymouth Barracuda (Grist)
Dodge Charger – Enduring Thunder (Ackerson)
Dodge Dynamite! (Grist)
Draw & Paint Cars – How to (Gardiner)
Drive on the Wild Side, A – 20 Extreme Driving Adventures From Around the World (Weaver)
Ducati 750 Bible, The (Falloon)
Ducati 750 SS 'round-case' 1974, The Book of the (Falloon)
Ducati 860, 900 and Mille Bible, The (Falloon)
Dune Buggy, Building A – The Essential Manual (Shakespeare)
Dune Buggy Files (Hale)
Dune Buggy Handbook (Hale)
East German Motor Vehicles in Pictures (Suhr/Weinreich)
Edward Turner: The Man Behind the Motorcycles (Clew)
Efficient Driver's Handbook, The (Moss)
Electric Cars – The Future is Now! (Linde)
Fast Ladies – Female Racing Drivers 1888 to 1970 (Bouzanquet)
Fate of the Sleeping Beauties, The (op de Weegh/Hottendorff/op de Weegh)
Ferrari 288 GTO, The Book of the (Sackey)
Fiat & Abarth 124 Spider & Coupé (Tipler)
Fiat & Abarth 500 & 600 2nd Edition (Bobbitt)
Fiats, Great Small (Ward)
Fine Art of the Motorcycle Engine, The (Peirce)
Ford F100/F150 Pick-up 1948-1996 (Ackerson)
Ford F150 Pick-up 1997-2005 (Ackerson)
Ford GT – Then, and Now (Streather)
Ford GT40 (Legate)
Ford In Miniature (Olson)
Ford Model Y (Roberts)
Ford Thunderbird From 1954, The Book of the (Long)
Formula 5000 Motor Racing, Back then ... and back now (Lawson)
Forza Minardi! (Vigar)
Funky Mopeds (Skelton)
GM In Miniature (Olson)
GT – The World's Best GT Cars 1953-73 (Dawson)
Hillclimbing & Sprinting – The Essential Manual (Short & Wilkinson)
Honda NSX (Long)
Intermeccanica – The Story of the Prancing Bull (McCredie & Reisner)
Jack Sears, The Official Biography of – Gentleman Jack (Gauld)
Jaguar, The Rise of (Price)
Jaguar XJ 220 – The Inside Story (Moreton)
Jaguar XJ-S (Long)
Jeep CJ (Ackerson)
Jeep Wrangler (Ackerson)
John Chatham – 'Mr Big Healey' – The Official Biography (Burr)
Karmann-Ghia Coupé & Convertible (Bobbitt)
Kawasaki Triples Bible, The (Walker)
Kris Meeke – Intercontinental Rally Challenge Champion (McBride)
Lamborghini Miura Bible, The (Sackey)
Lamborghini Urraco, The book of the (Landsem)
Lambretta Bible, The (Davies)
Lancia 037 (Collins)
Lancia Delta HF Integrale (Blaettel & Wagner)
Land Rover Series III Reborn (Porter)
Land Rover, The Half-ton Military (Cook)
Laverda Twins & Triples Bible 1968-1986 (Falloon)
Lea-Francis Story, The (Price)
Lexus Story, The (Long)
little book of smart, the New Edition (Jackson)
little book of microcars, the (Quellin)
Lola – The Illustrated History (1957-1977) (Starkey)
Lola – All the Sports Racing & Single-seater Racing Cars 1978-1997 (Starkey)
Lola T70 – The Racing History & Individual Chassis Record 4th Edition (Starkey)
Lotus 49 (Oliver)
Marketingmobiles, The Wonderful Wacky World of (Hale)
Mazda MX-5/Miata 1.6 Enthusiast's Workshop Manual (Grainger & Shoemark)
Mazda MX-5/Miata 1.8 Enthusiast's Workshop Manual (Grainger & Shoemark)
Mazda MX-5 Miata: The Book of the World's Favourite Sportscar (Long)
Mazda MX-5 Miata Roadster (Long)
Maximum Mini (Booij)
Mercedes-Benz SL – 113-series 1963-1971 (Long)
Mercedes-Benz SL & SLC – 107-series 1971-1989 (Long)
MGA (Price Williams)
MGB & MGB GT– Expert Guide (Auto-doc Series) (Williams)
MGB Electrical Systems Updated & Revised Edition (Astley)
Micro Caravans (Jenkinson)
Micro Trucks (Mort)
Microcars at Large! (Quellin)
Mini Cooper – The Real Thing! (Tipler)
Mitsubishi Lancer Evo, The Road Car & WRC Story (Long)
Montlhéry, The Story of the Paris Autodrome (Boddy)
Morgan Maverick (Lawrence)
Morris Minor, 60 Years on the Road (Newell)
Moto Guzzi Sport & Le Mans Bible, The (Falloon)
Motor Movies – The Posters! (Veysey)
Motor Racing – Reflections of a Lost Era (Carter)
Motorcycle Apprentice (Cakebread)
Motorcycle Road & Racing Chassis Designs (Noakes)
Motorhomes, The Illustrated History (Jenkinson)
Motorsport In colour, 1950s (Wainwright)
Nissan 300ZX & 350Z – The Z-Car Story (Long)
Nissan GT-R Supercar: Born to race (Gorodji)
Northeast American Sports Car Races 1950-1959 (O'Neil)
Off-Road Giants! – Heroes of 1960s Motorcycle Sport (Westlake)
Pass the Theory and Practical Driving Tests (Gibson & Hoole)
Pat Moss Carlsson Story, The – Harnessing Horsepower (Turner)
Peking to Paris 2007 (Young)
Plastic Toy Cars of the 1950s & 1960s (Ralston)
Pontiac Firebird (Cranswick)
Porsche Boxster (Long)
Porsche 356 (2nd Edition) (Long)
Porsche 908 (Födisch, Neßhöver, Roßbach, Schwarz & Roßbach)
Porsche 911 Carrera – The Last of the Evolution (Corlett)
Porsche 911R, RS & RSR, 4th Edition (Starkey)
Porsche 911, The Book of the (Long)
Porsche 911 – The Definitive History 1963-1971 (Long)
Porsche 911 – The Definitive History 1971-1977 (Long)
Porsche 911 – The Definitive History 1977-1987 (Long)
Porsche 911 – The Definitive History 1987-1997 (Long)
Porsche 911 – The Definitive History 1997-2004 (Long)
Porsche 911SC 'Super Carrera' – The Essential Companion (Streather)
Porsche 914 & 914-6: The Definitive History of the Road & Competition Cars (Long)
Porsche 924 (Long)
Porsche 928 (Long)
Porsche 944 (Long)
Porsche 964, 993 & 996 Data Plate Code Breaker (Streather)
Porsche 993 'King Of Porsche' – The Essential Companion (Streather)
Porsche 996 'Supreme Porsche' – The Essential Companion (Streather)
Porsche Racing Cars – 1953 to 1975 (Long)
Porsche Racing Cars – 1976 to 2005 (Long)
Porsche – The Rally Story (Meredith)
Porsche: Three Generations of Genius (Meredith)
Preston Tucker & Others (Linde)
RAC Rally Action! (Gardiner)
Rallye Sport Fords: The Inside Story (Moreton)
Redman, Jim – 6 Times World Motorcycle Champion: The Autobiography (Redman)
Roads with a View – England's greatest views and how to find them by road (Corfield)
Rolls-Royce Silver Shadow/Bentley T Series Corniche & Camargue Revised & Enlarged Edition (Bobbitt)
Rolls-Royce Silver Spirit, Silver Spur & Bentley Mulsanne 2nd Edition (Bobbitt)
Runways & Racers (O'Neil)
Russian Motor Vehicles – Soviet Limousines 1930-2003 (Kelly)
Russian Motor Vehicles – The Czarist Period 1784 to 1917 (Kelly)
RX-7 – Mazda's Rotary Engine Sportscar (Updated & Revised New Edition) (Long)
Scooters & Microcars, The A-Z of Popular (Dan)
Scooter Lifestyle (Grainger)
Singer Story: Cars, Commercial Vehicles, Bicycles & Motorcycle (Atkinson)
Sleeping Beauties USA – abandoned classic cars & trucks (Marek)
SM – Citroën's Maserati-engined Supercar (Long & Claverol)
Speedway – Auto racing's ghost tracks (Collins & Ireland)
Subaru Impreza: The Road Car And WRC Story (Long)
Supercar, How to Build your own (Thompson)
Tales from the Toolbox (Oliver)
Taxi! The Story of the 'London' Taxicab (Bobbitt)
Tinplate Toy Cars of the 1950s & 1960s (Ralston)
Toleman Story, The (Hilton)
Toyota Celica & Supra, The Book of Toyota's Sports Coupés (Long)
Toyota MR2 Coupés & Spyders (Long)
Triumph Bonneville!, Save the – The inside story of the Meriden Workers' Co-op (Rosamond)
Triumph Motorcycles & the Meriden Factory (Hancox)
Triumph Speed Twin & Thunderbird Bible (Woolridge)
Triumph Tiger Cub Bible (Estall)
Triumph Trophy Bible (Woolridge)
Triumph TR6 (Kimberley)
TWR Story, The – Group A (Hughes & Scott)
Unraced (Collins)
Velocette Motorcycles – MSS to Thruxton New Third Edition (Burris)
Virgil Exner – Visioneer: The Official Biography of Virgil M Exner Designer Extraordinaire (Grist)
Volkswagen Bus Book, The (Bobbitt)
Volkswagen Bus or Van to Camper, How to Convert (Porter)
Volkswagens of the World (Glen)
VW Beetle Cabriolet (Bobbitt)
VW Beetle – The Car of the 20th Century (Copping)
VW Bus – 40 Years of Splitties, Bays & Wedges (Copping)
VW Bus Book, The (Bobbitt)
VW Golf: Five Generations of Fun (Copping & Cservenka)
VW – The Air-cooled Era (Copping)
VW T5 Camper Conversion Manual (Porter)
VW Campers (Copping)
Works Minis, The Last (Purves & Brenchley)
Works Rally Mechanic (Moylan)

From Veloce Publishing's new imprints:

Battle Cry!
Soviet General & field rank officer uniforms: 1955 to 1991 (Streather)
Red & Soviet military & paramilitary services: female uniforms 1941 1991 (Streather)

Hubble & Hattie
Clever Dog! (O'Meara)
Complete Dog Massage Manual, The – Gentle Dog Care (Robertson)
Dinner with Rover (Paton-Ayre)
Dog Cookies (Schops)
Dog Games – Stimulating play to entertain your dog and you (Blenski)
Dog Relax – Relaxed dogs, relaxed owners (Pilguj)
Excercising your puppy: a gentle & natural approach (Robertson)
Know Your Dog – The guide to a beautiful relationship (Birmelin)
Living with an Older Dog (Alderton & Hall)
Motorway Walks (Rees)
My dog is blind – but lives life to the full! (Horsky)
Smellorama – nose games for dogs (Theby)
Swim to Recovery: The Animal Magic Way (Wong)
Waggy Tails & Wheelchairs (Epp)
Winston ... the dog who changed my life (Klute)
You and Your Border Terrier – The Essential Guide (Alderton)
You and Your Cockapoo – The Essential Guide (Alderton)

www.veloce.co.uk

First published in September 2010 by Veloce Publishing Limited, Veloce House, Parkway Farm Business Park, Middle Farm Way, Poundbury, Dorchester, Dorset, DT1 3AR, England.
Fax 01305 250479/e-mail info@veloce.co.uk/web www.veloce.co.uk or www.velocebooks.com. ISBN: 978-1-845842-46-8 UPC: 6-36847-04246-2

British Library Cataloguing in Publication Data – A catalogue record for this book is available from the British Library. Typesetting, design and page make-up all by Veloce Publishing Ltd on Apple Mac. Printed in India by Replika Press.

The British at INDIANAPOLIS

VELOCE PUBLISHING
THE PUBLISHER OF FINE AUTOMOTIVE BOOKS

Ian Wagstaff

CONTENTS

FOREWORD
BY DARIO FRANCHITTI

Winner Indianapolis 500: 2007 & 2010
IndyCar Series Champion: 2007 & 2009

There has been a massive amount of British influence on Indianapolis but, for me, it is Jim Clark's legacy that has been the biggest inspiration. Winning the Indianapolis 500, as he had done, was the highlight of my life. It is fun to win any race, that is why we compete, but this one is something different.

Although there had been British drivers and cars at the Speedway before then, it really all began with the rear-engined revolution in the 1960s. Now you cannot walk more than a couple of feet through Gasoline Alley without meeting someone from the UK, be it a driver, designer, engineer, mechanic, official or fan. 'Shop staff' like Andy Brown, Julian Roberston, and Allen McDonald have a huge effect on what happens at Indy and, in recent years, both Dan Wheldon and I have won the 500. This is going to keep going. There are a lot of talented, young British drivers who want to race an Indy car and there are plenty of opportunities for engineers and mechanics from the UK.

It is such an iconic race and one in which we from Britain have played a big part. So, it is great that a book has now been written about the British at Indianapolis both for the fans and for history buffs like myself. The following pages are full of in-depth stories about the many people from the UK that have made their mark there.

Dario Franchitti

Opposite and above: Jim Clark's win at Indianapolis in 1965 was not the first by a British citizen, nor even a British-born driver, but was arguably the most meaningful. The Scot's Lotus 38 was the first rear-engined car to head for Victory Lane. British influence on the race had become significant and has lasted to this day. (From original paintings by Jim Dugdale)

Dario Franchitti poses with Target Chip Ganassi engineer Andy Brown, the morning after the Scot's 2010 Indianapolis 500 victory. (Courtesy Andy Brown collection)

INTRODUCTION & ACKNOWLEDGEMENTS

For Gill

I confess to have been grinning when I walked in from the media centre balcony after the 2007 Indianapolis 500. I had just seen a British driver win America's greatest sporting spectacle. What was more, as I proudly pointed out to some US colleagues, it was the fourth consecutive single-seater (or open wheel, as they say in America) victory at the track for a driver from the United Kingdom.

The following day I found myself at the track's museum discussing the 1946 winning Thorne Engineering Special with a veteran fan. His interest in the car was that a friend had been one of the car's crew, mine that its driver had been born in England. The further one gets from home, the more patriotic one feels at sporting events. However, it did make me think that there was a logical successor to my book *The British at Le Mans* in the exploits of my fellow countrymen at Indianapolis.

It is, though, a very different story. The Le Mans tale is one of patriotism, of the wearing of British Racing Green and of a British spiritual take-over of a race in France. Indianapolis, by the very nature of its distant location, was always going to be a different matter. Unlike at Le Mans, it took many years for the British to have a major influence on the Indianapolis 500, even if one of their number was in at the very beginning, exactly one hundred years ago. This is more a story of individuals seeking either fleeting success or long-term fame in the US and, perhaps more significantly, of the engineering expertise that has grown up in what is known as Britain's motorsports valley. As such, there is less of an obvious structure to the story as British interest has waxed and waned. I hope that the following pages at least give a flavour of the UK's involvement. If nothing else, it may explain why,

such is the size of the expatriate British community in Indianapolis, that you get a better cup of tea there than most places in the US.

The varied nature of British involvement means that it has been impossible to give an overall picture of the Indianapolis 500's history. To put this story into context, I can would recommend the reader acquire the excellent tomes of Donald Davidson and Rick Shaffer, Rick Popely and L Spencer Riggs, Jack C Fox or Al Bloemker.

Quite what is meant by British had better be explained, given that the Nations' Cup, run as part of the old Champ Car series, erroneously made Scotland and the United Kingdom (rather than England) out to be separate countries. The entity concerned is the United Kingdom of Great Britain and Northern Ireland, which includes England, Scotland, Wales and Ulster. Having said that, I have been a trifle cavalier in my own approach. I have included all those who have been citizens of the UK, even if, as in the case of the 1916 Indianapolis 500 winner, he was born in Italy. To these I have added anyone born in Britain but who moved to the US, thus adding another outright winner of the event. To neglect these would be unfair; at least one of the engineers featured in the book has become a US citizen since I first started work on it. As far as cars and engines are concerned I have included anything manufactured in the UK. Not all are obvious. In one case alone, we have a Northamptonshire firm responsible for engines that have appeared bearing the brands of notable US, German, and Japanese vehicle manufacturers.

It may seem presumptuous for an Englishman to be writing a book on such an American institution, but I make no apologies.

Many born in the UK have been involved in the Indianapolis 500 and I only seek to record their efforts from, all right, I admit it, a biased stance (hence the English spellings unless quoting from a US periodical). I must thank one of their number in particular, Donald Davidson, who in the mid-1960s flew to the Indianapolis 500 with, already, an arguably greater knowledge of the race that any local. Without Donald's assistance and support the following pages would be very much the poorer. He was just one of the Indianapolis Motor Speedway staff who have aided the project and to them I must express my thanks. Their names are included below amongst the many who have either agreed to be interviewed at varying lengths or assisted in other ways. I now risk the sin of omission and to any that I may have missed, my apologies:

Tony Adamowicz; Kaaveh Akbari; Bruce Ashmore; Debbie Atkerson; Roger Bailey; Dillon Battistini; Derek Bell; Tino Belli; Nigel Bennett; Nigel Beresford; Jackie Bethel; Ben Bowlby; David Brabham; Sir Jack Brabham; Klint Briney; Eric Broadley; Andy Brown; Tom Brown; Paul J Bryant; Colin Bugler; Steve Burgess; Merrill Cain; Elizabeth Cannon; Dean Case; Clive Chapman; Beverly Charbonneau; John Church; Graham Clode; Mike Conway; David Cripps; Larry Curry; Derek Daly; Bob Dance; Nicki Dance; Arnold Davey; Donald Davidson; Gordon Day; Dawn DeBellis; Richard Dencer; Jim Dilamarter; Scott and Emma Dixon; Chris Ellis; Guy Faulkner; Nik Faulkner; Anne Fornoro; A J Foyt; Dario Franchitti; Andrew Garside; Nick Garside; Tony George; Graham Goodwin; Nick Goozee; Kim Green: Ron Green; Ken Gregory; John Griffin; Roger Griffiths; Dan and Evi Gurney; Lewis Hamilton; Tim Harms; Nick Harris; Andrew Heard; Dave Hillberry; David Hobbs; Tim Holloway; Clive Howell: Mario Illien; Eddie Jones; Glyn Jones; Graham Jones; Parnelli Jones; John Judd; Gordon Kirby; Jonny Kane; Mike Kitchel; Kelby Krauss; Al Larsen; Kathi Lauterbach; David Lazenby; Brian Lisles; Alex and Sam Lloyd; David Lloyd; Mary Ellen Loscar; Fiona Lovell; Allen McDonald; Ron McQueeney; Alan McCall; Les Mactaggart; Doug Magnon; John Manchester; Chris Mann; Pippa Mann; Darren Manning; Nigel Mansell; Alan Mertens; Mike Micheli; Neil Middleditch; Steve Miller; Lord Montagu of Beaulieu; Sir Stirling Moss; Chris Mower; Derek Mower; Fred Nation; Gary Neal; Sapphire Nichols; Andrew Noakes; Morris and Kathryn Nunn; Doug Nye; Chris and Debbie Paulsen; Martin Plowman; Richard Postins; John Pulford; Brian Redman; L Spencer Riggs; Dennis Reinbold; Adrian Reynard; Rick Rising-Moore: Julian Robertson; Tony Robinson; Gary Rodrigues; Ron Rose; Mickey Ryan; Benito Santos; Julie Schram; Chris Schwartz; Dave Scotney; Mark Scott; Susan Shrosbree; Stephen Slater; Allan Smith; Bradley Smith; Dominic Piers Smith; Guy Smith; Jim Smith; Sam Smith; Tony Southgate; Bob Sparshott; Emma Spearing; Tim Sullivan; Sir Jackie Stewart; Doug Stokes; Jana Strange; Ed and Sally Swart; Stephanie Sykes; John Tarring; Deb Taylor; Len Terry; Derek Tew; James Toseland; Terry Trammell; Mike Underwood; Jan Valentino; Barry Wanser; Jeff Ward; Tim Wardrop: Kathy Weida; Dan Wheldon; Keith Wiggins; Justin Wilson; James Winslow; Delano Wood; Billy Wooldridge; Gene Varnier and Matt Youson.

It only remains for me to also thank my publisher, Rod Grainger, for so readily agreeing to the whole idea, the family, Gill and Richard, for putting up with my obsession, and Tim who, in 2009, saw what it was all about.

Ian Wagstaff

BROOKLANDS PROLOGUE

The 1911 May 10 race meeting at Brooklands was much like any other that year. While motorsport on the continent of Europe had developed from the city-to-city races of the turn of the century, competition at the 3.25-mile, purpose-built, high banked track was still organised along horse racing lines. Indeed, when the track had opened in 1907 competitors' identities were determined by the drivers' coloured 'silks' as opposed to a number on the car. By 1911 the now traditional numbering system had been introduced but short match and handicap events still dominated the race card.

An overhead-valved engine Sunbeam, whimsically called 'Toodles II,' was arguably the star of the meeting. Driven by the poised Louis Coatalen, who had joined the Sunbeam Motor Car Company a couple of years previously as chief engineer, 'Toodles II' beat C A Bird's Napier in a five-mile match race and came first in two short handicap races. During the course of the day Coatalen also broke the 16hp half-mile, flying start record for the track with a speed of 86.16mph.

It is doubtful if many in the small crowd that Whitsun day in 1911 would have been aware of what was to happen twenty days later in Indiana, US. The previous year, car racing at the newly opened, 2.5-mile Indianapolis Motor Speedway had been along the same lines as that at Brooklands, with short races, some of them handicaps. On May 30 that was all to change with the introduction of a 500-mile race; an acceptance of a bigger picture that Brooklands was never able to encompass. It is true that the oval in the Surrey countryside did, starting in 1929, eventually host a 500-mile race, but even that was still a handicap event.

Indianapolis began to appeal to a wide audience while Brooklands stuck to a 'right crowd, no crowding' approach. Today, the weeds grow through what is left of the latter's mighty banking, while each May over a quarter of a million fans still crowd into the stadium that self-made businessman Carl Fisher built. (It has been a matter of conjecture whether Fisher was inspired by Brooklands when he first had the idea for his Speedway. However, while he did visit the older track it is most likely that he and Brooklands' founder, Hugh Locke King, simply had a similar idea at about the same time.)

In that Brooklands May meeting can be seen the seeds of how the Indianapolis was, as one author has witheringly put it, "made Brit." Coatalen was an enthusiastic publicist, as Sunbeam's eventual racing career bore out. Its cars set several long-distance records at Brooklands and, in the Indianapolis 500, Coatalen could see a further opportunity to underline the strength of his designs. A successor to 'Toodles II,' known as 'Toodles IV,' established a number of long-distance World Records in 1912 driven by Dario Resta, a name we shall come across again. Seeing its potential, Coatalen entered the car for the 1913 Indianapolis 500, the first British-built racer to contest the event, the forebear of the Lotuses, Lolas, Marches, and Reynards that were to come to dominate it.

Over a quarter of a million people still attend the
Indianapolis 500. This is 2004 with four Brits on the grid.
(Courtesy Indianapolis Motor Speedway)

At Brooklands, the grass now grows through the mighty
banking. (Author's collection)

PART ONE

1911-1960 – The first half century

1

PRE-WAR PIONEERS

"Not even under the trying conditions ... did he forget his native land ..."

A 50-piece band headed the column of militiamen marching in front of the packed Speedway grandstand. Soldiers carried high the flags of the nations about to be represented in the imminent Indianapolis 500-mile race. The crowds cheered as the Stars and Stripes were waved proudly. In this respect, the build-up to the 1915 contest was very little different to all those that have followed. Suddenly, someone wearing, as the *Indianapolis Star* put it, "... the uniform of a driver," rushed out from the pits. On reaching the Union Jack, he caught hold of one corner and "... pressing it to his lips held it there as he followed along with the parade."

The man in question was Sunbeam driver Noel van Raalte, described by the *Star* as "... an officer in the English army." The paper

The Speedway in 1910, the year in which Hughie Hughes, the first Englishman to race there, made his Indianapolis debut.
(Courtesy Indianapolis Motor Speedway)

was effusive about what it saw as his patriotic stance. "Not even under the trying conditions of the great motor marathon did he forget his native land and to it he paid final homage before embarking on the great struggle against time. The demonstration was so earnest, so impressive that for a second the spectators stopped their cheering to point to the man who, before them all, proclaimed his loyalty to the land of his birth."

England was by then fully engaged in the Great War, and only a couple of days earlier the same paper had reported that the British pre-Dreadnought, 12-inch gunned battleship, HMS Majestic, had been sunk, as would be learnt later, by the German submarine U21 in the Eastern Mediterranean.

Van Raalte was not the first Englishman to compete in the Indianapolis 500 but his action does provide an apt precursor to the British involvement in this unique motor race. Although quintessentially an American event, it is the British who have perhaps gate-crashed the party the most over the years.

Hughes poses in his Mercer prior to the inaugural 500-Mile International Sweepstakes.
(Courtesy Indianapolis Motor Speedway)

It was an involvement that had started four years prior to van Raalte's patriotic outburst. For the 1911 Indianapolis 500, the first ever such event, the grid was decided by how early the entry had

been made. Thus it was that car number thirty-six, a yellow and blue, virtually stock Mercer Raceabout, typical of the period with its box-like bonnet, artillery wheels, and racing number standing proud at the rear above the fuel tank, was placed as far back as the seventh row. The significance of car number thirty-six was that in it sat 25-year old Hughie Hughes, the first British-born driver to contest the Indianapolis 500. Hughes cannot have known that he was a trailblazer, or even cared, for he had possibly become a citizen of the United States by this time. However, the papers of the time regularly described him by the country of his birth.

'GH Hughes' as the *San Francisco Call* also named him, was apparently well thought of as a driver by his contemporaries. He "... has forged himself to the front in the last two years as one of the country's best pilots," proclaimed the *Indianapolis Star* in 1912. "(He) ... is an Englishman and is one of the old-school drivers of which few are now racing." Quite where he came from seems to be a mystery. The paper went on to state that he had driven a De Dietrich in the 1904 Gordon Bennett race "... in France." However, the records of that race, which actually took place in Germany, do not include him, in addition to which, as an Englishman, he would not have been able to drive a French De Dietrich, as the rules of the Gordon Bennett stipulated that car and driver had to be of the same nationality. The *San Francisco Call* had earlier described him as, "... fresh from his triumphs on the Brooklands track in England." No record appears to exist of him racing there, so make of this what you will.

Having arrived in the US in 1906, Hughes first came to prominence driving the Allen-Kingston in 24-hour races on Brighton Beach, New York, going on to drive Walter Christie's front-wheel-drive car on the dirt tracks. Even then the *San Francisco Call* was referring to him as, "... the famous racing driver."

By 1910 Hughes was the driver for the Parry Auto Company, a local Indianapolis operation established the year before by David Parry, who had been a partner with his brothers in the Parry Manufacturing Company, then one of the world's largest carriage factories. Car and driver made their Indianapolis debut at the race meeting the first week in September, a varied affair in which a total of twenty races were planned for the Saturday and Monday. First race for Hughes was the Saturday's 5-mile handicap, described by D Bruce Scott in his meticulous work on those early years as "... wild and confusing." Fifteen cars entered with Hughes setting off thirty-four seconds after the earliest starters. Despite being a handicap race there were few place changes, with Hughes classified sixth overall.

Hughes was out again on the Monday for a two-lap scratch race, this time for stock chassis with 231-300 cubic inch engines. Nine cars started, leaving eight when Joe Dawson dropped out with an engine problem. History records that Hughes was last of those eight. His second race of the day was another free-for-all, 5-lap handicap with seventeen starters. This time he finished in fifth.

Having completed a total of just twelve laps in 1910 Hughes – who now regarded himself as Mercer's number one driver – was back for 200 the next year. The rules at those early Indy 500s stated that, although there was prize money for the first twelve finishers, they had to complete the full 500 miles irrespective of how many times they had been lapped. Hughes in his factory-entered, 300 cubic inch Mercer kept going and finished in that all-important 12th place at an average speed of 67.73mph. Up front, winner Harroun had averaged 74.60mph. "The small end of the purse went to (Hughes)," was how the result was reported in *The Automobile*.

That November, Hughes was to win the Savannah Trophy in Georgia for Mercer. The race took place a few days before and on the same track as that year's Vanderbilt Cup. The *New York Times* headlined Hughes as saying that the winner for the main event, in which he was not entered, would be Victor Hemery. He was to be proved wrong for the race went to Ralph Mulford.

By the following May, Hughes' reputation was riding high. "Hughes is one of the most reliable drivers in the game and his big Mercer, a new creation built especially for this race, has made an impression on the rail birds and many predict that Hughes will be a winner. The Englishman has studied the track and he believes his tire wear has been reduced to a minimum," said the *Indianapolis Star* four days before the 1912 500. A day later it was reporting that 1911 winner Ray Harroun "... is stuck on Hughie Hughes' Mercer. Ray says that Hughes has the likeliest car in the race because it has a small engine and is shy on avoirdupois."

Before the race Hughes was asked what he would do with the $50,000 prize money should he win. "Buy a manor house and farm in merry England," he answered.

For the event Hughes found himself on the fourth row of the grid, having posted a speed of 81.81mph. His yellow, 301 cubic inch Mercer, this time the only one in the field, looked more like a racing car than the previous year with contemporary bodywork and wire spoke wheels. It is said that future Indianapolis Motor Speedway owner and Great War flying ace Eddie Rickenbacher (he was to change the spelling to Rickenbacker in 1918) was fascinated by the Mercer engine's vibration reducing, counterbalanced crankshaft.

Hughes races to third place in 1912. (Courtesy Indianapolis Motor Speedway)

The story of the race is all about how Ralph DePalma's Mercedes led, until mechanical problems started on the 197th lap, and how he pushed his car home. Most reports of the race barely mention that Hughes was running ninth at the end of the first 100 miles and up to a steady fourth by about half-distance, eventually finishing third, many minutes behind, and averaging 76.13mph – a speed higher than the previous year's winner. *The Horseless Age* did feel that because they were in the smallest cars in the race, Hughes, as well as a couple of Stutz drivers, "... probably deserve the most praise." Hughes, it said, "... drove his usual perfect race, and sent his wire-wheeled machine around the course at a consistent speed." It was felt that he might have finished even higher had it not been that, "... through an oversight" during the race, he ran out of petrol along the back straight coasting to a halt three quarters of a mile from the pits. He and his mechanic Eddie Pullen pushed the car in to be replenished. In all, Hughes made six stops, mainly due to tyre troubles.

At the finish a protest was by made by Stutz, which had contended that its driver, Charlie Merz, had finished third. The AAA officials retired to the Claypool Hotel to recheck the figures from their timing instruments. It was late that night before they could confirm that Hughes had, indeed, finished ahead of Merz, to claim a prize of $5000. That October, Hughes finished second in the 300-mile Vanderbilt Cup, run in the outskirts of Milwaukee, again using his smaller Mercer to good effect against much larger racers.

Driving for Mercer, Hughes was a regular in AAA (American

Automobile Association) National Championship races during this period, winning four races. Soon after their third place finish in the 500, he and the car were described as "The first star entry" for the Tacoma road race. "At the five-century sweepstakes, the Hughes-Mercer combination was one of the most feared in the entire contest … At Tacoma it should prove a dangerous contender," predicted the *New York Times*.

Wins took place in the 1911 Kane County Trophy and the 1912 Aurora Trophy, both at Elgin, as well as at Fairmont Park, Philadelphia in 1911. His car was put on display at the 1912 National Automobile Show at Madison Square Gardens, New York. "Cups won by Hughie Hughes and other drivers are piled on the yellow Mercer racer, which has such a sweeping career in the 300-cubic inch class events," observed the *New York Times*. He was back in front in 1914 for the Golden Potlach Trophy at Tacoma but now driving a Maxwell.

Hughes was to officially race just twice in the Indianapolis 500, although he was to be relief driver in 1913 for Bob Burman's Keeton and in 1915 for Billy Carlson's Maxwell. He took the finishing flag in the latter, the local press recording, "Tom Alley in a Duesenberg raced in only a few seconds behind Wilcox, with Hughie Hughes driving for Billy Carson in a Maxwell taking ninth place." In early May 1914 the *New York Times* reported that Hughes was a late entry in a Rayfield. Historian L Spencer Riggs recorded that this was the Hughes-Rayfield Special, a collaboration between Hughes and carburettor manufacturer William Rayfield. A contemporary photo shows a machine with a side radiator, well ahead of its time, set to the rear of a narrow, pointed bonnet. Hughes drove the six-cylinder car from Chrisman,

Illinois to Indianapolis just ten days before the 500. His practice times were easily quick enough to make the race. Then, on the eve of qualification, it seems that he took the car downtown. Whether he was showing off for a girl or for the press is now uncertain, but he over-revved the engine resulting in what the *New York Times* described as a destroyed crank bearing. The car was withdrawn and eventually sold to an amateur sportsman called Thompson. A year after his escapade with the Hughes-Rayfield, Hughes failed to qualify his FRP.

The Sunbeam 'Toodles' cars now make a reappearance in our story. 'Toodles V' was a V12, 9-litre, airship-engined single-seater that had made its way to America. Hughes entered it for the 1916 Corona Grand Prix in California. A fortnight before the event he was allowed to make a dawn trial run along the course. It is claimed that those not already awake were woken by the sound of the Sunbeam engine, and that virtually the whole city witnessed the run with its best lap of just over 100mph. Hughes did not finish the race itself, but reappeared with the car for a 150-mile race at the Ascot dirt track, coming home seventh.

Hughes was finally back at Indianapolis in late 1916 for the one-off Harvest Auto Racing Classic at which Louis Chevrolet was entered in a British-built Sunbeam. Driving a Hoskins Special, Hughes finished in the money in all three races, the 20-, 50-, and 100-mile contests. In the 50-mile race, "The Englishman showed some speed and for a single mile in the fifteenth lap led (Johnny) Aitken," reported the *Indianapolis Star*. He relentlessly raced the eventual winner to the end for a near photo finish; 0.28 seconds and around four feet. "On the last lap Hughes took the entire two and a half miles with the throttle wide

The Hughes-Rayfield Special has been described as arguably the most advanced car to be entered for the 1914 race. Frustratingly, Hughes destroyed the crankcase on the eve of his qualification run.
(Courtesy Indianapolis Motor Speedway)

open and his car wracking itself at every revolution. He gave Aitken the race of his life down the (final) stretch," said the *Star*. The pair had averaged almost 92mph. Hughes was also second to Aitken's Peugeot in the longest race, albeit nineteen seconds behind this time. The 100-mile contest was characterised by two battles; one of which was between Hughes and Ed Aleon, who raced under the pseudonym of 'Wilbur D'Alene' for third place. When Rickenbacher crashed on lap thirty-eight, the Englishman moved up into second, winning $2000. His prize for the shorter race had been just $500.

It was to be Hughes' last year. On December 2, driving his Hoskins, he was killed at a board-track in Uniontown, Pennsylvania. It was reported that he had run his car into the guardrail on the 62nd lap of the race because of engine trouble. He walked toward the press stand and had just arrived when fellow racer Frank Galvin lost control of his car and hit that structure. Hughes is said to have seen his danger but had no chance to escape, being killed instantly and buried in the wreckage. In announcing his death, the *New York Times* pointed out that the, "... English racing driver" had recently made his home in Los Angeles and had married a Miss Cruze of Boston.

If Britain's claim to Hughes is perhaps tenuous, there can be no doubting the nationality of the car that came fourth in the 500 of 1913. It may not have been in the country's racing colours of green (conflicting reports say it was painted black or grey) but car number nine certainly came from Wolverhampton, England. As such, it heralded the invasion that was to leave Britain's shores from the 1960s onwards. The car was a Sunbeam, a marque notable in that it was the only British company to win a major Grand Prix prior to 1957. As already introduced, this was 'Toodles IV.'

'Toodles,' incidentally, was Louis Coatalen's pet name for his wife, Olive. Sunbeam's meticulous racing historian, Anthony Heal, recorded how Coatalen reckoned 'Toodles IV' to have "The right combination of speed and staying power" to compete at Indianapolis although now two-years old. Originally a near standard 25/30hp model, the six-cylinder car had been developed since setting 15 World Records in 1911. Three more records had followed the next year. For Indianapolis, the car was given a shorter (10ft 7in) wheelbase, a new, streamlined, two-seat body and fitted with half-elliptic rear springs. The car was tested at Brooklands and then shipped from Liverpool for Frenchman Albert Guyot to use.

Guyot and Captain RFL Crossman, one of the drivers for the 1911 World Record attempts, who was to act as riding mechanic, sailed shortly after the car aboard La Provence, which left Le Havre just twenty days before the race. Although the well built Crossman was in Sunbeam's employ and the car had been prepared at the factory, it was said that it was a private entry; no-one was fooled.

The race was run in hot, gruelling conditions and both Guyot and Crossman suffered on their way to fourth place. Indeed, the

Riding mechanic Crossman, being well-built, had to squeeze himself into the Sunbeam's cockpit and was virtually unable to move for the next two days. (Courtesy Indianapolis Motor Speedway)

Englishman could hardly move for a couple of days afterwards. Nevertheless, they had succeeded in what they had set out to do and proved the reliability of the now ageing car. Heal recalled that the Sunbeam, "... ran with the greatest regularity," although journalist Massac Buist, writing at the time in *Autocar*, criticised the team for not showing the speed of the car. There were also some who hinted that, at least on this occasion, it might have been better if Crossman had been the driver.

Sunbeam was now to become a regular competitor at

Much interest was shown in Guyot's Sunbeam. (Courtesy Indianapolis Motor Speedway)

Chassagne retained his seat during this crash but mechanic Mitchell was thrown out into the long grass, without serious injury. (Courtesy Indianapolis Motor Speedway)

pits only to be withdrawn as spare wheels were not allowed to be carried. Grant, who had been driving to a predetermined speed about twenty seconds behind, moved steadily up the field to finish seventh having averaged 75.68mph.

Thanks to rain, the 1915 Indianapolis 500 was postponed for a couple of days and took place on May 31. The vast majority of British were otherwise engaged. A Zeppelin raided London that day while British troops had just taken Sphinxhaven in German East Africa. Nevertheless, two Grand Prix Sunbeams started, one of them British driven. Indeed, there were two drivers who could wave the Union flag that year. In the Peugeot camp was Dario Resta who, while born in Italy, had been raised in the UK from the age of two and was now a British national. The *Indianapolis Star* reported that in spite of heavy betting on Resta, as well as some of the local drivers, "... fans are not overlooking the Sunbeams."

One of these was driven by an Italian, Jean Porporato; the other was entered for an 'N Graham.' The pseudonym poorly disguised the identity of the Paddington-born Noel van Raalte, an aristocratic playboy whose family owned Brownsea Island; famous for being the location of the first Boy Scout camp and sited in Poole Harbour, the Dorset town of Poole being one that will come into our story again. In 1922, Van Raalte was to become the owner of the first production Bentley.

Indianapolis, continuing to race there as, in the words of the British Foreign Secretary Sir Edward Grey "The lights (were) going out all over Europe." For 1914, with the Great War still a couple of months away, the company entered a relatively small (4-litre) six-cylinder Grand Prix car from the previous year. The driver was another Frenchman, Jean Chassagne, and was accompanied by mechanic Percy Mitchell. A second Grand Prix Sunbeam was entered and driven by American, Harry Grant. Chassagne's Sunbeam crashed on its twentieth lap whilst in thirteenth place when an offside tyre burst. Mitchell was thrown out when the car overturned, landing in the soft grass while Chassagne was unhurt. The wheel was replaced and the car driven back to the

Despite the Union Flag, this is the Sunbeam of American Harry Grant, who had twice won the Vanderbilt Cup. (Courtesy Indianapolis Motor Speedway)

1915 entrant Noel van Raalte would also have been part of the Sunbeam team for the 1917 race that never happened. (Courtesy Indianapolis Motor Speedway)

back with his now outdated 1913 Grand Prix Sunbeam. He withdrew after 184 laps having been called in to fix his loose undershield. It was not Sunbeam's finest race, although a contemporary observer put it down to "... dogged bad luck" rather than "... unpreparedness."

Josef Christaens was the next to race a Sunbeam at Indianapolis. The 1916 car consisted of a new, 4.9-litre six-cylinder engine fitted to a 1914 chassis with longer subframe. His fourth place equalled Sunbeam's best, the Belgian having made just the one pit stop to change tyres. This was the year, though, that saw the first British winner at the Brickyard, a sobriquet that referred to its original surface of 3.2 million bricks. Dario Resta dominated the race and moved up one place better than his 1915 result using the same Peugeot (see Chapter 2). By the next May, the US would have been at war for just over a month.

There is a postscript concerning the British influence on the Indianapolis story that occurred before the US Government severed its relations with Berlin. Late in 1916, Coatelen met Eddie Rickenbacher and enquired if he would like to work with Sunbeam. The American driver duly travelled to the UK where British officialdom became suspicious of his German name. He worked for a week at Sunbeam's Wolverhampton factory before travelling to London for the weekend. Early in 1917, Sunbeam announced a plan to send three cars for Rickenbacher, Christaens, and Van Raalte to compete in the 500 but it was a race that was never to happen.

During his time in London Rickenbacher became aware of the airplanes that were flying from Brooklands. With his own country declaring war he returned across the Atlantic, inspired enough by what he had seen taking off from the field at Britain's own oval track to become a pilot himself and, by the end of the war, America's top scoring fighter 'ace.' From 1927 to 1945 he was also the title owner of the Indianapolis Motor Speedway.

While Resta gave notice of intent with a second place in his 1914 Grand Prix Peugeot, the Sunbeams had problems. The inexperienced van Raalte initially ran well and was up to seventh place at the halfway mark. However, plug changes, a lost bonnet, and a loose magneto bracket dropped him back. The *Indianapolis News* reported that he, "... almost quit the race when he lost his hood (*sic*) but Referee Pardington came to his rescue and told the patriotic Briton that his misfortune did not disqualify him."

Despite spending an hour in the pits and, "... after many troubles," van Raalte persevered to finish tenth and last and earn $1400 for his pains, one place behind Carlson's replacement driver Hughes. Porporato, who had been delayed with broken bonnet straps, was fifth with 100 miles to go when a piston seized. Harry Grant was also

---

THE INDIANAPOLIS 500

The Indianapolis Motor Speedway had been opened for two years before its inaugural 500-mile race was run in 1911. With the exception of the years of the Great War and the Second World War this has been held ever since, making it the oldest race to have been continually run on the same circuit. It is normally contested by a field of thirty-three cars, with riding mechanics being used in the early days.

The 2.5-mile track, a modern Circus Maximus with two long straights and four gently banked corners connected by two chutes, was an initiative of automotive parts businessman Carl Fisher. Since 1945, when it was saved by Terre Haute businessman, 'Tony' Hulman, it has been owned by the Hulman-George family.

Initially, the 500-mile race was sanctioned by the American Automobile Association, becoming a round of the AAA National Championship when that was first officially contested in 1916. In 1956, the national championship was taken over by the United States Auto Club. In 1979, the leading team owners formed Championship Auto Racing Teams (CART), which ran its own championship. The Indianapolis race, though, was still sanctioned by USAC. However, the CART teams continued to run in the Indianapolis 500 and after a brief hiatus it, too, counted for the new series.

In 1996, the then Speedway president Tony George caused controversy when he created the Indy Racing League, a new championship that would include the Indianapolis 500. CART continued with its Champ Car series, now without what had been its main race, and a split occurred in US open-wheel racing. This continued until 2008 when, with both series in decline, Champ Car was absorbed into the IRL.

2

THE ENGLISHMAN FROM LIVORNO – DARIO RESTA

"... the greatest race man in the world."

I n 1916, the Indianapolis 500 fell to a British citizen for the first time, only he was born in Italy and the race was just 300 miles long. He was also called Dario, which led to a coincidence ninety-one years later. Dario Resta hailed from Livorno, on the west coast of Italy but when he was only two-years old, his father, one time cavalry officer-cum-studio photographer Enrico, moved the family to Bayswater, London where he was brought up. His complexion gave a hint to his birth but his aristocratic English accent indicated his chosen nationality.

Backed by FR Fry of the famed chocolate manufacturer Fry's, Resta had taken up racing in his mid-twenties, competing at Brooklands, including the first meeting there where he finished third in the 30-mile Montagu Cup. He was to enter for the Grand Prix de l'Automobile Club de France (ACF) in 1908 at the wheel of an Austin, and then in 1912, 1913, and 1914 for Sunbeam. One of his Austin team-mates, Lord Brabazon of Tara, remembered that Resta wrecked three cars practising for the 1908 race, "Which annoyed Austin very much; for we had only five in all." As a result of the third accident, he was charged with dangerous driving and had to serve a month in prison after the race.

Hampered by an arm injury – the result of one of those crashes – and a slipping clutch, Resta finished a lowly 19th in his first Grand Prix but was placed fifth when the ACF resumed what is colloquially known as the French Grand Prix four years later again at Dieppe. That year the event was combined with the Coupe de L'Auto for 3.0-litre cars. All entries for this were automatically eligible for placings in the Grand Prix, as well as their own class. Resta's Sunbeam – he was now chief test driver for the firm – was one of three entered by the factory for this lesser category. A polished performance saw him lead the class from the eighth lap on the first day, at which point he was fourth overall behind just three of the mighty Grand Prix cars. On the final 47.84-mile lap of the second day he was still in fourth place and leading his class. However, team-mate Victor Rigal speeded up and, contrary to team spirit, overtook him. The performance of the 3.0-litre Sunbeams and Vauxhalls over those two days was a very early indication of what British cars could eventually do in a Grand Prix.

The following year at Amiens, Resta finished sixth overall, having been as high as fourth at one point before falling back with oil swamping his cockpit, due to a leaking reserve tank, which made it necessary to stop every four laps to replenish the sump. At Lyons in 1914, he was again soon up to fourth, despite the fact that the Sunbeams lacked the maximum speed of many of their rivals. Although he was to drop down the order, as the 20-lap race progressed he was back up to fifth at its conclusion.

Further races at Brooklands and elsewhere – in 1914 he was, for example, to win with Indianapolis veteran 'Toodles IV' at both Brooklands and Saltburn Sands – confirmed 'Dolly' Resta as one of Britain's leading racing drivers. However, an offer from US Peugeot

Horsepower at Indianapolis. In 1915 Resta's dark blue Peugeot battled DePalma's Mercedes. (Courtesy Indianapolis Motor Speedway)

Resta, seen here with riding mechanic Fred McCarthy, grimly determined before the start of the 1915 race. (Courtesy Indianapolis Motor Speedway)

importer Alphonse G Kaufman at the beginning of the Great War to race in America led to a phase in his career and a glorious year in which he could be regarded as the most successful driver then competing.

Resta moved to New York as a representative of Kaufman's Peugeot Auto Import Company and married American Mary Wishart, sister of the late Spencer who had driven in the first four Indianapolis 500s, promising his new wife that he would give up racing. That assurance did not last for long. He soon found success winning, for Peugeot, the 1915 American Grand Prize in San Francisco and then, two weeks later, the Vanderbilt Cup on the same course. 'A close relation' writing for *Motor Sport* in 1950 reckoned the, "Frequent spells of bad luck which had dogged him on so many occasions (in Europe) were (now) conspicuously absent." L Spencer Riggs recorded that, despite these performances, the Americans remained unconvinced and wondered how he would perform at "... a real racetrack"; Indianapolis.

Resta had entered the 1915 500, initially to drive a Sunbeam but then this was to change, perhaps understandably, to a Peugeot L76 belonging to his employer. Compared to Brooklands, the Speedway offered Resta few problems and he was quickly at home, qualifying for third place on the front row. For the first time, the race, originally scheduled for the Saturday, was delayed because of rain. Speedway policy then was not to run the event on a Sunday and the resulting wait saw pressure on accommodation and even, it was said, a shortage of food in the area.

The 500 itself turned out to be a close battle between Resta and the also Italian-born Ralph DePalma. The blue Peugeot was quicker on the straights, DePalma's Mercedes through the turns. During the early stages Resta had fought the Stutz team, leading on the opening circuit and between laps thirty-three and sixty-one. DePalma then moved up into the lead but Resta displaced him on lap 128 and, at one point was a lap in front, before a blown, right, rear tyre, the resulting brush with the outside wall, and a pit stop lost him the advantage. It was also reported that, in the last 150 miles, Resta had experienced a great deal of slack in his steering gear; a post-race examination finding the trouble to have been in the worm gear itself. At the finish there were four inches of free movement on the rim of the wheel. In the event, DePalma pulled away, although, two laps from the end, a broken connecting rod punched two holes in his crankcase. The engine was spewing oil as he nursed it to the finish, still able to beat Resta by over three minutes.

One item in the local press suggested that Resta had "... infringed upon the etiquette of clean sportsmanship when he was making his mad dash." It was said that he had tried to push DePalma into the wall at one point, but the victor made no complaint. Indeed, there was a suggestion that Resta had, himself, been forced close to the wall on the northeast turn by Johnny Aitken, who was that year appearing as a relief driver. The media was otherwise in praise of Resta's effort. "And then came Resta!" ran one headline. "Feared by his victories in the (United States) Grand Prix and Vanderbilt races, the English-Italian in his Peugeot drove a splendid race, and not until the last lap, when the checkered flag was flaunted across the track in front of DePalma, was he out of the battle for the capital prize."

The year that 'Brit Corner' burst into song, 2009. From the left Andrew Garside, Nick Garside, and Fiona Lovell. (Author's collection)

the start time was put back from 10.00am to early in the afternoon leaving a couple of cars still attempting to qualify at the hour the race would normally commence. Only twenty-one drivers started but DePalma was not amongst them, following a disagreement with the organisers over appearance money. Resta, however, was back with his Peugeot Auto Import Company entry. "The blue speed creation which the famous English-Italian pilot drove virtually was the same machine with which he forced Ralph DePalma to the finish here a year ago," wrote a local reporter. "It was the same machine he drove to victory in the Chicago contest a few months ago." It was also noted that the car had "... gone through many improvements ..." since first appearing in the US fourteen months previously. "The engine has been reconstructed under the personal supervision of the driver."

On race day, a crowd of between 65,000 and 70,000 ensured that the grandstands were full and the bleachers "... jammed to the rails." After it had been noted that the Italian flag was flying upside down and the misdemeanour rectified, the cars were dispatched, one at a time, and the drivers were introduced to the crowd before returning to the start line. Four bombs announced the race; two to send the drivers and mechanics back to their cars, a third to signal the start, and a fourth to send them on their way at precisely 1.28pm. Eddie Rickenbacher, in a Maxwell, took an immediate lead, driving furiously. By the end of the fourth lap he was a quarter of a mile ahead. On the sixth lap the Peugeots of Aitken and Resta drew a little closer, but two tours later the soon-to-be fighter ace had extended his lead to half a lap. Aitken and Resta continued to put on a great fight for second place, moving up when the Maxwell suffered a broken steering knuckle after nine laps. On the eighteenth lap Aitken pitted for a new tyre, and Resta sailed into the lead. At the 60-mile mark he was more than a lap ahead of the rest of the field, and by quarter-distance he had lapped everybody.

At the 175-mile mark Resta drove into the pits. It was reported that the pit manager, Arthur Hill, seemed to know, "... when the great driver was going to pull in." Fuel was poured in and the rear right tyre

Resta's fame now rose with wins on the board tracks at Mayfield and Sheepshead Bay, on one occasion becoming the first driver to cover 100 miles in less than an hour during a competition in the US.

The following year, Carl Fisher made the mistake of reducing the race distance to 300 miles in the belief that this was what the public wanted. He soon realised the error of his ways and, when racing returned after the Great War, the status quo was resumed. For the first time,the cars were lined up on the grid according to the day on which they had qualified, a system that continues, although modified, to this day. Resta, accompanied by (the then obligatory) riding mechanic Bob Dahnke, was on the outside of the front row. With the race shortened,

Resta and mechanic Bob Dahnke prior to their winning run in the 1916 500. The Italian-born Englishman was arguably the best racing driver competing during the Great War period. (Courtesy Indianapolis Motor Speedway)

changed in a rapid 1min 5sec before "Resta was off again on his mad dash for the prize." He was described as being, "... not only a masterful driver but also a mechanical tactician. (He) won because his machine was mechanically fit. He knew exactly how long his tires would 'stand up.' And he knew how many times he would be forced into the pits. Therein lies the secret of Resta's winning." Come the last lap it was noted that he was "simply joy-riding" at about 60mph in order to stay ahead of second place man 'Wilbur D'Alene.'

A British driver in a French car had won, which might go some way to explaining why the perhaps patriotic *Indianapolis Star* rather grudgingly stated that, "... extraordinary good luck kept Resta in the lead while others enjoyed misfortunes." The fans were also upset that Resta had driven straight into the garage area after his win, avoiding the victory celebrations. What they probably could not comprehend was that, unlike their approachable local heroes, Resta was a shy, modest individual. Another wrote, "Resta had the nerve. He had the stamina, the ability, and his sturdy blue racer flashed across the finish and into the rich purse offered by the speedway management."

It has been suggested that former rival Ralph DePalma recommended Resta for this drive in the Packard team for 1923. (Courtesy Indianapolis Motor Speedway)

Also in contrast to the comment about his luck, the *Star*'s front page proclaimed that Resta's, "... performance in the Peugeot yesterday stamps him as the greatest race man in the world." It was some claim, but it must be remembered that much of that world had long been at war. On the day of the race, warned by an intercepted signal that the German High Seas Fleet was about to leave harbour, British admiral John Jellicoe led the British Grand Fleet into the North Sea. The following day would see the protagonists engaged in the greatest surface ship engagement of all time, the Battle of Jutland. In December of the following year, the US itself declared war on Germany. Rumours that this was to happen had abounded earlier in the year, forcing Carl Fisher to abandon plans to run another 500. The race cars would not return until 1919; Resta not until 1923.

After the 500, Resta had done his best to live up to the media's claim, beating DePalma the next month on the board oval at Chicago, winning at Omaha in July, then Chicago again in October, before retrieving the Vanderbilt Cup at Santa Monica in November. The resulting 4100 points gave him the first officially contested AAA National Championship, the equivalent of today's IndyCar Series.

Although part of the aborted Sunbeam entry for 1919, Resta did not return to the Speedway until 1923; a comeback year after a period of retirement. This time he found himself as team-mate to DePalma, driving a hurriedly-prepared Packard. Apparently now less reserved, he received more publicity than on his previous appearances, but

the Speedway seemed changed and he knew few of the top drivers. Qualifying on the first possible day gave him third on the grid, even though he was only seventh quickest overall. He was to last for eighty-seven laps before a blown head gasket put his car out. That was the last Indy 500 for Britain's first winner. He returned to Europe to continue racing and was killed at Brooklands in the summer of 1924 while making a series of record attempts in a Grand Prix Sunbeam. At the beginning of the Railway Straight, the car's offside rear tyre left its rim. He held the initial skid but, with the front wheels on full lock, the car turned right round and hit the corrugated iron fence tail first. The petrol tank was split and the car caught fire, Resta being killed and his mechanic Bill Perkins seriously injured.

When Resta had won the AAA Championship in 1916 it had been a controversial result, assisted by the fact that his rival for the title, Johnny Aitken, had won the final deciding race only as a relief driver and, therefore, unable to score points. The fans had made their feelings clear about this and it is said that Resta lost much of his enthusiasm because of their reaction. However, reunited with Sunbeam, he appeared to be back to his old self. Indeed, he had been discussing a single-seat version of the Grand Prix car with Louis Coatalen, perhaps, it has been suggested, for use at Indianapolis. But for that tragic, September accident, the two most notable British names from Indy's early history might have returned to the Speedway ...

DONALD DAVIDSON

The young man from Salisbury, England created quite a stir. He had turned up at Indianapolis for the 1964 500; his first ever visit to the US and yet seemed to know considerably more about the race than the regulars at the Speedway. Donald Davidson had spent several years saving up the money to make the trip. During that time he had amassed a tremendous amount of information about the race, having what he was later told was a Selective Retentive Easy Access Memory. In other words, he could not be bothered with what did not interest him, but would "soak up, devour, and retain" what did. Inspired by 'the Memory Man,' Leslie Welch, the British radio entertainer, who would answer questions on sport thrown at him by a live audience, Davidson fantasised that a similar 'act' would go down well at Indy.

To this day, Davidson is in awe of the way in which the Speedway received him. He arrived on the first qualifying day to find that a genteel correspondence with Frances Derr, the IMS director of ticket sales ("she was like my aunt"), had resulted in his being given one of the desirable bronze badges that would grant him entry to the paddock. "Everybody was there and they were so accessible." News of Davidson's memory quickly got around. He would hang around the garages until about 10.00pm becoming something of an attraction in his suit, white shirt, and tie … and winkle picker shoes; "A style that never caught on here." Soon he was holding court as drivers were brought to him. "To my amazement, I was immediately taken into the inner circle. I could not believe how open and friendly everybody was."

Over a three-week period, Davidson met many of the legends that he had been reading about. Track owner Tony Hulman personally drove him back to his digs on three occasions. Jim Rathmann, the winner in 1960, even said that he was flying to Florida for a couple of days to meet up with some friends, none other than astronauts Gus Grissom and Gordon Cooper, and would Davidson like to go with him. It was not an isolated incident but there is still obvious regret in his voice when he says "And I didn't do it!"

Prior to his trip Davidson had been corresponding with a number of people, including Autosport magazine's Indianapolis 500 reporter Skip Lange, and Sid Collins, the voice of the IMS Radio Network. The latter took the young man under his wing and during the race Davidson was invited to be a guest on the air, being briefly asked to describe the career of one of the drivers, in this case 1932 winner Fred Frame. After about a minute a pit stop brought an end to his slot, and it was not until many years later that he discovered that the commentators had continued to talk about him for some time after he had left their booth.

A year later Davidson gave up his job as a cinema projectionist, applied for a green card, and purchased a one-way ticket to the States. He was welcomed back. Former 500 racer and now the competitions director of the United States Auto Club, English-born Henry Banks asked Davidson to visit him on the Thursday after the race. The next morning he started work for USAC not even knowing what he would be doing. To his delight it was to act as statistician, a role he undertook for many years.

Thanks to Collins he became part of the IMS Radio Network crew that season, a role that he is still performing. In 1966 WIBC, a prominent local radio station, invited him to host a fifteen-minute programme in which listeners would call in and pose questions to him. This was just a one-off but, in May 1971, he returned with his own programme, which continues to this day. Initially it was a quiz show where listeners would try to stump him, but now contains more anecdotal material about the drivers.

In 1997 Davidson left USAC to become the historian for the Indianapolis Motor Speedway, probably the only track in the world that has such a person on its payroll. Three days prior to the 2010 race, he was inducted into the Auto Racing Hall of Fame, just one of twenty-four living members, all but three of whom have participated in the 500. It was a significant honour. He believes that his life has been proof that you can follow your dreams. "It is said that the nobody remembers who came second and that you can't live in the past, but that is not true, I have made a career out of trivia."

Quintessentially British in jacket and tie, Donald Davidson was introduced in 1964 to one of the legends of the Speedway, Eddie Sachs. Tragically, Sachs was killed during that year's race. To their right is driver-turned-official Harry McQuinn, who acted as unofficial chaperon to Davidson. (Courtesy Jack Fox)

3

THE NOT-SO-ROARING TWENTIES

"No effort was made at speed."

Britain, no longer the undoubted superpower of Victorian times, was left reeling by the Great War. Racing at Brooklands did not recommence until April 1920, the resident-for-the-duration Royal Flying Corps having wreaked havoc on the track. The emphasis there was still on short handicap races. Sunbeam, though, seems to have had Indianapolis in its sights almost as soon as the war had ended. Three of the 4.0-litre six-cylinder cars were entered for the 1919 500 as early as January. Two were said to have turned up in the US during early May, with 1916 winner Dario Resta and Jean Chassagne nominated as the drivers. Neither car was scrutineered or officially timed, but on May 20 they were withdrawn. Quite why has remained a mystery, although it has been pointed out that their engine capacity was four cubic inches in excess of the race's 300-cubic inch limit.

One English driver did arrive at the Speedway in 1920. Jack Scales, who had driven in the 1914 Grand Prix de l'ACF for his then employer Fiat, and Jean Porporato entered the 500 with a pair of hastily prepared but conservative Gregoires. At Lyons, Scales was said to have, "... created favourable comment" before retiring with a broken camshaft drive. He and his Italian team-mate turned up late at Indianapolis, thanks to a shipping strike, and made frantic attempts to qualify the day before the race. Scales damaged a piston, which was repaired, but further problems hampered his attempt. In the near darkness, Proporato just managed to scramble into the race but it was too late for Scales.

Sunbeam's final assault on the 500 came in 1921. Louis Coatalen entered three 3-litre, straight 8-cylinder cars, an example of which made its debut at the Brooklands 1921 Easter meeting, winning the 3-litre Scratch Race in the hands of future Grand Prix victor Henry Seagrave. Their appearance was in keeping with the time, less like the pre-war monsters and more the look that would exemplify the early post-war years. To be precise only two were entered as Sunbeams, the other, differing only by the shape of its radiator, used the company's Talbot Darracq badge. Seven other 3-litre cars were also made for the Grand Prix de l'ACF.

It was hoped, at one stage, that Dario Resta might drive one of the STD cars but in the event none of the drivers were British. The 1914 500 winner, Frenchman Réné Thomas, and American Ora Haibe raced the Sunbeams, another Frenchman Andre Boillot, the Talbot Darracq. Thomas ran third until a water connection broke, Boillot retired with big-end failure, while Haibe soldiered on to finish fifth.

It was Sunbeam's last appearance at the Brickyard. The marque was to win Grands Prix, two Tourist Trophies, and three times take the World Land Speed Record, but it left Indianapolis virtually empty handed, with just the $11,700 that it had won there.

The years 1922 to 1926 saw a smattering of intriguing British drivers enter the 500, mainly better known for exploits elsewhere, and a charismatic British marque. First up was little, Bristol-born W Douglas Hawkes – who had raced at both Brooklands and on the Continent – in a factory-entered, basically production, 3-litre Bentley. This was still 1922, and the marque had yet to make its reputation at Le Mans. However, its cars were starting to appear abroad including,

Not Le Mans but Indianapolis. The 500 was the Bentley team's first international race. Riding mechanic H S 'Bertie' Browning accompanied driver Douglas Hawkes. (Courtesy Indianapolis Motor Speedway)

as WO (Walter Owen) Bentley himself said, at Indianapolis "... of all places."

"Oddly enough the famous American Indianapolis 500 miles was the first major event in which we entered; it was also our first major error," wrote Bentley. It was an event that was to prove a costly exercise for the Cricklewood-based company in sending both a professional driver and a mechanic with car. Bentley employee Hawkes was unable to keep pace with the Miller-engined cars then dominating the Speedway. Bentley's view was that, although Indianapolis had been dominated by European cars at one stage, it was now too specialised for all but "... experienced natives, a state of affairs that was to endure until the 1960s."

Said the *Indianapolis Star*, "The English Bentley driven by Douglas Hawkes of London has not shown enough speed at the brick yard (*sic*) to be considered a serious contender, although he is reported to have made a wonderful record at the Brooklands course in England. The aim of the English crew is to try and finish the machine in the top ten amongst whom the $50,000 prize money is to be divided, rather than go out to win." It was also, wrote Bentley later, "... to show the Americans what we were doing." Hawkes was the last of the nineteen who qualified on the first day of the trials with an average of 81.0mph, nearly 20mph down on the fastest time. On his first day at the track, local journalist W Blaine Patton had observed that "No effort was made at speed." Despite all this, it is said that the Americans were impressed by the Bentley's subsequent thirteenth place. Hawkes himself was due to drive a similar car in the Isle of Man Tourist Trophy on June 22 and only just made it back in time for the first practice.

The year 1923 saw an entry from the magnetic Count Louis Zborowski, who lived

The immaculate Zborowski was excited by the idea of the Indianapolis 500. (Courtesy Indianapolis Motor Speedway)

Two British drivers on the front two rows of the 1923 race. Resta is on the outside of the front line, Zborowski in the centre of the second. (Courtesy Indianapolis Motor Speedway)

on a country estate in Kent, England, and the return of Dario Resta. Zborowski, a British citizen, although the son of a Polish count and a wealthy American lady, had purchased one of the Bugattis that had been raced in the Grand Prix de l'ACF at Strasbourg the year before. It was to be one of a team of five cars from the French marque entered for Indianapolis that year. The race was something that Zborowski, a boating, model railway, and wireless enthusiast, had followed with interest, and which excited his racing ambitions. All the cars now had smart, offset single-seater bodies designed by French aviator engineer, Louis Becherau, who had been responsible for the wartime SPAD fighter planes. Zborowski's was painted bright blue with scarlet padding to the headrest. Another Briton, Clive Gallop – who, like Zborowski, had raced an Aston Martin at Strasbourg – was named as reserve for the team, and Dick Cooper was recruited as team manager.

Despite a sense of optimism, the members of the team quickly realised that their cars were not a match for those of the regulars. During his visit, Zborowski was to place an order for a Los Angeles-built Miller that he could take back across the Atlantic to race in that year's European Grand Prix at Monza. "Never ..." it was written at the time, "... in the history of racing sport has a foreign speed king come to America for a racing car."

The Count, a regular competitor at Brooklands like the other British drivers who started the 500 during this period, was fifth fastest in practice. It is said that he commenced the race, immaculate as

ever in tailored black overalls, driving hatless and with no goggles behind his small aero windscreen. *Autocar* reported that he "... steadily improved his position by sheer hard driving at the corners." On his tail sat team-mate Pierre de Vizcaya. On the forty-fourth lap a broken con rod put him out of the race. "His driving in (the) Indianapolis race, when his Bugatti met with ill-luck, will be remembered," said *Motor Sport*. Zborowski returned with the car to England, racing it at Brooklands and the Kop hillclimb near Princes Risborough, before his death driving for Mercedes at Monza the following year.

It was in 1924 that journalist Patton in his regular *Observed from the Speedway Pits* column reported, "Moss, the English driver, was on track for a few laps in the Barber-Warnock he is to use." Little can Patton have realised the ultimate significance to motor sport in those few words. Sir Stirling Moss may never have raced at the Brickyard but his father certainly did.

As the son recalled, Alfred, a dental student, had a great ambition to compete in the 500 and persuaded his father, Abe, that Indianapolis was the best place in the world to study dental bridgework. In the autumn of 1923, he arrived at the School of Dental Medicine at the University of Indiana. The young Moss could never have afforded to put himself in a position to enter the race but, in this way, he manoeuvred his father to do so.

Alfred had debuted at Brooklands in 1923 in an Anzani-engined Crouch. *Autocar* magazine reported his appearance favourably and that Easter he won the Private Competitors' Handicap. Another handicap victory followed later in the year and he went on to compete in the Junior Car Club's 200-Mile Race, where he retired with a blown gasket.

With this limited experience he talked his way into a drive with the Barber-Warnock Ford team for the 500, assisted by a letter of introduction from the Mercedes agent in the UK. The Barber-Warnock Specials were Frontenac-Fords, based on a Ford T chassis, designed by Louis Chevrolet, entered by a local Ford dealer and financed by Henry Ford himself. Moss presented his letter to Arthur Chevrolet, 'forgot' to retrieve it, and then went back for it four or five days later. By this time Chevrolet had lost it and, embarrassed, wrote a replacement of his own – "... probably a slightly more glowing one," says his son – that was sufficient for Moss to get the drive.

In practice, a tyre on Moss' car – said not to have been used for a couple of years – let go and bounced off the side of the track.

Like son, like father. Alfred Moss prepares to race. (Courtesy Indianapolis Motor Speedway)

However, the young Moss qualified twentieth and, in the race, finished sixteenth. At one point, sticking valves had been a problem. A pit stop on lap 138 saw the tappets adjusted and the rocker arms oiled, which seemed to cure the trouble. However, over-oiling resulted and a long stop made to change fouled plugs.

Sir Stirling recalls his father saying that such was the roughness of the track that he had to wear a strap around his waist for support. That Indy 500 was the highlight of Alfred's racing career. "He was very proud of it," said Sir Stirling, who admitted to having been inspired by his father's exploits at the Brickyard. "My father was referred to as 'the Earl of Moss,'" he added. It seems that Americans assumed most Englishmen to be aristocrats, for Hughie Hughes had sometimes been called, even in the newspapers, 'Lord Hughie.'

A year later, Moss was back in England where, presumably inspired by his Indy mount, he constructed his own Fronty-Ford-Speedsport, which was to win a Short Handicap race at the 1925 August Bank Holiday Brooklands meeting. He also acted as relief driver for Herbert Jones at the Speedway that year. During his time in America, the young dental student took part in a number of dirt track races. They were pretty tough, he was to tell his son. It is probable that he was the only Englishman to have raced at not only Indianapolis, but also on the dirt tracks that, prior to the British-led revolution of the 1960s, were an important step on the path to the 500 for many American drivers.

The three red Barber-Warnocks, including that of Alfred Moss, ready for the start. (Courtesy Indianapolis Motor Speedway)

On his marriage to the then Aileen Crauford in 1927, Moss gave up racing. However, it might be said that his influence on Indianapolis was not over yet. As will be seen, in the 1960s he was part of the group that had formed the British Racing Partnership (BRP), one of the final acts of which was to build a couple of cars, initially for the 1965 Indianapolis 500. "Papa ..." as he was known, "... was a genuine person," recalled BRP's chief designer Tony Robinson. "Polite, generous and jolly. Rarely did I see him lose his temper." However, he never spoke to Robinson about his Indy experience.

By the 1950s, Alfred, having become a highly successful dentist, was better known as the father of Stirling Moss. Father and son did talk about competing at Indianapolis but Stirling was far too busy racing in a whole variety of categories, including Formula One, to contemplate giving up the whole month of May. "I couldn't afford the time," he stated. Donald Davidson recalled seeing a telegram from car entrant John Zink offering Moss a drive for 1956 in the Watson used by Bob Sweikert to win the previous year. Moss sent a very polite reply saying that he was interested in racing at Indianapolis but only in a British car. Davidson also recalled that in the autumn of 1960, Moss was scheduled to test a Lotus at the Speedway but this was cancelled.

Finally, in 1961, Al Dean offered Moss a drive. Again the Englishman replied in a similar fashion to 1956. Dean countered with an offer to sponsor any British-built entry that Moss could line up. Stirling replied that it was too late for 1961 but that he was interested in talking about 1962. Before that could happen Moss' top line career had been ended by a horrific accident at Goodwood. 'Papa' remained the only Moss to race in the Indy 500, although a bearded Stirling was present in 1963 – as "a guest," he recalled.

Sir Stirling did compete in one oval race, the 1958 Race of Two Worlds at Monza, the second of two occasions when USAC Indy cars raced on the Italian track banked circuit. "It wasn't my cup of tea," he said. Driving a modified Maserati 420M known as the Eldorado Special, Moss finished fourth in the first of three heats, fifth in the second, but crashed out in the final heat when the Maserati's steering failed. In 1959, American Ralph Liguori failed to qualify the same Eldorado Italia car for the Indianapolis 500. Said Liguori, "I once tried to qualify a Maserati here. I think the only person who had ever driven it was an Englishman ..."

The Indianapolis press was pretty disparaging about the five foreign entries in 1926. All had originated in France, but two of them

The first of the Eldridge Specials, as driven by the talented London engineer, Ernest Eldridge, used a modified Amilcar 'Grand Sport' chassis. (Courtesy Indianapolis Motor Speedway)

had been built to his own design by Englishman E (Ernest) AD Eldridge. Eldridge, described in the Indianapolis press as, "... a British sportsman of considerable means," already had a reputation at Brooklands where he had averaged over 120mph with the mighty 21.7-litre FIAT 'Mephistopheles.' In 1924, he took the World Land Speed Record with the car.

The following year he turned his attention to the Grand Prix world. Based on Amilcar chassis with Anzani engines, his low-slung Eldridge Specials were built specifically for said category. They "... looked like a canoe turned upside down," observed the *Indianapolis News*. During the 1925 and 1926 seasons they competed in a number of top-level races, including the Grand Prix de l'ACF. Probably tempted by the prize money, he also entered the pair for himself and fellow Englishman, Douglas Hawkes – who, as the local press reminded its readers, had driven at Indy four years previously. "Hawkes is not a brilliant driver, as driving goes, but he'll be there when the hard going is over and have his car in good shape," was its verdict.

"The Eldridge Specials had been built in France but entered by an Englishman," said the *Indianapolis Star*. "It will be surprising if any one of the five (foreign cars) cross the wire first. One possibly may finish inside the money but the chances are against even this." The paper also inaccurately stated that "The Eldridge Specials had been built from the ground up especially for the present race." Eldridge had been active around this time record-breaking at France's own speed bowl, Montlhéry.

Also in the race was 1924 Le Mans 24-hour winner John Duff. He had been in the US for about two months, and it was said that he had travelled there to acquire an inside knowledge of American racing methods. "Duff has made a favorable impression among the drivers with whom he has come into contact. He has demonstrated in numerous ways that he is a thorough race driver in the time he has appeared on the local track."

Although Bentley – for whom he had won at La Sarthe – had competed here with Hawkes

THE BRITISH COMMONWEALTH

The British Empire, which once encompassed around one quarter of the world's population, has long since ceased to exist. However, in 1931 a number of Britain's former colonies joined together in a voluntary association known then as 'the British Commonwealth' and now as 'the Commonwealth of Nations.' The British sovereign is regarded as the symbolic head of this body, which currently has fifty-four members.

Drivers from four of these countries, in addition to the UK itself, have competed in the Indianapolis 500. Two, Canadian Jacques Villeneuve and New Zealander Scott Dixon, have won the race outright in 1995 and 2008 respectively. Dixon's compatriots, Denny Hulme and Graham McRae, and Australian Vern Schuppan have all won the Rookie of the Year award, as have Villeneuve and his fellow Canadian Alex Tagliani, and South African Tomas Scheckter.

Perhaps not surprisingly, excepting the British, Canada has supplied the most Commonwealth drivers for the race. If John Duff, born in China of Canadian parents, is included then the total for that country is fifteen. In addition, there have been seven Australians, four New Zealanders, and the sole South African.

Clockwise from above: Excluding the British themselves, just two drivers from the Commonwealth have won the Indianapolis 500; Jacques Villeneuve in 1995 … (Courtesy Indianapolis Motor Speedway)

… and New Zealand's Scott Dixon in 2008. (Author's collection)

Canada's Marty Roth hits the wall for the second year running in 2008. Roth was to sell his team to fellow Canadian Alex Tagliani's new FAZZT operation for 2010. (Author's collection)

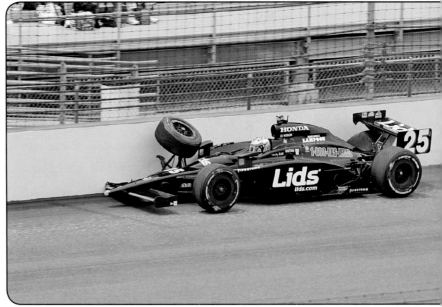

driving, Duff, another previous owner of 'Mephistopheles,' was at the wheel of a more conventional Miller. Born in China of Canadian parents, he had travelled across Russia, aged nineteen, to join the British Army during the Great War. Wounded in 1917, so far ahead of the Allied Lines that he was hit by so-called friendly fire, he had settled in England, racing at Brooklands, and establishing a Bentley dealership. Described by the Indianapolis press as a "famous English driver," he qualified the straight-eight, supercharged Miller-engined

Elcar Special (entered by the Elcar Automotive Co) in which Herbert Jones had been killed during the previous Thursday's trials. It was said that the team's pit and garage manager, Bill Hunt, made a "... heroic effort … to put the demolished car back into racing condition in such a short length of time. When it was wheeled off the track after hitting the wall and turning over two or three times it appeared a hopeless task. Close inspection, however, revealed that the engine had been uninjured."

Duff qualified the car at an average of 95.546mph, after recording better than 100mph on his first lap.

There was little to show from the British during the first half of the race. However, after 250 miles, Duff moved into ninth spot. He was still in that position when the race was stopped for rain on 160 laps, Duff having done 147. Eldridge, also described locally as, "... the English sportsman and manufacturer," was forced out on the 45th lap by carburettor trouble. (At one point during the race he had been temporarily relieved as driver by former wartime fighter pilot Herschel McKee). He then took over Hawkes' mount but was pushed off the track on the 91st lap, the last of the foreign cars to have been still running when its "... timing gears were put of out commission." The car was a full forty-four laps behind the leader.

The Eldridge Specials used 1.5-litre supercharged, four-cylinder Anzani side valve engines. Note the seven-year old reference to Resta, Dahnke, and the Sunbeam team on the garage door (see inset) – a partnership that never came to fruition. (Courtesy Indianapolis Motor Speedway)

The start in 1926 with three Britons on the grid; a number not seen in the race again until 1966. Duff's Elcar is at the very back, while the distinctively low Eldridge Specials can be seen in the centre of the line-up, towards the rear. (Courtesy Indianapolis Motor Speedway)

The local press were quick to show that they had been proved right. "The European entries were at no time serious contenders," said one commentator. "The five foreign cars which started failed to show much. Not a single one of the number was running at the finish," said another.

Eldridge subsequently entered the Specials for the board-track races at Altoona and Salem-Rockingham but failed to start on both occasions. He also tried a Miller while in the US and ran it at Atlantic

City before returning to Europe to make record attempts with it at Montlhéry. It was during these runs that he crashed and was left with serious head injuries and the loss of an eye. Despite this he was to return to record-breaking.

Duff, too, entered the Altoona and Salem races, having purchased the Elcar Special, finishing third in the 250-mile contest at the former, in front of 60,000 spectators. Thanks to a puncture at the Rockingham track, his car smashed into a guardrail and he was thrown out. As a result, he promised his wife, Clansa, that he would retire from racing.

Like Eldridge, Hawkes must also have been impressed by the Millers. In 1930, he bought a front-wheel-drive, 1.5-litre version and shipped it to Europe. Hawkes had a controlling interest in the Derby Company, which was based just outside Paris. Much work was done on the Miller, so much so that it became known as the Derby-Miller and subsequently the Derby Special. It proved a notable car, driven at Brooklands and Montlhéry by the formidable Gwenda Stewart, who was to become Hawkes' wife.

The British, though, had lost interest in the Indianapolis 500. The 1927 entry would be all American. Just two more English-born drivers would compete prior to the Second World War, one of them, Henry Banks, who had been brought up in the US, attempting to qualify on fourteen occasions and starting on six between 1936 and 1954. On the first occasion he became the first driver to pass a qualifying rookie test for the 500.

Banks, who was eventually to become USAC's significant director of competitions (where he was to hire a young Donald Davidson as keeper of records), won the AAA Championship in 1950 but only finished once in the top 10 at Indy. In 1951, driving Lindsey Hopkins' Blue Crown Special, he was placed sixth last of those to complete 200 laps. After his retirement from racing, Banks continued to return to the Speedway. Then, in 1959, he was controversially asked if he would like to replace the fired Duane Carter at USAC, which, three years earlier had replaced the AAA. At the time he was working for Ford's aircraft division. Banks flew to Indianapolis to discuss the position only to find on arrival that it was considered a 'done deal' at $15,000 a year.

The other British-born driver to appear in the 1930s, failed to qualify in 1939 and was only to compete in three 500s but, while Banks' career at the Speedway was a long one, his was brief. His name was George Robson.

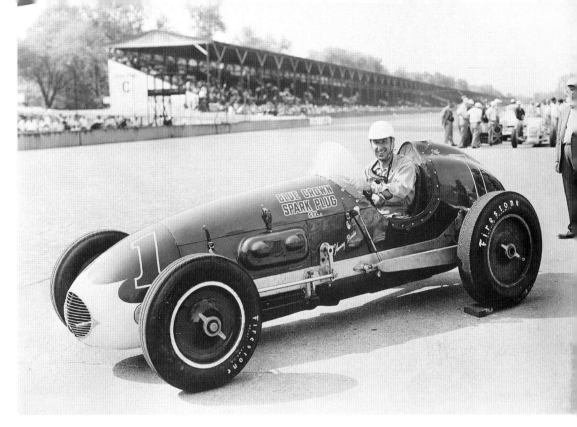

English-born Banks' highest place Indianapolis 500 finish came in 1951 when he was placed sixth in Lindsay Hopkins' Offy-engined Blue Crown Spark Plug Special. (Courtesy Indianapolis Motor Speedway)

In 1965 Banks (left) offered work to Donald Davidson, who was making his second trip to the States. Davidson was to remain at Indianapolis from then on. (Courtesy Jack Fox)

THE UNION JACK

The Union Jack 'flies' proudly about a mile and a half from the Speedway. To be precise there is a pub of that name at the far end of West 25th Street that not only bears the name of the flag of Great Britain but also has a British-born owner. Rick Rising-Moore commenced life in the Radcliffe Infirmary, Oxford, the son of an RAF mother and a Canadian serviceman who had met in Kings Lynn during the Second World War. With the hostilities over, the family moved to Canada where his father trained to be a veterinary surgeon. A tuberculosis problem in cattle meant a subsequent move to Indianapolis for eight Canadian vets, including Rising-Moore's father, on what should have been a one-year assignment. They all liked it and decided to stay.

Another of the vets ran a bagpipe band, the Gordon Pipers, of which the young Rick was a member. Speedway owner Tony Hulman sometimes attended its annual pipe festival and the band also played at the 500. (It also later became involved with Jim Clark.) Following service in the Vietnam War, he was asked where he would like to be posted and replied as near as possible to his grandmother in Weymouth, who he had not seen since he was three-years old. The subsequent posting was in Germany but he was able to travel to England on a number of occasions, becoming intrigued by "the British culture and my heritage." His grandfather had been in charge of the food and beverage services for the Flying Scotsman train, while another ancestor had been an architect in the time of Queen Victoria who "had to put his stamp on every pub that was built during her reign." Perhaps not surprisingly, he found himself in the catering business after leaving the military and became involved in the growth of the national restaurant chains, eventually building about twenty such outlets throughout the Mid West for himself and others.

In the early 1980s a pizza restaurant near to the Speedway was in trouble, and Rising-Moore, who watched his first 500 in 1964, saw an opportunity to take it over and open a premises near the track. Not only was this to be a bar but it could also be used as a gallery for Rising-Moore's friend, local motorsport artist Ron Burton. The Union Jack, as it was to become known "because of the British invasion," evolved into a meeting place for mechanics and racing personalities "like Graham Hill."

Over the past quarter century Rising-Moore has been able to witness the trends at the Speedway as those involved patronised his pub. "I think the British invasion legitimised racing, changing it from being just a show at county fairs to a real business."

Rick Rising-Moore keeps one of his friend, Jim Crawford's, helmets at the Union Jack bar. (Author's collection)

4

NEWCASTLE-BORN – GEORGE ROBSON

"We're not big people ..."

Thirty-six-year old George Robson from Maywood, California but born in Newcastle-upon-Tyne, England, was on his way from Los Angeles to compete in the Indianapolis 500 for the third time. He was, by his own admission, travelling too fast at 70mph and ran his Mercury into a ditch. "Robson is not a cautious road driver," *Philadelphia Daily News* sports reporter Lanse McCurley was to say later. It was not an auspicious start to the month of May, 1946. It was to end, though, with Robson averaging 114.82mph – slightly higher than his own prediction – on his way to victory in the first post-war race at the Brickyard.

The Robson family had moved from North East England to Toronto in 1910, the year after George's birth, but returned to the UK when the Great War started. George's father, also George, is recorded as an engine fitter on his son's birth certificate. When hostilities ceased, the family went back to Canada, before moving to Los Angeles where George and his brother, Hal, learnt the machinist trade in the family shop. Later, it was noted, though, that he would never interfere with his mechanics over a car, believing that to do so would be to disturb the harmony necessary for a team.

The friendly Robson cut a slender, 5ft 6in figure, 'bantamweight' was one way to describe him, a "... tousled-haired hotfoot in a

The Robson brothers (left-to-right Jimmy, Hal, and George) at Southgate Speedway, California, circa 1940. (Chalmers Davies photo, courtesy Don Radbruch)

George Robson cut his proverbial teeth racing sprint cars and midgets in California. (Courtesy Julie Schram collection)

Robson's first start in the Indy 500 was in Marty Keller's Offy-powered car. This was one of the vaunted front-drive machines that made up the 1935 Miller-Ford team. (Ted Wilson photo, courtesy Ed Slane collection)

home-made shirt," according to *Indianapolis Star* reporter Lloyd H Wilkins. Robson's wife, Marjorie, made the shirt herself to his specifications and specifically with short sleeves. Neither a smoker nor a drinker, he was described by her as a "family man." They had two children, George (twelve in 1946) and Beverly (six). Beverly does not remember much about her father, However, she does recall wanting to wear her white shoes to a racetrack. Margie told her absolutely not but Robson overrode her decision and told her "You go right ahead and wear them."

He played golf in his spare time, although he would not divulge his scores to the press. "Let's stick to racing," he would say.

"Modest and assuming," was how the *Indianapolis News* described him, "He neither dodges nor seeks publicity. When told he was to have a suite of rooms at one of Indianapolis' finer hotels, he remarked, 'We're not big people, we don't need any more than one room.'"

George had begun racing in 1931 at Riverside, Chowchilla, and Burbank. His mother was to recount years later how George and brother Hal made their debut at Chowchilla in a modified Ford roadster known as the "Galloping Bathtub." George progressed on the more prominent tracks, winning at the Huntingdon Beach and Southern Ascot Speedways, where three of the four Robson brothers, George, Hal, and Jimmy competed. Around 1936, the Robsons seemed to dominate Southern Ascot. Jimmy was badly injured at Oakland Speedway in 1941 but George and Hal, both of whom have

been described as "highly talented," raced on. (Hal, who was born in Canada, was to compete in the 500 three times from 1946 to 1948 and then fail to qualify in 1949 and 1953.)

In his first attempt, 1939, Robson initially qualified for the Indy 500 but was bumped from the field. In 1940, he both qualified and was classified in twenty-third position following shock absorber failure on his black Keller Special. This Offy-powered car, owned by Marty Keller, had originally been one of the famed 1935 front-engined Miller-

Ford team. The following year Leon Duray put in the first entry for the 500 with Robson named as his driver. Hal was expected to act as relief for Duray's Gilmore Red Lion Weil. The brothers were also taking their own midget with them to Indiana. "The Robsons are steady drivers, not as spectacular as some," said the press.

George's qualification performance improved up to sixteenth but an oil leak dropped him out after only sixty-six laps, one short of his 1940 total. He later relieved Tommy Hinnershitz, who went on

The first car entered for the 1941 race was Leon Duray's Gilmore Red Lion Special, to be driven by Robson. (Courtesy Indianapolis Motor Speedway)

Robson in front of one of the Indianapolis garages prior to the 1946 race. (Courtesy Julie Schram collection)

to finish tenth, in the same race. George and Hal returned to their machine shop in California where, for the duration of the war, they made parts for planes and ships. On May 7, 1946 they sold the shop and, the same day, left for Indianapolis.

Robson's car owner for May 1946 was Joel Thorne. It is said that he had to be asked four times before agreeing to drive one of the wealthy sportsman's Thorne Engineering Specials. Thorne entered two cars for 500, originally planning to drive one himself – he had already raced there thrice before the war. However, by May he was wheelchair bound, thanks to a broken leg resulting from a motorcycle accident in California, and was to sit in the pits throughout the race, directing the crew. Because of this, Robson nearly had an illustrious team-mate, for the drive was offered to pre-war Mercedes-Benz Grand Prix star Rudolf Caracciola who had originally, until customs difficulties intervened, hoped to race one of the 1.5-litre W165 Mercedes that had dominated the 1939 Grand Prix of Tripoli.

The German went out to practice in a cloth helmet, still allowed in Europe but not in the US. He was flagged in and Colonel Arthur Herrington, British-born but now chairman of the AAA (American Automobile Association) Contest Board, offered him a British Army tank driver's helmet. It was later in practice that Caracciola was hit, possibly by a bird, possibly something else, lost control and thrown from his car. It is generally reckoned that the English made helmet had saved the great driver's life.

Robert Arbuthnot displays the Union Flag in the Indianapolis paddock. (Courtesy The Lagonda Club)

Arbuthnot tries to find speed at the IMS in his Lagonda. (Courtesy The Lagonda Club)

The Adams-chassied Thorne Engineering Specials, in which Robson and Caracciola were entered, were typical pre-war, dug-out-of-mothballs racers. One of them had beaten what was by then a nine-year old lap record at the Speedway in 1937, recording 130.49mph in the hands of Jimmy Snyder. They had been designed and built by Art Sparks after he had sold the idea to Joel Thorne, and were unusual for the time in that the engines featured six-cylinders. Originally the displacement had been 337 cubic inch, but this was reduced to 183 when new rules were adopted in 1938. Uniquely, the engine maintained magnesium alloy castings throughout. Today, Robson's car sits in the Indianapolis Hall of Fame donated by its last owner Ray T Brady.

Veteran Indy 500 fan Paul J Bryant was a friend of Robson's chief mechanic, Eddie Offutt. He recalled Offutt, who had worked with

FORLORN ATTEMPTS

Two famous British names did appear on the Indianapolis 500 entry lists during the 1940s, although neither was to qualify. The first of these was actually another W O Bentley design and, bizarrely, a car that had already competed in the Le Mans 24-hours; surely the only one to have attempted to run in both races.

Two Lagonda V12s were entered for Le Mans in 1939, much to Bentley's disgust as he felt that they were insufficiently developed. The pair came an unsensational but steady third and fourth; the factory car of Arthur Dobson and Charles Brackenbury being the first of these, the private entry of Lords Selsdon and Waleran being the second. Motor Sport magazine was particularly enthusiastic about the result. "Britains (sic) Great Come Back at Le Mans" read the headline. "Big green British cars thundered round the course as in days of old" and "the workmanlike green cars represented Britain so worthily in the race," read the copy. The two cars were predicted to do even better in 1940. However, while the Indianapolis 500 may still have been able to run that year, Europe was now at war and the cars never returned to La Sarthe.

They did, though, race at the 1939 Brooklands August Bank Holiday meeting with Brackenbury, winning a three-lap handicap race. With the commencement of war they were stored in a block of flats in Staines. This was subsequently hit by a V1 flying bomb and the cars badly damaged. After the war, the remains were taken back to the factory: Brackenbury bought the works car and Scot, Robert Arbuthnot, a dapper member of a banking family and the owner of High Speed Motors, the other. Both cars needed new bodies and the latter appeared at the Elstree Speed Trials with what might be described as an odd looking body, still asymmetric but somewhat squashed.

One then has to wonder about Arbuthnot's next sporting entry. It may simply have been that the V12 Lagonda was built for endurance racing and that there was nothing but sprints and short races likely for it in the UK. Over in the US, however, there was a long-distance event, albeit hardly one for a tractable, road going sports car, the Indianapolis 500.

Arbuthnot accordingly shipped the Lagonda to America and towed it from the New York docks to Indiana, having an accident on the way. A problem arose when he took it out on the Speedway. Selsdon had managed 128.03mph around Brooklands with this very car but, for reasons that appear lost in the mists of time, Arbuthnot could not exceed about 106mph.

Whatever was wrong with the incongruous car, if anything, was perhaps never solved: On its way to the track for another run it came off the towrope and crashed. Arbuthnot returned to the UK and was, that August, killed in a road accident when a Buick coming towards his Peugeot burst a front tyre at speed and swerved into his path.

The car remained in the US and the next that is known of it John Fitch had bought it, competing with it at Watkins Glen. Car and engine were subsequently split up and Fitch continued to race it with a Ford V8 motor. After a chequered career, it eventually returned to Britain where it is extant, although now looking as it did in 1939.

The other great name to have made a fleeting appearance at this time was ERA, the builder of iconic voiturette cars (the forerunners of Formula 2) in the 1930s. A year after the Lagonda's failure, Leslie Brooke from Coventry acquired one of the two 'tiny' 1.5-litre E-type ERAs. These had been built just before and after the war as successors to the race winning A- through to D-types from the Lincolnshire company. They had, though, proved to be a disappointment. The wartime George Medal winner took his to Indianapolis in 1947 with future water speed record-breaker Norman Buckley as his mechanic but arrived late and failed to qualify, although attracting the attention of the press. "Our English cousin (is) gradually getting accustomed to the knack of driving our Speedway in his 90.8 cubic inch ERA, a six-cylinder job which has an engine speed of 8,000 revolutions per minute," wrote Pete DePaolo. "The ERA didn't make the grade," added Floyd Clymer. "Too bad, too … I'd like to see more foreign cars entered." Laurence Pomeroy thought the ERA of sufficient interest to his British readers to mention it in the first paragraph of his technical report on Indianapolis that appeared in The Motor.

On returning to Europe, Brooke nursed the ERA home in the British Empire Trophy on the Isle of Man, the first time that an E-type had finished a race. A failure they may have been but both E-tyres can still be seen to this day. GP1 was virtually destroyed having been engulfed in flames but was completely rebuilt using a third, spare chassis. GP2, Brooke's former car, still exists, and both have appeared at events such as the Goodwood Revival meeting.

A typical pose from Robson as he goes out to practice with the Thorne Engineering Special. (Courtesy Indianapolis Motor Speedway)

Harry Miller for many years, considered the Sparks engine to be one of the quickest and the Adams chassis one of the best, telling his driver "we can win this race, we have a fast and reliable race car." Robson was certainly quick in practice in the cleanly lined, blue car, posting fourth fastest time, but as he did this on the second day of qualifying he had to start in fifteenth place.

America had been starved of its 500 for many years and the crowds flocked to the Speedway on May 30, 1946, many of them unable to get in before the start. The *Indianapolis Star's* Sports Editor, W Blaine Patton, was still reporting the race, estimating the "wildly cheering" crowd that year to have been 165,000. "The sun shone, the sky was blue," said his paper. Metropolitan Opera star James Melton, unexpectedly and "wonderfully," sang *Back Home in Indiana*. The

spectators brought along "enormous jugs and thermos bottles" and the contents circulated freely. The women, mindful of possible sunburned noses, made themselves cone-shaped nose guards, presenting peculiar profiles to the rest of the crowd.

The British press was also in place. *Motor's* technical editor Laurence Pomeroy had arrived at the track early to collect technical data, while fellow Englishman John Dugdale was covering the event for *Autocar*. "It is interesting to note that our friends from a foreign country actually take more interest, especially technical interest, than many of our American publications, probably because motor competition of all kinds is of great interest to the average British motorist," wrote publisher Floyd Clymer.

A blistering pace was set from the start by Mauri Rose and Ralph

Hepburn but these and many others were forced out to leave only nine cars in at the end. During the early laps, it was reckoned that Robson was driving one car and coaching another, that of his brother. When Hal appeared to be in trouble George nodded encouragement; when he broke down he gave him a wave of condolence. From laps fity-six to sixty-eight and seventy-one to eighty-seven he ran at the front. On lap ninety-three Hepburn made his first pit stop; Robson, who had been running steadily, took the lead again and from then on was never headed. Behind, Jimmy Jackson tried desperately to close the gap after his one scheduled pit stop but was handicapped by carburettor trouble.

Prior to the 500 Robson had not competed in a supercharged car. Paul Bryant recalled the fact that Eddie Offutt had advised him on the handling of such a racer by describing the operation of a centrifugal 'blower.' When the impeller rotation reaches a critical rpm the boost pressure rises abruptly and the power output of the engine increases suddenly, causing the drive wheels to break traction. Offutt warned Robson to avoid opening the throttle fully when exiting a turn. "Wait until you reach straight line motion before calling for full power." Offutt was to relate that, viewing from the pits during the race, he saw Robson leaving Turn Four with his rear drive wheels breaking traction. He kept the car under control but Offutt grabbed a mallet used for striking knock-off hubs, ran onto the track and shook it in Robson's line-of-site. "I did just what you told me to not to do and I won't do it again," shouted Robson at his next pit stop.

Robson stopped just twice, on the 141st lap for fuel and a right rear tyre, and later for a split-second visit. He was told that Rex Mays, who had dropped out after twenty-six laps, would give him relief if required but he fully believed he could run the whole 500 miles without assistance. On the 167th lap Billy De Vore, who had been one of the last to qualify, hit the retaining wall when his throttle stuck. De Vore was to tragically reappear in Robson's story.

In the closing stages of the race Robson began to have trouble with his goggles but, as he recalled later, "I weathered it out. Those last twenty-five laps were sure something." Robson was 44.04 seconds ahead of the field as chief starter Seth Klein, from a stand high up, and his assistant from the pits both waved their chequered flags.

Writing himself in the *Indianapolis Star*, Robson later stated, "A magnificent little automobile, the best pit crew in the business, and that thing called 'racing luck' took me to that sweetest spot on earth – the winner's bullpen at the Indianapolis Motor Speedway." He described how the Thorne Engineering Special "... purred all the way without a hitch. The boys in my pit made my two stops for fuel and tires the briefest possible," he said, adding that he had been lucky not to have been near any of the day's accidents. Even when his brother Hal's Phillips-Miller Special threw a con rod on the home stretch about midway through the race it "... flew out of my way completely." He gave credit to the car's owner, Joe Thorne, mechanics Offut, Chickie Hirashima, Johnny Rae, and Jack Bailey. "They did everything from taping on my goggles to changing both the right tires all in a space of those minutes I spent in the pits. As far as winning is concerned – I think it is the greatest thing that ever happened. I have never been so happy."

Robson drove into the 'Bull Pen' in a state of near exhaustion, oil smeared and dirty. Initially he could only gulp and gasp before someone put the traditional quart of milk into his greasy hands. "That's good to get down," he said. The journalists crowded round, eager for some words from the latest Indy 500 winner. "I don't know what to say. I rode around the track twice trying to think of something to say," he eventually

Seth Klein waves the chequered flag from on high as Robson completes what should have been his final lap. (He went on to do a couple more.) (Courtesy Indianapolis Motor Speedway)

Robson drinks the victory milk in the fenced-in winner's enclosure known as the 'Bull Pen.' Wife Margie has already joined him, as has mechanic Chickie Hirashima (in white shirt to Margie's left). (Courtesy Indianapolis Motor Speedway)

Robson found it difficult to get it into his head that he had won the Indianapolis 500. The race, he said, was not "too tough." He reckoned that it would probably be now more difficult being the winner than it was actually doing the winning, saying that he had not been frightened during the race but certainly was by the crowds and the cameras. He was a shy individual who, when asked to sign an autograph, was likely to blush and say, "Me? Oh, golly." When asked how the race had affected him physically he would say that his fingers hurt … from signing too many autographs!

Second place finisher Jimmy Jackson complained that, contrary to AAA regulations, Robson had stayed in his car during a refuelling stop. Joel Thorne retorted by saying that Jackson was a "swell guy" but "I think somebody is putting bugs in his ears."

stated. Robson had, indeed, driven for 505 miles and the press put those extra laps down to his need to work out a speech of some kind.

The first to reach Robson was crewman Hirashima, who had been the riding mechanic for Jimmy Snyder when the latter had established the lap record in 1937. Once Hirashima had embraced Robson the victor was aided by Speedway president Wilbur Shaw in clearing a path to wife Margie. "I just knew you could do it," she said several times for the newsreels. Her husband could still hardly speak. Eventually, on being asked what he was now going to do, he replied, "I don't know what to do. I'm sure glad to be right here." Robson asked Shaw's help for something to say. "You drove a fine race. Nobody ever did a better job," was the three-time winner's contribution.

Robson's prize money was $42,350, of which he retained one third, car owner Thorne taking the rest. Among his other rewards was the Strauss and Co round-the-world airline ticket, and a one-year meal ticket from Wheeler's restaurant. He had broken a "six-cylinder jinx," his being the first victory for such a car since Ray Harroun's at the first 500 back in 1911. He also broke what might be seen as a second jinx. In both the 1940 and 1941 races he had been forced out at about 165 miles. "When I passed [that] today, I began to feel as if it might be my day," he recalled.

Robson was not the only British-born driver in the race that year. Early on Henry Banks was "riding the tail" of Paul Russo's car in his Automobile Shippers Special when the latter spun and hit the wall. Banks swerved in masterful fashion to avoid Russo, only to retire sixteen laps later with pinion shaft failure.

Robson now, unexpectedly, found himself centre stage. In the June he could be seen at the reopening of the Langhorne one-mile dirt circle, beating fellow Indy 500 winner Mauri Rose in a special, five-mile match race before coming second in a 100-mile race in Cliff Bergere's Noc-Out-Hose Clamp Special, this car having been the 1938 Indy 500 winner when known as the Burd Piston Ring Special. The next month he was back for a 20-lap Sprint car race. In a Weirich Offenhauser known as Poison Lil, he easily won his qualifying heat, and then narrowly lost out to Rex Mays in another frenetic five-lap match race. The main event was equally exciting, with Robson always fighting for the lead and winning as his rivals dropped out. Another 20-mile Sprint car contest in the August saw a repeat performance, with Robson dominating his preliminary heat and winning the feature event, having found an ideal groove up against the guardrail. Prior to the race, he also strapped a pair of JATO (Jet-fuel Assisted Take Off) rockets onto the side of Poison Lil and almost literally flew round

No victory banquet in 1946 but an outdoors affair at the track that afternoon after the race. 'Pop' Myers, vice president of the Speedway, who had been ticket manager at the track back in 1910, congratulates Robson. (Courtesy Julie Schram collection)

Champion heralded Robson's win. One of Robson's prizes was membership of the 100-Mile-an-Hour club sponsored by the sparkplug manufacturer. (Courtesy Julie Schram collection)

the track for an unofficial lap record of 108.1mph – the first time such a car had been driven on a dirt track. Langhorne historian L Spencer Riggs points out how much his David versus Goliath exploits at Langhorne drew the admiration of the local fans. Indeed, they would not let him go until well over an hour after his last victory. That month also saw him winning under threatening skies on the half-mile Williams Grove Speedway in Poison Lil. Most his racing following the Indianapolis win was in the east, although it was reported that he would be back west to race a midget at the Pasadena Rose bowl on August 13. "The entire Pacific coast racing fraternity will turn out en masse to give Robson a royal welcome," said the media.

After the 500, Robson had said that, with his winnings, he wanted to buy his own racing car and try for the 1947 AAA Championship. Asked if he would be back at Indianapolis for the following year's 500, Robson nodded his head and, with a grin, gave an emphatic "yes." However, just over three weeks after his last Langhorne win, he entered for the Labor Day race at the treacherous Lakewood Speedway, Atlanta, an event that attracted 38,500 spectators, including members of George's family. With only two miles to go, Billy De Vore had developed engine trouble. He decided to soldier on, driving slowly. Ted Horn was to say later that he should have been taken out of the race. The conditions were so dusty by this stage that Robson is

assumed not to have seen the impediment in time to avoid crashing into it. De Vore's car was thrown over a stone wall, but then George Barringer and Bud Bardowski both collided with Robson's car. Witnesses said that Robson had jumped out but was hit by another car, probably that of George Connor, as he tried to make his way to the guardrail. The United Press accused him of "... disregarding the unwritten law of the speedway," by doing so. Another report said that he had been thrown from the car, before staggering to his feet and then being hit. Race leader Horn, having seen the initial crash, made a heroic effort to flag the other cars down but the red clay dust was too thick. Both Robson and veteran Barringer were dead on arrival at Atlanta's Grady Hospital.

Earlier that day, as he sat in his car ready to start the 100-mile

Robson behind the wheel of 'Poison Lil' at Williams Grove Speedway, Pennsylvania, in 1946. (Frank Smith photo, courtesy Ed Slane collection)

Charles Goodacre about to set off on a preparatory lap ten minutes before the start of the Austin A90 record-breaking run. (Courtesy British Motor Industry Heritage Trust)

race, Robson had been approached by veteran AAA starter Austin Shay. Shay owned a filling station in Lebanon near the Williams Grove track, where Robson was scheduled to race again the following Sunday. "George, do me a favour," he is reported to have said. "When you come to the Grove next week, how about parking your car in my filling station for about an hour so I can invite my customers over to meet at Indianapolis winner?" Robson looked up, thought for a minute and then countered, "I'll go you one better, Austin. If you have a pair of coveralls handy, you can tell your customers the Indy winner will fill their gas tanks." It was not to be.

In the November, *Automotive Digest* published the points standings in the AAA National Drivers Championship as they stood, prior to the Lakewood meeting. In second place with 1,484 points was Robson. The asterisk that prefaced his name and denoted his death was stark. Horn, who headed the table, was to come second to Tony Bettenhausen the following year in the 100-mile George Robson Memorial Race at Goshen, NY. Rather like Robson after his 500 win, Bettenhausen kept going for a few extra laps after the chequered flag had appeared just to make sure that he had won.

AUSTIN ACROSS THE ATLANTIC

Austin may not be the first British car marque that springs to mind when one thinks of Indianapolis but, in 1949, an Austin A90 Atlantic convertible was driven round the Speedway for a total of 11,875 miles at an average speed of 70.68mph. It was, for the time, quite a remarkable achievement.

The idea was that of Alan Hess, Austin's public relations officer who recalled, in his book on the record attempt, that a fortnight before the (London) Motor Show he had put the idea to Leonard Lord, the company's chairman and managing director. In the crowded aisles of the exhibition, Lord gave the go-ahead.

For seven days the driving team of Hess and pre-war Austin racing drivers Dennis Buckley and Charles Goodacre pounded around the Brickyard, establishing or breaking fifty-three 3-litre class and ten unlimited class AAA 'stock car' records as they did so. The result, it was felt at the time, would enhance the prestige of Austin products and British cars in general worldwide. Suppliers such as Automotive Products, Dunlop, and Joseph Lucas also hoped to benefit from their success.

The absolutely standard 2660cc A90 had to withstand extremes of temperature that included intense heat, violent thunderstorms, torrential rain, hail, and snow. Local dogs ran around the track with what was described as "marked unconcern" while hurricane lamps marked out the four turns during the night. The drivers, who understandably found the experience fatiguing, drove with the hood down but the windows up. Their consumption of bananas and Coca-cola was said to be "phenomenal."

A first attempt was made at an average speed of 77mph but with around twenty new tyres being required per day, this was aborted after 2300 miles. The second attempt was far more successful, despite a variety of problems that included a holed piston and broken front hub spindle. The Motor reported that, because of the punishing nature of the track, the AAA officials were astounded that Austin had only brought one car for the attempt. "It was a fine achievement which should greatly enhance British prestige – and that of Austin in particular – in the US," said the press.

Two representatives of the media played important roles in the proceedings. Journalist and 1927 Le Mans 24-hour winner, S C H ('Sammy') Davis acted as team manager. The drivers were also entertained by the most unusual pit signals. Russell Brockbank, then Art Editor for Punch *and arguably the greatest of all automotive cartoonists, was on hand to change wheels. For the drivers, out on the track for three-hour spells, the chalk drawings that he sketched on a large blackboard for them to see as they drove past, must have come as a welcome relief. The versatile Brockbank also developed into a "first class cook" of eggs and bacon for them. His wife, Eileen, later said that changing the wheels at Indianapolis was the only time she remembered him getting his hands dirty, despite his love of cars.*

'Relieving boredom.' The great British cartoonist Russell Brockbank kept the Austin A90 drivers amused during their marathon run at Indianapolis.
(Courtesy The Brockbank Foundation)

AAA official Bill Vandewater flags off the start of the run.
(Courtesy British Motor Industry Heritage Trust)

PART TWO

The 1960s & 1970s – A technical revolution from Britain

5
COOPER AND THE REAR-ENGINED CAR

"It was an experience I wouldn't have missed for the world."

The 1950s are regarded by some as a golden age for Indy, but throughout this period the British showed no interest in the race. The Indy drivers of that era cut their teeth on the short ovals, in Sprint and Midget cars. What the British did was to change all that, although, ironically, Jack Brabham, the first to qualify a British car post-war at the Brickyard, learnt his craft racing Midgets in Australia. However, the British influence brought road racers to the 500, not only themselves but also other Europeans and South Americans, many of whom had come to the fore racing on British road circuits in lower formulae. The British also changed the very nature of the Indy car. You have to go back to 1982 for the last time a US-built car won the race.

The British understood the Indy 500 to be a great but arguably parochial American event, although it was not really on their radar. They proved this when, in 1978, the Indy cars raced in the UK and few turned up to watch. The Indy 500 is a remarkable institution but one you have to witness to truly appreciate, and Indiana is many thousands of miles away from the shores of Europe. For the British, 'the' race was their Grand Prix – usually at Silverstone – or perhaps the Le Mans 24-hours to which, in their thousands, they annually crossed the English Channel to watch. The sight of cars streaming through Turn One may have an effect on the cranial hairs but then so, too, does that of a sports car on the Mulsanne at 3.00am ... and they did not have to travel so far to see that.

It was at Le Mans that the British had really started to come to the fore as both drivers and racing car manufacturers. Then, in 1957,

a Vanwall driven by Tony Brooks and Stirling Moss won a World Championship event. A year later Vanwall took the inaugural World Manufacturers Championship, while Englishman Mike Hawthorn became the first of his nationality to win the driver's title. Cooper then took over the mantle and provided the rear-engined cars for Australian Jack Brabham to win the World Championship in 1959 and 1960. A British dominance of Grand Prix racing had started.

It can be said that it was only in 1961 that the British began to take any interest in what was happening at Indianapolis. From then on their influence became considerable, starting with a conversion of the field from mighty roadsters to rear-engined open wheelers. The faithful disparagingly called the latter 'funny cars.' There are some who have not, even now, forgiven the British for this. Joe Scalzo in his hymn of praise to the 'dinosaurs,' 'Indianapolis Roadsters 1952-1964,' talks of the "... miserable Ford-powered Lotuses and the other wiggle cars," "The little bastards that aren't that wonderful." He says of how the custodians of the 500 turned it over to Lotus boss Colin Chapman who, with others, obliterated the roadster and then, as Scalzo so tellingly puts it, "... made (the 500) Brit."

The forerunner of all this, a Cooper-Climax qualified for fifth row of the grid in 1961. It seemed incredibly small, the engine, a mere 2.7-litres, was, of all places, behind the driver ... and it was green. You just did not paint Indy cars green. It was like peanuts, it was bad luck. The British, though, had been painting their cars green ever since Englishman Charles Jarrott had discovered that Panhard had coloured his 1901 Paris-Berlin car that hue. As far as the French were concerned green was actually lucky, and they had painted his car that colour to nullify the fact that it had been allocated the number 13. The British took on green as their national colour, and it certainly did not seem to be doing them any harm in the early 1960s. (In Europe, cars in international races were supposed to appear in the national colours of their entrants. The US had been allocated white with blue stripes and blue numbers, not that anyone at Indianapolis, until Dan Gurney's Lotus 29 was painted in that scheme, would have noticed.)

There seemed to have been little understanding of each other's racing in those days. It was as if American Football and Rugby Union were about to merge without knowing it. Why else would Indy 500 winner Rodger Ward have taken an Offenhauser-powered Kurtis-Kraft Midget to Sebring for the US Grand Prix in 1959? He appears to have believed that the Midget's cornering ability would more than make up for the Grand Prix cars' power. In practice he was over ten seconds

slower than the next starter, who was driving another front-engined car using a dated Maserati 250F engine. To be fair to Ward, he took this setback good-naturedly. He also saw potential for the new breed of rear-engined Grand Prix cars at the track and worked on John Cooper, whose team leader, the now Sir Jack Brabham, was to win the World Championship that year. Brabham, though, recalled that he and Ward did not talk of Indy during their time together in Florida. He had certainly never thought of racing there and only knew of the race "... through magazines."

English-born, but US domiciled racing enthusiast Dr Frank Faulkner helped to organise an exploratory trip to Indianapolis for the Cooper team. "We dropped off ... just out of curiosity, to see how quickly we could get round in a conventional Cooper GP machine fitted with the then Formula One engine of 2.5-litres," wrote Brabham a year later. In fact, the team was in the US for a non-Championship

John Cooper tries out the Owen Maddox-designed T54 for size. (Courtesy Indianapolis Motor Speedway)

Brabham and Cooper sit for the camera backed by (left-to-right) Noddy Grohmann, Harry Stephen, Bob Smiley, Kimberly's pilot, Jim Kimberly, and Marshall Lewis. (Courtesy Indianapolis Motor Speedway)

Formula One race at Watkins Glen. The reception at Indianapolis was friendly, and Ward, who also drove the car, showed Brabham the accepted lines round the track. By the time the Australian had finished he had lapped fast enough to have qualified eighth for that year's race. The locals were astounded. The results were sufficiently encouraging to place an entry for the following year's 500. Faulkner had introduced the Cooper team to Jim Kimberly, head of the Kleenex operation, and he immediately offered to sponsor a special car. John Cooper was delighted.

A new car, designated the T54, was designed by Owen Maddox based on Cooper's Formula One machine. Significant changes included the right-hand fuel tank being smaller than the left, pushing the right-hand side suspensions out an inch from the chassis centre, and including the engine over eighteen degrees to the left. The understanding USAC technical committee waived its eight-foot minimum wheel base rule.

The main problems were tyres and power. The Grand Prix rubber had lasted a mere twelve laps during the test but Dunlop, which had never previously made a tyre for Indy, was intrigued by the challenge. Coventry-Climax, while concerned about reliability, stretched its World Championship winning FPF engine from 2.5- to 2.7-litres and set it to run on a methanol-based fuel rather than the aviation petrol demanded by the Formula One regulations. The engine now gave 252 rather than 240hp at 6300rpm. Brabham recalled that what was most important was an increase of 24hp at 5500rpm. Following the race, he reckoned that he could have done with another 100hp, observing that there was no British engine that could produce this.

The crew for this first British tilt at the 500 by a major British race car manufacturer since Sunbeam comprised Charles and John Cooper, Mike 'Noddy' Grohmann, Alf Francis, Bill James, and Tim Wall, with Coventry Climax's Leonard Lee also in attendance.

Despite being a twice World Champion, Brabham had had to undergo the mandatory rookie test. "It was very difficult," he recalled nearly fifty-five years later. "The regulations were stupid. I was supposed to average 100mph and just going around the track to look at it I was doing 130. The officials (mainly chief steward Harlan Fengler) went mad, called me in and gave me a big lecture."

Brabham had to commute between Indianapolis and Monte Carlo, with Kimberly arranging for private air travel to Chicago to connect with the trans-Atlantic flights. In the first practice session for the Monaco GP Brabham posted a 1m 44.0s lap. Theoretically, this would not have been good enough to qualify for the 16-strong grid but the World Champion had been guaranteed a start. He flew back to Indianapolis for another run at the Speedway and then it was back to Europe, with just an hour to spare, to start at the rear of the grid for

the Grand Prix. On lap thirty-nine he retired, his engine down to three cylinders. Sir Jack recalled that the commuting was "... very difficult but luckily I sleep well on an aeroplane."

At Indianapolis Brabham just had to qualify on the first day in order to get back to Monaco. "I played it pretty carefully," he said and qualified on the fifth row of the grid. Understandably tense before the race, the Australian found that once it had started "It wasn't half so frightening as I imagined it might have been." As the event progressed, so the limitations of the little car became evident. Although quicker than the regulars around the turns, there was never enough room to pass anyone in these sections, while down the straights the extra power of the roadsters enabled them to easily pull away. Brabham was probably up to about 160mph on the main straights but it was insufficient.

Dunlop Tyre's Vic Barlow had advised that the team would need to make three pit stops. However, the decision was made to go for two based on the fact that there would be plenty of rubber on the track left by the thirty-three entries. It was a mistake. Despite trying to preserve his tyres, Brabham was forced to make an unscheduled, third stop after 177 laps. He subsequently believed that had three stops been planned from the start he would have been able to go faster throughout the race. The pit stops were also desperately slow, thanks mainly to a wing nut on the offside rear wheel having been damaged during the first stop.

Brabham had one fright when the Offenhauser engine in Don Davis' Trevis, which he was trying to pass at the time, blew up causing the car to spin and bounce off the retaining wall, leaving debris on the track. Brabham steered the manoeuvrable little Cooper around this, interested to note that four of the far heavier roadsters behind him had failed to do so. In the end, the little green car came home ninth,

OFFICIAL ENTRY BLANK

INDIANAPOLIS MOTOR SPEEDWAY CORP.
INDIANAPOLIS, INDIANA

Enclosed is remittance of $500.00 entry fee for one car in race meet described herein. See Rule 2.

Date ___6th February___ 19__61__.

Name of Car ___Cooper-Climax___. Year Built ___1961___.

No. of Cylinders ___8___ Bore in Inches ___3.78___ Stroke ___3.74___ Inches

Piston Displacement ___167.6___ Cu. In. Supercharger? ___No___ Four or Two Stroke Cycle? ___Four___

Front, Rear or 4-Wheel Drive? ___Rear___ Gasoline, Diesel, or Turbine? ___Gasoline___

U.S.A.C. Car Registration No. ___-___ Program No. (Requested by Entrant) ___FIA/61/1___

Name of Owner ___Cooper Car Company Ltd.___ Program No. (Assigned by Speedway) ___1961/WC/1___

Address of Owner ___243 Ewell Road, Surbiton, Surrey, England.___

Name of Driver ___Jack Brabham.___ U.S.A.C. Registration No. ___-___

Address of Driver ___

Signature of Entrant ___[signature]___ FIA/61/1

P. O. Address ___The Cooper Car Company Ltd.,___
___243 Ewell Road, Surbiton, Surrey, England.___

Entries Close Midnight, April 15th, 1961.

THIS COPY FOR INDIANAPOLIS MOTOR SPEEDWAY CORPORATION   PLEASE RETURN WITH U.S.A.C. COPY

Cheshire-born racing enthusiast, Dr Frank Falkner, who assisted Cooper with its 1961 Indianapolis 500 project, had amongst his papers the team's entry form, signed by John Cooper. Falkner was also to introduce 1985 Indy winner Danny Sullivan to motor racing, presenting him with a course at the Jim Russell Racing Drivers School at Snetterton for his twenty-first birthday. (Courtesy Doug Stokes collection)

completing a full 200 laps and winning $7250; a satisfying result given that Brabham and Cooper had decided that anything in the top ten would be pleasing. "It was an experience I wouldn't have missed for the world," said Cooper.

How much impact had the Cooper made on the locals? "It was sort of impressive but the fact that the engine was so small and didn't have the horsepower meant that, although he (Brabham) made the race he wasn't that competitive," said Parnelli Jones, who shared rookie of the year with Bobby Marshman in 1961. "I was more worried about the guys I was racing against and not Jack at the time. Having said that, Jack Brabham was one hell of a race car driver. I later ran a few vintage races with him and I could still see that he had that desire to win."

It is interesting to read what Brabham wrote in the 1961 edition of *Motor Racing Year*. "I think that a front-engined car could be made to corner at Indianapolis as fast as the rear-engined car – using all-independent suspension, of course. But faster cornering would mean higher tyre wear, and so one gets into a viscous spiral. Frankly, I think the Indy Specials, tailored for just this one circuit, will take a lot of beating." It would, though, be just two years before they came under serious pressure ... from another British car. John Cooper wrote that when he and Brabham had arrived at Watkins Glen following the initial Indy test, one of the other team owners had "... come up and asked, 'What's it like?'" His name was Colin Chapman.

Quite a contrast; Brabham's little Cooper ahead of the Offy-engined Lesovsky of Paul Goldsmith. (Courtesy Indianapolis Motor Speedway)

The Cooper at the Indianapolis Motor Speedway museum is not Brabham's ground-breaker but a T53 that may have been used for Brabham's test at the track in 1960. It was also the spare car for the following year's 500 but did not leave the garage. (Author's collection)

MG AT THE SPEEDWAY

MG may be one of England's most charismatic motorsport marques but it is hardly a name that one would associate with the Indianapolis 500. Yet, in the mid-1960s, cars named the MG Liquid Suspension Specials ran at the Speedway. The chassis were built by Joe Huffaker and the engines were Offys but it was the suspension that led to the association with Abingdon.

In 1962 BMC launched what was to become its popular Morris 1100 small family saloon. Other BMC badges were gradually applied to the car, with an MG two-door version becoming available in the US. A particular feature of these cars was their Dr Alex Moulton-designed, interconnected 'Hydrolastic' suspension. Use was made of a fluid for the springing medium.

The San Francisco-based British Motor Car Company run by Kjell Qvale was an importer of MGs. The company operated a competition department under the control of Huffaker producing race cars usually with BMC engines but also entering the Indy 500 with one using a power plant from another famous British marque. Driven by Pedro Rodriguez, this was actually Jack Brabham's 1961 Indy car now with a 6-cylinder dohc Aston Martin engine. The legend 'BMC Aston Martin Cooper' down its flanks might have been a trifle confusing for a British observer. The Mexican was actually faster than Brabham had been two years earlier, but failed to qualify.

There was obviously no BMC engine that could be used at the Speedway, so instead Huffaker and the flamboyant Qvale looked to the suspension to maintain a link with the British for 1964. Three rear-engined cars that followed the lead given by Cooper and Lotus were built for the 1964 race. What made them different was the use of BMC Hydrolastic units from the 1100 in place of conventional springs. These, it was thought, would help reduce tyre wear while, by calling them MG Liquid Suspension Specials, Qvale could publicise his import business.

There is a story that the cars were going through technical inspection for the 500 when, too late to do anything before qualifying, it was discovered that the fuel cells were leaking. Qvale, in a very expensive Italian suit, crawled under the car pretending to show some detail to an interested party. He then let the oil drip onto his $3000 suite in order to keep it from appearing on the floor.

Rodriguez failed to qualify again after crashing one of the cars, but the other two, driven by Walt Hansgen and Bob Veith were placed a troubled thirteenth and nineteenth respectively having run well in the early stages, the latter in a car originally to have been entered by Sheraton-Thompson for A J Foyt. At one point both Veith and rookie Hansgen had been as high as third. The following year all three qualified, driven by Hansgen, Veith, and Jerry Grant, but none of them made it to the chequered flag.

Two of the cars qualified again in 1966, although they were no longer entered using the MG name. Four new monocoque Huffakers were also built using the same suspension, only one of them making the 500 grid. Bobby Unser took the latter to eighth place that year. One place ahead of him was Eddie Johnson in one of the older cars, now entered by Vatis Enterprises, the best finish at the Speedway for a Hydrolastic suspension car. A year later, Wally Dallenbach crashed a Vatis car in the first half of the race. The original spaceframe Hydrolastic cars certainly seemed to enjoy longevity with Dallenbach joined by Sam Sessions in 1968, the latter giving the cars their swansong in 1969 with a still Vatis-owned chassis.

Walt Hansgen ran as high as second in the 1964 Indianapolis 500 with a MG Liquid Suspension Special. It was a long way from Abingdon. (Courtesy Indianapolis Motor Speedway)

An unlikely inspiration for an Indy car, BMC's 1100 saloon. (Courtesy Marjorie Wagstaff)

GORDON KIRBY

A variety of British journalists have covered the Indianapolis 500 over the years but, in the main, UK magazines tend to use local scribes. Throughout the 1970s, 1980s, and early 1990s Autosport's man on the spot, Gordon Kirby, may have been North America-based but he hailed originally from Brighton, West Sussex.

Kirby's family had immigrated to Toronto when he was eight. His initial writing on the sport had revolved around road racing and he well recalls watching Stirling Moss win the 1961 Player's 200 at Mosport in his Lotus 19. As far as oval racing was concerned his sole experience was just a local, third of a mile affair. Then, in 1973 he was appointed Autosport's American correspondent and that meant covering the Indianapolis 500. Apart from that minor track in Canada, it was his first experience of an oval.

He learnt fast and was back the next season, and from then on every year until the advent of the IRL. "During that time the cars were incredibly fast and there were some great characters – Foyt, Andretti, Johncock, the Unsers." A couple of years after he first covered the race, Kirby was listening to Booby Unser. "I didn't really know him well at the time. He was carrying on and I told him that he was talking 'bullshit.'" On the face of it, that may not sound the ideal way to speak to an Indy legend. Unser was initially taken aback but the result was that the pair became good friends. Kirby was to go on to write biographies of the Unser family, Mario Andretti, Bobby Rahal, and, most recently, Rick Mears. His latest project is a detailed history of the Newman Haas team, which he is scheduled to finish in 2011. It is a work that was originally discussed with the late Paul Newman and which promises to be a truly definitive look at the team that has included Brits Nigel Mansell and Justin Wilson among its drivers.

Since the 'split,' Kirby visits to the Speedway have been less frequent and he has missed half a dozen of the IRL run 500s. He worries about its future. "You've got to get rid of spec racing," he said. Noting the ideas that had been put forward for the Indy car of the future he could see some possibilities, in particular for Ben Bowlby's DeltaWing concept (see chapter 22). The 'Catch 22' he saw, though, is that while there must be a change in the formula, it is difficult for him to imagine, with sponsorship income now at a premium, how the teams will ever be able to afford new cars.

English-born Gordon Kirby (right) and Rick Mears at an autograph signing session for his biography of the four-time Indy 500 winner. (Author's collection)

6

LOTUS TAKES UP THE CHALLENGE

"... they professionalised the whole thing."

"It was simple," recalled Dan Gurney. Simple it may have been but it was also pivotal to the seismic shift that took place at Indy during the 1960s. The tall, friendly Californian, as one of the Grand Prix stars of the era, could see that the rear-engined, lightweight technology of Formula One was the way to go. He was not isolated in his thinking but it was he who took what he regarded as the logical step of approaching Lotus boss Colin Chapman with the idea of building a car for the 500. As far as he was concerned, Chapman was the leading F1 designer of the time and the obvious person to take on Indianapolis. It was, Gurney said looking back over forty years, a "simple" decision.

Andrew Ferguson, competitions manager of Team Lotus from 1961 to 1969, in his seminal work, 'Team Lotus – the Indianapolis Years,' has left us with one of the best accounts ever of a motor sport campaign. As he pointed out, there were three companies involved in this. Two were American; engine supplier Ford and, from 1966, sponsor STP. The other was "Colin Chapman's miniscule British organisation, Lotus." Just ten days before the 1962 running, Gurney invited the Lotus founder to be his guest at the 500. The Cooper mid-engined influence could already be seen in Gurney's mount; a Buick V8-powered car built for former dragster and record-breaker Mickey Thompson by Englishman John Crosthwaite. Chapman could see how out-of-date the rest of the entry was – he felt he now knew what it must have been like to have watched the pre-war Mercedes-Benz and Auto Union Grand Prix cars.

There was no British involvement in the race that year, although,

By the time of Jim Clark's win, the IMS had taken to reproducing an image of the previous year's 500 victor on its admission tickets, a practice that continues today. (Courtesy Indianapolis Motor Speedway)

had he arrived earlier, Chapman might have witnessed both an English driver and a somewhat bizarre entry. While history records how the British brought rear-engined success to the Indy 500 during the mid-1960s, it is easy to by-pass the fact that there was a vain attempt to qualify an English-built front-engined racer – and a far from state of the art one at that. Pierre de Villiers and what have been described as a group of British beatniks – a most suitable phrase for those times – brought a 2.5-litre Alta-engined Formula One Connaught to the Speedway. A small British concern headed by Rodney Clarke and Mike Oliver, Connaught had come to prominence when the dental student Tony Brooks won the 1955 Syracuse Grand Prix. It was the first victory

Dan Gurney had already experienced a rear-engined car at the Brickyard in 1962, Mickey-Thompson's innovative special, which had been designed by Englishman John Crosthwaite. Inaccurately restored, this car now appears regularly in public, including here at the 2009 International Motorsport Industry Show in Indianapolis. (Author's collection)

for a British car in a Grand Prix – albeit a minor league one – since the 1920s. In World Championship racing, Brooks went on to be a six times winner but all the Connaughts could manage was a third place in the Italian Grand Prix of 1956, a couple of fourths, and a fifth. Their last appearance was that of the 'toothpaste tube' bodied Type C version which Paul Emery entered for Bob Said to race in the 1959 US Grand Prix. It was this car that de Villiers and his bunch of enthusiasts vainly and naively flogged around the Brickyard. The locals looked on with some amusement at their unprepared efforts.

The natives had also noticed the Cooper, and Mickey Thompson decided to do something about it. Thompson employed former Cooper and Lotus designer Crosthwaite to draw three rear-engined, Cooper-like cars for him. The versatile English driver Jack Fairman was engaged to pilot one of these machines, which received backing from Jim Kimberly, the supporter of the previous year's Cooper effort. Fairman had a busy schedule as development driver and having to pass his rookie test, and was unable to build up enough speed to qualify the car. He also tried out at least one conventional 'roadster' while it

Hands on hips; Jack Fairman surveys work being carried out on the hopelessly outclassed Connaught. (Courtesy Indianapolis Motor Speedway)

was perhaps inevitable that he should have a drive in the de Villiers Connaught, as he had raced for Connaught Engineering a number of times in the 1950s. It should perhaps be recorded that his laps in the de Villiers car meant that he was the last Briton to drive a front-engined car in practice for the Indianapolis 500, as well as the last man to start

a Formula One race with the engine in front of him when he qualified the Ferguson P99 for the British Grand Prix. Neither Fairman nor the Connaught were anywhere near making the grid for the Indy 500, but Fairman and the Ferguson will return to our story later.

We come back to Colin Chapman who, following his visit in

Clark and Chapman pose at Indianapolis with the Lotus-Coventry Climax 25 Formula One car that had just been raced by Trevor Taylor in the United States Grand Prix. It was the first time for over thirty years that a 1.5-litre car had been run at speed round the Brickyard. (Courtesy Indianapolis Motor Speedway)

1962, became inspired by the idea of racing at the 500. He and Dan Gurney approached Ford; the US carmaker was already thinking of a return to Indianapolis but was still undecided which chassis manufacturer it should work with and whether to use methanol or petrol. Then Jimmy Clark won the US Grand Prix with one of the revolutionary monocoque Lotus-Coventry Climax 25s and subsequently tested with team-mate Trevor Taylor's identical car at the Brickyard. The Ford engineers were impressed. With just 1.5-litres, the Lotus had been almost as fast as the Cooper in 1961. The decision was made, Ford was going to go with a V8 petrol engine – based on its Fairlane pushrod unit – for Lotus, and work started on the monocoque Lotus 29 that Len Terry detailed from Chapman's schemes.

Three cars were built that year for Clark and Gurney to drive, the latter of whom was to crash in qualifying, leading to his use of the 'Mule' prototype car in the race. (This is the car that is displayed in the Indianapolis Speedway museum liveried as Clark's own 1963 mount.) Practice was also not helped by the regulars' insistence, on seeing that the Lotus cars were running with Firestone's new 15-inch tyre, that they should be able to do so, too. Thus, there was some hasty casting of 15-inch wheels to pacify the rest of the field.

Early in the month there occurred what looked like a good omen when Lloyd Ruby set a new lap record at Trenton and led the Indy car regulars for some forty laps driving, of all things, an ex-F1 Lotus 18. Then Clark qualified for the 500 in fifth place and, with the roadsters scheduled to make more pit stops than the two 29s, things looked good.

Sure enough, as the roadsters made their first pit stops so Clark and Gurney swept into first and second places. At half distance, once the Lotus pair had made their own stops, Clark was still in second, some forty seconds behind Parnelli Jones' Watson-Offy. Jones made his second stop under yellow and kept the lead but

Gurney went testing at Indianapolis in the prototype Indy Lotus, 29/1. The 'stack-pipe' exhaust system was quickly replaced by a properly coupled 'snake-pit' manifolding exiting into twin tailpipes. (Courtesy Ford)

Gurney and Clark are dwarfed by the Offys in 1963. (Courtesy Ford)

Chapman, Clark, and Gurney (left-to-right) would seem to be at prayer. (Courtesy Ford)

Gurney seems astounded by Clark's way of checking tyre pressures. (Courtesy Sally Swart collection)

he could not pull away from the little green and yellow car. Gurney was now third.

By lap 177, the Scot was just five seconds adrift and Jones' Offenhauser was blowing smoke. His car was now leaking oil and Clark fell back. At this point Gurney also dropped back with a second stop for tyres and fuel and then a third for his rear wheels to be tightened. Chief steward Harlan Fengler had before the race warned that anyone dropping oil would be black-flagged but it was just not happening. Chapman remonstrated in vein. Eddie Sachs spun on the fluid that Fengler claimed was water and then crashed a lap later. Out came the yellow again, with lapped roadsters taking up the track between Jones and Clark. The green light came on with only seven laps to go and Clark could only claw back three of the 22 seconds, which he had now fallen back by. Runner-up Clark was gracious in defeat while the delayed Gurney drove home into seventh place.

Looking back, Jones does not believe that Clark was a threat to him. "I was quicker by over a mile an hour and at that time a mile an hour with a normally aspirated engine was tremendous. Everybody tried to blame me for the fact that the track was oily but it was oily all day long. Most of my oil was coming

Jim Clark's Lotus 29 is in stark contrast to the following roadster. (Courtesy Ford)

back on my exhaust pipe and onto my left rear tyre. Whether I should have been black-flagged – I don't think so. I had no idea that they were contemplating this and, to tell you the truth, I wouldn't have gone in anyway, not that close to the end of race. Remember I had led for most of the race and made three pits stops to Jimmy's one." In 1986 Jones was awarded the Kroger-sponsored Jim Clark Award for the fine example that he had set on and off the track at the IMS.

Lotus was to run the 29s at Milwaukee and Trenton later in 1963, with Clark leading the former from start to finish. The end of the roadster was inevitable. That end was delayed, though, thanks in part to some hastily redesigned Dunlop tyres. There were three Lotus-Fords in the 1964 Indy 500; Clark and Gurney in new 34s, and the rapid Bobby Marshman in the 29 that Gurney had crashed in qualifying the previous year and was now owned by Lindsey Hopkins. The 34s were little more than developed 29s, the main changes being quad-cam Ford V8s with Hilborn-derived fuel-injection in place of the carburettors and ZF transmission instead of Colotti. Despite Ford wanting to use Firestone tyres again, the other change was to Dunlop tyres; the British manufacturer having provided makeshift tyres that Lotus used in practice the year before, prior to going on to Firestones.

In qualifying all went well, very well in fact. Clark took the pole, the only Brit ever to do so, with Marshman at his side. Gurney was on the second row. Then it all went wrong, horribly wrong. Gurney carried out some full-load practice runs during which his tyres began to chunk. There was some frantic work over the Whitsun holiday as Dunlop made new tyres with a shallower and more stable tread pattern. Forty laps into a race that had been restarted after a ghastly lap two accident, Clark's left rear suspension collapsed. The tyres had been shedding tread, causing vibration and then component failure. At the time he had been at the front, having been swapping the lead with Marshman. The latter's Firestone-shod 29 had just retired with transmission oil leak. Just after half distance, concern over tyre wear meant that Gurney was brought in and his car withdrawn. Rodger Ward, the man who had encouraged Cooper, was to finish second in a US-built mid-engined car, but otherwise all the other top 10 classified drove good 'ole Offy-powered roadsters. As Chapman was to recall, Ford was far from happy.

At Milwaukee later that year, the two Americans who were last to win the Indy 500 for the roadster brigade, Jones and Foyt, took over two of the works 34s as Clark and Gurney were on World

Championship duty. Jones took pole and won, repeating the result the next month at Trenton when Clark returned. "Going from my roadster to that was like getting into a big go-kart," recalled Jones. "They put my number 98 on it. I could really appreciate how quick it was, how nice it handled and rode. A roadster would have seemed antiquated if I had had to get back into one."

The year ended tragically when in testing at Phoenix Marshman, who Lotus team members had described as a US version of Clark, suffered a fatal accident in what Andrew Ferguson believed was the Scot's second place car from 1963.

The British had, by the end of 1964, certainly arrived. "In my view they 'gentlemanised' the whole business of racing," said Rick Rising-Moore, the English-born owner of the Union Jack bar. "They brought this to a sport that was kind of wild and woolly. In my opinion, they professionalised the whole thing. When the English came they changed the whole attitude about racing. (Indianapolis Motor Speedway owner) 'Tony' Hulman was brilliant in encouraging that first wave to come over, although some of the older racers like A J Foyt were not too happy about that."

Said another of the 'old guard' Parnelli Jones, "I have always taken the attitude that everybody puts on their clothes the same way and it doesn't make any difference where you come from. However, it was good to see a little more world recognition such as we once had in the Indianapolis 500. Maybe we had got away from that. I didn't know much about Jimmy Clark until he came to Indy when I met him and Colin Chapman. I had the utmost respect for Chapman because of his creative ability. Jimmy took to the Indianapolis racetrack instantly like it was no big deal. At first he was making high approaches to the corner like you do on a road circuit. Then he started bringing it down a little bit and took to it like a duck to water. After I had beaten him that first year we became closer friends and I realised that, unlike Cooper, Lotus was here for real."

There are those who, to this day, believe that Parnelli Jones should have been black-flagged in 1963, leaving Clark and Lotus to take the 500 on their debut. However, it seems that what they did win was the respect of those who mattered like Jones. In 1965 they were to win far more. The British were in force by that year. On the grid were six Lotus cars, a pair of Lolas, likewise for BRP, and a lone Brabham and Ferguson. The three new Lotus 38s, two entered by Team Lotus and one by Dan Gurney's new All American Racers team, just looked right. To

these could be added a couple of old privately-entered Lotus 34s and a 29. Famous converts to the cause included former winners Foyt and Jones in extensively altered 34s, both of whom had Lola T80s as back up cars. To show that they meant business, three of the Lotuses locked out the front row of the grid, Foyt in his Ansted-Thompson Racing 34 edging out Clark for the pole. Gurney was on the outside. Foyt seemed to regard this as one up for America conveniently forgetting from where his chassis had originated. There was also a little matter of twenty-seven of the thirty-three starters being rear-engined – and who was responsible for leading that trend?

Clark led away at the start, backing off on lap two when he saw Foyt was determined to get through. "Let him get on with it," is how he recalled it to his biographer Graham Gauld. That did not last long, for Clark now reckoned Foyt was holding him up, and on lap three he was back in front. The expression that now comes to mind is 'game, set and match.' Clark would only now relinquish the lead during his first pit stop, leading for 190 of the 200 laps. It was not long before he was a whole lap up on Foyt and Jones in the J C Agajanian entry. Even his pursuers were driving Lotuses. By the end of the 500-mile race Clark – who had averaged a

Clark put his Lotus on pole for 1964, but on lap forty-seven his tyre was ripped to shreds. (Courtesy Ford)

Bobby Johns drove the second Lotus in 1965, finishing seventh as team leader. Clark went on to win. (Courtesy Ford)

record 150.633mph – was almost two laps ahead of Jones, Foyt having dropped out with transmission trouble. In fourth place was yet another Lotus, the two-year old 29 of Al Miller, while Bobby Johns in the second 'works' 38 finished seventh. Ensuring that half of the top ten cars had come from the UK, Al Unser finished ninth in Foyt's Lola.

It is impossible to overemphasise the significance of Clark's victory. His Lotus 38 was the first rear-engined car to have won the Indianapolis 500. He was also the first foreign national to win the race since Dario Resta in 1916 and a true born and bred Brit.

And another thing, the car was green, the first in such a hue to win the 500 since 1920. Hopefully, this should have proved a point to the superstitious locals. Having said that, they were probably happy to see that, thanks to the demands of sponsorship, the Team Lotus cars were in their last year of being painted green. However, the British were about to win again, whatever their colour.

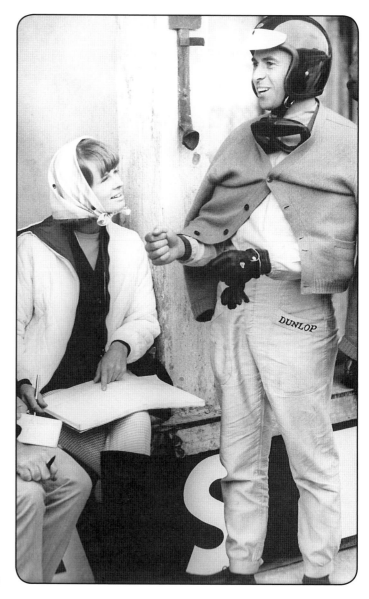

An upright Clark in the winner's enclosure. Chapman recounts how he got there. (Courtesy Ford)

Sally listens attentively to Jimmy. (Courtesy Sally Swart collection)

SALLY SWART

In 1965 Jim Clark notified Team Lotus competitions manager Andrew Ferguson that his girlfriend, Sally Stokes (now Sally Swart), would accompany him to all of his races. That meant not only the Grands Prix but also the Indianapolis 500. Sally recalled that, the year before, Clark had come back laughing from the Speedway. He had asked for a boiled egg at the Holiday Inn but was told that he could not have one because the egg-boiling machine had broken down. "He was amused and frustrated by the fact that they could not just put an egg into boiling water and time it."

Sally did not attend the whole month of May. "Jimmy used to say that it was horrendous, quite boring but very necessary because he had to set up for the 500." She recalled Clark telling her how much he liked the actual race at Indy "... because when I am in the lead, I have dollar signs flashing before my eyes." Being paid for leading a lap was new to him and, as Sally states, with a still infectious chuckle, "Being a Scot he liked to line his pockets."

On the day of the 500 Sally and Colin Chapman's wife Hazel joined Bobby Johns' family in the grandstands. Women were not allowed in the pits or garages then. Dave Lazenby reckoned that Sally and Hazel ought to be "... like the rest of the girls" and hang by their fingernails on the fencing round Victory Lane. "When the cars came down the straightaway for the first time, Bobby's sister started crying and I almost joined her. I had never thought to fear like that before. The Indy cars had big, fat fuel fillers which we were not used to; remember we did not have fuel stops in Formula One then. Colin, being Colin, redesigned the fuel feed from the Esso tank to improve fuel flow. To disguise this he wrapped the fuel hose in tiger stripes. Officials challenged him but he replied with Esso's advertising slogan of the time, 'I've put a tiger in my tank' and he got away with it."

Sally cannot remember how she and Hazel made their way across the track but they were eventually allowed into Victory Lane. At the subsequent post-race dinner and the festivities afterwards, Sally and Jimmy could tell that there was a "... little gap in the enthusiasm." Sally has her suspicions. "I didn't know the half of what had gone on but they had almost tried to prevent Jimmy from winning. Jim had known that and already warned me, 'They're not too enthusiastic that I'm here.' That was rather sad; it dampened the activities for us. However, I do know that he was welcomed in later years with more enthusiasm." Donald Davidson has pointed out that, whatever Clark told Sally about authority, the fans had immediately taken him to their hearts. However, even today, she believes that Parnelli Jones – now a friend and very close neighbour of Sally and her husband Ed Swart – should have been black-flagged by the USAC officials for shedding oil in 1963, and that Clark should have been given the win that year.

"After the race, I had my picture taken with Mario (Andretti), the Rookie of the Year and such a nice young man. Jimmy, I know, was very impressed with Mario's talent. He thought him very promising."

The next month Sally, Clark, and Mike Spence flew in Chapman's plane from Luton to the French Grand Prix at Clermont Ferrand. "There seemed to be quite a bit of activity at the airport. We had forgotten that the Paris Air Show was on at that time. The French Government had flown Yuri Gagarin (the first man to travel in space) down from Le Bourget to show off a new plane. There was a civic reception for him. We crept in at the back but it was known from our flight plan who we were. It was only a few weeks after Jimmy's Indy victory and we were invited into the party and plied with champagne.

"We saw somebody whisper in Gagarin's ear and he jumped up. It appeared he knew exactly who Jimmy was and that he had just won at Indy. He gave him a hug and a kiss – very unusual in those days – and I shook his hand. He seemed thrilled to meet Jimmy."

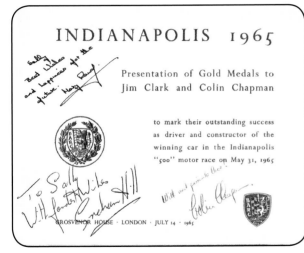

The British Automobile Racing Club presented Clark and Chapman with Gold Medals following the 500 victory. Chapman, Graham Hill, and Olympic Gold medal long jumper Mary Rand signed Sally Stokes' invitation card at the awards dinner. (Courtesy Sally Swart collection)

In 2009 Dario Franchitti invited Sally Swart to be his guest at the Long Beach Grand Prix. (Author's collection)

7
MADE TO ORDER

"We weren't designers as such ..."

The Cooper and early Lotus entries must be seen, more or less, as factory cars, although the latter was to sell on some of its into private hands. They were to be succeeded by machinery from a variety of production race car manufacturers, Lola, March, Reynard, and G-Force, who typified the British motorsport industry and changed the way that the Indianapolis teams sourced cars. By 1984, such was the emphasis on the customer car that Lotus was virtually shunned when it tried to come back with what would have been, in effect, a factory entry.

Lola first entered the fray in 1965 with T80s driven by Al Unser and Bud Tingelstad, and still had twenty-one cars in the field thirty-one years later. Late completion meant that the T80s suffered from a number of problems and were also-rans. In the field that year was another pair of purely customer cars from Britain, although in this case the manufacturer was in its last year of existence and, despite being a pioneer, was never to be part of the movement that was to come. BRP, the British Racing Partnership, was, in late 1964, about to fold its doors when American road racer Masten Gregory approached it with a request that it build two cars for the following year's Indianapolis 500. Gregory had raced for BRP in Formula One during the 1961 and 1962 seasons when the team entered Lotus 18/21 and 24 cars under the UDT Laystall Racing banner. (Jim Hall, a future Indianapolis 500 winning entrant, also drove for the team.) A year later, BRP had become a constructor in its own right, entering BRM-engined monocoques for Innes Ireland and Trevor Taylor.

The Partnership had been formed in the mid-1950s by 1924 Indy

European scene. Alfred Moss and a young Tony Robinson are flanked by legendary mechanic Alf Francis (left), who worked on the 1961 Indianapolis Cooper, and journalist Denis Jenkinson. (Courtesy Tony Robinson collection)

500 driver Alfred Moss and Ken Gregory (no relation to Masten) to run cars for the former's arguably more famous son Stirling. Gregory was, at the time, Stirling's manager. Claimed by Gregory to be the first Formula One team to have been fully sponsored, BRP had resorted to building its own cars when the introduction of the monocoque Lotus 25 in 1962 had made its own customer, space frame 24s obsolete.

Robinson (in suit) and Masten Gregory (in car) pose with the Highgate workforce. (Courtesy Tony Robinson collection)

mechanics and engineers. We weren't designers as such with a pen and paper; we were race car builders." In addition to Robinson, those involved included Bruce McIntosh, now with Gordon Murray Design, Rod Gueran, Stan Collier, and Peter Downie. Robinson admits that nobody at BRP had any experience of Indy and that he gleaned most of his information from books on the subject. However, other than such as the obvious like the Girling brakes, Armstrong suspension, Halibrand wheel and hubs, and a standard Morris rack-and-pinion steering, everything was designed or manufactured by the team. Even the driveshafts were designed by BRP but made by HRD of Wolverhampton.

The way that BRP had built the Formula One cars was to first make mock-ups, and the same process was used for the Indy cars. Using a jig bed that it had from its F1 cars, the team placed mock-up bulkheads at the front, centre, and rear. The mock-up engine and a gearbox casing were put in place and "... we ended up with the physical dimensions. We already knew Masten's size as he had already driven for us. We did not know, initially, who the other driver was going to be. Eventually we were told that it would be Johnny Boyd, who was taller than Masten, so we decided on a compromise size for the cockpit; a bit too large for Masten and a bit too small for Boyd. We could not afford to sacrifice too much unused cockpit area as we had to carry so much fuel."

Initially, the team did not know if the car would be fuelled by petrol or methanol. If the latter, it would have to carry a full seventy-five gallons in its rubber fuel bags to avoid an extra pit stop. It also proved difficult to obtain precise fuel consumption figures on the Ford engine. Six weeks was spent designing a car capable of incorporating seventy-five gallons by making use of cowl tanks and pressure refuelling connectors. And then a change in the regulations stated that such tanks and pressure refuelling were banned. That meant a loss of a precious ten gallons. Five of these were retrieved by extending the seat tank and making the car a little wider. There is a story attached to the fuel tanks, which were manufactured by Marston Excelsior. They could have been extremely expensive. However, Robinson, aware that money was tight, appealed to the better nature of the supplier's managing director John Harvey-Jones – later to become a noted 'trouble-shooter' on television – who agreed to a reduction in cost.

"Once we had manufactured the three bulkheads and tied the front and centre by two longitudinal bottom members from there on in

For 1963, the team undertook to build what was to be the second monocoque F1 car of its era. New cars were constructed for the 1964 season, however, the Formula One Constructors Association rejected BRP's overtures to become a member, and to benefit from its expenses and guaranteed start money, thus leaving Moss and Gregory with little option but to close down the operation.

Engineering director Tony Robinson recalled, "Masten asked us if we would be prepared to build him a car for Indianapolis at the end of 1964 when we were thinking of closing down. He had driven for us in Formula One and we had always had a good working relationship with him. He was a very sensible driver. However, we kicked the idea around before saying we could and we would." Alfred Moss was, perhaps understandably, said to be pleased by the thought of BRPs running at Indy.

"There was no reason not to do it," said Robinson. "We had the staff and the facilities, and 'half an idea' of what we were doing. I still had to go to North America for the end of season US and Mexican Grands Prix, so 'nipped over' to Indianapolis and picked up the regulations. I also went to Ford Motor Co in Detroit to see those in charge of the Ford Indy engine project. We organised a mock-up engine that was shared between ourselves and Lotus and Lola and also acquired a full-sized drawing of the engine."

Ask the Yorkshireman about the design of the car and he will reply that it was built rather than actually designed. "We were a team of

A bearded Stirling Moss did go to the Speedway, in 1963 – the year after his career-halting Goodwood crash. Jim Clark obviously has a point to make.
(Courtesy Indianapolis Motor Speedway)

we just had to bend up the internal shape of the cockpit area, clamp it, and drill it to the front and centre bulkheads," said Robinson. "It was all basically straightforward. It looked very much like a F1 car. We wanted to give it some nice cosmetic lines. The suspension was a beefed up version of what we used on the F1 car. There was no point in us being too daring and experimental."

Masten Gregory was responsible for the supply of the engines and the ZF gearboxes. There were delays with the delivery of the latter that

slowed down completion of the cars; Ken Gregory said that from the initial conversation with his namesake to delivery took five months. Eventually they were shipped to Indianapolis in the April, where they were taken over by an organisation that had been established by Masten Gregory's former stepfather George Bryant. The chief mechanic was George Salih who had built the low 1957 and 1958 Indy 500 winning Belond AP Special – tipping his car's Offenhauser engine on its side to reduce its frontal area – as well as having had a hand

Built in Highgate, delivered to Indianapolis, and, by 2009, being restored in Florida – Masten Gregory's BRP. (Courtesy Indianapolis Motor Speedway)

Chris Amon drives down the pit lane before trying in vain to qualify his BRP for the 1967 Indy 500. There are some significant entries at the bottom of the scoring pylon, indicating a danger of being 'bumped' from the grid. Three of these are former or future World Champions, including Graham Hill and Jackie Stewart. (Courtesy Indianapolis Motor Speedway)

"He's on it!" Indianapolis Motor Speedway owner Tony Hulman (far left), and celebrated announcer Tom Carnegie listen to Alfred Moss at the Oldtimers' barbeque in 1968. (Courtesy Indianapolis Motor Speedway)

Tony Robinson in 2009. (Author's collection)

in Lee Wallard's 1951 victory. Salih spent just one weekend at BRP's Highgate, London factory. It was agreed that two BRP mechanics would be supplied for the month of May, these being George Woodward and Jim Chapman, who was to stay in the US. The team manager was going to be one Stirling Moss, although, in the event, this did not happen. *Cars Illustrated* also thought that Robinson might attend but he was never to get to the Speedway again.

The cars were sent to the US less the engines, which were not ready in time. The piping installations had been carried out at Highgate, although these had to be modified once the cars got to America. The gearbox was also installed at Indianapolis. "It all went together, though, for both the cars qualified so you have to say it was a success," said Robinson.

In the event Gregory ran into an oil pressure problem, having run as high as fifth, while Boyd's car had gearbox troubles. Masten's performance, the quality of the cars, and the speed with which they were built by a team that had never seen the Speedway underlined the enthusiastic Robinson's undoubted abilities. Boyd ran in a BRP again in 1966, hitting the wall in turn one after five laps. However, that year's first lap wreck meant he was still classified as high as twenty-second. Carl Williams ran one of the cars in 1967, going a lot further until he, too, crashed after 189 laps. Grand Prix driver Chris Amon also tried to qualify a BRP in 1967. Some pretty big Formula One names – Jackie Stewart, Graham Hill, and Jochen Rindt – only just made it onto the grid that Bump Day. Both BRP Indy cars eventually ended up in the ownership of Thomas Acker who intended rebuilding them.

Cars Illustrated remarked at the time the two BRPs were being built that Ken Gregory would be going to Indianapolis to "... scout round (and) assess the market for further cars of this type." The cost for one of the quality built chassis would have been £8000. It did not happen for BRP but the market was certainly to open up for the British in the forthcoming years.

FERGUSON FOUR-WHEEL-DRIVE

In August 1963 Jack Fairman returned to the Speedway, reunited with the Ferguson P99 that he had started the British Grand Prix in two years earlier. Both Cooper and Lotus had placed their proverbial toes in the water by running Formula One cars around the track and now legendary entrant Andy Granatelli was doing so, too.

It was Stirling Moss who had first brought Granatelli's attention to the benefits of the Harry Ferguson four-wheel-drive system used in the P99. It might, he suggested, be a solution to the problem of transmitting the power of the Novi V8 engines that powered the American's cars. Contact followed with Tony Rolt who had been collaborating with Ferguson on the development of the 4WD system. Rolt, a habitual escapee who had finished the Second World War incarcerated in Colditz Castle, had been one of the UK's foremost sports car racers. He and Duncan Hamilton had famously won at Le Mans in 1953 with a Jaguar C-type.

As a result, the 2.5-litre Coventry-Climax engined P99 was shipped to Indianapolis. The car was no longer in the first flush of youth but Fairman lapped at over 141mph. Granatelli then wanted to see what an experienced Indy driver could do in the car. Bobby Marshman also took the car out quickly recording similar speeds. Although the car was running out of steam on the straights, Marshman reckoned he could go through the turns flat out. Granatelli was convinced and declared that he would be entering a 4WD Novi for the 1964 race. Ferguson duly initiated a design study for such a car, which would be known as a Studebaker-STP Special in deference to a new sponsor.

In direct contrast to the other British-built chassis that were starting to appear at the Brickyard, the resulting Ferguson was front-engined. Photographs taken at the time show Rolt at the Speedway in team apparel. The garish STP livery appears incongruous on the normally dapper, tall Major. American Bobby Unser, who was to win the Indy 500 three times in latter years, the first time at the wheel of a British-designed Eagle, qualified the car twenty-second in 1964 before being involved in the second lap accident that claimed two drivers' lives. The following year he was up to eighth in practice and ran in the top ten but went out after sixty-nine laps with a broken oil fitting. However, British eyes were probably elsewhere that year.

Ferguson was not finished with the Indianapolis 500. Although Granatelli claimed that little was left of its system for his 4WD STP Paxton turbine car, Ferguson did assist in its development. When Granatelli turned to Lotus for the next generation of turbine cars, the 1968 type 56, that, too, used the Ferguson transmission. Initially USAC banned four-wheel-drive for the following year, but relented as long as the wheel rims were no wider than 10 inches, compared with the 14 inches of the two-wheel-drive cars. Lotus and Ferguson were back for their final fling with the conventionally-powered 64. Mario Andretti should have driven one of them but destroyed it, switched to a Brabham-based two-wheel-drive Hawk ... and won.

The Ferguson P99 Formula One car was tested at the Speedway in 1963, driven by Jack Fairman and Bobby Marshman. (Courtesy Indianapolis Motor Speedway)

The tall Tony Rolt (third from right), arguably incongruous in his STP 'pyjamas.' (Courtesy Indianapolis Motor Speedway)

8

THE MEN IN GREEN

"I have never seen anything so fast in my life ..."

They were not Martians, even if, to the traditionalist Americans, they must have appeared as aliens. The Team Lotus mechanics were certainly green. At least their overalls and some of their cars were and to the superstitious locals this was an anathema. They also had long hair ...

The then crew cut Parnelli Jones recalled that, "(A J) Foyt and I decided that we were going to go over to the garage and trim their hair for them. The car was sitting up on blocks and one of them, I can't remember who, slithered underneath. It was a joke, some of them had probably laughed at the costumes we were wearing."

"The person they chased was Bob Sparshott," recalled David Lazenby who was one of the original Team Lotus Indy mechanics in 1963, acting as chief mechanic from 1964 to 1966. "Bob could move at an incredible rate. I have never seen anything so fast in my life as Bob with A J Foyt after him with a huge pair of scissors. Unbelievable!"

"A J grabbed hold of me and Parnelli had what looked like a pair of wallpaper shears. They could have chopped my hair off. They didn't do

Chapman and Clark pose with the men in green in 1965 (left-to-right); Dave Lazenby, Graham Clode, Peter Jackson of Specialised Mouldings, Bob Sparshott, Alan Moffat, and Jim Smith. Mike Underwood squats behind the car. (Courtesy Ford)

Jim Endruweit fires up the prototype Indy Lotus. (Courtesy Ford)

it but they frightened me to death," said Sparshott, the youngest of the Lotus mechanics in those days.

"We were in our mid-twenties and travelling to the US ten or eleven times a year. And, of course we were Englishmen in America and a lot of Americans had never met an Englishman at that time," said Lazenby. It was a time for extremely hard work, not to mention acetylene bombs, jacked up police cars, and other matters that are perhaps best glossed over. The hours certainly seemed longer than those worked by their US counterparts. "The Americans could not believe the way we worked," said Sparshott who was seconded from the Lotus Cortina team. "You got a funny look from (Colin) Chapman

if you showed a sign of weakness like wanting something to eat." Lazenby admitted, "It was quite sapping."

Jim Endruweit led the Lotus Indy mechanics during the first year at the Speedway. Indeed, it was he and fellow mechanic Dick Scammell who took Trevor Taylor's Lotus 25 Grand Prix car to Indianapolis for Jim Clark to have his first look at the track. Team Lotus competitions manager Andrew Ferguson recorded that Endruweit's first reaction was, "Where?" Although officially chief mechanic, the experienced Endruweit had managerial responsibilities and Indy was just one thing that he had to deal with. Lazenby was his senior Indy mechanic along with Colin Riley who had also switched from the Formula One team.

The British brought their Racing Green to Indianapolis. With Dan Gurney's car they also reminded the Americans that their national racing colours were white and blue. Such colour schemes were then de rigueur in Formula One but ignored at Indy. (Courtesy Ford)

recalled Lotus' second year at Indianapolis with less than affection. That, they said, was the year of disaster with the tyres and the platform. "Nobody would listen to me," said Underwood. "We had a (Len Terry-designed) jacking platform that would lift the whole car off the ground ... It had a static height of about four inches. You could get the car over it when you just pushed it over it, but when it had a driver in it just caught the jack." The following year, the Wood Brothers from NASCAR took over from what Ford, perhaps unfairly, saw as the rather tardy British pit crew. "It was a total disaster [in 1964]," said 'Laz.' "I couldn't leave America quickly enough."

Sparshott recalled that the Wood brothers at first could not understand what the team was saying. "We talked too fast for them." Conversely, the brothers spoke particularly slowly. He could not believe that they could be so slow in speech and yet so react so rapidly during a pit stop.

Lazenby recalled an incident when the track was closed at 6.00pm. He and Underwood found a pedestrian entrance to the circuit, which they measured and found just wide enough for the car to pass through. "We decided to take it out on the track," says Underwood. "It was hilarious." Lazenby was driving, seeing his way by the light of a large torch. After one lap "We rushed it into the garage because we knew this was all highly illegal, locked up, and rushed off before (Speedway superintendent) Clarence Cagle, who lived near the stadium, had time to get over and give us a rollicking ... but we got it the next morning." Cagle had certainly heard the noise of the Ford engine. "He guessed who it was, nobody else would dared to have done that." Lazenby added, "We had little incidents like that."

Lazenby had first come to the attention of Lotus after constructing a special that somebody had seen and said that, if he could build this, he should apply for a job with the company. He started there being paid 4/6 dollars an hour building Lotus Elites, but he had become bored working on the road cars when Jim Endruweit asked if he would like to work for Team Lotus, the racing arm. He took to Indianapolis like the proverbial duck to water. Endruweit, by contrast, hated the place.

Graham Clode and former aircraft technician Mike Underwood went into the Lotus Indy section for 1964. Clode originally joined Team Lotus to work on the Formula One cars. "One day I was asked if I minded giving a hand with the Indy cars as they were a bit behind ... and I stayed with them." With the increase of work that the section was experiencing, John Duxberry and Australian Jim Smith also joined the team.

Reminiscing many years later, Lazenby, Clode, and Underwood

"We had to do something to keep us amused," retorted Underwood.

In 1963 the two Bobs, Dance and Sparshott, were mechanics on the Lotus Cortina team commuting between England and the US as the cars were run in both countries. It was because of this that they, too, became involved in the Indianapolis story. Dance recalled them listening in to the 1963 race using short wave radio "... which came in and out." Within less than twelve months he and Sparshott were on the way to the Speedway themselves. "We were seconded in 1964 and 1965," said Sparshott, who was just twenty-one that year. "It was a real eye opener, a lot of fun."

Prior to qualifying in 1965, Bobby Johns had suffered "... a major shunt" at Indianapolis. Dance recalled that he and Jim Endruweit had just driven up Pacific Coast Highway One to Laguna Seca – where they were to run Jackie Stewart and Tony Hegbourne – treating their hire

Clark (second from left) in deep discussion with his mechanics, Dave Lazenby (sat on wheel), and Colin Riley. (Courtesy Ford)

One year Sparshott was given the job of signaller out on the pit wall. Timekeeper Cyril Audrey would give the times to another signaller next to him, who would then display these for the outer signaller. The cars were coming round fast and Sparshott had to be ready to get the board out as his came off Turn Four. "I missed one or two laps." Sparshott had to stay out on the wall for the whole three and a half hours of the race. "I was a bit nervous before the start of the race. I asked what happened if there was a crash and I was told just to duck down behind the (low) wall."

American response to the young Lotus team was, said Graham Clode, "variable." They superstitiously did not, though, approve of the way in which they were clad in green overalls. Early one May Clode and Jim Smith were weighing the car, which was just about on the limit. "The Americans would not believe us and at one point they locked us in the garage and would not let us out ... because we were wearing green!"

If 1964 had been an "absolute disaster" then, said Lazenby, "1965 was just like a wonderful, old clock ticking. We would work all day in the garage and, about half an hour before the track closed, we would push the car out and Jimmy would go a little bit faster than the day before. We would put the car in the garage, close the doors and return to work all the next day. Chapman kept writing enormous job lists. Everything was running well but he had to write them."

Lazenby also recalled how humid it was that May. "God, it was hot." The night before the race, the mechanics finished at about 10.30pm and returned to the Holiday Inn. Chapman heard them and, coming out of his room, asked what they were doing. "He was all ready to send us back to the garage," said Underwood. Lazenby, Clode, and Underwood had been joined by Arthur Birchall and Australians Jim Smith and Alan Mofatt that year. The following year, New Zealander Alan McCall from the Lotus Cortina section replaced Smith.

Underwood recalled an incident from 1965: "We pushed Bobby Johns out onto the apron and started the car up. 'Laz' waved him out but he didn't seem to turn the steering wheel and went into the car in front, pushing the wheel back into the chassis. We pushed the car back into the garage. Just at this point 'the old man' (Chapman) was coming through the tunnel. He wanted to know why we were going back as we hadn't even run. He went ballistic when he saw the damage. We stripped it down to the bare rack and I spent a day trying to pull the

car as if it had European handling and brakes. "We arrive at our garage with jangling noises coming from the car. The phone rang and it was the old man (Chapman) for Jim. 'We've shunted one of the Indy cars and we really could do with Bob and Bob again so get them on a flight *now*.'

"We arrived at the airport at about 8.30pm. Andrew Ferguson picked us up and I thought we were going to be taken straight to our hotel. Instead we went to the circuit, and into the garage where the boys were all flat out as if it were the middle of the day. David Lazenby said, 'Sort yourselves out a pair of overalls.' We finished at about midnight and then went to have something to eat. We had to be up at 7.00am and it went on like that." Dance recalled carrying out an "all nighter" on his thirtieth birthday. The two Bobs stayed for qualifying before returning to their Cortina duties. "I think we were quite pleased to leave then," said Dance. "It was like being in the forces."

"Being the youngest I was often given the jobs others didn't want," said Sparshott. "We had some special tubular wheel stands, designed for use when the wheels might still be on the car but not the springs and dampers. Dave Lazenby had lent one of our sets to A J Foyt but we wanted both our cars up on the stands. 'Laz' therefore sent me round to Foyt's garage to retrieve them. When I got there they were in the middle of an inquest. Foyt reckoned that he had been given the stands so I scarpered. 'Laz' went himself and confronted Foyt who ripped the stands out from under the car – it must have bent the rose joints – and he threw them out of the open door."

In Clark's absence, Mike Underwood sat in for him for the traditional front-row photograph. The British influence can be seen in the fact that Mario Andretti's Brawner (nearest camera) is a Brabham copy, while George Snider's Coyote was based on Bobby Johns' 1965 Lotus 38. (Courtesy Indianapolis Motor Speedway)

qualified." 'Laz' recalled that the cars had to be fitted with mesh under the engine so that, if it blew, parts did not drop out onto the track. He also remembers this was not very effective when, down the main straight, Unser blew his engine. "It went north, south, east, and west," says Clode. "We thought we had better get another engine so we nipped off to the engine builder, Louis Meyer, and asked for one. That was going to cost $24,000. 'Send the bill to Ford,' we said. We put the engine in and the next day, after just a couple of laps, Al was flying down the main straight and the engine went again. Back we went to Louis Meyer. So now we were on engine three."

As the team was pushing the gearbox into place, Underwood observed that it was "... a bit spongy." The quill shaft was too long and was pushing the crank forward. It was small wonder that the engines were blowing. "We got some thick washers and put them between the engine and the gearbox," says Lazenby. The team was now running out of time and the next day the time taken to change the engine was "... quite considerable." However, with the engine only held in by four bolts – the top two were not fitted – Unser qualified. Chapman sent a telegram observing how fast his team had changed the engine. "To this day, nobody has mentioned anything about the cost of those engines," says Lazenby. "Nobody has said a word." The mechanics just had not had the time to consult authority about their purchase.

In 1967 Mike Underwood took over as chief mechanic for the Indy section, supported by Arthur Birchall, Irishman Eamon Fullalove and Graham Bartils, Jim Pickles, and Welshman Hywel Absalom. Jim Endruweit, now racing manager, was, unhappily for him, also scheduled to be on the team and spend May at his least favourite circuit. For the final two years at Indianapolis the team looked very different to that of the early days, with Absalom, Birchall, and Pickles serving to the end, joined by Doug Garner and, in 1968, by Dick Scammell and Bill Cowe. In 1969, Bob Dance, Eamon Fullalove, and Graham Bartils returned to the fold along with Derek Mower, who had become a regular at Indianapolis, being succeed there by his son Chris, currently team manager at Panther Racing.

Dave Lazenby (left) and Colin Riley looking somewhat American outside the Indianapolis garages. (Courtesy Ford)

thing out again but I couldn't. That car ran in the race 3/8 inch shorter on the left-hand side."

In 1966, Clark qualified the first weekend but his new team-mate, Al Unser, did not. Chapman and Clark returned to England, the former leaving Lazenby with the somewhat obvious instructions to "Get him

The Chaparral was designed by Englishman John Barnard, and built by Bob Sparshott's B&S Fabrications in the UK. (Courtesy Indianapolis Motor Speedway)

before a return to England and Formula One. McLaren itself then asked him to go back to Indy in 1976, the year of Johnny Rutherford's second 500 victory. "They had got quite used to the British by then."

Sparshott was another to renew his involvement with the Indianapolis 500. British designer John Barnard had been approached by entrant Jim Hall, who had already won the 500 with a Lola, to design and build a Chaparral for the Speedway. The result was to be the revolutionary Chaparral 2K that brought 'ground effects' to Indy. Sparshott was now running BS Fabrications back in the UK, and Barnard had been insistent that the work be done in

Underwood pointed out that, other than Jim Clark, he was the only person to drive the H16-engined Lotus-BRM Type 42 Indy car. Underwood warmed it up for three laps at a Snetterton test before the Scot got in for another two and the complex engine let go. Underwood became disenchanted, particularly over the attempt to use the BRM H16 engine, and left after 1967. As he pointed out, changing from this to the Ford unit meant that the car grew by a full ten inches. He was no supporter of the engine from Bourne. After a brief time with Frank Williams and then with Len Terry, he became involved with the BRM Car-Am project, which took him back to the States. From there he moved back into Indy car racing, working as a mechanic for George Bignotti and the Vel's Parnelli team, running the Lola-based P J Colts for Al Unser and Joe Leonard. He just missed the team's 1970 Indy 500 victory but was there when Unser repeated the feat a year later. The locals certainly appreciated his forthright approach. Indeed, the Americans recognised the worth of the Team Lotus mechanics. George Bignotti approached Clode after he had left the team but he did not feel comfortable with the American way of life. Lindsey Hopkins tried to get Lazenby to join him, but he was persuaded to stay with Lotus. "Chapman could be quite persuasive."

For 1972, Underwood was reunited with former Lotus mechanics Eamon Fullalove and Graham Bartils (known respectively as 'Chalky' and 'Rabbit'; they all seemed to have nicknames, Underwood was 'Charlie Chins') who had worked under him at Indy in 1967. The task was to help build the McLaren look-alike Atlantas for Lloyd Ruby and Cale Yarborough. A short while with Indy innovator Smokey Yunick followed

this country. "I got to hear about this and made contact. I offered our services to build the car, although not knowing what plans he had," said Sparshott who had, during the previous year, 1978, run a Formula One McLaren.

There was no budget mentioned but the deal was done whereby BS would bill Barnard who then would bill Hall. American Gordon Kimball crossed the Atlantic to do the drawing under Barnard. BS Fabrications had a spare, vacant drawing office where a full-sized drawing board was installed. "As an engineer and a concept man, John was brilliant," to work with recalled Sparshott. "Everything that came off the board fitted and worked. It went together like a Swiss watch. I had never known anything like it before."

Clark's winning car of 1965 left Ford's museum in Detroit for restoration at Hethel. (Left-to-right;) Bob Sparshott, Graham Clode, Dave Lazenby, Len Terry, and Bob Dance were reunited with it. (Courtesy Graham Clode collection)

DEREK MOWER

Derek Mower – 'Joe 90' in Team Lotus-speak – spans the generation gap between the itinerant British mechanics of the 1960s and those who were to put down their roots in Indianapolis. Today, as will be seen, there are many British engineers living in and round the city. Those who worked for Cooper, Lotus, and the other British manufacturers that turned up at the Brickyard in the 1960s remained UK domiciled and flew back and forth over the Atlantic. Mower spent time in both camps.

A Team Lotus mechanic, he was part of its Indianapolis section in just the final year of the campaign, 1969. He was immediately attracted to Indy. Compared to Formula One, this was the place to be. Not only were the standard of living higher and the working hours shorter than in Grands Prix, Indianapolis was also a strange place. Mower recalled one dinner with Lotus designer Maurice Phillipe and fellow mechanic Doug Garner. Alcohol was prohibited at the restaurant ... in theory. The coffee pot came, Mower poured out the liquid and added milk, before realising that the pot's contents were red wine.

Mario Andretti was originally slated to drive for Lotus that year but, having crashed it, eventually piloted a Hawk to victory. In 1968 he had made his Formula One debut with the team, racing for them again in three Grands Prix during 1969. Mower worked with him during this time. At the end of 1971, having announced that he would be driving for Vel's Parnelli Jones Racing in the States, Andretti persuaded Mower and another Lotus engineer, John Baldwin, to go with him. Maurice Philippe also left the British team to design the new VPJs. Later they would be joined by yet further Lotus refugees Dick Scammel and Sid Carr. It was a small operation but heavily British. "We used to have an end of year party for all the team – that meant all eight of us."

On being invited to join VPJ, Mower waited until his daughter had been born and then, in January 1972, moved to the US. "I said to Mario that I would stay for two years ... then another two years ... then another two years ..." After three years with the Vel's Parnelli Jones team, Mower was appointed team manager of Bob Fletcher's Cobre Tire team, running such as Bobby Unser, Bill Vukovich Jnr, and Pancho Carter. He ultimately stayed in the US until 1986. In 1982, he was working on Gordon Smiley's car for Pat Patrick's team. His son Chris believes that it was Smiley's horrific, fatal accident in qualifying that made Mower question whether he wanted to stay in racing. He started a completely different business working on generators in the ranches around Phoenix but was drawn back into motorsport, eventually running a European Formula 3000 team with his son. Chris, as will be seen later, often accompanied him to the Speedway. Just over two decades later Mower Junior was back, initially with Conquest Racing and then as team manager at Panther Racing.

Three sets of parts were made, of which two were built into finished cars. The bodywork was manufactured by Specialist Mouldings. "We were all very enthusiastic and we knew that it was breaking new ground. It had some really nice things on it, including titanium gear lever and slug. This was a bit new to us."

Jim Hall was not best pleased with how much the car cost to build but, as Sparshott pointed out to him, it was not expensive to run. Barnard and Hall were to part company but the car created something of a stir when it first appeared in 1979, winning the following year now in the hands of Johnny Rutherford.

There was to be a postscript to the story for some of the Lotus mechanics. In 2008, Ford sent Clark's winning car – which had been for years in its Detroit museum, many of them in a seemingly unloved state – to Classic Team Lotus in Hethel to be rebuilt. Lazenby, Dance, Clode, and designer Len Terry were among those who were reunited with it there.

Derek Mower with Al Unser Sr's VPJ Eagle in 1974.
(Courtesy Chris Mower collection)

9

BRITAIN'S FINEST HOUR – JIM CLARK, GRAHAM HILL, AND JACKIE STEWART

"Jimmy was a horse whisperer."

Jim Clark, Graham Hill, and Jackie Stewart; together, they represent an era when the Grand Prix grids were green – with a splash of red – and the vast majority of drivers had Anglo-Saxon names. Between them, these three Brits won the World Championship seven times between 1962 and 1973. And, with just ten laps to go of the 1966 Indianapolis 500, they held a dominant one, two, three lead.

Clark, as recounted, was already a three-time Indy veteran with a win and a second place. The other two, despite their Grands Prix successes, were rookies as far as Indianapolis was concerned.

"Jimmy's driving skill was a God-given talent," recalled his former girlfriend, Sally Swart. "Heavily talented artists tend not to be well rounded and I think he was probably like that, but his mastery in a car made him a true artist. When he got out of one he almost became a different person. I once asked him how he made up his mind to turn the first corner and he laughed, 'that's automatic.' He did take time to make decisions.

"Jimmy was easy going but quiet and introverted. I liked to think of him as a 'dour' Scot although that is probably the wrong word. He seemed very aware of what his family would think of his actions and whether his father would approve. He always wanted to behave honourably. He liked to keep things low key and didn't make a fuss about himself."

"To me, Jimmy Clark was the greatest Formula driver ever to sit in a car," said four times Indy 500 winner, A J Foyt. "I saw him drive a stock car at Rockingham, a factory Ford that wasn't a good car but I think he ran in the top ten. Then he went to Trenton and Milwaukee

and ran real good. I reckon that he was one of the few Formula One drivers who would perform, whatever car you put him in. On top of that he was a nice guy."

Clark did know where to draw the line when he was in the States. L Spencer Riggs recalled seeing him at the high-banked Winchester track, said then to be the fastest half-mile circuit in the world. "His eyes were as big as saucers," said Riggs of the spectating Scot. If anybody expected to see Clark out on the track they would have been disappointed. "Jim didn't want anything to do with it."

"Jimmy was a horse whisperer," added Len Terry. "He was as smooth as silk. Jimmy and Dan Gurney had the same equipment at Indianapolis in 1963 but Dan could not do with it what Jimmy did. He was the best ever."

For 1966, Clark had been joined at the Speedway by two

Jim Clark in 1967. (Courtesy Ford)

Hill (centre left) had been present in 1993, although, unlike Clark (centre right), he did not start the race. (Courtesy Ford)

of his closest competitors in Grand Prix racing; one of them the Englishman who had pipped him to the World title in 1962, Graham Hill. As recounted, the Lotus 29 had not been the only 'funny car' at Indianapolis in 1963, there had been the car entered by Mickey Thompson. It had failed to finish but the hot rodder had new Chevrolet V8-powered cars built for the next season, the Harvey Aluminium Specials. In appearance they looked squashed, trodden upon by some careless giant. Being mid-engined it was perhaps fitting that two of the drivers originally signed to drive the cars were experienced Formula One racers, one of them the current World Champion, Hill.

The initial driver out on the first day of practice was Hill, who survived a spin to be first that year to pass the rookie test. Three days later he got too high on turn three, hit the wall, and spun down the chute. The moustachioed Englishman was unhurt, although the car had heavy right-hand side damage. He returned to Europe for Formula One testing but was back in Indianapolis later in the month. However, he made no attempt to qualify. British attention that year was all to be on Hill's archrival in F1, Clark. Hill's time at Indianapolis was yet to come. Three years later another English World Champion, John Surtees, was due to make his Indianapolis debut driving a Lola T90 for John Mecom. However, because of an enormous accident in a Can-Am race at Ste Jovite, he became unable to compete. Mecom's drivers were then to be Rodger Ward, Walt Hansgen, and Hill's BRM Formula One team-mate, Scotsman Jackie Stewart. In the April Hansgen was killed during the trials for the Le Mans 24-hours and, at the last minute, Hill was brought in to drive. In true Indianapolis style his car was know as the Red Ball Special, which, as Lola founder Eric Broadley recalled, "... was a gift" for a wit like Hill.

Jackie Stewart's first experience of the Speedway had been in the October before, when he had tried one of Mecom's well prepared cars "... to see if I wanted to do it or not. It was only really a reconnaissance and they were very fussy about my not going too fast, as they would do

Hardly the favourites, but Graham Hill and his Lola were to win the 1966 Indianapolis 500. (Courtesy Lola Cars)

with any rookie. I didn't feel uncomfortable with the walls. Everything felt OK." A number of luminaries were there to see the young Formula One driver that day, including circuit owner Tony Hulman and long time track superintendent Clarence Cagle. They must have watched with some interest for the Scot had taken the first of his twenty-seven Grand Prix victories just the month before and he was definitely seen as the 'coming man.' Canadian, Jim Dilamarter, then a 'gofer' with the Mecom team and later a leading figure with the Vel's Parnelli Jones operation, recalled how the now Sir Jackie would explain to mechanics George Bignotti and Brit, Jim Chapman how the car was handling. It seemed that his favourite expression was – to be said in a Scottish accent – "undoolating." This was still a clean-cut youngster, not the trend setting, long-haired epitome of the era that he was to become. In between qualifying and the race Dilamarter was transferred to Hill's car to work alongside its crew chief "another Britisher" George Woodward.

"I really enjoyed my times at Indianapolis, staying at the Speedway Motel – it was the Hotel de Paris of Indianapolis – and playing golf at

the circuit with such as Roger Penske." Like so many British, Sir Jackie now recalls just how long the May could be. Also like Brabham and Clark before him, he had the small matter of the Monaco Grand Prix to attend to and he flew back to Europe for what was to be the first World Championship race for the new 3-litre formula. Driving for BRM, he won the event by just over forty seconds and, thus, took an initial lead in the Championship.

At Indianapolis in 1966 Stewart found himself on the middle of the fourth row of the grid. Billy Foster, alongside him on the outside, hit the wall as the field took the flag; a massive accident ensued, although, thankfully, there were no major injuries. Stewart recalled that he was the last car through. "The big pile up was to play into our hands," said Lola founder Eric Broadley. "The fact that we had qualified so badly kept us out of the way."

One hour and twenty-four minutes later the race was resumed, and by lap seventeen Stewart's fellow Scot, Jim Clark, was in the lead. The previous year's winner had made the middle of the front row in qualifying but there was something very different about his Lotus.

The patriotic green had gone, replaced by the iconic red of sponsor STP, presumably to the relief of the superstitious locals. On lap sixty-five Clark spun, pitted, and lost the lead. Eighteen laps later he was back in front. This time he spun three times, missed contact with everyone and anything, and headed for the pits once more for fresh tyres. ("Spinning Takes Practice!" he said later.) American Lloyd Ruby was now in the lead but the Gallic clans were on his tail. Clark and Stewart were in pursuit and when Ruby pitted with an oil leak the younger of the two Scots moved up front. With eight laps to go he had more than a lap lead. "Jackie had the race won," recalled Parnelli Jones. Dilamarter, now assigned to Hill's pit, was wishing that he had not been transferred from Stewart's crew.

At this point though an oil scavage pump broke. "I switched the engine off before it seized and I coasted round to the exit of Turn Four," said Sir Jackie. At first he tried to push the car home thinking that he could get another lap. When he decided that it would be easier to walk the crowd showed appreciation of his efforts. Such had been his lead that he was still able to be classified in sixth place. "I felt that I had driven a good race so I didn't feel a great disappointment. You had to be good at drafting at Indianapolis then and I learnt a lot from those around me like

The ill-fated Mike Spence prepares to take out his Lotus turbine.
(Courtesy Indianapolis Motor Speedway)

Hill, far left, benefits from the first lap melee that eliminated eleven cars in 1966. (Courtesy Indianapolis Motor Speedway)

"Spinning Takes Practice," remarked Clark, in reference to sponsor STP.
(Courtesy Indianapolis Motor Speedway)

MIKE SPENCE

Mike Spence really should not have been at the Speedway in 1968. He had, after all, left Team Lotus at the end of 1965 after sixteen Grands Prix and a best result of third in Mexico, plus a win in the non-championship Race of Champions at Brands Hatch. His old team had entered Jim Clark and Graham Hill for the 500.

The unassuming Spence was now driving for Lotus' rival, BRM. In April 1968, his fate and that of his former team leader Clark became intertwined. (Three years earlier, Spence had 'led' the Formula One team and finished third at the Silverstone International Trophy while his 'number one' was away at Indianapolis.) He was entered for the BOAC 500 sports car race at Brands, sharing the new Cosworth DFV-engined Ford F3L with Bruce McLaren. The drivers should have been Clark and Graham Hill, but Colin Chapman had intervened and sent his men to an unimportant Formula Two event at Hockenheim. News filtered through of Clark's death during that race and Spence wondered what chance the rest had if a driver of Clark's talent had been killed.

Initially, it was announced that Jackie Stewart would replace his fellow Scot at the Speedway driving one of the turbine-engined Lotus 56s. However, Chapman also put Spence in the frame as a back up and he tested the car at Silverstone in the week leading up to the International Trophy there. BRM's Tony Rudd then gave permission for him to also test it at Indianapolis itself. At this point the European Formula Two scene intervened again. On his final practice lap at Jarama, Stewart left the road and damaged his wrist. He showed up for a physical at Indianapolis but a drive in the 500 was now off his agenda. Spence stepped up to partner Hill who, incidentally, he had replaced at BRM. It was a small world.

Spence was quickly on the pace at the Speedway, recording a practice time on May 7 about 0.5mph below the track record and telling the press that there was more to come. A race steward had said, though, that he was then running too high through the turns. A further 56 at the track that day was being driven by the inexperienced Greg Weld. Spence had initially been reluctant when Chapman had asked if he would evaluate Weld's mount to see if its lack of speed was down to driver or car. Tragically, he agreed to during the afternoon.

It was observed that, on his first lap he had gone higher than normal on his entry into Turn One. A lap later he was higher still and the chief observer had the yellow lights on before Spence had even made contact with the wall. For 300 feet the Lotus slid along the barrier and then hit it at forty-five degrees before continuing onwards and eventually halting in the middle of the track. The front right wheel, torn off but still retained by a track rod, had swung back, hit Spence's head and ripped off his helmet. He was immediately taken to the Methodist Hospital with serious head injuries. Andrew Ferguson recorded how he saw Jackie Stewart consoling an "ashen-faced" Chapman. Despite everybody's best efforts, Spence died that evening. Chapman, devastated by the loss of two such fine drivers within exactly a month, understandably issued a press statement that he wanted "nothing more to do with the 1968 Indianapolis race." It was not many days, though, before he was back.

"I was just enough of a practical engineer to reckon those new cars were not safe," said Parnelli Jones. "When Spence was killed that really made me realise I was making the right decision to quit driving Indy cars."

Over thirty British or British-born drivers have either practised for or raced in the Indianapolis 500. Mike Spence has the sad record of being the only one to have been killed at the Speedway.

With a few laps to go, Jackie Stewart looked the likely winner in 1966. His consolation would be the Rookie of the Year prize. (Courtesy Indianapolis Motor Speedway)

Roger McCluskey. The disappointment only came afterwards when I realised what I could so nearly have won so early in my career as a racing driver."

In his column in the short-lived British newspaper *Auto News*, Stewart that week described the race as "... a fantastic experience." Asked at the time why he had shut off his engine rather than go for broke with failing oil pressure, he replied that, as a Scot, he had been trying to protect his entrant's investment.

The laps leading up to this point must be regarded as the zenith of the British story at Indianapolis. Stewart, Clark, and Hill were in the first three places driving Lola, Lotus, and Lola respectively. It might be

Hill's 1966 Lola went on display at the Racing Car Show in Olympia, London, the following January. (Author's collection)

said that an American car, Lloyd Ruby's Eagle, had led the most laps, but even that had been designed by an Englishman, Len Terry. "Many of the critical blokes in our workshop were also British or Australian," Terry recalled. The situation was to lead Hill at the Victory Banquet to question whether there ought to be a trophy for the first American driver home. With Stewart's demise Clark and Hill swept into the first two places, or was it the other way round?

Stewart spent most of those last few laps walking back and confesses not to have been in a position to make judgement on the eventual result. "There was definitely consternation at the end," he recalled. "Chapman thought that Jimmy had won and Mecom thought that Graham had won." The timekeepers reckoned that Hill was the victor and so he became the first rookie winner since 1927, as well as the second consecutive victor from Britain. It was also the second leg of a unique achievement. With a victory at the Le Mans in 1972 sharing a Matra with Henri Pescarolo, Hill was to become the only man to have won the Formula One World Championship, the Indianapolis 500, and the Le Mans 24-hours

It is thought that Hill passed Clark about thirty laps before the end, but the Lotus team reckoned their man to have been ahead and that Hill had merely been unlapping himself. Both Brits drove into Victory Lane but it seems that a lap by Al Unser, whose lurid Day-Glo vermillion STP Lotus looked almost identical to Clark's, had been erroneously credited to the Scot. It was, proclaimed *Auto News*, "A glorious mix-up." Not everyone agrees with the result to this day. Clark's former girlfriend Sally Swart will still tell you that "Jimmy won at Indy three times" while according to Len Terry, "There is a very good chance that he won in 1966 as well as 1965." Perhaps they are understandably biased but as Terry recalled, "Chapman thought he had won and Jimmy thought he had won."

Hill used the Victory Banquet to complain that there were no doors on the toilets in the paddock area; it is a story that everyone from the time, including Stewart, will relate. "Everybody got a big charge out of that," recalled Parnelli Jones. The Americans saw no problem as women were banned from the garage area. However, next year the doors were in place. The British influence on the Indianapolis Motor Speedway has certainly been a major one.

Stewart was presented with the Rookie of

Aston Martin sent Broadley its congratulations after the 1966 Indy 500 win. The following year Aston-engined Lolas appeared at Le Mans, as they would do over four decades later. (Courtesy Lola Cars)

Graham Hill was to hit the wall after 110 laps of the 1968 race. (Courtesy Indianapolis Motor Speedway)

the Year award. With this came a variety of prizes, including a year's supply of butcher's meat "... which I never got." He was additionally presented with a blue Ford Thunderbird, "... which I did bring back." There was also one honour that the Scot received from the Hoosier state. A police car was once taking him to a speaking engagement when it had to detour to catch a car thief. The result was that he was made an honorary sheriff of Indiana.

In 1967, Stewart found his Mecom Lola to be uncompetitive and he was initially bumped from the field. Some pretty impressive names were finding it difficult to qualify that year. On the second weekend of qualifying he did manage to make it into the field but such are the rules at Indy that he was on the penultimate row of the grid. Dilamarter recalled how the team had to make a "superhuman effort" to get its

third car ready for him. "He drove his balls off to get that car into the race." Graham Hill, now with Lotus, was at the back of the grid, while even Jim Clark had only made the sixth row.

It was the year of Parnelli Jones domination with Andy Granatelli's first turbine car and another win for A J Foyt. Having started twenty-ninth, Stewart made a major charge through the field, ran as high as third and was catching Foyt when his Ford V8 lost oil pressure for the second successive year. "Parnelli was a smooth, top line racing driver, we got on well together. A J was a character. I always called them 'the pussy cat and the bear.'"

Stewart's fellow Brits fared even worse. It was a far cry from the previous year, with Hill dropping out with a burnt piston on lap twenty-three, and his new team-mate, Clark, twelve laps later. Having

Joe Leonard's Indy-leading Lotus 56/1 turbine car now resides in the Vel Miletich-Parnelli Jones Collection in California, along with Jim Clark's pole-winning Lotus 34/3 from 1964, the same car that Jones drove to second place a year later. (Author's collection)

witnessed two consecutive victories, the British would have to wait until 2005 to see another by one of their compatriots.

It would be Clark's last Indy 500. For many of his fans, the first they heard of his death the next year was over the Tannoy at the 1968 BOAC 500 sports car race. Sally Swart was at Zandvoort where her husband Ed was racing an Abarth. She was on her own at the time, sitting in the pits, when she heard a news flash on the radio. Her knowledge of the Dutch language was, at that stage, in its infancy. Clark's name was mentioned, coupled with the word 'overleden.' Worried, she rushed to her father-in-law who confirmed it meant the Scot had been killed in a minor Formula Two race at Hockenheim.

Stewart signed a contract to drive a gas turbine Lotus in 1968 but having damaged his wrist at a Formula Two meeting, had to withdraw.

Mike Spence, a former Lotus Grand Prix driver who was now with the Scot's old team BRM, took over the seat. A year later Sir Jackie was slated to drive a steam car for Bill Lear, a project that never came to fruition. That was not, though, the end of his involvement with the Speedway. From 1971 to 1986 he commentated on the 500 for ABC television, while in 1979 he drove the Ford Mustang pace car at the start. One could also point out Indy 500 winners Dario Franchitti, Juan Pablo Montoya, Gil de Ferran, and Helio Castroneves, all of whom in their early careers drove for Paul Stewart Racing, the team that Sir Jackie ran with his son. The track obviously has great memories for him, although he does say that during his time racing there "Coming back to the Riviera after the flat planes of Indiana was something of a cultural shock."

Maurice Philippe took over the design of the Lotus Indy cars from Len Terry. (Courtesy Chris Mower collection)

while Hill drove what was known as the 42F; a monocoque originally intended for the H16 but modified to take a Ford V8 four-cam, which has been described as "the most obscure Lotus." It did not even look right. Both cars failed.

However, it should be pointed out that it was an expatriate Englishman, Ken Wallis, who had designed the whale-like STP-Paxton while, as journalist 'Jabby' Crombac, who was close to Lotus, pointed out, the winning Coyote-Ford was "a blatant copy" of the Lotus 38. Clark even got to drive the turbine during a practice session and reported that this was going to be the car to win the 500. It was only the failure of a $6 ball bearing three laps from the end of the race that proved him wrong.

A year later and the British influence was as strong as ever. Indeed, Lotus and Andy

"I got to know the Hulman family. It was nice going to Indianapolis and they like having the Europeans over. My days were happy there. It was a task to thread the needle well there and there were specialists. Anybody who thinks that Indy is an easy trip is completely misinformed.

"It's still an enormous sporting event. I don't care who you are, you are still going to experience goose pimples when 'Gentleman start your engines' is said and 'Back Home in Indiana' is sung. It's an emotional place."

The domination of the 1967 race by Parnelli Jones' STP-Paxton turbine car and the eventual victory of A J Foyt's Coyote, coupled to what appeared a low-key effort from Lotus, would make it appear that the British influence was now waning. Lotus still desired to use the BRM H16 engine (see chapter sixteen), the failure of which left it to a certain extent in disarray. Clark had to make do with an ageing Type 38

Last Lotus at the Speedway; Art Pollard's Offy-powered conversion lasted only seven laps before it went out with a broken driveline. (Courtesy Indianapolis Motor Speedway)

Granatelli had combined and although the rules had been changed to peg back the turbines, the British team built such a car to run in STP colours. This was a period when Lotus racing cars appeared to take on a wedge shape; the type 61 Formula Ford and the highly successful type 72 Formula One were examples. However, perhaps the cleanest and sleekest was the Maurice Phillippe-designed Lotus 56 with its Pratt & Whitney engine. The final driver line-up was very different to that first envisaged. With the deaths of Clark and Mike Spence, and the indisposition of Stewart, Americans Joe Leonard and Art Pollard joined Graham Hill. The latter's suspension failed well into the race, but Leonard took the lead and seemed to be on his way to victory with nine laps left when fuel pump drive failure brought his car to a halt. Pollard was eliminated for the same reason and at about the same time. Still, one could point to the fact that winning Eagle did have a British designer in Tony Southgate.

Only one more Lotus was to appear in the 500. It was not, though, that the company had lost interest. With the limitations on turbines now too severe to contemplate running such a car, Lotus reverted to a conventional Ford V8 engine but retained four-wheel-drive for its final fling, the type 64. Mario Andretti was to drive one for Granatelli while the Formula One team of Hill and Jochen Rindt were to pilot two others. Andretti was very quick during practice but crashed heavily when a right rear hub failed. As an eventual result of this, the cars were withdrawn and Andretti went on to win the race in a Hawk. Chapman originally wanted the type 64s, which he saw as disasters, to be destroyed but they were returned to Hethel. All that was left was for Art Pollard to start the race in a type 56 that Granatelli had modified to take a turbocharged Offenhauser engine, retiring after just seven laps with a broken drive line. The saga of Lotus at Indianapolis was, it seemed, over. There was the type 96 ... but that is another story.

The unloved Lotus 96 poses outside Team Lotus' Ketteringham Hall headquarters. (Courtesy Gene Varnier collection)

THE UNWANTED LOTUS

In 1984, Cooper no longer existed as a racing car manufacturer while Lotus had not been back to the Speedway for fifteen years. Colin Chapman had suffered a fatal heart attack two years previously. It seemed that the pioneers of the rear-engined revolution had left the Indy scene.

It was at this point that English-born American businessman Roy Winklemann, best known in motor racing circles for his top-line Formula Two team of the 1960s, approached Team Lotus with a proposal to build a car for the CART Championship. With the Indy 500 then still part of that series, it could have brought Lotus back to the Brickyard. There was also a link that went right back in that Winklemann's number one driver in F2 had been Jochen Rindt, who had driven a factory Lotus in 1969 the final year of the team's Indy appearances, albeit an aborted one. Winkelmann now wanted to return to racing but rather than purchase a proprietary Lola or March, commissioned Lotus to build the type 96.

Australian Gene Varnier worked on the design of such a car under Gerard Ducarouge. The first that he heard of it was when he applied for a wage rise and was told that he could only have one if he would consent to work on another project in addition to the Formula One cars. The result was that he found himself assisting with what he described as "effectively a scaled up Formula One car." The idea was that it would use a Cosworth DFX engine actually prepared by Cosworth itself, a privilege that no other team had. In June Autosport had inaccurately speculated that use might be made of a Renault engine or even a derivative of a V6 Toyota turbo.

Sadly, it quickly became apparent that the establishment at CART would not take kindly to a car that was effectively a works effort with regard to both the chassis and the engine. Other than Penske, every other team purchased its cars and engines as conventional customers. No sponsor was forthcoming and no leading driver seemed interested. Varnier asked Ayrton Senna, who was with Team Lotus at the time, what he felt about driving an Indy car. "No way," replied the Brazilian, "Those guys are crazy." The project came to a halt before there was even a chance of an engine fire up, and Lotus was left with a proverbial white elephant ... except that it was green. Perhaps the superstitious Americans were right after all. "It was a good project. It's a shame it didn't happen," said Vernier.

It was, though, impossible to say that Lotus would never reappear at the Speedway. At the 2010 Autosport International Show the new Group Lotus director of motorsport, Claudio Berro, said that the company was "looking very seriously at Indycar." Given the current constraints of the formula, this appeared highly unlikely. However, Berro countered by saying "The chassis and engines are well established and will be there for a while longer, too. It does, though, give us a cost-effective way of both showing what we can achieve with our technical know-how and input, and it gives us an opportunity to brand and assist an existing team in a market that is of a lot of interest to us and in an area of the sport where Lotus has real heritage."

A couple of months later Lotus and Cosworth announced that they would, in fact, be bringing their two famed brands back to Indianapolis, albeit as technical and commercial partners of the KV Racing Technology team. The announcement confusingly referred to the car concerned, to be driven by Takuma Sato, as "the Lotus-Cosworth IndyCar" considering that it was, like every other car on the grid, a Dallara-Honda – but it was to be painted green and yellow.

At the beginning of 2010 it was said that there would be a Lotus-Cosworth at the Speedway that year, even if it was a Dallara-Honda. The car was, however, as can be seen in this shot taken at that year's Long Beach Grand Prix, green.
The new IndyCar rules packages announced in July 2010 stated that, although Dallara would continue to be the rolling chassis supplier, aero kits could be manufactured by anyone, and it was after these suppliers that the cars would be called. This led to speculation that the Lotus name really could be on its way back to Indianapolis. (Author's collection)

10

THE EAGLES' WINGS – LEN TERRY AND TONY SOUTHGATE

"It was all at arm's length then."

There may seem nothing British about Indianapolis 500 winner 'Frank Capua' but then his last lap victory was a work of fiction, the climax of the film '*Winning,*' arguably best remembered for the fact that it introduced actor Paul Newman to motor racing. Art did, though, reflect life in that the 1967 Eagle used by 'Capua' was painted to look like that raced by the real life 1968 victor, Bobby Unser, and both cars were the work of English designers, Len Terry and Tony Southgate respectively.

"It was a race that fascinated me; it was a one-off," said Terry who was the designer of the 1965 Indy 500 winning Lotus 38, as well as

Len Terry ... (Courtesy Charles Armstrong-Wilson)

... and Tony Southgate in 2009. (Author's collection)

By 1965 the Terry-designed Gilby had become a hillclimb car. It is also seen here at that year's RAC Championship round at Great Auclum. (Author's collection)

In 1958/59 Terry raced a Formula Junior car of his own design, the Terrier which made use of an outdated Ford side valve engine. The car still competes in historic racing and can be seen here at the Goodwood Revival meeting in 2009. (Author's collection)

the first of Dan Gurney's Eagles. He was talking not of the time when he was involved, but of back before the Second World War when, a teenager attending races at Crystal Palace and Brooklands, he would read accounts of the race in *Autocar, Motor,* and *Light Car* in his local library. "It became an ambition of mine to go to Indianapolis," he recalled. However, as the son of an engine driver, he never really thought that he would achieve this.

"Even then, I could see that the cars seemed to be behind the times," he said. This was surely even more so when he and Colin Chapman created the Lotus 29s that revolutionised the Speedway. Chapman had approached Terry in 1962 to replace designer Mike Costin, who was leaving to go full time at Cosworth. He had already had a period as chief designer at Lotus but had left following disagreements due to his position as a spokesman for the staff. Now, Chapman realised that he wanted him back. "Colin always needed an engineer behind him who was practical." Perhaps not surprisingly, given their history together, Terry was not really interested. "We were completely different personalities." However, by this time Chapman had been taken to Indianapolis by Gurney and told Terry that he was considering building a car for the 500. "It was that which decided me to go back and work for him again."

Like Chapman, Terry had cut his proverbial teeth in the 750 Motor Club. In the late 1950s he became a designer at Lotus for the first time. Dismissed by Chapman, he went to work for Sid and Keith Greene designing a sports racer and then a Formula One car, under the Gilby name. This low budget car had some modest success in lesser F1 events before becoming a hillclimb car and then ending its competition life in a sorry state sand racing in the Channel Islands. Historian Mike Lawrence reckons Terry's employment by Gilby to have "... signalled a change in the infrastructure of motor racing, which was to make Britain the foremost nation in the sport." Lawrence pointed out that, previously, a special builder would construct a car for

Terry was left to his own devices to design the Lotus 38. (Courtesy Ford)

himself and then, if successful, build replicas for customers. However, Terry "... was the first of a long line of designers who began with Lotus or Lola and were then employed by others." Terry's real influence on the sport as the man who designed the first rear-engined car to win at Indianapolis was still a few years in the future, and before returning to Lotus he was to build the Terrier Formula Junior car and design a Le Mans cars for Alpine.

He returned to Lotus in the September of 1962 "... and was immediately overburdened with work, which I didn't mind. I was working twelve and fourteen hour days but I was enjoying what I was doing and that was sitting at the drawing board." He became involved in redesigning the suspension for the rear of the Lotus Cortina, the Formula Junior Lotus 27, and also updating the World Championship winning 25 – a project that was to result in the 33 that gave Jim Clark a second title.

In 1963, Terry made his first visit to Indianapolis but recalled that the only reason he did this was because four more wheels and a complete set of suspension parts were required. "I took those across with me as personal luggage. That was the only reason Colin invited me to go there. Almost before the race was finished he had me on a helicopter to the airport on the pretext that there were Formula One things that needed seeing to. Of course, when I got home there was no such thing! He just didn't want me around." One gets the feeling that, even after all these years this still rankles, perhaps understandably

given the amount of work that he had been putting in. Prior to his departure from the track, Terry had been part of Clark's pit crew. His task was to operate the hydraulic lift, which raised the car for the wheels to be changed. "That was all I did."

Chapman laid down the schemes for the first two Indy Lotus cars, the 29 and the 34. "I just put his theories into practice." As time progressed so Chapman became more confident in his designer who, upset by the way he had unnecessarily been rushed back to Cheshunt from the Speedway, had made up his mind to leave once his three-year contract was up. "With the 38 (the 1965 500 winning car) he left me completely to my own devices. He gave me carte blanche on it. He was away on the Tasman Series at the time. Some of things I did may not have met with his approval but by the time he got back it was a fait accompli." Terry changed the concept of the Lotus Indy cars from being a 'bath tub' to having a full monocoque structure that formed a stressed-skin tube into which the driver slid. Use was made of Ford's latest 500bhp quad-cam V8 engine. With two pit stops now compulsory and use being made of a refuelling system with gravity towers, Terry adopted a three-cell fuel system with two large tanks on either side and a third behind the driver's seat. The result was to be one of the most significant cars in Indianapolis history.

Terry was not to see his car win in 1965. Dan Gurney had already asked him to design the first Formula One and Indy Eagles and, the very day after Clark took the chequered flag at the Speedway, Terry

The first Eagle to take off at the Speedway, Dan Gurney's 1966 Terry-designed car. (Courtesy Indianapolis Motor Speedway)

became part of Gurney's All American Racers, initially under a visitor's visa. Although in Terry's mind he had joined to design the Formula One car, it soon became obvious that the Goodyear money behind the operation was for the Indy version.

Unusually, learning that a car that he had designed had won the Indianapolis 500, "... did not really excite" Terry. "I had a certain amount of pride but I did not get emotional about it at all. The spur for me was drawing the thing. The cars were designed to win races and when they did that was only what they were supposed to have done." Terry's interest was always in the drawing, not the cars themselves. "Once the drawing was finished and the car complete I lost interest in it and became interested in the next project."

The performance of the Eagle Mk 2s – which Terry based on the Lotus 38 – almost resulted in a second straight win at the Brickyard for the English designer. Five qualified for the 1966 race. Gurney, himself, went out as a result of the first lap melee that year, but Lloyd Ruby led for a total of sixty-eight laps before a cam cover bolt worked loose.

Terry attended that year but watched from the stands with former colleague, Andrew Ferguson. Terry was simply a spectator, not involved at all in the running of the cars that he had designed.

As with Chapman, Terry did not have an easy relationship with Gurney but, in similar fashion, he left only to work with the tall California-based driver again a few years later. He does point out though, that the second time with AAR was only on a freelance basis. Terry left Gurney in October 1966 after just over a year, and although the following season's Mk 3 Indy Eagle was a development of the Mk 2 he does not regard it as one of his designs.

In 1969 Terry started producing the Leda Formula 5000 car and Gurney planned to be one of his customers. The order had come about as a result of meeting at the Indianapolis 500 that year when Terry had told Gurney of his plans. Terry may have been merely a spectator, but through Ferguson had a pass for Gasoline Alley and the pits. A delay in the production of the Ledas meant that the deal fell through but Gurney needed a designer for Indy. In the interim Gurney had been using another Englishman, Tony Southgate. Terry agreed to design the car and started work on it on the basis that it was only required to be suitable for the four-cylinder Offenhauser engine. "A month into the project Dan changed his mind and wanted it to accommodate the Ford V8 as well, and so I had to change the engine bay completely. A couple of weeks later he also said that it needed to accommodate his Gurney-Weslake engine." All the design work was done in England and then copies of the drawing sent to America where the parts would be made. As Gurney pointed out, the early Eagles may have had British designers but, unlike such as the Penske, Chaparral, and Galmer, they were American-built cars.

With only four months to work on it, the car finished up perhaps not as ideal as Terry would have wished. Gurney was not happy with it either. Nevertheless, it was to finish third in the 1970 Indy 500 driven by Gurney himself. So it cannot have been all bad.

Tony Southgate, Terry's successor following his first stint with Eagle, shares with Graham Hill the record of having won the Indianapolis 500, the Le Mans 24-hour race, and World Championship Grands Prix. His first success at the Brickyard came as a draftsman at Lola where he worked on the T90 that was, in Hill's hands, to win the 500 in 1966. "I was Eric Broadley's number two," recalls Southgate, "... but there were only three of us."

Like Terry, Lola founder Broadley and Lotus' Colin Chapman, Southgate had been a member of the 750 Motor Club. He worked initially at Lola on the Lola GT, leaving to join Brabham when Ford moved in on the project but returning to assist Broadley with the T70 Can-Am car and the T80, T90, and T92 Indy cars. That did not mean he got anywhere near the Brickyard. "It was all at arm's length then," he recalls. "We just used to wheel the cars out of the factory, take some photographs, and they would be gone."

The T80 was, he says, quite advanced for its day, unlike the first Indy car on which he had worked. He had assisted designer Ron Tauranac in the drawing office during a 10-month period at Brabham on the Zink-Urschel Trackburner – a tubular frame, Offy-powered car with which Jack was placed twentieth in 1964. "Ron never used to draw. He would come in and lean over the board and say he wanted this or that." To Southgate's mind, the Indy car was not much more than a large Formula One car with offset suspension and a fuel tank strapped to the side. "To be honest, we did not know that much about Indy. The car had teething problems but it must have shown promise because all the Americans started copying it." Southgate recalled that the Hawks built by Clint Brawner for 1965 were approved Brabham copies built using a wrecked Brabham chassis and Brabham drawings. Brawner's team, however, "... knew all about Indy" and, in 1969, a MkIII version of the Hawk won the 500.

Once the Brabham had been made it left the factory and Southgate never saw it again, "We had no feedback." As at Lola, there was no question of going to the race. Returning to Broadley's operation, Southgate again found himself drawing Indy cars. Broadley would carry out all the concept design work and then the drawing office, Southgate and ex-Ford man Mike Smith, would do

the rest. Unlike the Brabham, the monocoque Lola T80 was totally an Indianapolis car, it was not based on anything else. "It was vastly superior in terms of structure and safety to the Brabham. It was a nice car, very sound and straightforward."

As Southgate recalled, being a new project it took a while to get going, and in the 1965 500 Al Unser raced one to ninth place with Bud Tinglestad classified sixteenth, having run as high as third. It was the improved version, the T90, with its symmetrical suspension that could be used for road races and offset suspension for ovals such as Indianapolis, "... that really took off."

Although not present at the time, Southgate recalled the 1966 Indy victory. "There was this massive crash at the beginning but Graham manoeuvred through all the wreckage and came out in one piece. I was dead chuffed about our winning Indy, although, at the time, it did not mean much back in the UK." He persuaded a reluctant Broadley that celebratory stickers should be made for their road cars. "I went and got some made for about 50 pence." Southgate still owns a couple of these very basic, paper stickers.

LOLA-FORD
INDIANAPOLIS WINNER 1966
DRIVER: GRAHAM HILL .

Tony Southgate persuaded Eric Broadley that celebratory stickers should be made to honour the 1966 victory. The whole batch cost about 50 pence. (Courtesy Tony Southgate collection)

Southgate left Lola at the end of 1967 for the United States. Dan Gurney wanted him to design a new Formula One Eagle. However, Gurney's All American Racers team was also involved with the Indianapolis 500. "You worked on a variety of projects in those days. You didn't design just one car." The Formula One project folded and a new Indy car became the major focus. "By now I was a full designer," recalls Southgate. The first F1, Len Terry-designed Eagle had been a stylish car, distinguished by its beaked nose, "... but we wanted to move on from there." The 1968 Indy car was like a flattened version of this; with a coke bottle-shaped monocoque and with fuel concentrated in the middle of the car. The front bulkhead was flattened making possible a lower nose. It also featured outboard front suspension.

"Anyone could buy these cars," said Southgate. The result was that they appeared with a variety of engines. Gurney used his own engine; the pushrod V8 Gurney Weslake with low centre of gravity – "... the neatest package." This handled better on the road circuits but did not quite have the horsepower of its rivals, the Offenhauser or the Ford V8. Despite also being in the works team, Denny Hulme used the latter engine while Bobby Unser in the customer, Leader Card-entered car had an Offy. Unser was to win the 1968 race with Gurney second and Hulme fourth. Having not actually been to the track prior to 1968 it was, understated Southgate, "... a good introduction to Indy."

Southgate's wife, Sue, was in the grandstand for the race, along with some people from Eagle. When, on lap 191 Joe Leonard's Lotus turbine failed, a trio of Eagles came round in the first three positions. Sue remembers Eagle's works manager almost falling over into the fans in front such was his excitement.

CLockwise from right: Bobby Unser drives the Southgate-designed 1968 Eagle to victory. (Courtesy Indianapolis Motor Speedway); The Ford DOHC-engined version of Southgate's 1968 design. (Courtesy Tony Southgate collection); Tony and Sue Southgate at the Speedway in 1968. (Courtesy Tony Southgate collection)

"In my naivety I thought we went there to win but they were gob smacked. To be fair, Indy was *the* race; nothing came within a mile of it. At the start, when we were mulling around on the grid and I looked up at this cliff of people in the grandstands – it was incredible. That was when it came home to me, this is big. I hadn't experienced that at any other race at all," said Southgate.

Like other Europeans at the time, he was not too enamoured by the amount of time that had to be spent at the track. "It went on and on and on and ... You started off with the car going quite quickly. You then made a series of adjustments and slowed it down for about a week and then you sped up back to where you were! It was a show so they made it last."

For 1969, Southgate designed a completely different Eagle for Indianapolis. The 1968 model had a double curvature monocoque structure. "It looked pregnant in the middle," he said. Only one company in the US could undertake such prototype work and this supplier dried up, so Southgate was faced with designing a monocoque with single curvature panels. That meant a totally different structure but it did mean that AAR could manufacture it in-house at Santa Ana. The result had a wedge-shape inspired by the look of the previous year's turbine-powered Lotus 56. It was very flat with a low nose and high tail and a triangular section monocoque. "Designer types like me were interested in this shape." Wind tunnel testing was non-existent.

Southgate recalled that he made a couple of mistakes with this car. The main one concerned the shark's-type air intake underneath the flat nose with the air coming out from the side. He would have preferred the air to come out of an outlet on the top, as this would have cancelled out lift under the nose. "I knew though that Dan would give me a hard time about the heat getting into the cockpit." The result was that the car had "... a bit of lift" on the front and would go light at high speeds, resulting in understeer. The other problem concerned the head fairing. This was originally meant to have an air intake to the engine "... but I ran out of time and never got round to doing that." Years later, this was a route taken by many designers.

Gurney took the car to Indianapolis and, as Southgate recalled, "Dan is a great fiddler, a great character but a real finicky bloke." Southgate had just finished designing the car when he was approached by John Surtees, who had authority from Lou Stanley to offer him

1969 and 1970 Eagles, designed respectively by Southgate and Terry, and acquired by Doug Magnon for the Riverside International Automotive Museum. (Author's collection)

Tony Southgate with his second AAR design, the Eagle 'Santa Ana.' This original body shape tended to lift the nose and was modified prior to the 500. (Courtesy Tony Southgate collection)

TIM HOLLOWAY

"In the 1980s you did not work on just one car," said former March designer Tim Holloway. "Most of the office at March would be working on the Indy cars. My responsibility was the chassis and front end. During that time I never associated myself with any one particular team as I would have done in Formula 2 and F3000.

"I did go to Indianapolis once in the mid-1980s as customer support for testing. It was bit of an eye opener in that this lasted so long. People would have a push for a few days and then go back into the garage, recover, rebuild the car, and then have another push for a few more days. Everybody seemed to have a different plan. Testing at other races is always intense but it didn't seem that way at Indy. I was there to help generally and give out bits and pieces.

"We were having lots of problems at that stage with the rear suspension due to a funny rocker system on the back of the gearbox. It was being redesigned almost every day and bits shipped from the UK.

"Indy is inspiring as a place. I was quite awestruck. When the cars are running you realise just how quick they are, even on a track this big. I was there for a whole week but did not stay for qualifying."

Holloway and other former March colleagues went on to establish their own independent design company, two of these partners being Les Mactaggart and Tino Belli, now senior technical director for the IRL and a senior engineer at Andretti Autosport respectively. While these two are very much part of the Brits at Indy story, Holloway, now chief designer at Zytek Engineering, has not returned to the Brickyard since his March days.

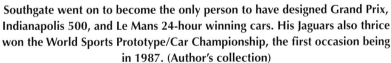

Southgate went on to become the only person to have designed Grand Prix, Indianapolis 500, and Le Mans 24-hour winning cars. His Jaguars also thrice won the World Sports Prototype/Car Championship, the first occasion being in 1987. (Author's collection)

Despite being involved in the design of the March Indy cars, Tim Holloway only once visited the Speedway. (Author's collection)

the job of chief designer at BRM. "I liked Indy but I wanted to be in Formula One so I said 'yes' immediately." He actually left at Indianapolis time and did not even stay long enough to see the race. "Once I had said I was leaving they weren't too interested in me!" Tony Southgate, who helped draw one Indy 500 winner and designed another, has, thus, only been present once at the race itself.

Ironically, having found that the car understeered during testing for the 500, Gurney cut a hole in the nose to let the air out. He also cut the front and removed the head fairing. The result, which looked more conventional, helped him to the runners up spot for a second year running.

11
BUILT IN BRITAIN
"... it became an important series for us ..."

Almost as suddenly as they had appeared, the British World Champions disappeared with Graham Hill failing to qualify in 1969. From then until the mid-1990s when the next arrived, the only drivers to wave the Union flag were David Hobbs and Jim Crawford. This is an era, though, of British engineers, expertise, and design. By 1986, every single one of the qualifiers was built in the UK. Having won the 500 in 1965 and 1966, British-manufactured cars were to repeat the exercise on six occasions between 1972 and 1981, and then every year from 1983 to 1997. Another victory occurred in 2000. Very often during this period a British-owned company built the winning engine. It was dominance in the true sense of the word.

Lola, Brabham and the sole Granatelli-entered Lotus kept the flag flying in 1969. Brabham, along with Ferguson, had been the first British manufacturer to follow Lotus to the Speedway, founder Jack returning to the scene of his historic 1961 run three years later with a car of his own; the Ron Taurenac-designed BT12 known as the Zink-Urschel Trackburner. Use was made of a conventional Offenhauser located in what was still an unconventional place, the rear. Neither Brabham nor Jim McElreath, who drove the car the following year, finished the race. McElreath had Ford power for 1966 and brought his Brabham home in third place, the highest 500 finish for the make. Two Brabhams started the 1968 race; one Offy-powered, the other with enlarged Repco V8 and driven by Jochen Rindt. Piston failure meant that the car only lasted five laps. Brabham was back as a driver the following year with Peter Revson as his team-mate and using Repco

Jack Brabham was back for the 1969 race, this time using a Repco engine. (Courtesy Indianapolis Motor Speedway)

engines again. Brabham returned for his final attempt in 1970 while cars bearing his name continued racing in the 500 until 1972, although none were able to match McElreath's high of 1966. However, it should be remembered that the 1969 Hawk, with which Mario Andretti scored his only Indy 500 victory, was an updated version of the car built by Clint Brawner, an approved and direct copy of the Brabham BT12.

Brabham was not the only Antipodean and former Cooper factory driver who left the team to start his own UK-based race car manufacturer. Bruce McLaren, the New Zealander who replaced him as Cooper number one, did likewise. In 1970 the first McLaren was seen at the Brickyard. Within twelve months the McLaren M16 was the fastest car there, although it would not be until 1972 that Mark Donohue took Roger Penske's version into Victory Lane.

McLaren director Phil Kerr had accompanied driver and fellow New Zealander Denny Hulme to Indianapolis in 1968 and had been impressed. He recorded that the race offered "distinct possibilities" for a team like Colnbrook-based McLaren. A year later members of the McLaren team, in the States for a Can-Am event, listened to the 500 on the radio and saw no reason why they should not build a car with which Hulme could win it. The result was the first McLaren Indy car, which was prepared for the 1970 race. The 2.6-litre t/c Offenhauser M15 drew heavily on the ultra-successful M8 Can-Am car. The team was proud of its new aluminium monocoque chassis that contrasted with its antiquated four-cylinder engine. Writing in *Autocar*, Eoin Young said how it was strange to be using a power plant that was descended from the Miller of 1931. Bruce McLaren, who two years earlier had tested a turbine car for Goodyear at the Speedway, claimed it was like having four 500cc Cooper-Norton Formula Three engines tied together.

McLaren and Hulme tested the car at Goodwood and the former's enthusiasm for the project was evident for all to see. The company also established McLaren Engines, a base in Livonia, Michigan to serve as an operational base for its Indy car and Can-Am programmes.

Initial practice at Indianapolis went well until Hulme was severely burnt when his fuel filler cap came open, allowing methanol to pour into the cockpit. His fellow New Zealander Chris Amon, who had been testing the M15, was uncomfortable with Indianapolis' unforgiving walls and a new line-up – Americans Peter Revson and Carl Williams – had to be found for the team. Both acquitted themselves well, and

the cars, which won a Society of Automotive Engineers award for their design, were then sold to Gilmore Broadcasting. Kerr pointed out that McLaren himself was proud of that award. However, the day after he returned from the States, the likeable New Zealander was dead, having lost control of his Can-Am M8D when its rear bodywork broke free during testing at Goodwood.

On the way back to the UK, McLaren and British designer Gordon Coppuck had been discussing ways of learning from the promising M15, Coppuck believing that several shapes should be investigated. The result was the wedge-shaped M16, one of the most attractive cars to race at the Speedway, and one of the most effective. If the M15 had drawn on lessons learnt, the M16 was to teach others. 'Gulf orange' works cars were entered for Revson and Hulme, while a third was sold to Roger Penske for Mark Donohue to drive. The two Americans put their cars on the front row of the grid, with Hulme in fourth place. Donohue built up a huge lead in the early stages of the race, although Revson, who had been disputing second place, fell back, unhappy with his car's handling, while Hulme spun. The dream ended, at least for the time being, when the blue Penske car suffered a major transmission failure. Revson fought back to second. Perhaps not surprisingly, Penske purchased two new M16Bs for the following season.

Revson and Donohue again made the front row of the grid for 1972. The former chased Bobby Unser's Eagle during the opening laps before both retired and Penske's other driver, Gary Bettenhausen, took over at the front. For lap after lap it looked as if, at last, a member of the Bettenhausen clan would win the Indy 500. Then, with seventeen

During the 1970s, McLaren was the most successful of the British-based constructors, winning the Indianapolis 500 on three occasions. Johnny Rutherford, seen here in 1974, was behind the wheel on the two occasions when victory went to a factory version. (Courtesy Indianapolis Motor Speedway)

Mark Donohue's blue McLaren chases down Sam Sessions' Gene White Racing Lola in 1972. Donohue was to give Roger Penske his first victory. Sessions was to finish fourth, last of those on 200 laps, and second British-built car. (Courtesy Indianapolis Motor Speedway)

tours to go, his engine gave up the contest and Bettenhausen's team-mate, the patient Donohue, inherited the lead. McLaren had won the Indy 500 at just its third attempt.

McLarens remained at the forefront of Indy throughout the 1970s, their final appearance being in 1981 when Vern Schuppan drove Theodore Racing's car – one of the three McLarens entered that year – to third place. Johnny Rutherford underlined their effectiveness with a first, second, and then another first place for Team McLaren in the years 1974 to 1976, while Tom Sneva scored a couple of second places in 1977 and 1980. A variety of privately-entered McLarens also graced the fields during these times.

Rutherford recorded how McLaren engine man, Englishman Roger

Bailey, who will feature again in these pages, built a strong qualifying engine for the 1973 race. "Bailey could really make an engine run," he wrote. That was a bad year at the Speedway, though. Art Pollard, who had driven the last Lotus to race at the Speedway, was killed in practice while one of the McLaren privateers, Salt Walther was badly burnt when his car crashed at the start. Rain then delayed the restart until the Wednesday when Roger McCluskey was the highest finishing McLaren driver in third place. Rutherford was happy just to have survived in ninth.

The following year saw Rutherford second fastest in qualifying but twenty-fifth on the grid thanks to a controversial interpretation of the rules by new chief steward Tom Binford. Nevertheless, with "... a

The full-scale master mould of the Lola T80 at Specialised Mouldings. (Courtesy Lola Cars)

great car," he was able to duel for the lead with A J Foyt and Bobby Unser; his run to eventual victory being made easier when his fellow Texan was black-flagged for blowing oil. The following year, Rutherford was right behind winner Unser when rain brought out the red flags on lap 174. It rained again the following year. The red flags came out after 102 laps, but this time Rutherford's beautifully handling M16 was in the lead. On both winning occasions his chief mechanic was a Welshman, Denis Daviss.

McLaren replaced its workhorse M16 with a Cosworth DFX-powered car, the M24. Driving one for Penske in 1977, Tom Sneva was the first to lap at over 200mph during qualifying, although Rutherford and three others had exceeded that figure in practice. Despite Sneva's pole, his subsequent second that year and his second place in Jerry O'Connell's car in 1980, McLaren had, though, won its last Indy 500.

Today, McLaren races solely in Formula One. However, this UK-based operation spanned the gap between the pioneers of the 1960s and the ubiquitous British manufacturers of the 1980s, winning three 500s and adding lustre to the story of the British at Indianapolis.

The decade changed with a spate of British-built victories for Lola, Penske, and Chaparral. Lola had been absent since its last Indy 500 in 1972. However, it was back with a single car in 1978 ... and won. The company had first appeared at the Speedway in 1965 with the T80s. "George Bignotti had approached me to build the cars," recalled Lola founder Eric Broadley. "We had plenty to do but you grabbed what you could. Indianapolis was a strange place, still old fashioned, which was rather nice. It still had a roadster mind-set with the teams going there in May, putting a car together, building the engine, and then going racing. Then we Europeans arrived and screwed things up for them by making it expensive.

"We approached the design of an Indy car in the same way we would have that of a road racing car, except in 1965 we had offset suspension. That was a waste of time, but that was how it was. Theoretically, it should have been an advantage but nobody ever exploited it as they should have done. It was banned before anyone really understood its potential."

In 1966 Lola returned with a car, the T90 that incorporated lessons learnt from what had been a difficult debut. "I found those first two

Lolas were first pushed out onto the Indianapolis grid in 1965. (Courtesy Lola Cars)

Eric Broadley (hands in pockets) shares a moment of humour with Al Unser Sr. (Courtesy Lola Cars)

years very interesting," mused Broadley, who was present in the pits on both occasions. "People would arrive with the most peculiar cars."

That season the aluminium monocoque cars were ready in plenty of time, and delivered to the John Mecom team for the season's opening race in March at Phoenix. As already related, three were entered for the 500; Graham Hill and Jackie Stewart driving Ford-engined versions, American Rodger Ward an Offenhauser-powered car – the Englishman taking the win. "I didn't expect to be so successful so early on," said Broadley.

The T92 which appeared the following year was substantially the same as the T90, but with detail changes and a different cockpit surround. USAC officials felt that the changes were insufficient for a new number and so, for them, the cars were known as T90 MkIIs. Lolas continued to appear on the Indy 500 grid until 1973, with seconds for Al Unser (1967) and Mark Donohue (1970), plus a third for Bobby Unser (1969). For 1968 Lola persuaded Hewland to build a four-wheel-drive gearbox for its T150. In order to save weight, Broadley had used magnesium for the outer skin of the tub. He was watching at Turn One early in the race when the Al Retzlaff-entered car's hub broke. "The shower of sparks that came off this tub was astronomic. I didn't use magnesium again after that." In the following year Vel Miletich and Parnelli Jones bought out Retzlaff, acquiring both his mechanic, George Bignotti, and the Lola, which Bignotti converted to two-wheel-drive. By 1970 it was sufficiently modified to be renamed as a P J Colt, copies of it twice winning the 500, by that stage though, Lola had nothing to do with the car.

When Lola reappeared in 1978 it was to surpass anything it had achieved before, even with the T90. The Jim Hall-entered, Cosworth DFX-engined T500 did not just win the 1978 Indianapolis 500, it took all three 500-mile races on that year's calendar. "Last Sunday's result put the seal on the superiority of British motor racing engineering in the USAC arena," said *Autosport* following the Indy win, pointing out that the car had also used a Hewland gearbox. Broadley recalled its driver, Al Unser, as being one of the most analytical that he had worked with.

In the 1980s, as will be seen, Lola followed March into becoming a genuine production car manufacturer for CART. "In the 1980s and 1990s it became an important series for us and I went to many of the races ... which was murder," said Broadley. In all, he reckoned to have crossed the Atlantic between 200 and 300 times. Sometimes over thirty cars would be built in a year, with a

Bud Tingelstad, who had driven one of the original Indy Lolas in 1965, qualified Vel's Parnelli Jones Lola T152 eighteenth in 1969. (Courtesy Indianapolis Motor Speedway)

'INDY LOLA' WINS AT MONZA

Although the history books record numerous wins for Lola, including three at Indianapolis, its name does not appear in the lists of Grand Prix victors. The initiated, though, know this to be a travesty, and John Surtees has been at pains to point out that his last minute victory in the 1967 Italian Grand Prix was really at the wheel of a Lola, the Honda RA300 or 'Hondola' of legend. A Honda it may have been named. However, as Surtees stated, it was actually a Lola Indianapolis chassis adapted to take Honda's engine and gearbox. Surtees – who had been due to drive a Lola T90 at Indianapolis in 1966 before his Ste Jovite Can-Am accident – and Broadley saw the T90 as an ideal way of overcoming Honda's tardy chassis development. "We've got to do something," said Surtees. Tony Southgate recalled that the Hondola was made in about a month. "We literally grafted the Honda engine and transmission into the back of a spare Indy monocoque." Surtees may not have driven at the Brickyard but he did have a famous victory at Monza, and in what was a Lola in all but name.

Al Unser Sr's solitary Lola dominated the three 500-mile races in 1978. His win at the Speedway was the first for a Cosworth-engined car.
(Courtesy Ford)

peak of thirty-eight T91/00s; each year Dick Simon would ensure that he took delivery of the first chassis, Bobby Rahal wanted the thirteenth. "The heyday of supplying Indy cars was good while it lasted, but these things never last for ever."

Eric Broadley in conversation with the author during late 2009.
(Courtesy Sam Smith)

PART THREE

1980-1996 – Domination of the British manufacturers

12

THE LONE ENGLISHMAN – DAVID HOBBS

"... so Mark and I ate free for the whole month."

Margaret Hobbs flew from the UK for the 1973 Indianapolis 500. It is still not possible to fly direct to the city from London but then it was even more complex. One of her flights was delayed and she had to overnight in New York. On the shuttle bus the next morning she was chatted up by handsome, young Eastern Airlines pilot, Jim Darnold, himself a "big Indy fan." On hearing her accent and discovering the purpose of her visit, he said he knew who she would be "rooting for." Darnold, while not knowing the identity of the lady he was talking to, was aware that there would be only one British driver in the field, David Hobbs.

Throughout the 1970s, indeed from Graham Hill's last drive at Indy in 1968 through to Jim Crawford's debut in 1985, Leamington Spa-born Hobbs was the sole British driver representative in the 500. Darnold, who subsequently kept in touch with David and his wife Margaret, would probably have been aware that Hobbs was one of only two non-US citizens in the race that year, a norm for those days.

The early 1970s saw a sprouting of big wings and huge leaps in speed and, while it may not have been British drivers leading, it was the British McLarens that were to the forefront of this. Hobbs, already a veteran of three Grands Prix, was in North America in 1970 competing in Formula 5000 for John Surtees' team. Despite having joined the championship at the halfway point in both this year and the previous, he had twice managed to finish in the top three. That winter he had a call from the Roger Penske team asking if he would like to run with it for 1971, driving a Ferrari in long-distance races as well as competing at Indianapolis.

"I said that I would. Then it got a bit more complicated," Hobbs recalled. "I met Roger at the Dorchester Hotel in London with Mark Donohue who, probably because of his Irish roots, was not very fond of English people. However, I had beaten him two or three times the year before so had got on their radar screen."

The problem was that the Surtees team used Firestone tyres while Penske was contracted to Goodyear, meaning that he would not be able to remain with Surtees in F5000 if he chose to sign with Penske. The latter overcame the problem by arranging for Hobbs to replace John Cannon in Carl Hogan's F5000 car, thus enabling him to become a Goodyear driver. "So ..." said Hobbs, "... I left Surtees, which caused an awful rumpus, and went to join Hogan and Penske, winning the F5000 championship that year with the former."

In those days Indy was, as Hobbs remembered, "... the full done deal." He continued, "We went down there at the end of April and stayed at the Howard Johnston about a mile north of the track where Intersterstate's I-465 and I-65 meet. My first experience of the Speedway was the next day and I was pretty well overawed by the whole thing."

Hobbs stated that he could not believe how friendly all the drivers, particularly Johnny Rutherford, were "... although A J Foyt wasn't exactly the guy you would cosy up to. He didn't like English people then." It was clear to Hobbs, though, that the drivers "... lived a complete sort of cocoon where the Indy 500 was the only thing in their entire lives. It was the only race and everything else, even the USAC Championship, was nice to take but just foreplay for Indy. I found that

Hobbs found himself in a Penske-entered Lola for his debut drive at Indianapolis. (Courtesy Indianapolis Motor Speedway)

a bit strange, although I had felt a bit that way myself about Le Mans. These guys were just so obsessed with Indy."

He found the track "overawing," although he reckoned it was more suited to road racers than to the tail-out dirt track drivers who traditionally found their way to the 500. "I thought it was going to be like Daytona but it isn't; it hasn't got much camber to it at all. It is like four of the old Abbey Curve or Stowe Corners at Silverstone. So driving it wasn't too difficult. I found this going round and round an oval not exactly boring, but it wasn't like a road course. You couldn't slide the tail out. You had to make a long apex. If you went high and then tried to cut down it wouldn't work. But you still had to let the car go out to the wall, not drive it out there."

Hobbs was down to drive the blue Lola that was raced to second place the previous year by Donohue. "It had a big, old Ford engine and a huge turbocharger. I learnt to drive Indy style. You left foot braked and tried to keep the throttle open otherwise it took for ever to wind the turbocharger up again." Penske team leader Donohue now had one of the new McLarens and was repeatedly quicker than both the factory drivers, which, recalls Hobbs "... upset [McLaren director] Teddy Mayer a bit."

The sheer amount of practice time was a novelty to a road racer like Hobbs but "I just kept my head down and did about 2000 miles of practice." He worked with 'Lou,' a former Shelby engineer. "We used to go across the road to the bar in the shopping centre because he fancied one of the ladies there. On one occasion we had drunk far too much together the evening before and I really did not feel like driving. I came into the pits and told Lou. He answered that he fully understood and then told Penske that there was a problem with the car and it needed bringing back into the garage to be examined ..."

Hobbs had no trouble in feeding either. A restaurant had awarded a dinner for two, every night, for the fastest driver of the day. Donohue was repeatedly the quickest "... so Mark and I ate free for the whole month. It was quite a good little restaurant."

So the month of May proceeded with Donohue dominant, the two works McLarens just behind, while Hobbs "... lurked around in about seventh or eighth place." On qualifying day he was only fractionally slower than Donohue had been the previous year with the same car, although he admits that he found the experience "... pretty nerve wracking. You had just four laps and you didn't want to screw up or hit the wall.

"In those days the engine was expendable in qualifying so you jacked the boost up so that it was almost infinite. In my car, you would go down the straight at about 215mph but the average speed was about 170mph. You had to slow up a lot for the corners then. I find it hard to believe how these guys now go flat out all the way round. It just doesn't seem right to me." At around lunchtime Hobb's team-mate recorded "a cracking time." Then, over the loudspeaker, the team heard the voice of announcer Tom Carnegie saying that Peter Revson had just set a new track record in his factory McLaren. "Mark was devastated," recalled Hobbs.

"What astounded me was that every day for practice there would be a smattering of people there – probably about 25,000 of them. Come qualifying day Roger had said we had to be there early to beat the traffic. I pointed out that it was only qualifying but there was a massive traffic jam everywhere. At about 8.00am I walked out onto the pit lane and the grandstands seemed absolutely full. There were 250,000 there for qualifying; the biggest single day sporting event in the world was the Indy 500, the second was the first day of Indy 500 qualifying. I will never forget the scene that met me as I walked out of the tunnel onto the pit lane. It was a dammed impressive sight."

Hobbs can remember little about the race itself, although he points out how "staggeringly" different the car felt between empty and full tanks, tanks which in those days held seventy-five gallons of alcohol fuel. A pit stop to replenish this dropped him back to about twenty-eighth place with Rick Muther's elderly Hawk right behind him. "Coming out of turn four on lap 113 I heard this almighty clattering and banging and I thought the engine had blown. I had missed the pit entry – which was very narrow in those days. I was looking in my mirror so I could ease over onto the grass at Turn One but I couldn't see Muther. 'What the hell's happened to him,' I thought, as he had been right behind me.

"Of course, when my car blew up and slowed down he gave a great wrench on the wheel and hit the inside wall. While I was looking in the mirror he was coming at me and hit me at about 7 o'clock. I was punted into the wall. Shit was flying everywhere, the wheels and the radiator and tanks burst. He was sent spinning down the road and nearly turned over. I stood up in the car with my visor covered in oil. I put it up and looked back towards Turn Four and set off for the pit wall. In those days we were all so worried about fire. I had near enough seventy-five gallons of fuel on board. Boy, I so nearly misjudged it. I own a picture of me leaping onto the pit wall with A J Foyt only just missing my back foot. It was really close. I was laughing but Roger was pretty pissed as he thought I had crashed. I pointed out that the engine had blown up." In fact, the transmission had broken.

Meanwhile Donohue had a commanding lead, a lead that was also brought to an end with a broken transmission. Some laps later, Mike Mosley spun into the abandoned McLaren, taking Bobby Unser with him. As Hobbs, who reckons he could so easily have been a candidate for rookie of the year, recalls, Penske had plummeted to a certain first and a probable fifth to two wrecked cars. "For some extraordinary reason – it was so un-Roger like – the team had decided to put some lightweight gears in the gearbox for the race. We had done so many miles in testing with no problems but both cars had gearboxes let go in the race. I don't think that Roger Penske has ever had such an unlucky year," summed up Hobbs.

As part of his agreement with Penske, Hobbs had been due to compete in the other two 500s at Pocono and Ontario. However, Penske, understandably, saw no point in replacing the Lola, which had been around 10mph off the pace, with anything other than another McLaren. According to Hobbs, Mayer was prepared to replace Donohue's car but would not sell Penske a second one.

Hobbs did not race at Indianapolis in 1972. However, in 1973 Roy Woods, a wealthy Texan oilman, secured "this incredible" sponsorship from Carling Black Label beer. This was "... for his entire team to do everything, Can-Am, F5000 and Indianapolis. He wanted me to drive in all of them. I already had a good deal with Carl Hogan for F5000 (Hobbs won the championship in 1971), which I wanted to carry on with but I did drive the Can-Am and Indy cars. Again we planned to compete at Indianapolis, Pocono and Ontario."

The team made use of a customer Eagle with turbocharged Offenhauser. "Dan Gurney, when he had seen the wings on the McLaren, thought if we are going to put wings on a car we ought to put real wings on and speeds had rocketed up." The 4-cylinder Offenhauser was, as Hobbs recalls, a different kettle of fish to the Ford: bags of torque and a slightly smaller turbo. "There was not much throttle response. Obviously, the corners were much quicker now because of the wings."

One of the two Woods' mechanics had considerable experience of road racing with such as Jaguar enthusiast Bob Tulius but had no experience of Indy at all. "The other was an Indy mechanic but all he knew about was the footprint of the tyre. It was a case of the blind leading the blind when it came to setting the car up." It was not, he says "... a particularly happy time. The mechanics and I did not gel at all and I was hardly an experienced oval driver."

The race was to be what Hobbs rightly describes as a "nightmare" event. Rain and a serious accident triggered when McLaren privateer Salt Walther flew up into the catch fencing just as the green flag was dropped. The race was stopped and then the rains came. They returned the following day, and it was not until the Wednesday that the race was started again. Hobbs had been caught up in that incident. "Fuel was just spraying everywhere – alight. It was all over the road. You could see the alcohol blue flames so well because it was such a dark, cloudy day. I was coming through from where I had been on the grid. I squeezed right over to the pit wall and pulled up on the grass at the end of the pit lane, just flabbergasted. I have been quoted as saying I could not understand how thirty-three of the so-called best drivers in the world could not get down to Turn One, which Mario Andretti was very upset about."

The race itself was also red-flagged on lap fifty-seven following a massive accident, which proved ultimately fatal for Swede Savage and crewman Armando Teran. Once the race got going again, "I was going like hell and passing all sorts of people. I am not sure where I got up to but I was humming down the back straight at about 200mph when the engine suddenly stopped dead. So, I pushed the clutch in, freewheeled into pits and said the engine has stopped. The Offy had a magneto

Alcohol-fuelled. Hobbs took the Carling Black Label sponsorship to McLaren for 1974. (Courtesy Indianapolis Motor Speedway)

Hobbs prior to his final run at Indianapolis. He had just qualified "by the skin of my teeth."
(Courtesy Indianapolis Motor Speedway)

Carling Black Label's money was "blown" with no success in any formula and there was no sponsorship from that quarter for Roy Woods in 1974. However, there were those in the marketing department who had been impressed by the Indianapolis hype and wanted to stay with Hobbs himself. "A writer called Dick Van De Feen contacted McLaren and the money was taken there." Hobbs now found himself a factory driver. "Ironically, that season my car was fully sponsored and Johnny Rutherford's wasn't."

The rules had changed slightly and far less fuel could be carried. Wings were also cut down. "I ran pretty well in practice but not so well in qualifying – not even as quick as the morning before. I qualified ninth. When the race started the setup of the car seemed to have gone away. I don't know if some 'expert' at McLaren had decided to change something. The big thing in those days was tyre stagger – it was the talk of the pit lane. I didn't like cars that oversteered. The tyres could be massively different then. When the race started the car felt loose to me. I was no good through Turns Three and Four. I struggled and struggled and then foolishly decided to make a pit stop to change the stagger. No sooner had I started off again than the yellow flags came out. The net result was that I finished fifth. There was nobody that day who would have beaten Rutherford but I might have finished second or third."

Hobbs admits that, short of racing that year, he was not in shape and became tired as the 500 progressed. "My neck started to give up." However, one result of the race was that, when Mike Hailwood broke his leg at the Nürburgring driving the Yardley McLaren, Hobbs was able to negotiate with Teddy Mayer to replace him in the Austrian and Italian Grands Prix.

The last time Hobbs competed at Indianapolis was "a disaster." In 1976 he drove for George Walther, father of Salt whose accident had brought the race to a premature halt two years before, and owner of the Dayton Steel Foundry. "A lovely old guy" recalled Hobbs. "They called me up. I wasn't doing much that year but I didn't particularly want to do it. I said no but they offered 2000 bucks. I made the fatal mistake of

ignition. They found out that had broken. They put a new one in and, by an absolute miracle, fitted it dead, spot on. Off I went but I was about twenty laps down and was eventually classified eleventh." On lap 129 the omnipresent rain returned and four laps later the red flag came out for the last time.

saying make it 5000 and I'll do it. They said yes; I should have asked for 10,000."

As it was Dayton Walther's McLaren-Offenhauser kept breaking down in practice and, as Hobbs recalled, "I just qualified by the skin of my teeth. We had fiddled and faffed about and then I put a new set of tyres on, was five mph quicker, and got in.

The race was no better. "Even on the pace lap the bloody thing kept dropping out of gear. Then it sprang a water leak. I was out in a handful of laps. It was just a dreadful experience, not a good way to end my Indy career. On reflection I wished I had driven more there. There was lot more money, a lot more fame. Nobody knew who drove F5000 but everybody knew who drove Indy cars."

Hobbs still reflects on the way in which the Indy drivers were held in such regard, but road racers of the calibre of fellow F5000 champion and brilliant sports car driver Brian Redman, hardly known. He recalls his remark that though Redman had won more races than Wally Dallenbach had eaten hot dinners, the latter was far better known. "This got back to Wally who pointed out to me that he had eaten quite a few hot dinners; we had a laugh about that."

Hobbs, who was to win the Trans-Am Championship in 1983 and was to compete in the Le Mans 24-hours twenty times, went on to become a Formula One commentator, first for *ESPN* and then for *SPEEDtv*. However, he has never seen the Indy 500, except from the wheel of a car.

PROWLING AROUND INDY

The name of Jaguar is more likely to be associated with Le Mans than Indianapolis, yet the famous British marque has been seen at the Speedway. The first five Formula One Grands Prix at the track featured entries from the Cosworth V10-powered Jaguars. These were hardly Jaguars in the true sense, this being the brand that Ford used when it took over the Stewart Grand Prix team. That they eventually were called Red Bulls, after an energy drink, perhaps proves a point about the vagaries of F1 identities. Nevertheless, it should be recorded that their drivers included Brits Justin Wilson, who was to race in the 500 itself before the decade was out, Eddie Irvine, and Johnny Herbert. Their best place was Irvine's fifth in 2001.

Back in 1957 a true Jaguar had taken to the track. This was a D-type sports car owned by Jack Ensley, president of Jaguar Midwest Distributors Inc. (Indianapolis), and it was driven there by Pat O'Connor in a feasibility test. Ensley and Bob Sweikert had finished third in the car the year before at Sebring. O'Connor also took the pole for the 500 in 1957 but perished twelve months later on the first lap of the race.

In 1993 ten Jaguar XJ220s were prepared by Tom Walkinshaw Racing to take part in what was to be known as the Fast Masters Challenge: a televised extravaganza for ESPN involving mainly retired drivers, including Englishmen Derek Bell, Brian Redman, and former Indy 500 contestant David Hobbs – in effect three of Britain's greatest ever sports car racers. The event took place to the north west of the city at the Indianapolis Raceway Park (now known as O'Reilly Raceway Park), the scene of the annual Night Before the 500 Midget race. The IRP had a road course but, strangely, use was made of its oval, with a dogleg included, cutting out Turn One, a grand total of 0.75 miles. The result was mayhem and some very battered, very expensive cars. Redman and Hobbs finished the final in third and fourth places respectively.

Redman remembered the event well. "There were fifty drivers over the age of fifty and there were two or three 'heats' over different weekends. Eventually, they had, I think, ten finalists. David (Hobbs) and I were in that group. The race was run at night. About two thirds of the way through, a marker cone was knocked onto the track. Eagerly jumping on the excuse to throw a yellow flag, we all bunched up. In the lead, from memory, was Bobby Unser followed by David Pearson. Parnelli Jones and George Follmer were behind them. After three laps or so under the yellow, and getting ready to go green, I saw lights from behind approaching rapidly. I accelerated as hard as I could, but David came past going at least 50mph faster. As he approached Follmer and Jones, they also must have seen him coming and closed up together side-by-side. Unfortunately, they were a bit too quick and hit each other. Parnelli went off to the right and hit the wall, George stopped on the left as the automatic crash protector cut power from the battery. David went into the lead, was black-flagged, and then sent to the back. I finished third, behind Unser and Pearson ... thanks David!"

Perhaps then it is not surprising that Hobbs reckoned his memories of the competition to be vague. "I did at least get through to the final. After a run behind the safety car I set off a bit too soon and somehow seemed to run into Parnelli Jones and George Follmer, or at least caused a hell of a mix up. In the end, David Pearson won from Bobby Unser, underlying just how good those guys were. Strange cars to them and a very strange track, very short and tight; we only used the bottom three gears.

"It was a great idea and it would be good if we could have some sort of senior's events like that for television, but the costs would be very high, not like putting a golf match on at all."

Derek Bell did not qualify for the final so his recollections differ somewhat from the above. The aspect that remains in his mind is that, each day he and wife, Misti, shared meals and the car to the track with Paul Newman; really getting to know the actor. "The Jag was OK but on that 'karting' track we only used second and third gear. So, it was not memorable but another part of life's rich pattern!"

A final word from Redman that illustrates the gulf between the European road racers of his time and the American oval specialists: "In the bar one night, a guy who was an ex-NASCAR racer said, 'Brian, can I ask you a question? Whadaya do when yus come off da banking into da infield?' 'Well, I change into first gear.' 'You mean you change to third, then second, then first?" 'Nope, I change straight into first.' A lengthy silence followed, then, 'How the hell do ya do dat?'

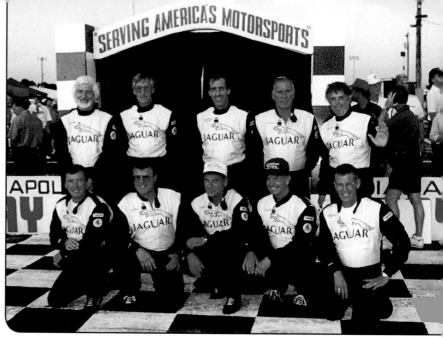

The Indianapolis Raceway Park (now the O'Reilly Raceway Park) normally plays host to more suitable cars, such as these Midgets at the annual 'Night Before the 500' meeting. In 1993, a field of far from appropriate Jaguar XJ220s was let loose on the track. (Author's collection)

David Hobbs (centre rear) and Brian Redman (right rear) in illustrious company at the IPR. (Courtesy David Hobbs collection)

Jack Ensley's Jaguar D-type XKD 538 is seen here at the Speedway in 1957, although young ladies seemed to have usurped Pat O'Connor's place in the cockpit. (Courtesy Indianapolis Motor Speedway)

13

THE INDY CARS ARE COMING!

"I guess I'm cornering much slower ..."

'The Indy Cars are coming!' proclaimed the pre-race publicity. Sixty-seven years after the first Indianapolis 500, a full field of Indy cars were being shipped to the UK to compete in two rounds of the then USAC Citicorp Cup. Motor Circuit Developments, the owner of Brands Hatch, was to promote the races but they were to be held at both Brands and Silverstone.

In 1978 Indy cars mainly raced on ovals and that meant, as it is said in cricket, that rain stopped play. Even today, that is the case on the ovals; something that Dario Franchitti must have been pleased about when a downpour stopped the 2007 race not long after he took the lead. In England, the teams would be racing on road courses but there was no such thing as rain tyres. And, of course, it often rains in England.

MCD boss John Webb took a big gamble to bring the Indy cars to Britain. An inner core of enthusiasts was excited by the prospect but would they appeal to a wider audience? "To offer the public something completely new is always a risk but *Autosport* considers this venture tremendously exciting. At a time when many forms of international motor racing are falling by the wayside, we are now being offered the fastest cars in the world," said one of the two UK weekly motor racing publications. It was hoped that the races would become a permanent feature on the calendar. Rick Mears and Tom Sneva had already tested the latter's Indianapolis pole-winning Penske PC6 at Brands in the August and indicated that such cars would be more spectacular than the norm experienced in UK-based single-seater racing. There was even the promise of plenty of overtaking from the narrow wheeled, turbocharged cars.

It was never going to be easy though. The September and October races punctuated a busy end of season schedule for the USAC teams, which would have to adapt its cars for road racing; fitting locking differentials, smaller turbochargers, different pedal assemblies, and increased suspension travel. Goodyear was also

Steve Krisiloff and Wildcat heading for the Silverstone start/finish line. (Author's collection)

having to supply what was its first real batch of US road racing tyres. The races were additionally crucial to the destination of the 1978 Citicorp Cup, America's premier open wheel series, being rounds sixteen and seventeen of an 18-race schedule. The British fans were promised at least one pit stop, full course yellows and a pace car, all commonplace now but not found in European single-seater racing in those days.

Qualification for the sixteen places on the two grids was via a special session at Michigan Speedway. The resulting line-up might have been described as stellar. Six of the drivers had won, or were to win, the Indianapolis 500. A J Foyt was to make what was one of only two racing appearances in the UK. Brothers Al and Bobby Unser were to start, the latter, it was promised, in a modified Eagle. Johnny Rutherford and Gordon Johncock, who were both to be multiple Indy 500 winners, were included, as was the reigning USAC champion, Tom Sneva. The quiet Hawaiian Danny Ongais was regarded as the favourite. Perhaps it as a sign of those times that only two of the sixteen

were aged below thirty; one of them that year's Indy 500 rookie of the year, Rick Mears, who was destined to become one of the greatest of all Indy drivers. Two of them, Sneva and Al Unser, were still in the running for the Citicorp Cup. Unser had an eighty-four point lead with just the three races remaining. The scoring was complicated but based on the length of the race. Hence a win at Silverstone, which was regarded as a 150-mile event, was worth 300 points, while 240 points were to be awarded to the victor at Brands Hatch, which was scored as a 120-miler.

The late 1970s were a period of zero interest in Indy from British drivers but there were six UK-manufactured cars in the line-up; the two Poole-built Penskes of Mears and Sneva, Al Unser's Lola, Rutherford's factory McLaren M24B plus M24s for Wally Dallenbach, and the controversial Salt Walther. The Lola T500 had been particularly successful that year with Unser having won all of the three 500-miles on the Citicorp Cup trail, including Indianapolis. Eight of the cars used the British Cosworth DFX engine, then taking over from the venerable

Three decades after their 'close encounter' at Silverstone, Tim Wagstaff met A J Foyt at Indianapolis. (Author's collection)

American Offenhausers. These included Ongais' Parnelli and Bobby Unser's Eagle, as well as the British-built cars.

The MCD publicity machine under television presenter-to-be Mike Smith did its best to promote the two races, and the festivities included scrutineering for the Brands race at the Jubilee Gardens on London's South Bank. In preparation for it all, the British race directors for the two meetings, Pete Browning, and Pierre Aumonier travelled to the US to witness the USAC race at Texas World Speedway. A dozen USAC officials were also to be integrated into the British race organising teams. The Americans even came with their own commentator, the legendary Chris Economaki.

It rained a lot at Silverstone that year. It rained on the Grand Prix-like grid of the International Trophy. Within a few laps most of the 'superstars' had spun off, leaving just four cars running and the race to be halted prematurely. It rained on the British Motor Cycle Grand Prix and the official lap charters lost control of what was happening in the 500cc race. "Who do you think has won?" commentator Murray Walker asked those who huddled in the grandstands. (Many years later the author asked Kenny Roberts if he actually had won the race. "I don't know," he replied. "But once I had my hands on the trophy they weren't getting it back!")

It also rained on Saturday, September 30.

The rain first arrived on the Thursday, at exactly the time that the Indy cars were due out on track for their first session. With no wet weather tyres and the ever-present dangers of blown engines caused through wheelspin, there was little incentive for drivers to venture forth despite their enthusiasm for the track. "Man, you can go off here and not hit anything for ten minutes," observed Johncock. By lunchtime on the Friday the track was dry enough, and the spectacle began. Ongais was particularly breathtaking as he annihilated the Formula One track record. The Hawaiian, who had already driven a Grand Prix car at Silverstone, said this was more fun. "I guess I'm cornering much slower, but it doesn't feel that way." Down the long Hangar Straight he was recording a top speed of 203mph. The next day the precipitation was back, and by mid-afternoon still manifested itself as intermittent drizzle, meaning that the race start would be delayed by twenty-four hours. Foyt drolly commented that they could always hand cut slicks to run in the rain …

During the afternoon, track dryers on loan from the nearby Santa Pod drag strip had whooshed their way round the 2.932-mile circuit. The marshals had also been encouraged to take their cars out on the track to help dry it out. Others stood around in rain until the early evening before being stood down. The notion of a 'rain check' was not known in the UK, and some marshals were unable or unwilling to return the following day. A Sunday club meeting at Mallory Park accounted for a number. This meant that when the race did actually get going on the Sunday it was somewhat under-marshalled. Gill Wagstaff, wife of the author, who was then Silverstone's press and promotions manager,

decided that she would attend on the Sunday, bringing with her their five month-old son Tim. As the race started so she went for a walk, pushing offspring in an old-fashioned pram up what was, in fact, the deserted back straight of Silverstone's club circuit. Eventually, with no marshals nearby and not knowing where she was, she arrived at the junction of the club and Grand Prix circuits, Becketts Corner. At this point, a car – "A red car, number fourteen," she said on her return to the press office – blasted past. She beat a hasty retreat. Thirty-one years later the pram's former passenger attended his first Indianapolis 500 where he met the driver of "number fourteen," one A J Foyt.

The weather looked a little better on the Sunday and the sparse crowd was treated to a spectacular start, with Ongais snatching what seemed an inevitable lead. Within two laps the yellows came out, perhaps commonplace today but then a novelty for a British race. Johncock, who had spun, caught up the tail of the pack and racing resumed. Foyt, who had been tenth on the grid, was moving up but Ongais was breaking away from the field, setting a new outright lap record on lap four. A lap later a halfshaft broke on his Parnelli and he crept into the pits. Now Al Unser built up a sizeable lead. Foyt meanwhile, had made an early pit stop. Those unused to such an activity assumed him to be in trouble but after what the refuelling virgins saw as a "miraculous" 10.43 seconds halt he was on his way. How European perception of a pit stop was to change. Unser, by contrast, left it too late to pit and had to crawl back with hardly any fuel left. Johncock took over and virtually the same thing happened to him. Lack of running time at the track had caused some of the teams to miscalculate the amount of fuel required. The lead went to Bobby Unser for one lap before pitting, and then to Mears who had already refuelled. There had already been five leaders and the grid had been only sixteen strong, yet there was still one more to come. Foyt was closing in on the young Mears and the pair went side-by-side, the

111

Spike Gelhausen aims his Eagle at the Woodcote chicane. (Author's collection)

Penske driver only just hanging on to the lead before the dreaded rain returned and the pace car led the field into the pits.

Half an hour later and the cars were back out, although the clouds still threatened. Foyt was all over Mears at the restart, taking him after a couple of laps and pulling out a three second lead. Finally, Walther did what he had been threatening to do for some time and went off at Copse, the rain intervened again and a halt called to the proceedings. Only thirty laps were run but considerably more overtaking had taken place than had occurred in the previous year's British Grand Prix at the same track; a race of sixty-eight laps with twenty-six cars. Those few fans present could also go home saying that they

The fans at Silverstone were able to watch multiple Indy 500 winners, such as McLaren driver Johnny Rutherford from Texas. (Author's collection)

had seen the "mighty" A J Foyt win an Indy car race. "These guys are real men," observed spectator Neil Martin.

"We weren't really set up for road racing and we hadn't really known what we would need. However, I was running second, pretty good," recalled Foyt. "I had my own motor (a dohc engine assembled by the A J Foyt Engine Corporation in Houston, Texas) and Coyote car, and I was having trouble getting past the Cosworth-powered Penske. Jackie Stewart had told me that on the back straightaway (the Hanger Straight) where you turn in (Stowe Corner) you can drive in a lot deeper. That was where I was pitching and that was probably how I won the race. I hoped that Jackie hadn't lied to me, 'cos I drove in awful fast and awful deep and would have ended up in the grandstands with all the people if he had. That really was a misleading corner.

"I enjoyed being in Britain. It was my only race at Silverstone. I went there as a rookie and I won. The first time to I'd been to England I was there for a sports car race at Brands Hatch, and I had hit the fence on the first lap. I wouldn't have minded seeing the Indy cars return to the UK. We had a lot of fun over there. I didn't care for having to wear a necktie for breakfast. People seemed to want to wear a necktie everywhere they went."

The next day was fine in southern England. Around 5000 people turned up to see the Indy cars on parade at London's Jubilee Gardens. Sadly, only 10,190 paying spectators had been at Silverstone the day before. Quentin Spurring, writing in *Autosport*, urged his readers to attend the subsequent Brands Hatch race. If the crowd was below 30,000 then MCD would not break even on the project and the Indy cars would not return. "We assure you that this would be a tragedy," wrote "Q," who had caught the cork from Foyt's victory champagne, which the Texan duly signed – a memento he retains to this day. (In 1986 Spurring was meant to attend the Indianapolis 500 itself. Rain on the Sunday forced a postponement of the race and he rescheduled his flight home. It rained again on the Monday and he could no longer delay his return. The 500 did not actually happen until the following Saturday. However, *Autosport* that week did at least have a photograph of its editor standing in the rain on the line of bricks. He would not see an Indianapolis 500 until 1993.)

The decision was taken to hold the Brands Hatch event not on the Grand Prix circuit but on the original, kidney-shaped track where spectators could witness all fifteen cars (one had crashed in practice) throughout the 100-lap race. Following a suggestion that Spurring

Indy cars seen for the first and only time en masse at a paddock in Kent. (Author's collection)

Rick Mears on the grid at Brands, pondering before a race he was to win. (Author's collection)

Hawaiian Danny Ongais was again the class of the field at Brands Hatch. (Author's collection)

Bobby Unser rounds Paddock Bend. (Author's collection)

made to John Webb, the 1.2036-mile track was evermore to be officially known as the Brands Indy circuit. The circuit was arguably less suitable than Silverstone, although at least the weather was decent and, again, the painfully shy Danny Ongais was the class of the field. This time he led for most of the race and was ahead by more than a lap when he retired, unable to select fourth gear. Foyt's Coyote was too heavy for him to be in contention this time and Mears, having lost out to him at the Northamptonshire track was the lucky recipient of the ultimate lead when Ongais dropped out. (Pole man Al Unser had exited from the race almost immediately after the start with an exploded clutch.)

For those who had not seen racing outside of the UK, and for some of those who had, the Indy cars had been a revelation. "Come back, USAC," pleaded *Autosport*. However, not everybody had been impressed and there were some dissenting voices in the magazine's correspondence pages. The normally enthusiastic journalist Denis Jenkinson actually thought

Brands' commentator Brian Jones conveys to the fans the ambience on the Brands podium. Danny Ongais, Gordon Johncock, and Rick Mears are the drivers (left-to-right). (Author's collection)

Oval racing comes to the UK. Twice the Champ cars raced at Rockingham. (Courtesy Kingpin Media)

the initiative "misguided" and wrote in *Motor Sport* that "Running Indianapolis cars on a typical Formula One circuit sounded as optimistic as entering a Shire horse in the Grand National." If that be so, there were some Shire horses.

Whatever, true Indy cars were never to return to Britain. In 1996, the then championship organising body CART was effectively thrown out of Indianapolis itself by the creation of the Indy Racing League. Strictly speaking, the Lolas and Reynards that contested the Champ Car series could, therefore, no longer be considered Indy cars. In 2001 and 2002 they raced on the new 1.5-mile oval at Rockingham, on the outskirts of the Northamptonshire town of Corby, the first such track to have been built in the UK since Brooklands. The inaugural year must have been déjà vu to those who had been at Silverstone in 1978 as rain prevented action on the Thursday and Friday and the race itself was shortened from 208 to 168 laps. Penske's Gil de Ferran dramatically overtook Kenny Brack on the final bend having only just relinquished the lead a lap before. A year later, the Champ Cars returned for a full

500km, with Dario Franchitti (Reynard), who had been ninth in 2001, taking a home win, engineered by fellow Briton Allen MacDonald. Another Brit, Darren Manning, came ninth, this time driving the one-off Team St George entry.

With less spectator interest than had been hoped for and dispute between CART and the race organisers, that could have been it for US open-wheel racers in Britain. However, there was one last hurrah in 2003 when another round of the CART series was held on the Brands Hatch 'Indy' circuit. If, after the spectacle of Silverstone, the Brands Hatch race in 1978 had been a little disappointing with its fewer overtaking possibilities, the 2003 event was dire. In the week before, series president Chris Pook promised overtaking. He was wrong. A total of about 40,000 people turned up to see Sebastian Bourdais lead all the way, trailed by a procession that made no attempt at passing, and which included Manning in fifteenth. If there had been those desperate for the Indy cars to return in 1979, there was to be far less enthusiasm for Champ Car to come back a quarter of a century later.

GUY FAULKNER

On being elected Governor of Indiana, Mitch Daniels could see how important a motorsport 'cluster' would be to his state. A significant person who has subsequently helped to achieve this is an English academic from the University of Westminster. Part of Daniels' drive was to throw out a challenge to higher education. In 2006, Indiana State University at Terre Haute, about an hour's drive from Indianapolis, then looking for an identity, responded and turned to senior lecturer Guy Faulkner to head up a motorsport initiative.

Faulkner had first become fascinated by the business of motorsport through his son, Niki, who desired to become a racing driver. He had contacted the UK's Motorsport Industry Association to ask what it was doing about education. Finding that it knew little about the subject, Faulkner volunteered to write a discussion paper, as a result of which he became closely involved with the rise of MIA and UK Government interest in the subject. He was also to learn through the UK's Higher Education Funding Council of an innovative motorsport education programme at East Tennessee State University and Bristol Motor Speedway. The council provided six month funding for him to research it.

His experience in this led to the ISU asking him to carry out a feasibility study and then, impressed by the result, enquiring of the University of Westminster if Faulkner could be spared to establish a programme. The London-based university responded by sending him on a two and a half year secondment as director of motorsports initiatives.

Faulkner took a multi-disciplinary approach, although the basis of the programme was the shortage of engineers and that, by sucking in people through the charisma of motorsport, this could be alleviated by increasing interest at not only higher education level but also through the schools. It would also, it was felt, assist in the development of the cluster.

Faulkner decided that the programme – which is funded by the Lilly Foundation – needed its own laboratory and, in Terre Haute's half-mile dirt track, the ISU found the ideal location. Today, its interns basically run the facility. To act as a catalyst for the students, the ISU also runs its own division three dragster team; Team Sycamore Racing, in which the students operate every aspect from the engineering to the publicity. In its first year the car made it to the Nationals, winning prizes for both the best engineering team and best-prepared car. Today, the ISU is a member of the Motorsport Knowledge Exchange, which is based at Oxford Brookes University in England.

Indiana State University turned to Englishman Guy Faulkner to lead its motorsport initiative. (Author's collection)

Faulkner reckoned his programme had an ideal laboratory on its doorstep, the Terre Haute 'Action Track.' (Author's collection)

14

THE TIME OF MARCH

"Gordon showed us the way, and what the difference was between a Formula One car and an Indy car."

With Lola's 1978 win in the 500 began a long spate of victories by British-built cars, interrupted only by Wildcat in 1982. The year before that had seen a new name on the Indy grid, March. Like McLaren, it took just three years for the cars from Bicester to win their first 500. For five years they reigned supreme, often representing the vast majority of the field.

The 1980s and 1990s are, in the main, years in which drivers from the American continent won in British-built cars. By 1981 March was no longer the fresh-faced youngster that had burst onto the scene just over ten years previously, taking on everything from Formula Three to One, and even managing to win the odd Grand Prix. It was to be a pivotal year for the company, which at the start had been facing financial problems. One of the founders, Robin Herd, was to admit that it found its American market by accident.

The year before it had built a Formula Two derived car called the Orbiter for entrant Sherman Armstrong. This Ian Reed design failed to qualify for the 500. However, George Bignotti travelled to March's Bicester factory to help supervise modifications to the car, immediately

All but two of the cars on the 1984 grid were Marches. Howdy Holmes (41) leads the field from pole man, Tom Sneva (1) and Rick Mears (6). In the second row Gordon Johncock is the filling in an Andretti sandwich with father Mario's Lola on the outside and son Michael's nearest to the pits. Mears was to win by two laps. (Courtesy Indianapolis Motor Speedway)

gelling with the company's Dave Reeves, who was to eventually become its managing director. Between them they discussed the ideal Indy car but the money was just not available, although a Bignotti-sorted Orbiter did come third in the final round of the championship. Then, in late December, American Don Whittington turned up at Bicester, not that anyone there had heard of him but he had the money to buy four Indy cars. A few weeks later, Bignotti had also found the cash to go ahead, and the March 81C became a reality.

Gordon Coppuck, designer of the 500 winning McLaren M16, briefly joined the company carrying out groundwork on the car, which used a beefed-up version of the March 811 Formula One tub. While the 811, a copy of the Williams FW07, basically failed, the 81C did anything but. "Gordon showed us the way, and what the difference was between a Formula One car and an Indy car," said Alan Mertens, who was to replace Reed as March's chief Indy car designer. Tom Sneva in the Bignotti and Dan Cotter car was the fastest qualifier at Indianapolis, although, as he did not set the time on the first day, did not take the pole. In the race, Sneva and the Whittington brothers failed to finish, but a point had been made. A gentleman by the name of A J Foyt abandoned his own Coyotes and purchased an 81C, becoming the first person to win an Indy car race for March at a lacklustre Ponoco 500. Sneva also won two races, including, significantly, the last of the season. March was on its way; the next year it was to sell twenty cars, with America becoming its main market.

The 82C was a user-friendly update of the previous year's car with a Hewland DG400-based longitudinal gearbox replacing the troublesome Weismann transverse box. Seventeen were to start the Indianapolis 500, with Pancho Carter's the best finisher in third place. Gordon Johncock's victory in a Wildcat was to be the last for an American-built car. Penske had the quickest entry that year but you could not buy one of its latest cars and so March, which, with Sneva, Hector Rebacque, and rookie Bobby Rahal, had won a number of other races, became the inevitable, indeed the only, place to buy a production Indy racer. However, perhaps it was no coincidence that what was to be billed as the 1000th March to be built, an 83C, was destined for Foyt.

The 83C was another update of the original design but now with a March transverse gearbox. Mertens recalls, "In our early days there it was pretty easy to be successful at Indy as there wasn't much competition. We were only competing against ourselves. However, we were under pressure to make each Indy car more

successful than the last, and just as it was getting difficult along came Adrian Newey, who was just a genius." Newey, now a multi-Grand Prix winner with Williams, McLaren and Red Bull, was to become a significant force as far as Indianapolis was concerned.

March boss, Robin Herd, engineered Teo Fabi for Forsythe Racing for the 1983 500. The Italian rookie took pole and disappeared off into the distance at the start. He surrendered the lead at his pit stop and dropped out after his second when, given the 'go' sign prematurely, he tried to leave with his fuel apparatus still engaged. However, in the closing laps, Tom Sneva despatched Unsers father and son to score March's first of five consecutive victories. Eighteen Marches had started the race, along with six Penskes and two Lolas. Bignotti-Cotter had also tried out a Morris Nunn Theodore, although it did not qualify. British domination was on its way; the following year just two starters would be built outside of England. In fact, only four were not manufactured in Bicester. Significantly, Penske bought an 83C for evaluation, and also a pair of 84Cs. One of them was to win the 500 driven by Rick Mears, with every one of the thirteen finishers using a March chassis. March's money worries were, at least for the time being, over.

March's IndyCars tended to be designed by committee but it was a pretty illustrious committee, containing at various times; Mertens, Newey, Reeves, Tim Holloway, and, on one occasion, Ralph Bellamy. Mertens describes Reeves as "... one of the unsung heroes" of March's early days with these cars. He was, at the time, the factory manager but he "... had a lot of good ideas and sometimes he would bully us into accepting them. The work ethic that he imposed on us was very good."

The committee's 84C may have dominated the grid but it was now up against Nigel Bennett at Lola and its successor had to be good. The battle was now on with the Huntingdon-based firm. "The year 1985

Penske's new recruit Danny Sullivan gave victory in 1985 to the now familiar combination of March and Cosworth. (Courtesy Ford)

was the first that Adrian and I basically lived in each other's pockets working on the 85C," said Mertens. "We fell into a pattern where he would do all the aerodynamics and give me an envelope in which I would design the mechanical car. This would then filter down into the drawing offices for all the detail work."

The number of Lolas grew from the single pair seen over the previous two years, but March order books were still full with forty-four Indy cars sold for 1985. Customer faith was rewarded; the 85C was one of the best of all March Indy cars. Ironically, while the lesser 84C had dominated the result at the 500, there were 'only' six Marches in the top ten in 1985, with Mario Andretti's Lola close behind Danny Sullivan's Penske-entered March at the end. Elsewhere, Lola seemed to be leading the way, but March driver Bobby Rahal just managed to give the make its first CART Championship. The trouble was that while the Lolas were working straight from the box, it took time for the teams to get Marches right.

Wind tunnel work ensured that Newey's pointed-nosed 86C was even quicker than its predecessor. With cars entered by six of CART's best teams, as opposed to Lola's three, March had an excellent year, winning all but three races. The articulate Rahal, who had first come to prominence at the wheel of a March, won a rain-postponed 500 in which every single car had been built in England. Rahal, in the Truesports entry, had taken the lead from Kevin Cogan on lap 198, diving inside the latter's Patrick Racing car on the restart after a two-lap caution period. He then powered away, setting the fastest lap on his final tour – the first time this had ever been done by the winner of the 500. It was an emotional victory. The team's owner, Jim Trueman, who was suffering from terminal cancer, died just eleven days later.

During its time producing Indy cars, March was a major pioneer in the development of crash testing, which it carried out at Cranfield. "We went from single skin aluminium to aluminium honeycomb chassis, and from the top being carbon aluminium honeycomb and the bottom aluminium honeycomb, and we took crash testing very seriously," said Mertens. In particular, attention was given to eradicating serious feet injuries. The company had "a huge fight" with Indy's governing body to get it to accept a carbon route.

Bobby Rahal (3) was a major figure in March's early success. In 1986, he narrowly beat Kevin Cogan's car (7) into second as Marches filled the first four places, the only cars to complete 200 laps. (Courtesy Indianapolis Motor Speedway)

Roberto Guerrero's fourth place in 1986 was the lowest of his three Indianapolis starts at that point. All had been in Marches. (Courtesy Indianapolis Motor Speedway)

GALMER

During the 1980s and 1990s even the seemingly American cars were built in Britain. In addition to the Penskes and the Chaparral, the 1992 500 winning Galmer was constructed in England, like March in the then motorsport hub of Bicester.

At the 1988 Indianapolis, Alan Mertens had a motor home meeting with Rick Galles and Al Unser Jr where he was asked what his ambitions were for the future and what it would cost to hire him. "I said my ambition was to start my own company and to design and build my own race cars. They looked at each other and Galles asked Junior what he thought and he said 'Yeah, go for it.'" The result was Galmer Engineering, based in former March premises in Bicester, which initially worked as an operational research and development facility for the Galles team.

Mertens admits that a serious illness in his family meant that he initially took his eye off the ball prior to the 1989 500. However, thanks partially to an understanding Unser Jr, "I shook myself out of it," and during the week after qualifying their Lola was turned into what the driver described as one of the best race cars that he had ever had at Indianapolis. Unser Jr bided his time in the race until the closing laps "... when he just took off. We were going to clean up." For Mertens it looked like being a strange but happy ending to what had been a traumatic month. With less than two laps to go "Little Al" and Emerson Fittipaldi were fighting it out for the lead six laps ahead of the rest, the Galles car just in front. Then Unser was momentarily baulked and the Brazilian slipped ahead. Into Turn Three Fittipaldi drifted up the apron and his Penske brushed the Lola's left rear wheel. Unser spun, hit the wall and slid down into the infield. Fittipaldi maintained control and went on to win. "Knowing what we had gone through, that destroyed it for us. Then we went through the most miserable season."

However, a win at the very end of the year set them up for 1990 when the CART Championship fell to the, by now, Galles Kraco team. By 1991 March had disappeared from the field, leaving Lola, Penske, and Ohio-based Truesports as the only chassis manufacturers. That year the decision was made for Galmer to manufacture its own car, the Chevrolet-powered G92.

"We had a good data base from the 1991 Lola and we integrated a lot of its mechanical parts into the design. However, we wanted to break the conventional Indy car mould so we had a more futuristic shape." There were, though, some basic things wrong with the initial design. Work had been done in the quarter-scale wind tunnel at MIRA but when the team commenced testing it found that the car was performing unpredictably.

Former March and Brabham engineer Andy Brown was, at the time, looking to set up a Formula Three team and the opportunity arose for this to be based at the Bicester facility. "Like a lot of dreams," the F3 idea did not happen. However, it was at this point that Galmer's aerodynamicist, Bernie Marcus, left. "The car was not working well and there were problems with the front wing stalling on road courses," recalled Brown. His background with British Aerospace had been aerodynamics so Mertens asked him to look at this. As assistant technical director, Brown joined to run the design side in the UK while Mertens spent most of his time in the US looking after the race engineering. "Andy was brilliant," said Mertens. "He helped to solve a lot of the aero problems but there were some that we could not do anything about as they were inherent in the build of the car."

It was also found that the bell housing was not stiff enough, which meant that some of the structural integrity was lost. That did not hurt it on road and street courses but it certainly did on high-speed ovals. The exhaust and twin waste gate systems were used to blow the air as it came out of the back of the tunnel, which meant that when the driver was on and off the accelerator it was changing the centre of pressure of the car. Again, this worked for it on street and road courses but not the ovals.

Two of the G92 cars were on the grid for the 1992 season, with Danny Sullivan winning third time out at Long Beach. The 500 fell to Unser Jr, giving Mertens a sixth victory at the Brickyard to add to the five he had won with March. For Unser it had been unfinished business. In the closing stages, another son of a famous father, Michael Andretti, had a healthy lead in his Lola. On lap 189 he was out with a broken fuel pump, leaving Unser in the lead. This time he had not Fittipaldi but Scott Goodyear in Brit, Derrick Walker's Lola to contend with. As the pair exited Turn Four for the final time, the Canadian feinted right and tried to slingshot past Unser, failing by 0.043 seconds; the slimmest margin in Indy 500 history. "It was a very satisfying feeling to win at Indy in a car of your own manufacture," said Brown.

He also recalled that the car "... did not have a particularly good press. I think a lot of that was due to the fact that the pre-season testing did not go well. I remember Mario Andretti saying that we might as well pack it in and not turn up." However, the problems were pinpointed before the season started, using the Leyton House wind tunnel at Brackley. "We called in a lot of favours from our F1 contacts," said Brown.

A development of the Leyton House front wing was installed on the car, although it could not be made available in time for the first race of the season at Surfers Paradise. However, having realised the problem, the team overloaded the rear wing and ended up qualifying on the front row of the grid. "I'm sure that must have silenced people like Mario Andretti. But for a downpour towards the end, when we were running first and second, we could have won in Australia but we did so soon at Long Beach. And we led the championship with three races to go, so I find it very hard to understand, and equally galling, as to why the car had such bad press, although I admit that we did have some problems with it."

"It was a good consistent runner but the front end was too reactive," said Australian designer Gene Varnier, who worked with the team and had already been involved with the aborted Lotus 96.

"It did have its shortcomings,' added Brown, "... particularly on the short ovals, and there are those who would say that we were lucky to win Indy as Michael had it stitched up with ten laps. However, winning Indy first time is verging on unique."

By the end of the season Galles Kraco was in with a reasonable chance of the championship, but the introduction for the last two races of a tub, built as an investigation into the more stringent 1993 safety rules, just exaggerated the issues with the car's torsionally soft bell housing. Unser would finish well down the order in these final two races, and this limited him to third place overall in the points.

"We were looking good for 1993," said Brown. "The numbers in the wind tunnel were excellent. In fact, I didn't see numbers to beat them until we put the 1996 Reynard in the tunnel." However, the money was not available to develop the car any further and in the November the operation was reduced to a skeleton crew. "We had even got as far as ordering the material for the buck for the tub when the order came down for us to stop work"

Bruce McCaw entered Dominic Dobson in the year old Galmer for the 500. "We took a lot of pleasure in the fact that it qualified the fastest of the year old cars," said Brown. Dobson finished twenty-third but that, along with Al Unser Jr's win and Danny Sullivan's fifth the year before, were the only appearances of the Oxfordshire-built Galmers at Indianapolis.

Former March and Lola designers Alan Mertens (left) and Bruce Ashmore (centre) seen spreading the word about their BAT IndyCar project at Long Beach in 2010. (Author's collection)

A Galmer G92 ready to leave Bicester for the US. (Courtesy Gene Varnier collection)

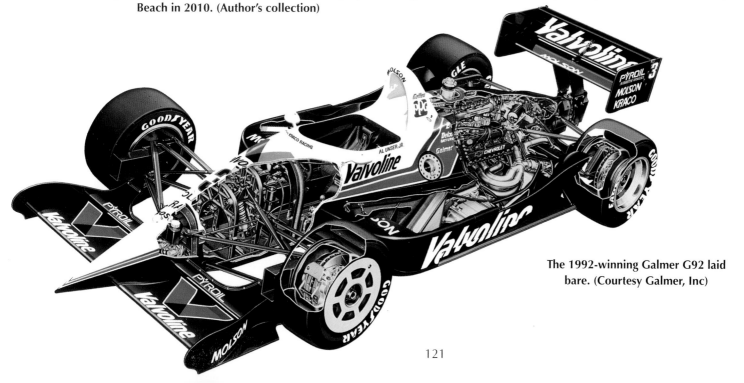

The 1992-winning Galmer G92 laid bare. (Courtesy Galmer, Inc)

For much of the 1980s Mario Andretti fought the Marches with a Lola. There were only four cars from Bicester by 1989, the year that this shot of Andretti's Ilmor Chevrolet-engined car was taken. (Courtesy Lola Cars)

Up to 1987, with the exception of the odd Buick-powered version, March Indy cars had been powered by the Cosworth DFX engine. Now two more British-built V8s had become available; the Chevrolet-badged Ilmor (which had appeared the year before behind the Alan Jenkins-designed Penske PC-15), and the Brabham-Honda-styled Judd. It did not make any difference to the Indy 500 result though. Penske entered three Marches; two of them with the Ilmor engine but it was the third, the Cosworth-motivated one of Al Unser Sr, that won. Now towards the end of an illustrious career, he had been called in at the last minute to replace the injured Danny Ongais. His car was an 86C which the team had originally no intention of using. Indeed, it had been booked to appear on display that weekend in the lobby of a hotel near Penske's Reading, Pennsylvania base.

By now Mertens and Newey were becoming frustrated with the politics at March and plotting to form their own breakaway company

– to build IndyCars and take the business away from their employer. They were in discussion with a couple of team owners, one of whom, Mertens believes, tipped off Herd about what was happening. "Robin dragged us up to his office and sat us down but the stupid thing about it was that he let Adrian go and kept me!"

Newey left to engineer Mario Andretti's Newman Haas Lola and Tino Belli took over his aero work on the IndyCars. The proverbial writing was now on the wall. Andretti had taken the pole for the 500 with four of the front two rows having driven Lolas. Even Rahal was now at the wheel of such a car. The fact that, at the chequered flag, there were five Marches up front did not halt an exodus away from the make. The 87C proved to be a handful, particularly now that Goodyear had decided to use a radial tyre at Indianapolis. "The tyres were giving up in the middle of the corners," recalled Mertens. Lola was also treating its customers much better than March – customers

THE REPUBLIC OF IRELAND

Not everyone from the British Isles can be described as British. In 1916 what is now known as the Republic of Ireland declared its independence from Britain, although it would be a few years before this was recognised. Just two drivers, Derek Daly and Michael Roe, from the country have attempted to qualify for the Indianapolis 500. Daly started the race six times, including in 1985, the year that compatriot Roe, who never made the grid, was bumped by three-times winner Johnny Rutherford.

At the end of 1982, Formula One driver Daly had become intrigued by the speed of oval races and, having just been divorced, was looking for a "complete change of lifestyle." He fetched up in Indianapolis hardly knowing anyone, having driven an Indy Car at Phoenix in the November. He secured a drive for 1983 with a husband and wife team, Herb and Rose Wysard. The following year he drove for Tony Bettenhausen in a March so slow that he eventually retired it, the only time that he was ever to do so for handling reasons. Later in the season he was badly hurt in a massive 207mph crash at Michigan that, he recalled, left him in pain for two and a half years. During that time he underwent nine operations. His first race following the crash was the 1985 Indy 500. Unable to bend his ankle up, he had to have inch and a half heel lifts built into his racing boots. Sponsored by an Austrian beer, he qualified and was then bumped off the grid. The team owner then bought a Lola from A J Foyt, which Daly proceeded to qualify "... and then the cheque bounced." Daly recalls that it was easier for him to drive than it was to walk that year, and he was classified twelfth, his only actual finish in an Indy 500.

He was still not back in full-time racing the following year, and an attempt to qualify for the 500 came to nought when it started to rain on the third lap of his run. In 1987, he raised the small sum of $200,000 in eleven days from three businessmen who he had never met before to secure a drive with Pat Kehoe. It was his first year with a Buick engine … and it blew up. He was to return to full-time Indy car racing with the Raynor Garage Doors team but had problems in his last two Indy 500s. A television commentator's position now beckoned, which has continued at the 500 to this day. "Indianapolis turned out not to be just somewhere I raced but where I lived and worked."

Derek Daly with Lola-Judd in 1989. (Courtesy Indianapolis Motor Speedway)

The Englishman, the American, and the Irishman. Derek Daly (right) in recent conversation with team owner Keith Wiggins (left), and 1998 Indy 500 winner Eddie Cheever. (Author's collection)

the 88C work effectively, winning four races and finishing second in the championship.

Mertens remembered "... getting a lot of grief from the March customers." At Long Beach they had a meeting into which they called him to say that they felt Galles now had an unfair advantage in using the designer of the car. Mertens pointed out that his loyalty had to be to the team that was now paying his wages.

By 1989 there would be only four Marches on the grid at the Speedway and by 1991 there would be none left. Those final years saw just Porsche- and Alfa Romeo-engined Marches – the only time that the make did not use British engines. The two car manufacturers had chosen March; the former to replace its own chassis, the latter from scratch, for their Indy 500 tilts.

At Indianapolis Teo Fabi's compact, Gordon Coppuck and Tino Belli designed March 89P was second fastest in practice through the turns and twenty eighth quickest on the straights, which says something about both the chassis and the engine. Le Mans winner Al Holbert had been behind the project but had been killed in an aircraft crash and Englishman Derrick Walker was now the team's principal. Tino Belli's low-profile car for the following year was controversial; being made entirely from carbon fibre, a material that had come into use in Formula One. The cars were thus stronger and safer than the norm. To this point carbon fibre had been used for the upper portion of the Indy car tubs but not the whole car and CART, which at the time sanctioned all the Indy car races except the Indianapolis 500, declared the new car temporarily illegal. Walker protested but March had to rebuild the tubs to contain an "acceptable" amount of aluminium honeycomb. Neither March nor Porsche would return to Indianapolis.

John Baldwin and Maurice Philippe were responsible for the Alfa-Romeo-engined car, the 89CE. In contrast to the 89P, it appeared almost bulbous. It was also lamentably slow. Morris Nunn, who, in partnership with Pat Patrick and Jim McGee, ran the two cars for Roberto Guerrero and Al Unser Sr in 1990, recalled that the engine was " ... a disaster. Big Al went out for one lap at the Speedway, came in and said 'The engine's shit!'" The rear wing also fell off as the car entered Turn Four. For the British chassis manufacturer that, for five years, had totally dominated results at the Brickyard, it was an unfortunate ending.

were beginning to notice late delivery or that parts would not fit if their car was less competitive. In addition, an opportunity to sign Nigel Bennett in mid-1987 was missed. Mertens designed a car for 1988 that was technically beyond the average Indy team to use. If it was setup correctly it could be extremely quick over a lap or so before, being over sensitive, it would fall away. There were other problems with the car, and sales fell to twenty that year. Mertens, disillusioned with March, quit to join Rick Galles' team and engineer an 88C for Al Unser Jr. A few weeks before he had left March, the company had been visited by Ed Nathman, then Galles' team manager/engineer. On hearing that Mertens had quit, he called up and suggested he work for Galles. "His logic was who better to have as the team's resident engineer than the designer of the car that it was running."

Mertens had regularly attended the 500 as a designer, "... partly to soak up the flack from the customers, partly to collate their feedback." During this time he did not actually engineer any of the cars "... although I may have looked over the occasion shoulder and made a grunt or remark." Thus, 1988 was his debut as an engineer.

He admitted that he was nervous of committing himself to a race team, never having race-engineered a car. However, he and Unser Jr, who respected the fact that Mertens had once raced himself (in Formula Ford) quickly gelled. The result was a spectacular season for the Galles team, although Penske had returned to his own chassis and won the 500 with Rick Mears. Only Galles seemed to be able to make

15

THE BRAVEST OF THE BRAVE – JIM CRAWFORD

"His injuries were almost irreparable."

Napoleon Bonaparte nicknamed Marshal Michel Ney the "bravest of the brave" after the battle of Friedland. It is a sobriquet that could be used for Jim Crawford. Team owner John Menard certainly referred to him as "... the bravest man I ever knew." Crawford raced at the Brickyard from 1985 to 1993, on all but one occasion the sole British driver. In that time he led for eight laps and finished no higher than sixth but his is a name to remember, alongside those of his fellow Scots Clark, Stewart, and Franchitti.

It was on lap ninety-four of the 1988 race that Crawford took the lead – the only non-Penske driver to do so that year – in a year-old, Mac Tools-sponsored Lola-Buick entered by drag racing legend Kenny Bernstein. Eight laps later, the top three cars pitted under yellow and he fell back to third. Despite a second stop to plug a leaking transmission, he stayed on the lead lap and retained that position. On lap 168 he

Jim Crawford as he will be remembered, totally committed and well below the white line.
(Courtesy Mark Scott collection)

moved back into second and became involved in a scrap to stay there with former World Champion Emerson Fittipaldi. Jim was fighting a car that was not handling well on the normal line. Dropping to a very low racing groove, he was using the entire apron and sometimes getting two wheels on the grass.

Five laps before the end of the race Crawford, who had a strong local following, made an unscheduled pit stop due to a deflating tyre. He took on fuel and new tyres but a baulking wheel nut extended his stay and he dropped back to sixth position. At the end of the race, the scoring pylon credited him with still being in third but the official results confirmed the sixth place. Even so, Crawford was euphoric and the crowd cheered him. This was a man who still needed a cane to walk and who was in constant pain following horrific injuries sustained in practice the year before. It was a remarkable performance.

The Dunfermline-born – but with a thick Lancashire accent – Crawford came to fore in Formula Atlantic in the UK working as a mechanic to keep himself in the sport. Having won the Southern Organs title with a March that he had built up himself, he was given a Chevron factory seat for 1975. By the time of the British Grand Prix, despite his inexperience, he was offered a drive in a works Lotus. The factory was still using the Lotus 72, which had proved a World Championship winner in the hands of Jochen Rindt and Fittipaldi but was now well past its sell by date. Crawford was signed by team manager Peter Warr, whose idea was to offer a small amount of money and a test drive to a couple of rising stars in exchange for their exclusive services for a limited amount of time. Crawford spun off in the wet conditions at Silverstone and finished thirteenth when he returned three Grands Prix later to contest the Italian GP at Monza.

For a while his career took a downward turn and he raced in a variety of categories, including a return to Formula Atlantic and then Formula Two at both British and European level, winning ten races in the national series. In 1982, he took the low-key British Formula One Championship before moving to North American to compete in the Can-Am series – twice finishing second in that championship with a total of five wins.

Crawford's first appearance at the Brickyard came in 1984 at the wheel of the British-built, Ed Wachs Motor Sports Theodore, having already finished fourth in the Long Beach Grand Prix that year. "Jim Crawford of Scotland will be practicing in No 68, which is his oval car," said the official Speedway bulletin. "The No 78, originally thought to be his oval car, is actually his road racing mount and will be used as a back-up. The No 68 is a Theodore/Cosworth. No 78 is an RK Theodore/Cosworth." Whatever the car, Crawford was yellow-flagged by his crew in qualifying having only achieved a 197.585mph lap. The last day of qualifying was rained out and, despite having a mount that was considered capable of making the grid, he was forced to sit the race out.

The following year he took part in seven CART races as well as debuting in the 500 for Wysard Racing. He actually qualified on the first day but a technical inspection suggested that his Lola was 20lb underweight. The car was disqualified and that, it seemed, was that for the Scot. However, another team sold entry space to Herb and Rose Wysard, which made it possible for him to enter again in a new Lola-Cosworth. With this he qualified in the last hour of the final day at 205.525mph. Crawford's crew accordingly painted '410-plus' above his garage as the qualifying speed – the total of the two runs combined. In the event, his Canadian Tire-sponsored car fell victim to electrical gremlins with fifty-eight laps to go.

Of qualifying Crawford was to say: "You can feel the pressure building. You've got to concentrate and think to yourself, man, don't worry, close your eyes and pretend you're somewhere else for a while, because the pressure of the Indy 500 can get to anybody."

Crawford in conversation with fellow Brit, Roger Bailey, during practice prior to his crash in 1987. (Courtesy Mark Scott collection)

Crawford and Scott deep in discussion. Scott recalled it was probably about which pub to go to! (Courtesy Mark Scott collection)

1986 saw him as a last minute replacement for John Paul Junior in the ASC Incorporated March 86C. The team originally wanted Gordon Johncock to stand in for him but he could not be available quickly enough. "A week ago last Wednesday I was in Dallas ...," said Crawford to the *Indianapolis Star*. "... I was going to come round with my helmet and hope and try to get a drive. But then Roman Kuzma called and I was on the plane that night."

The laconic Crawford now had the mighty Buick power that would motivate him for all but his last Indy start. There is an irony in this in that, while he was the sole UK-born driver for most of his career at the Speedway, his Buick-powered cars have been described, particularly following later work by Bob Riley, as the ones that were the least British and the most American during this period. In Saturday qualifying, Crawford was first out but the last to make the grid, thanks to an exploded turbocharger. "It was a case of clean all the system out, put in a new engine, a new turbo, and start again," he said. It took just three hours, although Crawford reckoned it seemed more like six. All was to no avail as, in the race, a blown head gasket put his March out after seventy laps, having run strongly in the top ten. "He was phenomenally quick," recalled the then March aerodynamicist Tino Belli. "He got in the car and was on the pace immediately."

Crawford nearly was not the lone Brit that year as former Grand Prix driver Rupert Keegan also tried to qualify a March in 1986, but never really looked like doing so.

It was in 1987 that Crawford fell victim to the undoubted dangers of the Speedway, driving a year-old March-Buick promoting Pat Patrick's American Racing Series. He had been running quickly in practice, clocking 215mph at one point. On Saturday, May 9 at 2.25pm he made an attempt to qualify but was waved off after three laps having been no faster than 206.825mph. At 3.55pm he was back out, although, as he had been sitting in line, the needle had fallen off his chronometric rev counter. As he took the green on the main straight the Scot was pulling 234mph. Then, in the middle of Turn One, he spun once and hit the wall with the right-hand side of the car and slid 860 feet through the short south chute. "I remember every second of it. To cut a long story short, I was going too fast into the turn and the car wouldn't physically go round it," he recalled with honesty. Crawford was trapped in the car for some time. Dr Henry Bock, the Speedway's medical director reported that he had sustained dislocation and fractures of both ankles, and a fracture of the lower right shinbone. He was rushed to the Methodist Hospital where Dr Terry Trammell, the famed surgeon who had worked on so many Indy car drivers, undertook a five-hour operation. "His injuries were almost irreparable," said Trammel. "His first round of surgery was about limb saving." Crawford was to talk of Trammel's "miracle healing" but the injuries that he had sustained were to trouble him for the rest of his life.

Trammell recalled that when Crawford had been out of hospital for some weeks he got tangled up with something in his apartment, fell, and re-broke one of his fractures; it was never to heal cleanly after that. "He was so bloody stubborn that he wouldn't use a wheelchair." During the 1988 race a screw that still remained in Crawford's leg was coming loose at the point where his ankle was in contact with the cockpit. He developed a technique using more leg and less ankle on the throttle and refused to blame his legs for anything. To add to the drama, his then wife Sheila was expecting their son, Geoffrey, about the time of race day.

Crawford's friend Mark Scott started as chief mechanic for the Buick Indy engine development team in 1987. He recalled: "His injuries were so bad. They were a constant problem. Trammell and his team did a remarkable job considering what was left of his feet and ankles, but he was continually having to have treatment. It was early days and they were finding out what could and could not be done." Scott – who pointed out that the Indianapolis Motor Speedway greatly assisted with the medical expenses after the crash – visited him in the hospital's emergency department, where, ignoring the severity of his injuries, Crawford asked for a case of Bud Light when asked how he was.

Despite the accident, Crawford was able to return to his duties as development driver for the Buick engine project and was, as recorded above, back at the Speedway the following May. "He was in a year of recuperation," recalls Scott. "It had become apparent that, with his injuries, it would have been difficult for him to do any road course work. That narrowed his options. The people at General Motors and the Kenny Bernstein team thought the world of him. By the end of 1989 he was probably as fully recovered as he would get.

"Jim's focus became oval racing and the Buick programme was his best option," he adds. "He was always very interested in the technical side of things, which is probably why he enjoyed the Buick work.

The US Air Force awarded Crawford a set of wings for this one. Amazingly, he emerged without any serious injuries this time.
(Courtesy Indianapolis Motor Speedway)

It was the same for me, working within an engine programme that was different to everyone else."

"He was test pilot for Buick," recalled another close friend, the English-born Rick Rising-Moore, who runs the Union Jack bar. "That project did not work out but he was paid well. He was happy to be involved with General Motors and GM liked him. He had a good sense of engineering. He could be working in there with the guys. He believed in teamwork. Once they started listening to him the performance level went up."

Said Scott, "Because he had such an extensive background as a race mechanic, he knew exactly what we were having to put up with and were trying to achieve, so you never felt under pressure from him. His mechanical sympathy made him ideal when it came to feedback. And he turned out to be really quick as well, which helped! He was often faster than the car that we gave him." If he had any one shortcoming, reckoned Scott, it would have been his shyness. "He was one of the few drivers that I have worked with who had complete confidence in the crew ... until you screwed up. He was like Nikki Lauda in that. You knew he would be a constant in the performance of the car. It made it simpler to set it up."

Boost rules meant that the Buick was uncompetitive away from Indianapolis but Crawford's injuries would, anyway, have ruled him out of competing on a road circuit. After his great 1988 performance, something in which Trammell took great pride, Crawford spent another four years with the Buick engine, qualifying fourth in 1989 but finishing no higher than fifteenth the year later.

In 1989, he was thought to be a candidate for pole position having run at nearly 226mph. The team sought for even more speed and made last minute adjustments to the Buick engine. Now it would not run correctly, and real last minute work was required before Crawford was able to qualify at what must have seemed 'just' 221mph. During the second week of practice the qualified car, running in race setup, suffered a left rear suspension arm failure in Turn Three, with a resulting crash. It was described as one of the hardest hits at the track in recent memory. Although briefly unconscious, Crawford was unscathed and quipped on his return from the hospital that he felt "... like a James Bond cocktail, stirred by not shaken."

Said Trammell, "In his second accident he didn't break anything ... as far as they could tell, because he had been so broken the first time." Crawford was insistent on leaving the hospital that evening and, with no one else available, asked Trammell, with whom he had now developed a close relationship, if he could give him a ride back to his apartment. "When we got there I asked him which door was his. He replied that it was on the third floor. He reckoned that he could walk but he was sore and bruised. He took two steps and turned white. I put him on my back and carried him up three flights but I couldn't pick him high enough so he was dragging his feet. When we got to the apartment, I just dumped him and lay on the couch because I thought I was going to die! I don't know how long I stayed there that night."

While most thought there was insufficient time, the Bernstein team sent the badly damaged Lola back to England for repair, and thus allow Crawford to retain his fourth place grid slot. It was said that this was to cost Bernstein more than a new Lola chassis. Before the tub was shipped to Huntingdon, Crawford had attached a note for the Lola people, "Please fix my car. I've bent it a bit." Never had Lola been asked to mend such a badly damaged car, but a team of five worked a total of 140 man hours and the tub was back clearing customs in Chicago the evening before Carburetion Day. "Miracles take a few days, the impossible, a little longer," said a sign that the Lola boys had pasted to the tub. "We fixed it, Good Luck," said another at the back of the cockpit with the names of the quintet.

The Bernstein team re-assembled the car overnight, and by the end of the next day's practice session Crawford was up to 214mph. He and crew chief Scott seemed confident that they could find more speed for the race, and by mid-contest Jim was running fourth putting in laps at 218mph, despite a clutch failure meaning push starts at each pit stop. Unfortunately, a rod let go on the 136th lap and the brave saga was over. As the car rolled back towards the pits, so the crowd rose to applause.

"After the 1989 race Kenny Bernstein did not know if he could continue," said Scott. He and Bob Riley had left to form their own operation and been contracted by John Menard to run Crawford in 1990 using a 1989 car. "I can't remember why but for some reason we didn't like the 1990 car. I think in hindsight we were wrong. It made it tough for him to get into the race and, of course, he had that spectacular accident. I think they sell more photos of that accident at the Speedway than any other! But, typical Jim, he just shook it off and went down the pub." Just over a week before the race, Crawford had lost control of his Lola in Turn One and spun backwards along the outside wall before sailing off down the south chute – about twelve to fifteen feet off the ground – and landing the right way up, sliding onto the grass. The Scot emerged without any major injuries and went on to qualify at 212.200mph, although a very loose car in the race meant that he struggled and finished seventeen laps behind the winner.

"He even got a set of wings from the US Air Force when he did that high fly in Turn One," recalled Rising-Moore. "I think he got higher than anyone has ever done in a race car at Indy." Trammell was more reflective, "I get visibly concerned when I see one of them that has been tenuously put back together smack the wall like Crawford did," he said to the New York Times.

In 1992, Crawford set an unofficial track lap record in practice of 233.433mph. That year in the run up to the race Jim and team-mate Roberto Guerrero were the ones to ape, the former actually opening up the 230mph club. His race, though, only lasted seventy-four laps before he spun his Quaker State Lola in front of Rick Mears and hit the wall going backwards.

Crawford's final start in the 500 came in 1993. Entrant Bernstein was still racing, and making his first full-time foray into the complete PPG Indy Car series with sponsorship from Budweiser. An ambitious three-car assault on Indianapolis was planned, which backfired when Buick stopped development of its V6 engine and the team had to use Ilmor-Chevrolet motivation. The team's organisation was stretched at the Speedway and Crawford had a torrid time. Life was not made easier when, after designer Bruce Ashmore made his move from Lola to Reynard, Bernstein's race engineer, John Travis, another Englishman, was recalled to the UK to work on Lola's 1994 contender. On lap sixteen of the race, Crawford, running towards the back of the pack, spun in Turn Two but managed to avoid any contact. Having started thirty-first he finished in twenty-fourth place, eight laps behind the winner. Crawford was back with Buick power in 1994 and 1995, failing to qualify on both occasions.

"In 1994 Bob (Riley) and I decided we wanted to go back to the Speedway," said Scott. "It was just the lowest budget. We had a 1990 car, which was just eligible, and only one and a half engines. Jim did everything he could but the weather got hotter and hotter. We realised that if we kept going he would only end up flinging the car into the crowd so we withdrew. As it was about the only thing I could ask him, I queried when he came in what the car was like in traffic. 'I am the traffic,' he replied. It was just a lack of a decent car that Jim didn't get in that year; it was just too old. Bob and I were just two blokes entering a car for the 500 but it was just an expensive way of getting a really good parking space." Within a year, the Speedway had seen the last of one of its bravest contenders. The Scot retired from racing and became a charter fishing boat captain in Florida.

Crawford with Bob Riley and Mark Scott's team in their expensive parking place of 1994. (Courtesy Mark Scott collection)

"In my view Jim knew no limits, nothing rattled him," said Rising-Moore, who sometimes chauffeured Crawford around Indianapolis in the years after his accidents. "I worked his pit board for several years. He told me once, 'It's just a formality that you are out there; I am going to go as fast as I damn well can.'

"He was one of the most incredible human beings I ever met. There wasn't a mean bone in his body. There were no airs about him. Not to take anything away from Jimmy Clark but around here we called him 'The Flying Scot' or 'Gentleman Jim Crawford.' Not that he

Mark Scott with one of the rare Riley & Scott IndyCars. (Author's collection)

MARK SCOTT

Englishman Mark Scott had been an engine builder with McLaren Formula One, visiting the US with the team, but "with no intention of staying." However, when Tyler Alexander and Teddy Mayer put together Mayer Motor Racing to run in the 1984 Indianapolis 500, they invited a number of their former colleagues to join them. Scott was one, although he still thought he would only be in America for one year. However, "I enjoyed living in Pontiac and the money in Indy Car racing was much better than in F1." At the end of the year the Indy Car programme finished but most of the team stayed in the country with Scott, going on to work for a variety of people including BMW and Forsythe Racing.

In the mid-1980s Pat Patrick and Roger Bailey set up a team in Michigan to run the Buick Indy engine programme, employing a number of English mechanics including Scott, who had known Bailey from their time together at McLaren. Being chief mechanic for the project brought him into contact with Jim Crawford.

Scott, with Bob Riley, founded Riley & Scott in 1990, the company being best known for the sports cars that won the 24-hours of Daytona on three occasions. It was one of three manufacturers selected to build chassis for the new Indy Racing league in 1997 but never had the success of G-Force or Dallara. Stan Wattles qualified one for Indianapolis in 1998, crashing early on, while Raul Boesel finished twelfth the following year. That was it as far as the marque's appearances at Indy were concerned, although Buddy Lazier did use one to win at Phoenix in 2000. By then Reynard had acquired the company. Scott, now a US citizen, moved on to found Indianapolis-based Prototype Development, one of the company's projects having been to restore a 1967 Lola T90 – "which came to us as a stack of loose tub skins and rusty bulkheads" – for Lola Cars. This was followed in 2008 by a replica of Graham Hill's 1966 winning Lola, the actual car having been destroyed many years ago.

BILLY WOOLDRIDGE

Fabricator Billy Wooldridge commenced his career at Arch Motors building space frame chassis. He graduated to Lola in 1968 and then Shadow, before setting up his own company, Magnum Engineering, servicing the racing industry. In the early 1980s Theodore Racing approached him with regard to its Indy car project. That took him to the US but the team soon disbanded, and he joined Provimi Veal, which was running Derek Daly.

Wooldridge then returned to the UK, but in late 1986 Morris Nunn invited him to work with Granatelli Racing. When Vince Granatelli moved the team to Phoenix, Wooldridge was reluctant to go with him. "I'm a limey white boy; it's far too hot in Phoenix." This led to a period with Hemelgarn Racing, and then the Jaguar sports car team, before joining Riley & Scott. Another period with Morris Nunn followed, initially in Champ Car, and then the IRL.

Wooldridge was eventually reunited with Scott at Prototype Development, initially running the IRL wind tunnel programme for General Motors and working with a third Englishman John Jackson. It was he who was responsible for building the 1966 Graham Hill Lola replica. "Billy was able to pull that one out of his hat," said Scott.

was a Donald Davidson but he also knew much about the history of this place. It was somewhere that he wanted to be."

Rising-Moore had first met Crawford when he and Sheila had made a visit to the former's Union Jack pub. A year or so later, the Scot invited him to his Florida home. On one of Crawford's last visits to the Union Jack he had his traditional silver Indianapolis 500 badge with him. He told Rising-Moore to throw it into the bar's fish tank. It is still there to this day. "We had a couple of beers and he said 'I think I am all in.' He was really hobbling about by that time. After he had his accident I could see the agony in his face."

Crawford was in a tremendous amount of pain right from the day of the accident for the rest of his life. "He could not get on with the pain killers, they made him feel too bad," said Mark Scott. "He did not want to get hooked on them. Many of the drivers who had had incidents had briefed him on that. So he would tend to self medicate with more drink than perhaps he should have done."

Rising-Moore took him once more to see Trammell. The surgeon suggested that Crawford "hang on for another year" by which time technology might have caught up enough to help his plight. "But it just didn't happen." For Trammell, who had always been able to help his patients, it was particularly poignant.

Not long before Crawford died, Trammell rang him up to say that some major advances had been made in what he could do. There might be a chance that he could improve his feet and get rid of some of the pain. He suggested that Crawford travel to Indianapolis to see if he was an appropriate candidate. Scott picked him and first took him to his workshop near the airport. "He looked terrible, he just looked grey. There was just this one chance that Trammell could do something, so he had all his records with him."

What was not known at the time was that when one of the original skin grafts was made it was from a cadaver that had hepatitis. A culmination of this and the effects of drink had damaged Crawford's liver. The state of his internal organs was such that the surgeon realised he would not survive further treatment. "We discussed ways to improve his situation, but it was impossible," said Trammell.

"It was strange, but he came back from that meeting with

Bill Wooldridge at work restoring a Lola T90. (Courtesy Mark Scott collection)

Trammell as if a huge weight had been lifted from his shoulders," recalled Rising-Moore. "He looked really good. It was as if he had dropped ten years off his life, and he was quite chirpy on the way back to Florida." The next Scott knew, Crawford had been found dead in his apartment at Tierre Verde with liver failure. "He knew there was no real way around the pain but I suspect there was nothing deliberate. His organs just would not take it."

Rising-Moore recalled putting a pin badge of Crawford up on the wall at his vacation cottage in northern Ontario that day, August 6, 2002. The Scot was due to spend some time there but about an hour later he received a call to say that Crawford had died. "He sacrificed his body for the sport," states Rising-Moore. "There is no question about that."

16

BRITISH HORSEPOWER

"What to do ...?"

For ten years, commencing in 1978, the Cosworth DFX engine from Northampton ruled at Indianapolis, arguably the greatest display of British supremacy ever seen at the Speedway. To cap it, the winning Reynards in the final two years before the advent of the Indy Racing League were powered by Cosworth XB engines. During the period in-between there were six Chevrolet victories and a sole win for a Mercedes-Benz. Did this mean that the British had lost the edge? Not a bit of it. These power units, despite their names, also originated in Northamptonshire, although, in this case, from the firm of Ilmor.

The story, though, does not finish with the arrival of the IRL. In 2004 Honda took its first ever victory at the Speedway, followed up a year later by powering Dan Wheldon to victory, after which it became the sole engine supplier for the League. Honda, Japanese? Never believe what the brand appears to tell you. Like the Chevrolets and Mercedes-Benz before them, these Hondas came from Ilmor's Brixworth works. The name of Ilmor has never actually appeared on a winning Indy 500 engine, but by 2009 it had thirteen victories under its belt.

Apart from the early days of the IRL, British-manufactured engines have, for thirty years, ruled over Indianapolis. However, it was to be a long time before the names of Cosworth and Ilmor were to become part of Indy folklore. Prior to the 1970s, a British engine on the grid for the 500 meant that it powered a British chassis. First up was the 6107cc Sunbeam engine fitted to 'Toodles IV' in 1913. Its six cylinders had been cast in two blocks of three and its side valves were operated

The Cosworth DFS was the final version of the DFX that ruled the Speedway for many years. (Courtesy Lola Cars)

by a camshaft on the near side, with a single Claudel carburettor on the offside. A 450 cu in limit was placed on entries for the following year. To overcome this, Sunbeam decided to use its rather small dry sump, six-cylinder 4.5-litre-engined Grand Prix car for the 1914 race. With a premium on acceleration, twin Claudel Hobson carburettors were fitted, while engine cooling was improved by fitting twin water outlet manifolds on the cylinder head.

For the 1916 race Sunbeam used a new 152bhp twin overhead camshaft, four valves per cylinder, 4.9-litre, six-cylinder engine that was said to show the influence of Ernest Henry, who had designed the engines of the Indy 500 winning Peugeots. When Sunbeam returned after the war, the 500's capacity limit had been reduced to 183 cu in, which coincided with the Grand Prix 3-litre formula. The Sunbeams for 1921 had dry sump straight-eight aluminium engines with steel liners and four valves per cylinder. Like the 1916 engines, they featured camshafts driven by a train of straight-toothed pinions, although, unlike the earlier unit, the five main bearings and the big ends were plain. Experiments were carried out with both two and four carburettors, with four horizontal Claudels being used for the 500.

The following year saw another British engine in the entry, the virtually production 4-cylinder, 3-litre in Hawkes' Bentley. From then on, we have to look to 1961 for the next British power unit to make the grid. Robert Arbuthnot and Leslie Brooke had been unable to make the grid with their V12 Lagonda and straight-six ERA-engined cars. Likewise, the de Villiers team and then Pedro Rodriguez, who failed to qualify Connaught and Cooper cars that used, respectively, straight 4-cylinder Alta and 6-cylinder Aston Martin engines.

The Lotus and Lola entries that so changed the Indy 500 in the 1960s were reliant on US-made engines. However, the little Cooper that started the rear-engined revolution was British through and through. The grid in 1960 was totally Offenhauser-powered. In 1961 there was the one interloper, the Cooper's Coventry Climax engine. The company dominated Formula One and many other forms of racing for a while but this was the only time one of its engines appeared in the Indy 500. Charles and John Cooper persuaded Climax to increase the size of the 2.5-litre FPF engine that had won two World Championships to 2.7-litres. Climax did so with a certain reluctance, pointing out that it was not happy about potential reliability. Using a 50/50 methanol/AvGas mix, the engine delivered an extra 25hp at 5000rpm compared to the 2.5-litre. Despite the manufacturer's fears, it also finished its one and only 500.

For 1966, Formula One rules had been changed to accept 3-litre engines, and Tony Rudd and Geoff Johnson went over the proverbial top by designing a H16 unit for BRM; essentially two flat-eight engines one above the other. Lotus was also to use the engine and, with the promise of great power, Colin Chapman was easily persuaded to take a 4.2-litre version of the unit for his next Indy car, the type 42. Power was one thing, weight was another, and Lotus' new designer Maurice Philippe found that it was even heavier than had originally been stated. The problem plagued the H16 engines, which were not ready for the 1966 500, so Lotus reverted to its type 38s. (The H16 was essentially a failure in F1, although Jim Clark did use one in his Lotus 43 to win

the 1966 United States Grand Prix.) An ungainly type 42 did appear at Indianapolis the following year but a much longer Ford V8 had replaced the engine from Bourne.

Two engines which had an Anglo element did make the grid in the 1960s. One of the three Eagles entered in 1967, that of future World Champion Jochen Rindt, used a Ford pushrod V8 with special cylinder heads from Gurney-Weslake, drawn at Weslake's Rye, Sussex base but cast in Pennsylvania. Dan Gurney, himself, was to use such an engine to come second in 1968 and 1969. Rindt was also the first person to use a Brabham-Repco V8 at the Speedway. Although this 4.2-litre unit, based on the 3-litre Formula One engine, was built in Australia, much of the design work was carried out by Englishman John Judd who, as an apprentice draftsman, had worked on Brabham's 2.7-litre Climax engine for the 1961 500. He recalled designing the metering unit for the Indy Repco, "... persuading Lucas to do something it thought impossible."

Judd's own company, Engine Developments, went on to prepare Cosworth DFX engines. Then, in 1987, the Galles team's Marches appeared at the Speedway powered by Judd-designed "Brabham-Honda" V8s; Honda's first, although unofficial, foray into Indy car racing. The engine was a 2.65-litre turbocharged version of Judd's 3-litre normally-aspirated F3000 power unit. Sir Jack Brabham was involved both as a shareholder in Engine Developments and a consultant to Honda, which put up the money, cast the blocks, and supplied the engine management technology. The following year, Honda having passed over the major castings, the engines became simply known as Judds. From 1987 to 1991 they ran at the Speedway, the best result being third in 1989 when one was used to power Raul Boesel's Lola.

Twelve years previously, the first Cosworth had appeared at the Speedway powering Al Unser's Parnelli. Parnelli Jones, the man who had prevented the British from winning in 1963, had entered a car with what was to become the most successful Indy engine ever to leave the shores of Albion; the soon to be called DFX. In 1983 the whole field, with just one exception, used this unit.

The story arguably begins with an American who has done more to bring about the British engine dominance of the 500 than anyone else, Roger Penske. In 1972 he had asked Cosworth to build a batch of short-stroke, low compression versions of its remarkably successful DFV V8 Formula One engine with a view to turbocharging them. It was a project that never got off the ground. However, another leading Indy car team, Vel's Parnelli Jones, was also interested in the DFV, as it was about to build its own Formula One car. Although there was little success to come for VPJ during its two years of Grand Prix racing, it had been attracted to the low cost and high reliability of the Cosworth engine, and so asked Indy car engine builder Larry Slutter to look at the possibility of turbocharging one. The 3.0-litre engine was reduced to the obligatory 2.65-litres using a short-stroke crankshaft developed by Cosworth for the Penske project. This was fitted to the VPJ6 – little more than a converted VPJ F1 car – designed by Maurice Philippe and then revised by his fellow Englishman John Barnard. At Indianapolis Al Unser finished seventh at its wheel and then went on to win the Pocono 500 the following month.

McLaren was the next to fit the engine and Cosworth, which up to this point had little to do with it, decided to build an "official" version. Slutter was poached by the British company to run a satellite operation in Torrance, California. Components were shipped back to Northampton where complete turbocharged engines, now known as DFXs, could be assembled.

Great success followed with the first Indy 500 win coming in 1978, thanks to Al Unser, now in a Lola. A severe reduction of boost pressure introduced by USAC in 1979, intended to keep the old Offenhauser engines competitive against the new upstart, actually helped the DFX's reliability, and so it thrived. By the mid-1980s it had a near monopoly of the 500, just missing a complete grid in 1983 when all but one of the starters were powered by Cosworth engines.

Paul Morgan and Swiss-born Mario Illien were employed at Cosworth; the former the liaison engineer between the company and the Indy car teams, while Illien was engaged in Formula One and had designed the revision for the DFV, known as the DFY. They had decided that they would like to work together but, as Illien recalled, "What to do and where to find the money?" At the time, their existing employer was dominating Indy, and so they felt that "This was the place to start." They called Roger Penske and asked if he might be interested. He responded in the affirmative and asked for a budget and timetable. Within a few days these had been handwritten and submitted, and the pair summoned to Penske's home. A meeting of about two hours resulted in a handshake and the instruction, "let's go!"

The new company, Ilmor, was started in January 1984. In the October, still during the design phase, Chevrolet came on board to lend its name to the engine, taking on twenty-five per cent of the company. Illien was still not convinced that Indy Car was the way that he wanted to go but in 1985 he attended his first Indianapolis 500 and was "fascinated." He now felt that this was the right way forward, although he lately admitted that Ilmor had a difficult start. There were some at Cosworth who felt that there was too much of the DFX in the new engine, while it did not help that the then current Penske, the Alan Jenkins-designed PC15, was not one of Poole's finest. However, Illien reckoned that he and Morgan proved a point to Penske by persuading him to test the engine in a year-old March.

Penske had exclusive rights to the engine in 1986 but the following year it was also supplied to Newman Haas and Patrick Racing. The first win came at Long Beach with Mario Andretti. Then came a question over reliability, with a torsion problem between crank and camshafts and breaking valve springs. At Indianapolis Andretti, with a comfortable lead, eased off. Illien said what was discovered later was that he was cruising around a natural frequency of the valve

Mario Illien was not initially convinced that IndyCar was the way to go. (Author's collection)

Chevrolet by name, Ilmor by nature. (Courtesy Lola Cars)

THE BRITS AND ETHANOL

In 2006, the Indy Racing League threw down a challenge; it had made the decision to run on 100 per cent ethanol. Given that Indy cars had raced using an alcohol fuel (methanol) for many years, this initially looked a simple move for Ilmor, which, apart from the trackside calibration, carried out the work for its customer, Honda. However, testing proved that there were issues of power loss and cooling that first had to be overcome.

IRL senior technical director, Les Mactaggart: "We attacked the problem in two stages. In 2006 we ran with a blend of ninety per cent methanol and ten per cent ethanol. This allowed us to make the transition as smoothly as we could. We had the balance of the year to do the development needed for ninety-eight per cent fuel grade ethanol. The burden was on the engine supplier to achieve that; the bulk of the work was on re-mapping."

So far, so good. However, there was far more to it as was discovered. Mactaggart's fellow Englishman, Roger Griffiths of Honda explained. "The first foray was to see how the existing 3.0-litre engine worked on ethanol. Two things were apparent; one was that the engine performance was down, which was not unexpected, the other that the amount of heat rejected by the engine was greater."

Honda presented the findings to the IRL, saying that the down-turn in performance would probably be fine for oval racing, as it would only take four or five miles per hour off the speed of the cars, but not road courses where the cars might look slow. "At this point we had three options," Griffiths continued, "To increase the capacity of the engine, to go for a greater state of tune, or to run it faster. At the same time, we were looking at how we could reduce the cost of the programme. One way of doing that was to increase engine life. The second two options ran against that. We therefore did a study on what capacity increase would be necessary to retain the performance. Three and a half litres seemed to be a reasonable number. The nice thing about going back to that capacity was that we could quite quickly build an engine as we still had some left over components from a couple of years ago.

"The ethanol 3.5-litre was not ...," pointed out Griffiths, "... the same engine as we had in 2003. Between switching from 3.0 to 3.5-litres we learnt a lot about crankshaft design. There was also a connecting rod design change. Perhaps the most obvious difference has been to the fuel system, this being simplified to help with cost and reliability."

spring. "If he had gone hard he would not have had that problem." Illien subsequently designed a damper system that "overnight" fixed the early problems of the engine. It was transformed from being marginal to very successful. Cosworth tried to respond, with a short stroke DFS version of its famed V8, but the basic design's days were over.

Although the DFX and DFS had been born out of the Ford-financed DFV, they were never supported by the carmaker. In 1992, the blue oval was back at Indianapolis as Ford co-operated with Cosworth on its next Indy car engine, the XB. Steve Miller, now Ilmor Engineering managing director and formerly with Cosworth, "... lived through the demise of the DFX and then we got going with the XB engine." This unit, unlike the DFX, was designed by Stuart Grove from scratch to be a 2.65-litre engine, and was thus lighter and smaller. Miller, who led the project, recalled the difficulty of marketing the engine against the now entrenched Ilmor. Following the failures of the Alfa Romeo and Porsche projects, no-one seemed prepared to break ranks. "I wore out a lot of shoe leather trying to sell the XB." Eventually, Newman Haas was persuaded to fund a car with Lola and some backing from Ford. The engine immediately

Ilmor carried out much of the work that enabled the IRL to run on ethanol. (Author's collection)

The Mercedes-Benz-badged pushrod engine caught the opposition by surprise when it arrived at the Speedway. Despite its name, it was another Northamptonshire creation. (Courtesy Indianapolis Motor Speedway)

proved competitive, powering Nigel Mansell to the championship in only its second year, and the Indy 500 winners in 1995 and 1996.

Meanwhile, Chevrolet had been looking to reduce its involvement, which Ilmor felt would mean the loss of its competitive edge. Eventually in 1993, the budget had fallen by so much that Ilmor pulled out, although the third version of its Chevrolet engine, the C, won the 500 that year with six Cosworth XBs in tow. "We were in free-fall for a while," recalled Illien. However, in the November, all that changed with the entry of Mercedes-Benz into the fray, initially to talk about Formula One.

USAC had changed the rules regarding pushrod engines and, that July, Penske, Illien, and Morgan decided that the time had come to design one. Penske asked how powerful the engine could be. Illien guessed 940hp. In the end it was to produce 1024hp. Illien did enquire if Chevrolet would be interested in such a unit, although it already had the Buick programme. "You just stay with the racing engine," was the response. "We know everything about pushrods."

"It was the most intense programme that we ever undertook."

Design work commenced in July, and, by the end of January, an engine was on the dyno. Everything was carried out in secrecy with misleading names – such as "Pontiac" – being put on the drawings to ensure that suppliers could not give the game away. Although Ilmor was now speaking to Mercedes-Benz about F1, it was not until April that the German carmaker got to hear about the pushrod engine. However, a visit by the principals to Stuttgart in April resulted in it coming on board on the one condition that Penske used the engine in all three of his cars. "It was a late bonus," said Illien.

Penske designer Nigel Bennett recalled the period with what he described, tongue firmly in cheek, as "the cheat engine." A couple of years previously, he had been talking to Morgan about the production-based Buicks that were setting very fast qualifying times at Indianapolis because "... they were allowed their own ridiculous capacity and boost rules, which gave them more horsepower than we could achieve." Bennett suggested that Ilmor "... take a Buick and really do something with it." At the time Morgan turned down the idea, but today Bennett wonders if the conversation had been the germ of an idea that resulted in the pushrod Mercedes engine.

"It was an amazing project," he stated. "The engine was tested at Nazareth, and every time it blew up parts had to be flown back to Brixworth on Concorde. The first time it achieved a full 500 miles was during the first weekend that we ran at Indianapolis." Illien says that the initial problem (gudgeon pin failure) was due to the cold ambient temperatures experienced during testing.

Illien was convinced that there would be only one shot with the beautiful sounding, pushrod engine before it was banned. The rules were changed after Al Unser Jr had driven the Mercedes-motivated Penske PC23 to victory, but only to change the boost. It was no problem to Ilmor, which took on orders from other teams. "Then USAC realised these buggers don't give up and we were completely banned."

Recalled Penske Cars' managing director, Nick Goozee, "It was only because of the secrecy that we were able to keep within the walls of Penske and Ilmor that that project worked as it did. If the opposition in America had got wind of what we were doing, then it would have been stopped very early. It was only because we produced it out of a hat at Indianapolis that it worked."

Steve Miller joined Ilmor from Cosworth.
(Author's collection)

Honda became sole supplier to the IRL, enabling Ilmor to once again dominate the Speedway.
(Author's collection)

ROGER GRIFFITHS

Englishman, Roger Griffiths is Honda's man at Indy. He joined Honda Performance Development in 2003 as Race Team Technical Leader. In addition to his work with the Indy Racing League, to which Honda is the exclusive engine supplier with its Ilmor-designed and -built engine, Griffiths has also been in charge of trackside operations for the Acura engine programme in the American Le Mans Series.

From 1992 to 1994 Griffiths worked at the Nissan European Technology Centre. This was followed by two stints at Cosworth Racing, working on Formula One programmes with Sauber and Minardi, and time at Ray Mallock Ltd, Ascari Cars and, in 2003, as a senior development engineer at Aston Martin Motorsport.

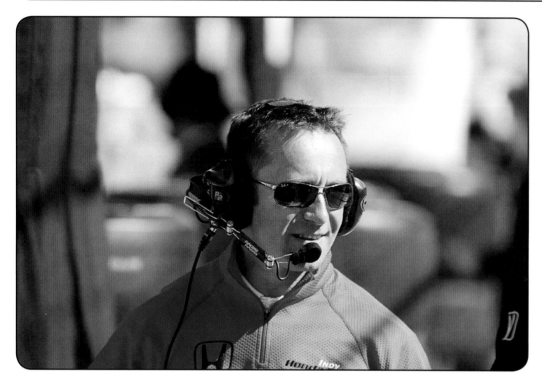

Englishman Roger Griffiths, seen here in the pit lane at the Speedway, became Honda's Race Team technical leader in both IndyCar and sports car racing. (Author's collection)

By 2001 Steve Miller joined Ilmor. This was the brief period when the IRL rules meant that only GM (originally badged as Oldsmobile) and Infiniti engines were being used. However, Penske returned to the Speedway that year and brought back with it its old partner, Ilmor, to supply some specific engine components, mainly for the fuel system. Ilmor also started designing an IRL engine speculatively. Miller and Paul Ray had come up with the idea and "... ran it past the flagpole" with Morgan and Illien. Morgan pointed out that they were the second ones to suggest it, Roger Penske having done so only that weekend. "We were pushing on an open door."

Honda had left CART, and seemingly US open wheel racing, while Toyota had announced that it would be competing in the IRL. In the autumn of 2001 Honda started "tentative talks" about returning with Ilmor. Following the horror of September 11, the idea was "... put on ice and we felt that was an opportunity gone." However, the following spring it was revived and an agreement signed in the May. Ilmor was faced with a tight time-scale to ensure that the V8 engine would be ready for racing in 2003.

Almost all the parts for the H19R as it is known – with the exception of the pistons and a few small items – are manufactured at, or sourced out of, the Brixworth facility. All the initial design and performance development was also carried out in Northamptonshire where the design control still resides. The IRL engine was the first time that Honda ever subcontracted a major engine programme. After powering the 2004 and 2005 Indy 500 winners, Honda became the sole engine supplier to the IndyCar Series in 2006. By the end of 2009, Ilmor had supplied eighty-five Honda units; initially of 3.5-litres, then 3.0-litres, and finally back to 3.5-litres to accommodate the use of ethanol fuel.

17

THE POOLE PIRATES

"It worked pretty well."

When it comes to sporting prowess most towns and cities in England are known for their soccer teams. Not so the south coast location of Poole. This is a speedway town, and in more ways than one. Its Wimborne Road track may be an oval but it measures a mere 299.1 metres (327.1 yards) and is covered in shale. Opened in 1948, this is speedway as the British recognise the word – four motorbike riders racing for just four laps, and usually for team honours. This is the home of the Poole Pirates, winners of the country's top league titles on five occasions.

However, there is a second 'speedway' aspect to the town. For a period, the crowd at Wimborne Road stadium included interested spectators from a local engineering firm. Riders from the team, including six times World Champion Tony Rickardsson, would also visit that company's factory. The interest was logical; it was in Poole that no fewer than seven Indianapolis 500 winning cars were built, for the firm in question was Penske Cars.

For many years at the Indianapolis Motor Speedway, it seemed that Penskes were the only American cars that could withstand the

Poole has been a speedway town in more ways than one. (Author's collection)

**The Penske PC-6 has been described as iconic.
(Courtesy Gould Inc)**

onslaught of the Marches, Lolas, and Reynards from Britain. Yet, while the Penskes appeared to have an American identity, every one of them was built in the Dorset town. Given the race car expertise to be found in the UK, it is perhaps not surprising that Roger Penske's eponymous operation should have chosen the country as its manufacturing base. Less obvious is why it should have picked Poole, a town many miles away from what has since become known as Britain's 'Motorsports Valley.'

The reason for the location goes back to the team's then sponsor, the First National City Bank's desire for exposure in Europe, which led to it persuading Penske to enter Formula One. Graham McRae's Poole-based Formula 5000 operation was subsequently acquired. The town's port was felt to be useful but also, because of Penske's already well-established reputation in Indy Car and Can-Am racing, he wanted to, as Penske Cars former managing director Nick Goozee put it, "... move into Formula One quietly." Poole was considered to be sufficiently far away from the hub of F1. Manufacturing started in 1974 with a win for Ulsterman John Watson in the Austrian Grand Prix in 1976. At the end of that year, Penske, finding it difficult to run a Formula One team in Europe while concentrating on his business empire in the States, withdrew from Grands Prix but decided to retain the manufacturing facility in Poole. Indy cars were now to be constructed there using the expertise that had been built up. Prior to this Penske had been purchasing such cars from Lola and McLaren.

Perhaps not surprisingly, the first Indy car built at Poole, the PC5, was a derivative of the McLaren M24. The staff, recalls Goozee, was very small but the car towards the end of the year helped Tom Sneva to the 1977 USAC Championship. Goozee described its successor, the PC6, as being one of the most iconic of Indy cars. Like the earlier Penskes, this was designed by Englishman Geoff Ferris. It was with the PC6 that Penske made its first Indianapolis appearance as a manufacturer, Sneva finishing second that year having taken the pole.

Ferris was the key figure at Poole during that stage, indeed was the first employee of Penske Cars. He had previously worked at Lotus under Colin Chapman before going to Brabham. The other figure of note at the time was Scot Derrick Walker. Having run the Formula One team he took over the running of the company as general manager in 1977, until moving to Team Penske itself three years later. Walker was to become a noted Indy Car entrant in his own right, as recorded elsewhere. With Walker's move to the US, Ferris found himself in the dual role of chief designer and general manager. That was probably too great a load to put on one man, and so in 1983 Goozee took over the general manager's position. He had been with the company for almost a decade having started as a fabricator and mechanic. Ferris could again concentrate on the design, and was ultimately responsible for all the Penskes up to and including the PC12. He then designed the gearboxes for the subsequent Penskes prior to his retirement.

The year 1979 was the first in which a true ground effects car turned up at the IMS. The Chaparral was yet another with an American identity but designed and built in the UK, as outlined in chapter eight. Ferris' PC7 was perhaps more semi-ground effects, sporting sidepods that contained the underwing. Three had been built for Bobby

**Nick Goozee became Penske Cars' general manager in 1983, having started with the company as a fabricator and mechanic.
(Author's collection)**

CLIVE HOWELL

March and Lola's country of origin, as well as Penske Cars' base, meant that there were plenty of British mechanics around in the 1980s. For example, Al Unser's Penske-entered March had an English chief mechanic when it won in 1987. Clive Howell had been a British Aerospace apprentice at Brooklands. With Brabham based "... just down the road ..." and a mother, Kath who was said company's secretary, he found himself helping out there; something that morphed into a full-time job. Derrick Walker was chief mechanic at Brabham then, and sometime after he had left to join Penske he rang Howell to ask him if he wanted to work in America. He did, married a local girl, Mary, and worked his way through the ranks at Penske, becoming general manager for the team in 1998. He was still with the team in 2010, acting as race strategist for Will Power as he led the IZOD IndyCar championship.

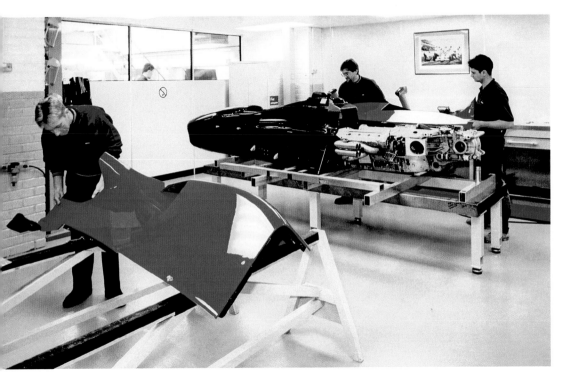

Penske Cars' body assembly shop. (Courtesy Nick Goozee collection)

A Ferris design returned to the Indy victory lane in 1981, though, with Bobby Unser driving a PC9B. For the following two years Penske could do no better than second place: first with Mears in a PC10 in what was the closest finish to date, and then with Al Unser Sr a year later in a PC11.

Ferris stood down in 1984. The PC12 had proved uncompetitive and Goozee recalled, "I had to go and buy March 84Cs. We very quickly adapted these and won the Indianapolis 500 (with Mears) about three weeks after we had taken delivery of the cars." Looking for a new designer, Goozee found that he was faced with two options. One was Rory Byrne, who was then working on the Toleman F1. Ted Toleman, however, asked his workforce to hang in with the struggling team and Byrne, having agreed to join Penske, changed his mind. Frank Williams advised Goozee to consider Merseysider Alan Jenkins who was, at the time, working as an assistant to John Barnard at McLaren. Jenkins designed the McLaren Formula One-based PC15 and PC16 but both were unsuccessful and the team continued to use Marches at Indianapolis, with Jenkins engineering Danny Sullivan's win in 1985 using one of the Bicester-built cars.

Even when Penske bought customer tubs as opposed to building its own, Penske Cars would still model the rest of the car with great precision, and taking into consideration the different tracks. "I think we exceeded 200 wishbones for one season for two cars and a spare," said Goozee. "We regularly changed and disposed of the suspension after three races. This was quite common in Formula One but rare in Indy Car racing."

In 1986 Jenkins was replaced by Nigel Bennett, whose days with Penske are recounted in the next chapter. That decade was to be, in Goozee's words, "... the most successful period for Team Penske by far." During this period Penske Cars sold cars to customers, including

Unser and Rick Mears. In the event, Mears qualified one of the older PC6s and put it on pole, Unser in a PC7 was on the second row.

With Jackie Stewart pulling off the track in the pace car, Al Unser shot ahead in the yellow Chaparral and proceeded to dominate the first half of the race. A melted transmission seal put him out on lap 105, after which brother Bobby took over and seemed to be on his way to victory. There was no doubt that ground effects was now the way to go, and it was the British-built cars that were to the forefront. In the event, the PC7 lost fourth gear and Mears moved into the lead on lap 182 with the older Penske. The first victory for a Poole-built car was about to happen.

British ground effects expertise was much in evidence the next year, with the Penske PC9 the first true such car from Poole. Johnny Rutherford was now at the wheel of the Chaparral and took both the pole and the win. Mears was first of the PC9s in fifth place, one behind Gordon Johncock's PC6 and one ahead of Pancho Carter's PC7.

Composite assembly at Poole. (Courtesy Nick Goozee collection)

Patrick Racing. It was with one of these cars that Emerson Fittipaldi won the 500 in 1989, a second consecutive victory for a Poole-built vehicle. This highlighted a problem that Penske Cars had in selling cars to Team Penske's competitors. The last time that this happened was for Bettenhausen Motorsports in 1993. The problem arose again in the late 1990s when Penske Cars looked like becoming one of the three chassis suppliers to the Indy Racing League. However, there were objections about this from some of the other IRL teams. Team Penske was the Poole operation's main customer and principal means of financial support: its own requirements had to be paramount so, thereafter, despite its ability to build customer cars, it concentrated solely on Team Penske.

The 1994 season and, in particular, the Indy 500 win with the Mercedes-Benz pushrod engine, was, said Goozee, "particularly exciting." However, there is a danger inherent in such success that not enough effort is put into the following season. "Reynard had worked doubly hard to get back at us for 1995 and we ignominiously failed to qualify at Indianapolis. That was the beginning of the worst period for

Penske Cars." Nigel Bennett retired from Penske at the end of 1996, by which time the split between Champ Car and the IRL had occurred and, staying with the former, Penske Cars was, temporarily, no longer involved in the Indianapolis 500. It did return to the Brickyard in 2001, but as a customer of the Italian race car manufacturer Dallara, and thus out of the story of the British at Indianapolis. Roger Penske had been considering the merits of keeping Penske Cars operational. During 1999 there were moves to form a liaison with Reynard, and to look at an IRL project, but nothing came of this and, eventually, the premises were sold to precision machining company Aerotech.

Goozee believed that, in the 1990s, Penske Cars was regarded as the equal of any of the Formula One manufacturers. Liaison was common between Poole and such as McLaren and Williams. Goozee had worked with Ron Dennis earlier in his career, and was also to form a friendship with Martin Whitmarsh, which enabled Penske to have direct access to McLaren's research centre in Woking. At the same time, McLaren borrowed Penske Indy cars for examination. During the 1990s F1 was looking at Indy Car ground effects with much interest.

Penske Cars staff assemble in 2005, not long before the UK operation was closed. (Courtesy Nick Goozee collection)

An F1 McLaren would also find its way to Poole, which Penske was able to use for reference. During the previous decade, Penske had used the Williams wind tunnel in Didcot and, in return, supplied that team with Penske shocks, another offshoot the Penske empire had just started producing. None of its competitors ever had such close relationships with Formula One. Former Penske Cars technical director, Nigel Beresford recalled, "Nick was really good at bringing along young guys and giving them an opportunity. We had a tremendous, young group of engineers."

Goozee reckoned that the company was the first motor racing manufacturer to use CAD. In 1984, it formed a sponsorship agreement with the then Computer Vision. The building that it moved into that year had a CAD system installed with a dedicated hard drive room and one workstation. A number of the Formula One designers – including Ferrari's John Barnard and Williams' Patrick Head – paid a visit to take a look. "It was very crude in those days, at best had just the ability to make a coloured image of a car and spin it around. It was still much

quicker to design by pencil and board. All the Penske designers did their schemes on a 14ft drawing board. When we started Geoff Ferris did all the drawing. By the time we had finished designing with the PC27 (a post-split Champ Car) we had fourteen people in the design team."

Initially, Penske Cars had run out of two 1500 sq ft units on a small industrial estate. In 1987 it moved to the Upton Industrial Estate and a 5000 sq ft facility. There it continued until 1994 when the company moved to a 12,000 sq ft base, two doors away. Over the following years extensions were built that took the total to 36,000 sq ft. At its peak in 1991, Penske Cars had ninety-three employees. However, this meant that costs were running too high and staff numbers were first reduced to 60 and then, in later years, to forty-eight. "Part of the reason for this was that we were able to become much more efficient at our manufacturing." However, with an increasingly unfavourable exchange rate and, with the team now running Dallaras, a reduced added value, the UK operation ultimately became too expensive to continue and everything was consolidated under one roof in the States during 2006.

THE SPEEDWAY BIKE

Motorcycle speedway reminded Nick Goozee of his time in motor racing during the early 1960s, and perhaps it was nostalgia for those days that attracted him to Penske Cars' local 'dirt track' in Poole. However, Goozee did not content himself with spectating. He set out to show the speedway world just what could be achieved using Penske's leading edge, Indy car technology.

The standard speedway bike is a basic item, built to a cost. There is little that you can do to it; you certainly cannot fit brakes or rear suspension. Yet Goozee could see that, if the standards that Penske Cars applied to its Indy cars were to be used on building one, the result would "... completely transform the world of speedway."

In 2003 Poole Pirates team manager Neil Middleditch telephoned him to say that World Champion Tony Rickardsson was keen to visit Penske's premises. That evening Goozee found himself at a speedway meeting for the first time. "Casually, I said to Tony 'Do you know, I reckon we could build a far better bike for you. Would you be interested in working with me?'"

The following day the pair met again. Goozee offered to fund the cost of a first bike – it should be noted that this was always a private project of his and never a Penske Cars one. The idea was that, if this worked, Penske Cars would be engaged as a contractor to build more. He gathered together a dozen relevant Penske staff and asked who would like to be involved in the project. "It's evening and weekend work only," he pointed out.

A twist rig was made for a conventional Jawa speedway bike and all the weak spots worked out, as well as what happened under certain loading conditions. From that, "We saw immense opportunity to design and build a new frame, but we had to approach the project as if we were designing an Indy car. Very quickly, we were able to see that the chassis was particularly weak in the rear subframe and round about the headstock. What we had to do was make a bike rigid enough not to shimmy but flexible enough that it gave the rider a sense of feel."

A prototype bike was built, named the "Middlo" after Middleditch and his father Ken, a noted rider of the 1950s. This was ready for testing on the day of the season's first meeting of 2004. The Swede took out both the Middlo and a Jawa. They were so different that he was not at first sure that he wanted to ride the Middlo again. "When he first tried it, Tony could barely get it round the corner because it drove so hard," recalled Middleditch. "It was just pure traction." The engineering was initially so good that the bike was too rigid. Rickardsson, however, mounted it for one last attempt and decided the potential was such that he would ride in that evening's meeting. He won every heat that he lined up for, scoring maximum points. From then on he continued to use the prototype, soon winning World Championship Grands Prix with it. The result was that he ordered eight more frames from Goozee. While the prototype had been built out of hours, for the production run Rickardsson became a customer of Penske Cars until he retired from Speedway in 2006 to race cars in the Porsche Carrera Cup Scandinavia.

A headstock was designed whereby the mechanic could move the forks backwards, forwards – thus lengthening the wheelbase – and laterally, or keep them in a neutral position. The forks could be offset by 1.5 degrees, which Rickardsson found on short tracks a great advantage. "Speedway is all about turning," said Middleditch. "And that is what the Middlo brought to the sport. Anything goes in a straight line."

The top competitors began to approach Goozee to see if he would also supply them "... but they, understandably, didn't want to pay the money." The riders could buy a complete Czech-built chassis ready to put an engine in for about £500. Rickardsson paid four times this amount for each of his Middlos. It was almost impossible for them to have become commercially viable and Goozee eventually dropped the project.

Having a Formula One car constructor in Poole naturally excited the interest of the local press in Penske Cars' early days. However, in 1978 when the Indy cars – including two Penskes – raced at Silverstone, the then Mayor of Poole was amongst those attending the meeting. "It excited him sufficiently that he, and then subsequently all the Mayors of Poole, adopted us. Poole was in a period of regeneration and they regarded us and Sunseeker boats as being the noteworthy local companies. It became common practice that every new Mayor visited us. Winning first a Grand Prix and then the Indianapolis 500 from an area of the south coast that was fairly bereft of motorsport made us something of a celebrity organisation," said Goozee.

Poole Pirates team manager, Neil Middleditch, and the 'Middlo.'
(Author's collection)

18

THE BATTLE OF BRITONS – NIGEL BENNETT AND BRUCE ASHMORE

"I was playing catch up ..."

"He was surely a good 'enemy,'" is how Bruce Ashmore summed up the struggle in which he engaged with fellow designer Nigel Bennett during the late 1980s and early 1990s. The pair had both worked at Lola with Bennett leaving in 1987 to eventually join Penske. That year was the last of March's five-year winning streak. Now began a battle of two Britons with Bennett and Ashmore personifying a dogged Penske versus Lola contest.

Ashmore had been a couple of years into his apprenticeship at Lola when, in 1978, the decision was made to return to Indy. "I was just a lad in the drawing office but everybody was drafted

Bruce Ashmore still lives and works in Indianapolis ... (Author's collection)

in. It was the biggest car that I had been involved in." He recalled, "We were trying to go after reliability. The T500 was a chunky, strong car. It was not particularly quick, it won the three 500s (including Indianapolis) on reliability." Despite the success of the T500, the phones did not ring the following year at Lola. A couple more of what was basically the same car were built in 1980, and that was it until 1983. That year Lola and Carl Haas combined forces, and the T700 was built using the same design team as that for the T500. Mario Andretti was to be the driver. Initially, the chassis was, recalled Ashmore, "terrible." Said its pilot, "This car's got leprosy and you're trying to cure it with a Band-Aid." The team did not give up on it though. Mid-season the chassis was

... while Nigel Bennett has retired but still lives not many miles from the old Penske Cars factory. (Author's collection)

Bobby Rahal joined the Lola camp, where he was engineered by Ashmore. (Courtesy Lola cars)

stiffened and a one-piece underwing installed, considerably improving its performance.

For the following year Nigel Bennett was hired. "We had another set of eyes that had recently been on Formula One," said Ashmore. A proper wind tunnel programme was initiated, the result being about twice the downforce of the previous year's car. The car was quick out of the box and, although Andretti retired at Indianapolis, he won the championship.

Former Firestone tyre engineer Bennett had experienced Formula One through Hesketh, Lotus, and Ensign. During his spell at Lotus he had worked with Mario Andretti, and it was perhaps then that the seed of his time at Indianapolis were sown. That arguably started to sprout when he and Ralph Bellamy designed a carbon top chassis for the Ensign N180 Formula One car. When Bellamy left Ensign, Bennett designed the F1 N181 and N182. "We started the year with $600,000 total sponsorship and a staff of thirteen people, then ran out of money which led to an Indy car project for (George) Bignotti." Morris Nunn's

operation converted two of the F1 cars to Indy car specification to gain income and keep people employed.

Bennett remembers that the Indy 'Theodore' – as Nunn's cars were now known following an association with Teddy Yip – was "... better than the Marches of the time." Only a solitary example was ever raced, and that on one occasion. The car was never developed but he believes that the design was potentially "pretty competitive." It was basically an adaptation of the F1 car, something made easy by the similarity of the Cosworth DFV and DFX engines, and using a March transverse gearbox. At this point Mario Andretti returns to the story. The Theodore was also very stiff, and caught the attention of Andretti and the Newman Haas team who were having problems with their all-aluminium construction Lola. The former Indy 500 winner, now back in Indy cars, was partially responsible in persuading Lola to take on his former race engineer when the latter left Ensign.

At Lola – then a cost orientated company and "... a big learning experience for me" – Bennett worked with, and was partly paid by, Newman Haas. This included race engineering, certainly at Indianapolis with his first 500 being the 1983 race. "I have a horrific memory of the amount of time wasted every year at Indianapolis. I used to loath it, not having enough to do for too many days, interspersed by engineering excitement. Getting meaningful testing done was very difficult, as every ten to fifteen laps the car had to pushed away from the pit to be refuelled, as pit refuelling was not allowed in practice."

Bruce Ashmore described the 1983 T700 as a "real dog" when it was first taken out. However, by the end of the year it had won at Elkhart Lake, "... which we achieved mainly by increasing the stiffness of the chassis and adding sealing and moulded carbon underwings." Ashmore believes that, during Lola's early days of wind tunnel use, "We did not really know if reducing the drag or adding downforce was going to make a car go faster, so we did a lot of testing. We often misled ourselves. The wind tunnels and the models weren't that good. There were a lot of cars at that time that just did not work and we built some at Lola." Even today, Lola founder Eric Broadley believes that, "There is a load of bullshit talked about wind tunnels."

Long time Lola employee Dave Scotney recalled how the T700 had to be rushed through. He, John Church, and Neil Marshall, who was in charge of Indy car assembly, had built a wooden monocoque identical to the car. Broadley walked round a corner into the secret area in which this was being created accompanied by Mario Andretti, who was expecting to see the real thing. "I hope it doesn't suffer from woodworm," said the American. Church was to take over assembly of the Indy cars from Marshall in 1989 until 1996. He usually attended Pole Day for the 500 but never the race itself. In fact, the trio recalled how none of them actually attended the race, but would watch it on the television in the Lola canteen.

For 1985 Lola produced a development of the previous year's T800. These, though, were the years in which March had a stranglehold on first place at the 500, and Andretti finished second. A rule change for 1986 left Lola, said Ashmore, "... with a black eye. We were in a real battle with March and Adrian Newey and Alan Mertens came up with a really nice car. We spent a lot of time with the regulations people and we thought we were on top of all the changes, which had been brought in to slow the cars down. Then we looked at the opposition and we were so far behind. Our car did not have enough downforce. It was big. It was heavy." Perhaps Bennett and Ashmore

learnt from that car; their battles in the years to come would indicate that they did so.

The 1987 car was "a complete make over." Bobby Rahal's team had joined the Lola camp and, while Bennett continued to work with Newman Haas, Ashmore looked after Rahal. The latter won the championship, while Andretti took the pole at Indianapolis, led most of the race but fell out when a valve spring broke.

Bennett, who was to be present at twelve Indy 500s, left Lola to set up his own Indy car design operation with Ray Wardle. A potential sponsor was in place but this fell through and he was head hunted to be chief designer for Penske, which had been experiencing limited success in recent years with its own designs. Bennett became a contractor for Penske, never actually being employed by the company. He was, with his leather patched sports jacket, in the words of Penske's Nick Goozee, "The last of the gentlemen designers."

Although one of his Lolas had won the 1985 championship, it was not until he joined the Poole-based company that Bennett was to design an Indy 500 winner; Rick Mears 1988 victory with the PC17 being the first of five for the Englishman. Bennett now regarded himself very much as a specialist Indy car designer. The PC17 was a logical development of everything that Bennett had learnt at Lola, including the basics such as suspension geometry and weight distribution. "I also always tried to make a car that looked reasonably pretty. I think that aesthetics are important. A good-looking car is right for morale among mechanics and the team."

Ashmore had taken over from Bennett as chief designer at Lola. "After three years working with him, I reckoned I knew the way he

A Lola T88 at Huntingdon. They proved slower than the Penskes. (Courtesy Lola Cars)

Bennett's Penskes have the best two places on the grid, thanks to Emerson Fittipaldi (1) and Rick Mears (2), though Arie Luyendyk (30) will give Ashmore the last laugh in 1990. (Courtesy Indianapolis Motor Speedway)

thought," said Ashmore but, for a while, this seemed to be to no avail. He confessed that he initially made the mistake of carrying on with a car that Bennett had started designing. Perhaps it is not surprising that Bennett and Penske came out on top at Indy that year. "We won some races with the T88/00 but everything revolved around Indy at that time, so you compromised on all the other tracks to make sure you were fast there. We had put everything into lowering the centre of gravity and making it stiffer and more reliable but we were slower than the Penskes," Ashmore recalled. The time carried out in the wind tunnel was, accordingly, increased for the 1989 car. "We lowered the centre of gravity further and made sure that there was less frictional drag by

working on the transmission, the wheel bearings, and the uprights. It was a little bit quicker than the previous year but the Penskes had moved up another step. So I then put everything into aerodynamics." The Lola T88/00 had featured a hypoid gearbox. "We got rid of the hypoid for 1989. It was a much better car but we were still behind the Penskes. I was playing catch up with those guys."

There were six Lolas in the top seven in 1989 – it was just that two laps ahead of the field was Emerson Fittipaldi's Penske. In the struggle for the Borg Warner Trophy the two camps worked with different design philosophies. One of Ashmore's leitmotifs had been to try and make a car with a minimum number of components. Wishbones, for instance, were generally non-handed. "I would force the design into being like that. I think this came from the time of drawing by hand. I also started in a machine shop so I knew how hard it was to setup and make a component. The fewer components, the shorter time that you needed to make the car or the fewer people that you needed to do so. You could get it on the track before anyone else and start testing it," said Ashmore. "I remember when Penske and Lolas used to line up together on the front row of the grid at Indianapolis, with almost exactly the same speeds. One year I caught Roger Penske examining our car. He looked down at the top wishbone and the brackets that held it onto the tub. He could see each bracket was the same piece and the lower wishbone brackets were similar to the top. He shook his head and then looked at the complexity of his car. Every wishbone bracket was different and the bolts were in at different angles. He just looked over at me and smiled."

For 1990, Ashmore "... sat down with Eric (Broadley) and we had a real brainstorm." The result was that the T90/00 was a major departure from the previous year's effort. Ashmore, understandably, described it as his favourite design, for it was the car with which he was at last to beat Bennett. "It won the pole and the fastest ever Indy 500 with Arie Luyendyk, and the championship with Al Unser Jr., but it was more than just that."

The T90/00 had the minimum chassis size – the side pods were minimum height and maximum width. The wheelbase was stretched to give more room for the components. The turbo was moved so that the engine cover was lower. Ashmore took out all the adjustment for the suspension geometry as this had been affecting the aerodynamics. It was a 100 per cent aerodynamic project. "The Indy 500 is fast so I decided we had to have the lowest drag and the most downforce.

"My driving force has always been aerodynamics. I would compromise anything for this. I would not worry about such as raising the centre of gravity or increasing the

Luyendyk leads Rocky Moran's older Lola and Al Unser Jr in another example of Ashmore's finest. (Courtesy Lola Cars)

ASHMORE'S GOLD CROWN

There is a certain irony in what Bruce Ashmore was up to towards the end of the 2000s. Traditionally, the route to the Indy 500 had been via the short oval tracks that abound throughout the US. Then the 1960s saw the start of a trend that has led to the vast majority of today's Indy car drivers coming up through road racing. There are a number of reasons for this, the British influence having been one. In the 1970s the (then USAC) national championship ceased being run over a variety of tracks from dirt to the Brickyard itself, becoming confined to the longer, paved ovals. That did not help. At the same time the British and Commonwealth drivers were showing how quickly they could adapt to the Indianapolis track. This was not surprising. It is less of an oval and more of four, linked road racing bends.

Proof of how the status quo changed can be seen by examining a list of winners for the Hoosier 100, which traditionally takes place just before the Indy 500 on the 1-mile dirt track at the Indiana State Fair Ground, not far north east of the Speedway. In the first twenty-two contests the race was won eighteen times by a driver who had or was to win the 500. Since then, very few of the winners have even contested the 500. At the 2009 Hoosier 100, a British presence lurked in the paddock. Bruce Ashmore was engineering the RW (Rotondo Weirich) Beast-Toyota of Shane Hmiel, and there was more to Ashmore's interest than just looking after one car.

Tony George's stated aim in launching the Indy Racing League was to bring the short track racers back to the Speedway. As such it failed. However, the dream is still there, and Ashmore's latest project is an attempt to provide a final and missing rung in a ladder that could bring American drivers back to the Indianapolis 500.

Ashmore has become series coordinator for the projected Gold Crown Championship, which, he claims, could be the answer to those who bemoan the dominance of the overseas drivers in the Indy Car Series. Gold Crown is to be part of a ladder system of open wheel racing for drivers aspiring to the Indy 500. Its cars are tube-framed, front-engined, solid axle, single-seaters, specially designed to race on both superspeedways and road courses – tradition combined with a modern look. The engines are to be the same 800hp V8s used by the Silver Crown cars that contest the Hoosier 100. Two examples were on display at the inaugural Indianapolis Motorsport Industry Show in December 2009.

After an initial meeting of potential owners, production of cars was announced with four different chassis constructors, including Bruce's own Ashmore Design. Testing and development was to follow in 2010 with a 10-race programme scheduled for the year after.

Ashmore engineered Shane Hmiel's Beast to third in the 2009 Hoosier 100 at the Indiana State Fairground. (Author's collection)

Two examples of Ashmore's Gold Crown cars made their debut at the 2009 International Motorsports Industry Show in Indianapolis. (Author's collection)

weight." You can see where the influence comes from. The last year of Ashmore's apprenticeship at Lola, 1980, was spent in the drawing office. The Lotus 79 had proved that ground effects were the way to go and "Aerodynamics had become the big thing." Lola had just started

to make use of the quarter-scale wind tunnel at Imperial College, London. "However, I did not worry so much about this with the 1990 Indy car. I had saved a lot of weight on the mechanical components but we had more bodywork so it was still a little bit overweight. The one-piece underwing was much stiffer and heavier. There were many gaps and leaks on the previous car so I designed this one so that all the suspension was on top of the underwing. It was such a big jump from the car before. It came out of the frustration of finishing second at Indy all the time," said Ashmore.

Ashmore's 1991 design was more reliable, with seven cars in the top eight at Indy. First place, though, looked strangely familiar, one of Bennett's Penskes, driven this time by Rick Mears. The suspension was moved for the 1992 Lola, thus making it easier to work on. "That was another year in which we should have won the 500. It was just above freezing and the tyres were like rocks," he said. There were some changes made for 1993 to meet new rules but all were essentially developments of the T90/00.

Following the Galmer victory of 1992, Bennett and Penske were back on top for 1993 with Fittipaldi again winning the 500. However, it is the following year's Penske PC23 that is one of Bennett's favourite designs. It swept the board in the championship. "We had extraordinarily good traction, so much so that the opposition accused us unfairly of having traction control." Using the Mercedes-Benz pushrod engine, it took the 500. The Mercedes version was, he said, a major design project on its own, without even taking into consideration the work that Ilmor did on the engine. It required different gearbox, radiators, and bodywork.

If there is any race that Bennett would prefer to forget it is the following season's Indianapolis 500. Having won so convincingly in 1994, the Penske team went testing at Indianapolis in high wind conditions. Nobody could exceed 212mph and "... our drivers were totally spooked by the wind." It was hardly a good start to the month of May. The previous year Fittipaldi had been almost a lap ahead of the field when he went low trying to lap eventual winner Al Unser Jr. He hit the apron white line and lost the back end ... and the race. For 1995 he had demanded a car that was not going to go loose on him on the ovals. "He asked me to design a front anti-roll bar for Phoenix that would be exceptionally stiff. He won the race and loved it. Then we went to Indianapolis with it and the car understeered, so we started putting on more and more front wing. All that did was to make the

Bennett describes the so-called 'stock-block' version of the Penske PC23 as a major design project in its own right. (Courtesy Indianapolis Motor Speedway)

Rahal returned to Lola for 1995, finishing third behind two Reynards. (Courtesy Lola Cars)

On the first qualifying day, Unser ran three of the four qualifying laps before Roger Penske, thinking that he was not going fast enough to make the grid, aborted the attempt. In retrospect, Bennett says that was a mistake because Unser's times on the first three laps were quick enough, and he would have qualified. During the second week Penske "... had lost faith in our ability to solve the problem." He duly purchased a Reynard "... and that didn't work too well either, so he borrowed two Lolas, but none of the drivers could qualify in anything. To me, that proved that they had been totally spooked by the whole situation."

Bennett recalled Penske asking him if he minded the team purchasing a Reynard, "... as he didn't think we had the time to get the Penske up to speed. I said I did but he bought one anyway! It was an horrific month." Paul Tracy was not with the team that year for Indianapolis but he came back and tested for the car at the Speedway, just after the end of the season. "We had a normal front bar on. He did 232mph and said, 'I can't see what your problem was.'"

Bennett regards himself as not being particularly creative but more of a developer; analysing what may have gone wrong and drivers' feedback and then working out where he could improve the car – a one step at a time approach. During his time with Penske, his work on a new car would start around April or May with an extensive wind tunnel programme at Southampton University. "This took up about eighteen weeks in the year, which was a contrast to when I was at Lola when we had a very restricted wind tunnel programme. The wind tunnel was the basis of Penske's research at that time. The overall programme was well organised with a set date being decided early on for the car's delivery." It was a goal that, Bennett believes was rightly set – leading to much discussion between design team and management. Generally, the car would be delivered to the airport on time but it meant

Lola versus Reynard in 1995. Scott Pruett in the latest from Huntingdon leads Stefan Johansson in a year-old car from Bicester. (Courtesy Lola Cars)

car loose on entry, and still have the exit understeer. It seems amazing now that we didn't get to grips with the problem but days lost to bad weather and reliability problems meant less running and the drivers no longer had any confidence."

that the team had to be very structured with its design and build programme, with weekly production meetings. "It worked pretty well."

Following a final involvement with Indy car racing as a consultant to G-Force, where John Biddlecombe recalled, "He was an absolute pleasure to work with," Bennett retired to the Dorset countryside, not far from Penske Cars' former premises. Ashmore meanwhile, had left Lola after seventeen years. Straight after the 1993 500 he had moved to Reynard. Adrian Reynard and Chip Ganassi had joined forces as Reynard North America, the idea being to give the British company (yet another located in Bicester) a stable base in the US. Reynard – who had first been taken to Indianapolis by his father in 1964, touring the track in a minibus – was introduced to Ashmore at the 1993 500, and the pair agreed to catch up in England. Reynard recalled that, at the subsequent meeting in The Green Man pub near Silverstone, he was flattered to learn that Ashmore was willing to work with his company.

Ashmore's actual task was to run Reynard North America – as well as test with Michael Andretti – working for Ganassi. In addition, while Australian Malcolm Oastler designed the bodywork and chassis for the new Reynard Indy Car, Ashmore was responsible for the suspension geometry. The pair had complementary talents and eventually worked well together. Carl Haas slapped in a lawsuit, which came to nothing, claiming that Ashmore had appropriated Newman Haas intellectual information. It was settled by Ashmore simply writing a letter. It was

at this point that he moved to Indianapolis to live. "I had been flying across the Atlantic twenty to twenty-five times a year, and never with the family. I really liked America, and I wanted to get closer to the development."

In 2010 Ashmore underlined his commitment to the city when, in association with fellow British-born IndyCar winning designers, Alan Mertens and Tim Wardrop, he announced the BAT project. This was the fifth – including Lola and Brit Ben Bowlby's DeltaWing – bid submitted to the IRL to create the IndyCar of 2012. The experience behind the project was impressive. The skills were also complimentary, with Mertens known for his mechanical design ability and Ashmore for his aero work. If successful in its bid, BAT stated that it would design and build the entire car within a 30-mile radius of the Indianapolis Motor Speedway. The team was also working on a further plan to expand the race car industry that once thrived in the area.

Reynard kept up its ability to win first time out in a new formula when one of its Cosworth XB-engined cars came first at Surfers Paradise. However, at Indianapolis Jacques Villeneuve could only finish second to a Penske. It must have been déjà vu for Ashmore. Adrian Reynard recalled that his company had prepared well for Indy

The year 1996 was the last in which the whole field was built in the UK. Buddy Lazier's Reynard led home Davy Jones' Lola, both 1995 models. One of the Lolas in a lacklustre field even went back to 1992. (Courtesy Indianapolis Motor Speedway)

NIGEL BERESFORD

"Out of the blue" in the October of 1991, Tyrrell Formula One race engineer Nigel Beresford received a letter from Penske Cars' Nick Goozee saying that he had heard he might be interested in working in America. The result was that he became Rick Mears' engineer for the 1992 season, running him in the 500 that year, and Paul Tracy in 1993 and 1994.

Beresford, the son of former Lola and McLaren mechanic Don Beresford, and Tracy were absent from Penske for 1995, the Englishman having returned to Tyrrell. However, when Tracy went back the following season he asked for Beresford. The split had by now occurred, so that meant no Indianapolis 500 for a while but Beresford soon became head of engineering at Penske Cars' Poole operation, and then technical director.

Penske returned to the race in 2001 but it was not until 2007 that Beresford found himself back there, engineering Ryan Briscoe for the Luczo Dragon team, which was basically a Penske satellite operation, part owned by Roger Penske's son, Jay. In 2008, Beresford missed the 500, being wholly involved on Penske's ALMS Porsche project. In 2009 Penske ran three cars again, and Beresford returned to engineer Will Power. "Indianapolis represents the biggest challenge in race engineering," he observed.

While most of Indy's British engineers have relocated to the US, Beresford has continued to live in Dorset, England, a long-distance "commuter."

Nigel Beresford outside the former Penske Cars premises in Poole. (Author's collection)

Car racing, so it had not been a surprise when it won its first race in the series. He admitted that, because of this, it was perhaps more of a shock to him when his cars failed to win their first 500, beaten by the appearance of the Mercedes-Benz pushrod engine.

Reynard realised that he needed to concentrate on the Indy programme if he was to win the 500, so, like Ashmore, he "... exported my family to America." He bought a house in Noblesville, just north of Indianapolis, from Derek Daly and "... made a commitment to ensure that we weren't beaten again the next year." He made sure that he understood not only the setup of the Speedway but also all of the teams. "Thus when we started 1995 we felt we were better prepared, although the race is still a lottery."

In 1995 Canadian Villeneuve went one place better than the previous season, winning the 500 for Players-Team Green ahead of fellow Reynard driver Christian Fittipaldi. Other than the British themselves, it was the first time that a driver from the Commonwealth of Nations had won the race. Reynard watched the race from the Turn One grandstands accompanied by his parents and in-laws. Then came the IRL/CART split but there was one last hurrah for the Bicester firm. For its first year the IRL ran existing CART-style Reynard 951s and Lola T500/00s, and with Reynard again present, Buddy Lazier, fighting the effects of a back injury, came first in a 951 entered by Ron Hemelgarn.

In 1996, to demonstrate his commitment to Indianapolis, Reynard became responsible for the building of an open jet wind tunnel there; the pioneering Auto Research Center. At the time there was only one other moving ground wind tunnel in the US. The tunnel was instantly successful, and it was not long before the teams wanted to make use of it. Reynard reckons that the wind tunnel models his company made constituted its second highest production run.

Reynard, by then, was working with Tony George's technical team on the transition to IRL formula cars, designing a common engine interface. However, it made better business sense to stay with Champ Car, and so 1996 was the last time that either Reynard or his cars attended the 500. The familiar British manufacturers had all left the scene and in 1997 it would be up to a "new boy on the block."

19

THE WORLD CHAMPION –
NIGEL MANSELL

"It is still the craziest accident I have ever had ..."

By the early 1990s the drivers may have mainly been in British cars but most of them were American. Then out of Europe there came another Englishman. This was not any Brit but the reigning World Champion, Nigel Mansell. If the 500 had again become parochial after the excitement of the 1960s, it was now being thrust back into the World spotlight. "Nigel ..." recalled Bruce Ashmore, "... raised the game."

Unable to agree a deal with Williams, despite having just won the 1992 Formula One World Championship for the team, the forthright Englishman had decided to accept an offer from Carl Haas to join the Indy Car operation that Haas owned with actor Paul Newman. Retirement was being considered by Mansell, who had recently moved to a new home in Florida, but he could see the possibility of making history. Just before the Portuguese Grand Prix, he signed for the American team and then went on to win the race at Estoril, scoring enough points to give him the record for a single season.

"The Newman Haas team was a great one," recalled Mansell. Perhaps his greatest memory of that time was "having fun" with Newman, who he describes as having been "motivational." However, Mansell believes that it was not all plain sailing for the team. "Mario (Andretti, his team-mate at Newman Hass) was under great pressure with (his son) Michael racing for McLaren in Formula One. I was winning the championship in America while Michael (who he believes was a much more accomplished driver than his brief F1 record indicates) was having a bad time of it in Europe. I believe it was tough for Mario to see me as his team-mate."

Four British World Champions have raced in the Indianapolis 500; (from the front of painting) Nigel Mansell, Jim Clark, Graham Hill, and Jackie Stewart. (Original painting by R S Day – reproduced by kind permission of *Bodyshop Magazine*)

Even before he had arrived at Indianapolis, Mansell had made his mark on the Indy Car scene. He took the first round of the PPG Indy Car World Series. Maybe that was not so surprising; it was on a street circuit, Surfers Paradise, and he was, after all, the reigning world

Prior to his arrival at Indianapolis, Nigel Mansell had established himself as one of the leading Grand Prix drivers of the era. (Author's collection)

champion. He was also on Commonwealth territory, the Australian race being the only round of the so-called 'World' series to be held outside North America. The last time a driver had won on his debut in an Indy Car race had been that other Englishman, Graham Hill, at Indianapolis in 1966.

Phoenix was Mansell's first ever oval race meeting and he crashed heavily in practice, having to miss the event. It was, perhaps, an unusual start for a man who was to dominate the ovals that year. "When I asked A J Foyt for advice on how to race on an oval he said, 'Boy, don't turn right. Yaw'll eat concrete.' A J was very helpful, as was Rick Mears who told me that there were two types of oval driver, those that had hit the wall and those that were going to." Mansell believes, though, that most of the American drivers "... did not want outsiders coming in and competing with them." Now, he observes, it is very different.

Injured or not, Mansell was back for Long Beach, finishing an exhausted third. Then came Indianapolis. "It was very, very different. It was a superspeedway but with little banking, so unlike Michigan where I was to win the 500 mile later in the year. I was impressed by just how many fans could be seated around the circuit.

"It was very technical. You even had to look at the flags on the

Mansell; 1993 – still every inch an Englishman but now an Indy car driver. (Courtesy British Racing Drivers Club)

corners to see which way the wind was blowing. You did not want to go barrelling into a corner at 240mph and get oversteer or understeer that you were not ready for. You really had to gather a lot of information before you even went out on the track."

May started well for Mansell. Back surgery brought about by the crash at Phoenix caused him to miss the first few days of practice but, on his first day at the track, he was quickly up to speed in his Kmart/Texaco Havoline Lola, achieving the fourth fastest time. Qualifying was a little disappointing, and his average of

MORRIS NUNN

Morris Nunn, christened 'Mo' by the press, had raced in Formula Two and Three before founding race car constructor Ensign in 1970. A line of successful cars was followed by a move into Formula One for the 1973 season. Over the next decade, those such as Chris Amon, Jacky Ickx, and Clay Regazzoni were to drive Ensigns – a best result being fourth at the 1981 Brazilian Grand Prix.

Ties with financier Teddy Yip led to Ensign being merged with his Theodore team for 1983 and using the Theodore name. That year the company built a Nigel Bennett-designed Indy car for Bignotti-Cotter. The team also had Marches, and Tom Sneva proved slightly quicker in one of these. His times in the Nunn-built car would have easily put him on the grid as well, but the March was chosen. Sneva went on to win. At the end of 1983 Nunn parted company with Yip. He decided to go to Phoenix for the last race of the year. There, he was offered a job with the Bignotti-Cotter team – well paid he was surprised to find – the idea being that he would bring his road racing experience to the operation. However, he was to find that he often clashed with George Bignotti, and in 1985 he returned to work with Theodore on an Indy car project, which, through lack of funding, never really got off the ground.

In 1986, Nunn was back in the US to work for Newman Haas Racing and Mario Andretti. "But I could not stand to stay in Chicago during the winter." He also found the Italian-American difficult to work with, and left at the end of the year. (Andretti did, however, call him a while later and ask if he would go back.) Now, with a reputation for being able to sort out an Indy car, Nunn was approached by Patrick Racing to oversee Emerson Fittipaldi. The pair had raced together in the 1960s and quickly gelled. The result was victory for the revived Brazilian, in both the Indianapolis 500 and CART Championship for 1989. "He was the opposite to Mario," in the way that he listened to his engineer. "Just drive the car, tell me how you can't go quicker and I'll fix it," Nunn said.

Nunn recalled Pat Patrick instructing the crew to unnecessarily fill up Fittipaldi's tank at the final pit stop. "I wondered what was going on. I went berserk." Patrick apologised, admitting that he was nervous. Al Unser Jr was able to catch and pass a puzzled Fittipaldi who felt that he must be down on power. "We didn't tell him that he was full of gas. I don't know if he knows to this day," said Nunn. The Brazilian did not, though, give up and, with 'Little Al' spinning on the last lap, won the race in his Ilmor-engined Penske, full tank or not.

Patrick was to sell his team to Chip Ganassi, and went on in partnership with Nunn and Jim McGee to run the unfortunate Alfa Romeo programme using March chassis. From there, Nunn went, himself, to Ganassi, staying with the team for eight years, during which he oversaw four consecutive, post-split CART titles.

"I was going to retire after the 1999 season but Mercedes came to me and said would I start a (CART) team." When the three-year Mercedes deal came to an end, Mo Nunn Racing switched to Honda, and then Toyota. In 2002 he was back at the Speedway, having decided to run one car in Champ Car and the other in the IRL. Driving a G-Force for Nunn, Felipe Giaffone led that year's 500 briefly on four occasions, before coming home third. The following year, Mo Nunn Racing returned with two Panoz G-Forces for Giaffone and Tora Takagi, the team finally running at the 500 in 2004 with Jeff Simmons. By this time Nunn, as owner, was no longer engineering the cars himself. The team disbanded after 2005, although Nunn continued to be involved for a while as a technical advisor to Target Chip Ganassi Racing.

Having closed his own team, Morris Nunn became a technical advisor to Target Chip Ganassi Racing. (Courtesy Target Chip Ganassi Racing/Getty Images)

220.255mph could only put him on the third row of the grid.

In the early stages nothing indicated this was Mansell's first oval race, although he did over shoot his pit on a scheduled stop. By lap 174 he was running in third, then pulling off the manoeuvre of the race when he surged past former World Champions Mario Andretti and Emerson Fittipaldi for the lead.

The fairy tale, though, did not happen and Mansell is happy to point out that how he lost that lead was down to inexperience. How he was put in that position is another matter. Lyn St James stopped at the entrance to the pit

**Mansell's arrival at Indianapolis caused a media stir.
(Courtesy Indianapolis Motor Speedway)**

The Englishman's own take on what happened is thus: "Indianapolis had a different governing body then with its own rules, which you had to learn about ... and how it imposed them. Fair play did not always come into it. I went there twice, and both times was affected by yellow flags. They threw one when Lyn St James was in the pit lane. What had that got to do with what was going on out on the circuit ... except perhaps a rookie was out there winning the 500? I got jumped on the restart with a few laps to go. It was very disappointing to see the footage played back. There was no reason to put out a full course yellow, it was nonsense. However, you can't fight the system, it is what it is."

It should be pointed out that Mansell does add that, during his time in Indy Car, "The officials, by and large, and apart from a couple, were good."

lane and the yellows came out. Fittipaldi and Arie Luyendyk, then in second and third places, were old hands at this restart business, and Mansell stood little chance when the race turned to green.

Mansell continued to push, and even sideswiped the retaining wall on the exit of Turn Two. He got away with just leaving a black

**Mansell immediately took to the Speedway.
(Courtesy Indianapolis Motor Speedway)**

A year later and Mansell's Lola now bears the number one of the reigning champion. (Courtesy Lola Cars)

mark on the wall and finished in a fighting third place. 'Rookie of the Year' can be a strange term at Indianapolis. Mansell took the honour that year. Three true Brits have won it; Mansell was the reigning World Champion at the time, Jim Clark was in his first Championship winning year, while even Jackie Stewart was a Grand Prix winner when he took said prize.

From now on Mansell won every oval race of 1993, finishing the season as Indy Car champion. It was arguably the most successful 'rookie' season in Indy Car history. "Winning the CART Championship the year after the World Championship was something very special," he recalled. Mansell even believes that he changed driver thinking with regard to overtaking on the outside on an oval. One commentator observing that Mansell was attempting such a manoeuvre, stated that it was not possible to do so. His fellow commentator pointed out that he just had. "I wouldn't recommend it ..." said Mansell, "... but you had to do it if you were a true racer."

Mansell could not carry his momentum into the following year, in which three pole positions were the sum of his achievements. Looking back over the two years, though, he observes, "It was a great experience that I feel richer for doing. It was definitely something special."

The Indianapolis 500 was arguably the nadir of his 1994 season. Mansell can also be pretty forthright about what happened that year. Having qualified in seventh spot, he had gone a lap down by the ninety-second tour; the reason was that he had been given a stop-and-go-penalty for illegally passing Raul Boesel in the pit lane during the first round of stops. It is something that he still questions. The alleged infringement took place right at the end of the pit lane. He and Eddie Cheever were already up to speed when Boesel was just starting to accelerate from his stall. As Mansell said at the time, he was faced with the choice of overtaking him or braking hard and causing an accident.

Following the penalty, Mansell became the fastest man on the track. When the yellows came out for an incident in Turn One it was an opportunity to make up that lost lap, but instead it turned out very differently, for the most bizarre of reasons. As the cars slipped into the pit entry lane on the inside of

"We weren't even on the race track!" (Courtesy Indianapolis Motor Speedway)

Turn Three, so rookie Dennis Vitolo misjudged his speed. His Lola hit the left rear wheel of John Andretti's similar car and flew through the air backwards, narrowly missing a couple of other cars, before landing

159

on Mansell's engine cover. The Englishman leapt from his Lola to be enveloped by a fire marshal. How he subsequently reacted – storming off before the doctors could finish their examination – is said to have won him little sympathy from the local fans but you have to see his point. "Your heart goes out to Mansell," said one of the commentators over the airwaves.

Even today, the incident still rankles. "What was so disgusting was that Vitolo caused an accident when we had already done a lap under full course yellow, and we weren't even on the race track but on part of the infield. He did not slow down enough, hit the car in front of him, went airborne, and then landed on top of me. There's one thing to have a racing incident under green but another to have a horrendous accident when you are following a pace car. It is still the craziest accident I have ever had in my life. It leaves you stunned."

Mansell never went back to Indy. Vitolo did just once, qualifying twenty-eighth on the mainly lacklustre grid of 1997 and eventually finishing a troubled fifteenth, still running but twenty-seven laps behind the winner.

Mansell in 2009 getting ready to return to racing. (Author's collection)

Mansell never went back to the Speedway after Vitolo ended his 1995 race, but the American did return in 1997. (Author's collection)

JOHN MANCHESTER

John Manchester thought that he was going out to Indianapolis in 1985 to look after drivetrains for Dick Simon Racing. It was a logical assumption, given that he had been working for Alan Smith Engines for around six years. However, on arrival he found that he was to be a complete mechanic, something of a proverbial baptism of fire given that he had never worked on race car chassis before. Not long prior to the Indianapolis 500 it got worse. "By the way ...," he was told, "... you will be changing wheels during the race."

"I had never held a wheel gun before," he recalled. "I remember kneeling there, waiting for the car to come in. I remember how it came to a stop and how the brake dust fell away, but I really do not remember actually changing the wheel. I felt so on show and that everybody in the grandstand must be looking at me."

Manchester had come out to Indianapolis on the recommendation of a former colleague at Alan Smith's, Barry Foulds. He was based to the west of the Speedway, in Clermont near Simon's workshop, and was made to feel at home by visits to the Union Jack bar with such as Foulds, Morris Nunn, and Formula One designer Gary Anderson, who was then chief engineer for the Galles team. "We drank what was claimed to be British beer, but it obviously wasn't."

Manchester was impressed by the sheer size of the Speedway, and by the way the crowd could actually sound out over the engines. He had the opportunity to stay on in the US but, with wife Hazel employed in England, he made his way back to Alan Smith's at the end of the season, staying on when the company was acquired by Zytek Engineering and becoming the company's operations director.

In 2009, Mansell made a surprise return to the circuits driving the Team LNT Zytek LMP1 at the Silverstone 1000km. The following season, Beechdean Mansell Motorsport was formed and an entry for the Le Mans 24-hours was accepted for Mansell and his sons, Greg and Leo, driving a similar car. A slow puncture just four laps into the race caused Mansell Sr to crash sideways into the wall on the fast section between the Mulsanne and Indianapolis corners. He was taken to the medical centre for checks and, therefore, although the Zytek was not badly damaged, he was unable to drive it back to the pits to carry out the necessary repairs, thus forcing retirement. (Author's collection)

PART FOUR

1997 to the present – The Indy Racing League era

20

EFFECTS OF THE INDY RACING LEAGUE

"Telling the world was quite bizarre."

The year 1996 saw the infamous 'split' in US open wheel racing with the formation of the Indy Racing League (IRL). The CART series would no longer include the Indianapolis 500 schedule, and so ceases to be of relevance to this tale. The politics do not concern it either, but what arguably does is the effect that it had on British entries. One of the then Indianapolis boss Tony George's intentions was to reverse the trend started by the Brits back in the 1960s, and make the 500 once again the preserve of American drivers brought up on the short ovals. In this he ultimately failed – 2009's record number of British drivers being just one example of this.

What the spilt did do was bring an end to the long-standing domination of the Indy 500 by British chassis. In 1996, all the cars were manufactured in England. The following year the number was down to fourteen, although the first three spots were still taken by UK-built cars. By 2008, every single car would be Italian.

The first year of the IRL was a liminal one. The formula's new cars were not yet ready and so the field comprised a hotch potch of Champ Car spec Lolas and Reynards. From the British

Two thirds of the front row in 1997 were G-Forces, with Arie Luyendyk (5) and Tony Stewart (2) taking the first two spots. (Author's collection)

163

1997 was the first year for a long time that less than half the field had been built in Britain. Nevertheless, fourteen were G-Forces. (Author's collection)

point of view, its only real significance was that it was the final time these highly successful makes competed at the Speedway. Victory went, for the second year running, to a Reynard. For a ninth time, a Lola filled second spot. There was one other relevance for the British. Entrant Bill Tempero dropped his original driver, David Kudrave, in favour of Justin Bell, the son of multi-Le Mans winner Derek Bell, who was also present at the track. However, the Englishman was unable to get his four year old Lola into the field. On the Thursday before final qualifying, he announced that there just was not enough time to find a competitive ride and pass his rookie test. That year's *Indianapolis Year Book* quoted him as saying, "This is how my week has been. It's a bit like Michelle Pfeiffer knocking on your motel door and then saying, 'Oops, wrong room!'" Father Derek recalled two "painful days" watching the younger Bell trying to crack 200mph as his turbochargers kept blowing. He admitted to not having been too upset when his son withdrew.

The IRL set down the design for its new formula and authorised three manufacturers to build the chassis. All were new to the Speedway. In fact, the British member of the trio, G-Force, was new to most people, although it had worked on Thrust SSC; Andy Green's supersonic World Land Speed Record-breaker. There was also a British involvement in one of the others, Mark Scott being a director of the Riley & Scott operation. However, that marque was only to be represented twice in the 500, both times with singleton entries.

G-Force evolved out of the demise of Onyx Formula One. During 1990 a number of its former employees became Chip Ganassi Racing Ltd – a research and development facility established in Fontwell, West Sussex, England – initially to work on Ganassi's Indy Car Lolas. When Ganassi changed to Reynard it was felt that the operation was no longer needed. Thus, in 1992 it broke away to become G-Force with John Biddlecombe, Simon Kingdom-Butcher, and James Morton as the directors, carrying out subcontract fabrication work for Formula One teams. The subsequent involvement with Thrust SSC enabled the company to grow. One of the other founders, Ken Anderson, returned in 1996 having been working on the rules package for the new IRL car, and, with Lola and Reynard seemingly uninterested in a cost cap formula, G-Force was invited to pitch to the new organisation. With funding coming up front from the Speedway's owner, Tony George, ex-Penske Cars fabricator Biddlecombe did not have to think long before agreeing to become a manufacturer. Anderson became technical director. (Eric Broadley recalled that the advent of the IRL "spoilt the business" for Lola. The company had, in fact, pitched to become one of the IRL's chassis suppliers but Broadley came under much opposition from his US distributor, Carl Haas, who was firmly in the CART camp. "So, I backed off.")

"Telling the world – on April 1 – was quite bizarre," recalled Biddlecombe. "Who is G-Force," asked a member of the media. "We've never heard of them." Long time Indy entrant Dick Simon

LES MACTAGGART

One of the leading figures throughout the years of the IRL has been Englishman Les Mactaggart. He had been a principal engineer with British Leyland up to 1979, subsequently joining March as project manager for its sports cars and then for the Indy cars, producing the 83C through to the 88C. In 1988 he joined the Leyton House F1 team as factory manager. Two years later, he became part of a design manufacturing company, working with Robin Herd, Tim Holloway, and Tino Belli. Their first customer was Fondmetal in 1990, followed by Larousse. In 1995/6 the company carried out development work for the Forsythe Champ Car team.

In 1996 Mactaggart was mowing the lawn in his backyard. His wife came out to tell him, "There's a man called Tony George on the phone for you." George informed him that he was having cars built in the UK and Italy for a new series, the Indy Racing League, and he did not know whether he would have enough in time for the first race at Walt Disney World. "If you are not too busy, would you mind overseeing the operation?" Mactaggart took this on a part-time basis, working as technical consultant liaising with G-Force and Dallara on the regulations for the following years. The arrangement continued up to 2005 with Mactaggart commuting from the UK to every race. As the season became more condensed, this became a problem, so the family decided to relocate and Mactaggart assumed the role of senior technical director. His tasks included running the technical inspection process for both Indy Cars and Indy Lights, and the production of the rule book, as well as working on the technical strategy for the future. With major changes scheduled to the IndyCar formula, it was a pivotal role.

Les Mactaggart was mowing his lawn when the call came from Tony George. (Author's collection)

Part of Mactaggart's work at the IRL has been to ensure that drivers are now far safer in the event of a crash. The construction of the cars has been improved to this end and a SAFER (Steel and Foam Energy Reduction) crash barrier installed at the Speedway. (Author's collection)

certainly had, and was able to reply positively before Biddlecombe even had a chance. It was going to be difficult to promote a company that had never built a race car before, especially as its main rival was going to be the highly experienced Italian firm, Dallara. However, George ensured that the orders were split evenly.

In the run up to the first race of 1997, G-Force and Dallara played cat and mouse with design, the British manufacturer arriving at Walt Disney World, Orlando with a well-made, lighter car, thus enabling its teams to use ballast. A lock-out of the podium at the opening race for G-Force saw one of the leading Dallara teams, that of A J Foyt, immediately change ship. (Biddlecombe took every employee to that race as a reward for hard work, although all of them had to carry parts.) It was the beginning of an excellent year for G-Force;

with Arie Luyendyk heading Scott Goodyear and Scottish-born Jeff Ward at the rain delayed 500 for a G-Force one, two, three. The IRL championship also fell to G-Force driver, Tony Stewart. It should have been plain sailing from then on but commercial pressures were at work and Stewart's team owner, John Menard, purchased Dallaras for the next season on cost. Not as financially sound as the well-established Italian firm, G-Force cold not match the price. It was the beginning of Dallara's eventual stranglehold on the series and the end of British pre-eminence. It would take a while, though, and there were still three more G-Force Indy 500 victories to come, Juan Pablo Montoya's win in 2000 temporarily re-uniting Ganassi with the Sussex operation. Anderson had now left G-Force and Paul Burgess had become chief designer, with Nigel Bennett acting as consultant.

There have, effectively, been three generations of the G-Force/Panoz design.
(Courtesy Elan Motorsport Technologies)

2004. By now, though, the cars had lost their British identity. In 2002 the design office, while staying in the UK, had moved to Kimbolton, Cambridgeshire with Simon Marshall designing the 2003 version. However, the Fontwell base was closed down. In early 2003, a few of the carbon tubs were manufactured in the UK by SPA Design but these were then shipped to Elan Motorsports in Braselton, Georgia, where the finished cars were assembled. Elan's chief design engineer, Andrew Kendon, pointed out that, although the company is American, there was a strong British presence in the factory, with at the time over sixty per cent of the production employees being British nationals, with a mix of former G-Force and Lola employees. Biddlecombe left in 2005 and G-Force's old premises were taken over by his and Kingdom-Butcher's new company, Global Technologies Racing.

For 2003 the name of the cars was changed to G-Force Panoz. Two years later the name was simply Panoz; the cars were now truly American and so drop from our story. It may be that they were the final Indy cars to have been built in Britain, the last of a long line that included twenty-five winners over a period of thirty-five years. In February 2010, the IRL issued a statement that it was considering designs from four companies for the 2012 season. One of these was three times winner Lola, which said it had presented a "total solutions package" to the IRL Board. Its design focused on safety, engine adaptability, and weight reduction, with a proposed 1380lb against the then current Dallara's 1540lb. Head of special projects Peter McCool's team was also suggesting a dual-bodystyle approach, with two aero performance balanced cars using a common chassis, which should be able to compete in close formation. Different engines could be used for both styles, while the chassis could also be adapted for Indy Lights. The company had additionally looked at a number of futuristic options, suggesting that the best might be deferred to appear "as a next iteration option."

Even if Lola had won the contract, the cars would not have been manufactured in Huntingdon. One of the IRL's stipulations was that they would have to be "built in the US, preferably at an Indiana-based facility." In the event the contract to build the chassis was awarded to the incumbent Dallara, although other firms were invited to provide aerodynamic kits for the cars.

The sole aerodynamicist on that 2000 Indy 500 winning G-Force was Dominic Piers Smith, straight out of Imperial College. By coincidence he had replaced another Dominic Smith in the post. Although the younger Smith had been involved in a project for the Ferrari F1 team at Imperial, this was his first real job, and he was given "almost a blank sheet of paper." He immediately found a loophole in the rules. Twenty-five cars had been built before the IRL objected to his interpretation and the twenty-five had to be rebuilt. The design took a performance hit because of this, but still proved successful, and Smith was at Indianapolis to see his creation win first time there – "a massive experience" for one so new to the business. With the G-Force operation likely to move to the USA, Formula One beckoned, and Smith joined what was then BAR, going on to lead its aerodynamics team as it became the World Championship winning Brawn operation, and then Mercedes GP, as well as finding the time to be a concert pianist and be featured in *BBC Music Magazine*.

G-Force was on its way to losing its British identity. Don Panoz' Elan Motorsports Technologies Group had bought the company, although the founding trio still had key executive roles. In 2003, Biddlecombe was concerned that the IRL wanted a third manufacturer, and Lola nearly came on board but was unable to agree terms. G-Force had another couple of decent years with Gil de Ferran winning the 500 for Penske in 2003 and Buddy Rice for Rahal-Letterman in

G-Force's first appearance at the 500 had also seen the debut of a notable Glasgow-born driver, Jeff Ward. (Ward's family had moved to America when he was about two-years old, landing up at Rotondo Beach, California knowing nobody.) The others who hailed from Scotland, Clark, Stewart, Crawford, and Franchitti, all made their names on four wheels but Ward was different. Long before his

John Biddlecombe still operates from G-Force's old Fontwell premises. (Author's collection)

appearance at the Speedway he had established himself as a peerless motocross rider and was to become the first to win every major AMA national championship.

During his time in motocross Ward became friendly with Paul Tracy, accompanying him one time to the 500 when Tracy was driving for Penske. When the time came to, initially, retire from motocross, Ward still felt that he wanted to race and Indy Cars seemed "... the obvious route" to take. At the end of 1992 he purchased an Indy Lights car and, with Tracy's assistance, entered that championship, running in it up to and including 1996. His Indy Lights team in 1995, Arizona Motorsports, had run Al Unser Sr in practice for the 500 the year before with an old Lola, which was still in the workshop. The decision was made to take the car to rookie orientation and to give Ward some track time at the Speedway. Arizona Motorsports was based at Indianapolis and there were still miles on the engine, so it was not going to cost the team much. At that point Ward had only participated in between twenty-five and thirty car races. There were some impressive rookies that year but he "felt pretty good," so the decision was made that he should attempt to qualify for the big race. "I wasn't really mentally ready for it. It was a lot of pressure but I think it was a good step in my career. I was able to feel what Indy was all about." On bubble day he was right in the action, although feeling that perhaps he should not be there, given that this was the year when the Penskes were even failing to qualify. "We didn't make it but in hindsight that was probably good because I did not have the experience to run in the race. The pressure was never the same as that first year."

While Ward could see no opening in CART, the launch of the IRL did have possibilities. Former Grand Prix driver Eddie Cheever was looking to run a second car in the 1997 500 and Ward had some funding, so a deal was worked out. It was not, though, to be his first IRL race. In Florida, and with his racing kit for the following week's Daytona 24-hours, Ward decided to attend the season opener at Walt Disney World. "I was just hanging around when Davy Jones had his big crash." Car owner Rick Galles asked Ward if he could take over his G-Force for the next day. "I hadn't had any practice so they gave me eight laps before the qualifying." Impressively, he qualified eighth out of the nineteen starters. He then ran near the head of the field before clutch problems intervened. Hopes of staying with the team were dashed when the more experienced Kenny Brack came along with sponsorship. The next race would, therefore, be the Indy 500 with FirstPlus Team Cheever.

Ward had to wait a little longer to start his first 500 than expected. As the beginning of the race drew near, a B2 Stealth bomber flew the length of the main straight. With dark clouds looming just above it, it was a menacing sight. Then those clouds dropped their load and the race was postponed for twenty-four hours. On the Monday, just fifteen laps were run before heavy rain returned. It would be the Tuesday before 200 laps could be completed. "The anticipation was painful," recalled Ward. Having qualified in seventh position, following a practice crash caused by an oil leak, he had already moved up a few spots during those aborted fifteen laps. "It's a nerve wracking place, anyway."

Following the restart, Ward quickly got into groove, his G-Force "... feeling comfortable all day." On lap 142 he took the lead, losing it to Arie Luyendyk but then reclaiming it on lap 169. For twenty-four more laps he headed the field. His fuel adjuster was not working, though, and it was impossible to lean the engine out to save fuel. The others were conserving fuel while Ward went off "like a rabbit." On lap 193 he pitted, the hope being that others would have to do the same. Yellows enabled the Treadway Racing G-Forces of Luyendyk and Scott Goodyear to stay out and, as they went nose to tail for the chequered

One of Lola's concept sketches for the IndyCar of 2012. (Courtesy Lola Cars)

TIM WARDROP

Former March, Williams, McLaren, Wolf, and ATS development and design engineer Tim Waldrop is one of the most experienced of all the British to have engineered at the Speedway. Between 1985 and 2007 he acted as a dedicated race engineer at no fewer than twenty-three Indianapolis 500s, a record number for a Brit.

Chichester-born Wardrop's first involvement with the race was working on Gordon Johncock's 1982 winning Wildcat, the last victory by an American-built car. During his latter years at March he worked exclusively on Indy cars and was contracted as race engineer to the Kraco Racing, Gurney/Curb Racing, Hemelgarn, and Porsche Motorsport teams; his final project with the company having been with the Porsche-engined March 89P. For two seasons he carried out design and development at Galmer Engineering, undertaking some of the initial work on what was to become the 1992 winning Galmer G92. However, he was head-hunted by Derrick Walker and Porsche in 1990, to try and sort out the March-Porsche 90P that had been designed during his time away from the Bicester-based manufacturer. It was, he recalled, "probably the worst racing car I had ever seen."

With Walker and Gordon Coppuck he then formed Adrem Engineering, which was based at the former March Engineering facility. During this time he was contracted out as race engineer for Derrick Walker's eponymous Indy Car team. As such, he worked with Will T Ribbs when he became the first Afro-American to start the Indianapolis 500, and with Scott Goodyear the year he came so tantalisingly close to winning the race, pipped by that Galmer. Ribbs' qualification for the 1991 race gave Wardrop "... the most pleasure. It was my finest hour."

A highly successful relationship with Arie Luyendyk began in 1995 when Wardrop engineered the Dutch driver and Scott Brayton at Team Menard. The pair qualified second and first respectively for the Indy 500 that year. Wardrop then went with Luyendyk to Treadway Racing, during which time the Dutchman set the all-time single-lap and four-laps qualifying and practice lap records, the latter at 239.26mph, twice put the car on pole, and also scored his second 500 victory. "People used to say that Arie and I must be brothers," said Wardrop.

That win in 1997 had been with a G-Force, and Wardrop went on to become technical director of the manufacturer's IRL programme. That meant his involvement in another Indy 500 win in his role as technical consultant/race engineer to Juan Pablo Montoya and the Ganassi team in 2000. The following seven seasons saw him continue in these positions with a variety of teams. During this time, he was reunited with Luyendyk and also assisted fellow Englishman Darren Manning. In 2007 ill health forced a temporary retirement but he was back in 2009 helping PDM Racing to win races in Indy Lights. At the beginning of the following year it was announced that he would, along with Bruce Ashmore and Alan Mertens, be one of the partners in the BAT bid to design and build the next Indy car.

flag, so Ward could only follow them for third place, with lapped cars in between. Consolation came in the form of the Rookie of the Year award; of the four British-born drivers to have won this, three were born in Scotland. "It was a great day. I had a good chance to win but for circumstances at the end."

Having started at the age of thirty-three, Ward was to compete in seven Indy 500s. "I still consider myself as a motocrosser that happened to race cars," he said. However, while he reckons to have found it strange every time he got into a race car as opposed to onto a bike, he understands that "Indianapolis gets into your soul." In 1999 he finished second, leading briefly on laps 151 to 153 for Pagan Racing. A year later, driving for A J Foyt, he was fourth, back in a G-Force after a year with Dallara. Six consecutive races came to an end in 2002 (the year that he won the Boomtown 500 at Texas) with a ninth place for Target Chip Ganassi. In 2005 he raced there for a last time, retiring his Vision Racing Dallara on lap ninety-two with handling problems.

Although he did not return for the 500, Ward was back at Indianapolis for the MotoGPs as a radio commentator. In his first year at the Speedway, he had been the only British-born driver. In his last, there were four – one of them, Dan Wheldon, taking the Borg Warner Trophy. For the British, times had changed.

Some great Scottish-born drivers have competed in the Indy 500, although Jeff Ward's family moved to California when he was still young. (Courtesy Indianapolis Motor Speedway)

21

FRONT PAGE NEWS – DAN WHELDON

"The guy is an Indianapolis natural."

In 1999, Dan Wheldon was racing in the US Formula Ford 2000 series in the same team as Mark Dismore Jr. He was invited to attend the Indianapolis 500 by Dismore's father, also Mark, who was driving in the event. "It absolutely blew my mind," he recalled. "I had been to the British Grand Prix but the size of this event and the energy that surrounded it just blew me away. I said to Junior. 'I'm going to race in this event one day and win it.' We still joke about that."

Six years later, the lad from Emberton, Buckinghamshire became first Englishman since Graham Hill in 1966 to win the race. "It doesn't matter if you have been born and raised in England, you think you know how big the Indianapolis 500 is. Having said that, I didn't really realise the magnitude of the event until I went there in 1999," he later stated.

It had been in Wheldon's mind to compete in the British Formula Three championship in 1999 but he had nowhere near the budget required. He did test, and was quick enough to become excited about the prospect, but with the money available it was never going to happen. "I also toyed with Formula Renault but didn't even have the budget for that." The previous year he had raced a factory Formula Ford Van Diemen and it was that manufacturer's founder, Ralph Firman, who suggested that he might cross the Atlantic and try the Formula Ford 2000 championship in the US. "He said that I should do a test and then worry about the money after. I did the test, liked the car, and the team and thought about the potential for the next couple of years." Wheldon then talked to Firman, and Primus Racing team owner and Van Diemen importer, John Baytos, about how little money he had and they said, "We'll make it work."

At first Wheldon found it difficult to adjust to the way of life in North America. Returning to the UK on a regular basis, he still hankered after Formula Three. "I was going back and forth instead of concentrating. Baytos sat me down and gave me a wake up call." The team owner pointed out that, without anywhere near the budget to do F3, he needed to get it out of his system and concentrate on what he was doing in America. In the US, he said, there were already people interested in doing deals with him. Wheldon nearly did one with Walker Racing to run in the 2002 Indy 500. However, that never happened and his first appearance in the race was the following year as a member of the front-running Andretti Green Racing team.

Wheldon's first test at the Brickyard was the day before Mario Andretti had the well-publicised 'flip' that put a stop to any comeback. "Just being around people at AGR,

The Union Flag flies high over Indianapolis for the first time since 1966. Car owners Michael Andretti (right) and British-born Kim Green sit on the side pods. (Courtesy Indianapolis Motor Speedway)

the team." Wheldon believes that it was through those at AGR that he learnt to respect the event. He began to delve into its history. "The way that these big names talked about it made me realise that this must be a very, very special event. Everybody who has come here has just fallen in love with it. The energy and the atmosphere that you feel here on race day is like nothing else. I have been privileged to go to the Super Bowl but even that does not have the energy. How can it? You have got a two-and-a-half-mile raceway surrounded by grandstands that are absolutely full of people."

Others may have different views on the length of the month of May but Wheldon believed that it should not be shortened. "It's part of the history. One of the things that makes this ever so very special is the fact that you are at the racetrack for basically a month. That build up to the event is what makes it so exceptional. A lot of the people who don't make it out to the track until race day still look at the news every night to see what is going on."

Wheldon also believes that what the teams learn running during May can be taken on to the other racetracks where they do not get the same chance to practice. "Its incredibly important to be on track as much as you can."

Like his fellow British 500 winner, Dario Franchitti, Wheldon believed "... the majority of the field would prefer to come first in the Indianapolis 500 than the championship," although he was to do both in 2005. He reckoned that winning the race propelled him into the latter part of the season. "Your confidence feeds the whole team."

Wheldon's first year at the Speedway did not end as well as it had started. He crashed upside down trying to defend against Sam Hornish. "He dropped back from me on a restart and then took a run at me, so I tried to block him. Everything goes so fast for a rookie. You are learning so much, and the Speedway is a difficult racetrack to learn as there is no margin for error. However, I was like a sponge. I tried to take in everything from the team. That helped a lot for the following year when I knew what to expect. In your first 500 you have no idea about the dirty air, how long the race is, how many pits stops you are likely to make, and how much you can change you car during those stops."

There was pressure on Wheldon being the driver brought into the team to replace Michael Andretti. However, fellow Brit Tino Belli, who was his race engineer that year, recalls that he was fast all month and upset not to get the pole. "He wanted to withdraw his time but the team decided it was sensible to accept his second row place. He then carried himself very well in the race. It was a wonderful experience. The guy is an Indianapolis natural."

Wheldon found that there was "... a tremendous difference" for him between the 2003 and 2004 races. Indeed, he nearly won the latter. The second year, "... everything seemed to happen a bit slower." He led briefly at one point in the early stages before the red flag came out for rain on lap twenty-seven. Six laps after the restart he was overtaken but continued in a battle for the front spot for some time after the half-distance. When the rains came back on lap 180, Wheldon was in third place, capping off what had been described as a fine month.

like Michael and Mario Andretti, made me realise just what an unbelievably important event the 500 is." The younger Andretti, despite a tremendously successful career, had never won the race. It was thought that this would be his last time in the event and there was much pressure on the operation. "You could feel a vibe throughout

Wheldon in 2008. (Author's collection)

A year later it was to get so much better. "I had an unbelievably fast car in 2005 right from the moment we rolled it off the truck; with the exception of qualifying, when we were just slow. We had made a mistake and we could not understand why. It was not until about 5.40pm, and I had already done one run, that we figured out what it was."

Unfortunately, it was too late for the AGR team to get Wheldon's Dallara-Honda back in the line. Despite having been quickest on many of the days leading up to qualifying, he was left languishing in sixteenth place on the grid. However, "By that stage I was happy that

we had figured out what was wrong with the car and that we were going to be fast in the race."

His race engineer, Eddie Jones, remembered that the team practiced well with the main focus during this period being on the race car. "We just knew how crucial it was. We weren't particularly focussed on qualifying, and when it came to that we weren't very competitive. Poor Dan was initially furious; he is so competitive. However, both Dan and myself had an air of confidence. We knew that we had a really good race car and Dan was at the top of his game. Once we had got over the disappointment of qualifying he wasn't that concerned about being back in sixteenth."

"I can describe the race in very simple terms," said Jones. "I think Dan's march to the front was controlled, measured, and frankly inevitable. I think he was destined to win that day. In many ways the rest of the season was like that." Inexorably, Wheldon worked his way through the field. He and Jones had already talked about the patience needed for Indy. "It can take quite a few laps to set someone up for a pass," the engineer had reminded him. A full three-quarters of the way through the race he took the lead for the first time, holding it for eleven laps, and then swapping it with Vitor Meira and Danica Patrick as the pit stops played out. He was leading at the time of the final caution period. With just ten laps to go the race went green and, to everyone's amazement, Patrick moved to his outside and out–accelerated him into Turn One. The reaction of the partisan crowd would suggest that they were more eager to witness an inaugural female victory in the Indy 500, rather than the first British win for nearly forty years. Four laps later Wheldon reclaimed the lead, holding it to the end and a total prize money of $1,537,805. It was his third consecutive win that year, and one of the six that took him to the Indy Car championship.

Wheldon recalled, "After the race I was so excited about getting back to the team. For Andretti Green it was their first win in the 500. Michael had been so close as a driver. It was one of those times when you just wanted to be with everybody. AGR had about one hundred employees then and everyone contributed to that win. When you have dreamed of winning something for so long there are so many emotions that you feel. It's pretty difficult to take in. Given the number of great names that have not won here, I thought that winning it once would satisfy you but the feeling you get from that makes you so determined to win it again. However, it so, so difficult."

For the British, it was a double victory thanks to Eddie Jones. "On the podium we were jumping up and down and someone mentioned British driver, British engineer. It hadn't dawned on us before," said Wheldon.

The then Andretti Green Racing joint team owner, Kim Green, recalled, "... that it was not an easy win" for Wheldon. Green was running Tony Kanaan's car that year. He believed that both this and the other AGR car of Dario Franchitti were better than Wheldon's. Franchitti and Kanaan ran up front for most of the day. However, Green believes that he and Kyle Moyer, who was controlling Kanaan's pit, were running "slightly" conservative strategies and did not gamble as much on fuel at the last pit stop. "Track position ended up playing a big part in what happened. Once Dario and Tony were back in the

British joy knows no bounds. (Courtesy Indianapolis Motor Speedway)

pack the cars did not feel so good, and so we were unable to make our way back up to the front."

Every year Green studies the films from the inboard cameras for the whole race. "There was no commentary; it was just Dan in the cockpit, the sound, and watching what he did for the whole race. He worked his tail off for 500 miles in many challenging situations to get his car handling right, to get round people, and through traffic. He won the race fair and square with a lot of hard driving. At one point he was coming through Turn Four, full speed, and was about to go beneath the car ahead when it suddenly decided to go into the pits. Dan had to therefore go into the pit entrance and then back onto the racetrack before the entrance to the pit lane. It was the kind of thing that could have ended up in disaster. It was one of the greatest races that I have been involved in as a team member."

"Dan is very courageous, he leaves nothing on the table,"

observed Andy Brown who was later to engineer him at Target Chip Ganassi Racing. He is the sort of driver you want to work with. It makes you step up when the driver is putting his all in."

During the years that he was with AGR, Wheldon was really the junior driver. "Having team-mates like Dario, Tony, and Brian Herta, and a mentor such as Michael Andretti, was really helpful in the years that he was with us," said Green. "He was a sponge and he needed to be. He watched and listened. He is his own person and that's got strengths and weaknesses but during the 2004 season he learned so much, especially the number of times he finished a close second to Tony Kanaan. In 2005 he really blossomed, starting off the season at St Petersburg winning not with the fastest car but by being at the right place at the right time. A lot of winning is about confidence and I think that gave Dan great momentum going into the rest of the season."

Wheldon recalled the response to his Indy 500 win that he

found in the UK. When he first went to the US, the only other British drivers of note racing single-seaters there were Dario Franchitti and, in Indy Lights, Guy Smith and Jonny Kane. The media there, which had not commented on any of his previous wins, now took notice and *The Times*, for one, had a dominant photo of him drinking the milk on its front page. "I even had a very nice note from Nigel Mansell," he says. Another Brit who had led the race, Jackie Stewart, also sent a message. "When you get notes from people who you respect like that, it is another realisation that you have won such a great race."

Wheldon was now being recognised in public. "Tell people that you are an Indy Car driver and it often means very little; tell them you are an Indianapolis 500 winner and you get a totally different response. People's perception of you changes. I was young when I won it [twenty-five] and it did a lot for my career."

His name was linked with the third driver role at Formula One team BAR. "I definitely want to try it someday ..." he said "... but now isn't the time to talk about it." Formula One may have seemed important to the European press but would becoming the Friday practice driver for a mid-pack team really have been progress for an Indy 500 winner? One doubts it would have been seen that way in the US.

"It did not feel that you were working at Andretti Green.

Having dominated the 2006 race only to puncture, Wheldon again led laps in 2007, but was involved in Marco Andretti's accident at the end.
(Courtesy Indianapolis Motor Speedway)

TOM BROWN

Scottish engineer Tom Brown had been working at Poole for Penske in the 1990s when the company sold some Nigel Bennett-designed cars to Tony Bettenhausen Jr. Brown was assigned to assist the team, his first race being the Indianapolis 500 itself. After a second season he returned to Dorset to work with Bennett, also commuting to engineer works driver Emerson Fittipaldi for three years.

At the end of this period, Bettenhausen enticed Brown to work full-time for him in the US. When the former was killed in a plane accident, Brown had to keep the team alive, running both the race team and the engineering. "That was a tough assignment." He persuaded fellow Brit Keith Wiggins to join him, and together they created the HVM team.

When the team's Herdez sponsorship ended there was not much money remaining in the company, and so Brown left to join the PKV and then Forsythe operations until the end of the CART series. In 2008 he was asked by Indianapolis-based Sarah Fisher Racing to work on a couple of races "... and thoroughly enjoyed it." At the Indy 500 he engineered Fisher, herself. "As a small team you couldn't make a single mistake – you couldn't recover from one."

In just eighteen months Sarah Fisher Racing was to go from "just one of everything" to three cars and much larger premises. Brown has great respect for what Fisher has achieved. For the 2010 season he joined her team full-time, excited by the fact it appeared to be one of the few that was actually growing. He would also, hopefully, be running the newest Brit at the Indianapolis 500, Jay Howard. "It's not just another race track," he said of the Speedway. "Everything we do is centred around that one race."

Tom Brown in late 2009 at Sarah Fisher's new workshop. (Author's collection)

Not quite the correct line. Wheldon helped launch a Wii and Nintendo Indy game in the IMS media centre a few days before the 2007 race. (Author's collection)

Everything was such fun," said Wheldon. However, at the end of his championship year he moved to the Target Chip Ganassi team, just failing to take the title for a second consecutive season when he lost out on a tiebreaker to Sam Hornish. That year's Indy 500 made him realise just how much winning the event the previous year had meant. Wheldon simply dominated the race only to suffer a flat tyre towards the end. "It broke my heart."

In the middle of a tough month, he qualified his Dallara on the outside of the front row. His new team could not find the speed of the Penske operation in qualifying trim, so the decision was made to concentrate on the race setup. It was not until Bump Day that the

Wheldon moved to Panther in 2009. His National Guard livery was pretty obvious at the start of the season; the camouflage was yet to come. He is seen here at Long Beach. (Author's collection)

Wheldon is inside Tony Kanaan as they dive into Turn One during practice for the 2009 race. (Courtesy Tim Wagstaff)

team finally figured out what was wrong with the car. "Up to that point we just hadn't been able to make it work as well as we would have liked over a full fuel stint." After this the car was transformed. "It felt very comfortable on Carburetion Day, and then on race day it was absolutely phenomenal."

Come race day, and on lap ten, Wheldon stormed into the lead and began to run away with the race in what appeared to be the strongest car in the field. For much of the event team-mate Scott Dixon protected his position from second spot, eventually earning a drive-through penalty for what was said to be blocking.

Said Wheldon, "I remember Chip (Ganassi) coming on the radio and telling me to be careful to save fuel because my pace was far higher than anyone else, and I replied that I was in the leanest position

you could be in. I was still pulling away; it was the best feeling ever; being able to overtake cars at will and then hearing the lead increase. It went up – two seconds, four seconds, twelve seconds. I increased to nineteen seconds at one point. It was almost too easy. Then I picked up a flat tyre. That crushed me."

"It was a very hot Indy and we made the correct decisions as to what to do with the car," says his engineer that year, Andy Brown. "That was very pleasing from a personal standpoint. The puncture before the final pit stop meant that we had to make the stop early. People have said we had to make that stop anyway, so what did we lose? We lost a lap and a half coping with that puncture. The tyre pressure sensor on the right rear had failed so we only had Dan's word for it that he had a puncture. However, we could see from the steering

The camouflage might work were it not for the yellow highlights. Aided by a highly efficient pit crew Wheldon, seen here in Turn Two, finished second in 2009. It was his best result of the season. (Author's collection)

trace coming over the telemetry that something was not right. He had a massive moment coming out of Turn Four so we had to call him in. We then lost too much time changing his tyres so that we were not best placed for the final laps. To dominate like we did and not win made it one of my most disappointing 500s." Fourth place was scant reward for the driver who had led a total of 148 laps. "Everything has to go your way in this race. At one point I almost lapped Sam Hornish and he won the race," said Wheldon

In 2007 and 2008 Wheldon was again fast and led laps. In the first of these Andy Brown recalled that he became frustrated as the team experimented during practice with different wheelbases. In the event, Wheldon became caught up in Marco Andretti's crash on the back

In 2009, despite being British, Wheldon embraced the National Guard sponsorship, becoming active with the National Guard Youth Foundation. (Author's collection)

straight just before rain brought the proceedings to a final halt. In 2008 he was second on the grid, and was able to take the lead by lap three. He lost this during the first caution of the day, only to quickly regain it and hold it until lap thirty-six. Wheldon then began to trade the front spot with team-mate Dixon until his car became loose, causing him to drop back into the pack. The handling problem meant an eventual twelfth position. At the end of the season he was replaced in the Target Chip Ganassi team by fellow Brit Dario Franchitti, returning to Panther Racing, which had given him his first two races in the IRL back in 2002.

The month of May for 2009 was by far the most difficult one that Wheldon had had to date. For almost the whole of the time he was suffering from a loose car. "It has been mentally draining," he said in the run up to the race. Towards the end of the Sunday practice the week before the event, he felt a little bit of headway had been made with a "ton of downforce" dialled into the car. He had never used Carburetion Day as a practice event before, simply as a shake-down, but felt that this time it would be necessary.

Having started back in eighteenth place, Wheldon steadily advanced through the field, thanks in the main to some highly efficient pit stops. At the penultimate restart he was up to fifth, quickly passing Paul Tracy for fourth. At the next pit stop former team-mate Scot Dixon was held up, and so the Englishman moved up to third. Then Penske's Ryan Briscoe was forced to pit and third became second. It would be tempting to suggest that it was only a lack of laps left that prevented

Wheldon from marching to the front but that would be to deny Helio Castroneves' undoubted dominance of the final miles. In fact, the closing minutes for Wheldon were more a matter of holding off Danica Patrick than fighting for the lead. Nevertheless, the second place was a great result for the Panther team, which was no longer regarded as one of the series' front-runners. "I can honestly say the team executed 100 per cent," said Wheldon. "The pit crew was phenomenal. They made my job incredibly easy all day because they made me spot after spot in the pits. I think everyone on the team should be incredibly proud."

For the 2009 Indy 500, Wheldon's Dallara had been decked out in the grey camouflage colours of the National Guard. He has become a spokesman for the Youth Challenge programme that the National Guard is part of, a role that he takes very seriously. "It seemed a little different talking in a press conference room about something other than racing. A lot of the things that the troops value, I value, too. I have had a great relationship with them. They have been so supportive of the programme," he said.

"How come we have a limey representing our National Guard?," enquired a local photographer. Had he seen Wheldon with the programme's youngsters he would not have needed to ask. His personality makes him a natural with them. They do not seem concerned that he hails from the other side of the Atlantic. One thing is sure is that he has become an integral part of the race that he so much enjoys.

XTRAC

The importance of Indianapolis is such to motorsport suppliers that over the years a number of British companies have established operations in the town. Leading performance transmission supplier Xtrac is one such.

Andrew Heard, now vice president of Xtrac Inc and then lead design engineer on Xtrac's Reynard Champ Car project, first became involved with the US in 1998. To support Reynard, he decided to attend a number of test sessions and races. The resulting direct contact with end users helped the company develop its product. For 2000, Xtrac was awarded the contract to become sole supplier of gearboxes to the IRL, replacing the heavy EMCO units. The company was able to improve on the serviceability, weight, and crash worthiness of the previous 'box. The original IRL contract for three years was renewed, and then the company was allowed a little more freedom on the layout of the transmission. Although around seventy per cent of the parts were retained, the length of the transmission was shortened, for safety reasons, by fourteen inches. Heard points out that, when British driver Mike Conway hit the concrete wall backwards at 200g in 2009, his gearbox survived undamaged.

Throughout 1999 Heard was commuting back and forth. His load increased with the addition of the IRL and there were times when he attended Champ Car and IRL races on the same weekend. There came a point where Xtrac managing director Peter Digby reckoned he ought to stay out in the States. The initial plan was that this should be for just the six months of the racing season, but that half-year naturally extended and Heard has been Indianapolis-based ever since.

At first, Xtrac's then US distributor Motorsport Spares assisted with office space on Gasoline Alley, next to HVM. It was apparent that the company, also a distributor for other UK firms such as AP Racing, SPA, and GKN, did a good job for Xtrac at the racetrack. However, the need was beginning to be felt for it to have a US base of its own and so, in January 2003, Xtrac moved into a 6500sq ft building on West 80th Street with a staff of four. It was not the first British company to have made such a move. Exhaust systems manufacturer Good Fabrications had established an Indianapolis operation during a point in the 1990s when it supplied to virtually every team on the Indy grid.

By 2004, Xtrac had also become involved in the Grand-Am series and then Touring Cars in the US. By 2009 the head count had grown to twelve. That year the company also started to assemble product in Indianapolis as well as at its Thatcham, England headquarters.

In 2007 Xtrac was also approached by the IRL with regard to a paddle-shift gear change system. Two systems were considered; one British, the Zytek EGS (Electrically-assisted Gear Shift), the other the French Megaline's pneumatic AGS (Assisted Gear Shift) version. The choice, Digby recalled, was "very close" with Megaline just getting the nod. After a series of tests, Xtrac distributed systems to all the teams "and then ...," recalled senior engineer Andrew McDougal, another Brit who headed the project, "... we were told they needed more." The IRL had absorbed Champ Car and the number of cars had risen. However, Xtrac was ahead of the game and had already produced an extra thirty kits five weeks before the announcement of the so-called 'unification.'

Xtrac now runs an end of the year competition that is connected to its contingency sponsorship. For each race of the IRL championship, the highest finishing car displaying its decals on either side of the attenuator on the back of the car receives an award. The driver with the most of those awards at the end of the year, which in 2009 was Englishman Dan Wheldon, then receives an additional $5000 bonus.

Xtrac became sole gearbox supplier to IndyCar. (Author's collection)

Led in the US by Andrew Heard, Xtrac has enjoyed a highly successful relationship with the IndyCar Series. (Author's collection)

22

EX-PAT ENGINEERS

"If Indy teaches you one thing, it is patience."

"Mario Andretti had a secret weapon in winning pole position at the Indianapolis Motor Speedway," said the *Indianapolis Star* in 1987. "It was an Englishman named Adrian Newey, the engineer on his Lola." Newey may have returned to Europe to design Formula One cars, most recently the Red Bulls, but he was just one of the British engineers who had begun to populate the Brickyard in the wake of the Cooper and Lotus mechanics.

The British mechanics who descended upon Indianapolis in the 1960s tended to be in their twenties; youngsters who spent part of their lives flying across the Atlantic. By the twenty-first century the situation was different. The British engineers were likely to be more mature, and domiciled in America. With a number of the teams, including front-runners Target Chip Ganassi, Andretti Green Racing (which was to become Andretti Autosport for 2010), and Panther Racing, based not many miles from the Speedway, that meant living in Indianapolis itself. A community of expatriates has built up there with, in 2009, eight British engineers working for just the three teams mentioned.

Andretti Green Racing certainly had a very British feel to it during the victory years of 2005 and 2007. Both the winning drivers, Dan Wheldon and Dario Franchitti, had fellow Brits as their engineers in Eddie Jones and Allen McDonald respectively. But there was more to it than that: even the team's then joint owner, Kim Green, despite claiming to be Australian, would admit to having a British passport.

Green's father had been a farmer in Somerset. After World War Two, he emigrated to Australia to make a fresh start there. Kim's three

Kim Green, joint owner of Andretti Green Racing until the end of 2009, is Australian in all but birth and passport, which shows him to be yet another Brit. (Author's collection

elder siblings, including Barry who ran Team Green in Champ Car, were all born there. In 1953, Green's parents returned to England with thoughts of re-establishing themselves on the family farm. In 1954, Green was born in Wells. However, his father had decided that life was easier in Australia than having to work with his brothers, and Kim celebrated his first birthday on an Australia-borne ship.

He has only returned to the UK a couple of times since, but never became an Australian citizen. When he first started in racing and

Eddie Jones was the first of two Englishmen in recent years to engineer a Brit to victory at the Indy 500. (Author's collection)

needed to travel abroad, there just was not enough time to change nationality and it was easier to get a British passport. "It's what I have travelled on ever since ... even though I consider myself an Australian."

Despite Green's undoubted 'Down Under' accent, one could hear plenty of British voices at Andretti Green Racing (AGR) during this period. In addition to Jones and McDonald, there was also Tino Belli; another example of a Brit with an Italian name – although in this case Welsh. It was, however, the Londoner with the Welsh name but Irish parents, Eddie Jones, who was the first of these engineers to taste success at the Brickyard with AGR.

Many of the Brits working at Indy came from Formula One. Jones can go further than that. His father Aiden Jones built a Grand Prix car, the Shannon; which retired on the first lap of its only GP, the 1966 British. Eddie grew up around racing and also remembers his father

as team manager and design consultant to the Scirocco-Powell team. Prior to this he had been a mechanic with Anglo-American Racing, which had entered cars for such as Stirling Moss and Dan Gurney. The team recognized that Jones Senior had some bright ideas about design, and gave him the opportunity to build the Cooper T59-based Aiden-Cooper, which ran in a few non-championship Formula One races during 1962. It was notable for being the first F1 car to be designed with side radiators (shades of Hughie Hughes' 1914 car), although this was replaced by a conventional nose cone before the season started.

Eddie started racing himself, latterly in Formula Super Vee both in Europe and the US. Father and son built their own car, again called a Shannon. In those days the formula was considered a stepping-stone to Indy cars in the States. "I really had high hopes." Halfway through 1983 he was offered the works Anson drive, replacing one Arie

Allen McDonald is famed for his detailed briefing documents. (Author's collection)

Luyendyk who went on to twice win the Indy 500. However, a huge accident at Pocono, in which he badly broke both legs, effectively ended his driving career.

Now over thirty, Jones returned to the UK to attend Imperial College, London, gaining a degree in aeronautical engineering. Once graduated, he went to work for Ron Taurenac. The next stage was to move back to the US and join a partnership that produced Shannon Sports 2000s. In 1996 he ran and engineered an Indy Lights team. At the end of the year he was approached by Barry Green to run Team Green's Indy Lights programme. During the next couple of years he ran various drivers, including Ulsterman Jonny Kane.

In 2001 Michael Andretti joined the operation, and Jones became his engineer in CART and the IRL. Back in 1983, a young Andretti had won the Formula Super Vee race at Long Beach. Jones had come fifth

that day. On Andretti's initial retirement after the 2003 500, Jones took over as Dan Wheldon's engineer, Tino Belli having worked with the Englishman prior to that. "In 2004 we really started getting it together, then a year later we won it all. At the 500 that year Jones and Wheldon both 'felt that it would be our day.' I had a sense of an unstoppable force," recalled Jones.

After Wheldon left the team, Jones became Marco Andretti's engineer; only losing out on a second victory when Sam Hornish pipped the nineteen-year old on the line. After three years with Andretti, Jones moved within the team to engineer Danica Patrick. "Look how Danica improved in 2009," said Wheldon. "I think a lot of that had to be put down to Eddie Jones."

"Eddie is unbelievable," he added. "There is no bullshit with him. He gave me great race cars and I had supreme confidence in him.

Our relationship was such that I could come into the pits and I did not even need to speak but he would know what to do with the race car. I have never had that with anyone else. When you explained something you felt through the wheel he understood because he has driven himself. He became a great friend."

Two years after the English duo of Wheldon and Jones took the Indy 500, a second AGR-entered British pairing was victorious in the race, Dario Franchitti and his engineer Allen McDonald. The latter, another Londoner, is one with a Formula One background having joined Brabham in 1984. He had attended the University Colleges of Swansea and of London, sponsored by the Royal Corps of Naval Instructors. That meant two years training at the Royal Naval College in Plymouth, and even some sea time. After five years at Brabham McDonald went to work for Arrows, which was to become Footwork, also spending a season with Paul Stewart Racing.

From his time at PSR he came to know staff at Reynard, and it was they who said that any time he wanted to work in the United States they would be happy to help. "This took my interest. It would be back to a smaller environment where you could have a deeper interest in developing the car and work in a more level playing field."

Moving to America, he first plied his trade with the PacWest team in Champ Car engineering English driver Mark Blundell, winning three races in his first year. In 2002 McDonald moved to what was then Team Green where he was reunited with Dario Franchitti, engineering the Scot right up to the time that he left AGR in 2007. Franchitti recalled that he spent about eighteen months trying to persuade the loyal McDonald to join the team. Like Wheldon and Jones, Franchitti and McDonald were to become friends as well as colleagues.

A number of his fellow engineers have said that they joined the IRL for Indianapolis but that was not initially the case with McDonald. "I remember talking to Andy Brown and he said that when you go to Indy it makes the hairs on your head stand on end. He loved it from the moment he first went there. I didn't feel that at first and it took years for it to get under my skin but now I absolutely love it."

The attraction for McDonald was the "closer engineering group and being more involved in the development of the cars." He admits that, when he first went to the Brickyard "the place kind of scared me. As an engineer it is difficult to get a grasp of what exactly it needs. It's so different from European racing."

To add to McDonald's difficulties, the team was still competing in CART but had bought some IRL Dallaras. "We took them to Indy and tried to make them work. We were really behind. We worked hard to solve the problem of going quickly at Indy but we certainly hadn't by qualifying because we were second day qualifiers. Dario's run when he finally qualified was a terrifying thing to watch."

McDonald feels that, as race day approached, Team Green started to get a hang of the Speedway "and we had pretty decent race cars." However, not helped by a controversial yellow flag decision that robbed Team Green's Paul Tracy of a win, he "was pleased to be leaving the track" at the end of the event. "It didn't do much for me then."

A year later the now Andretti Green Racing joined the IRL full-time "and it was forced on me to get a better idea of what high speed ovals were about," said McDonald. Slowly he got into this form of racing and to understand its subtleties. "I think this may have been equally true of Dario, and perhaps I held him back in that respect."

McDonald and Franchitti were, though, to become adept at the Speedway, resulting in the rain swept win of 2007. "We had a great team that worked well," recalled the driver, "Allen and I had our brains in sync."

The following year McDonald moved within the team to become its communications engineer for the 500. It seemed like a good idea to have someone "to oil the wheels" between the four AGR entries and their individual engineers but, in hindsight, he feels that it did not work; "I certainly missed the race engineering." For 2009 he returned to such a position with Tony Kanaan, before leaving at the end of the season to become chief race engineer at FAZZT; the new team for which Alex Tagliani was to drive.

"Allen's a great race engineer, switched on but with no ego. We were together for six years, starting in Champ Car, and built up a very strong relationship," recalled Franchitti. "His is a very organised person in his work and has a thirty to forty page briefing document at each race, which has become famous. That proved really helpful in my win at the 500. I think it helped not just our car but all the cars in the team. The month at Indy may be a long time but people can still panic and that document was something we could always go back to if the conditions changed."

The third of AGR's British engineers, Tino Belli, was first at the Speedway in 1986 as an aerodynamicist for March. Robin Herd took him to the Indy 500 to work with the official March works team of Danny Ongais and John Paul Jr but circumstances ensured that the latter would be unable to start. "I was a rookie engineer with a crew that was cobbled up and no driver." As recounted, Paul was replaced by Brit Jim Crawford at the last minute.

The following year Belli was seconded to the then Barry Green

Tino Belli first went to the Speedway when working for March. (Courtesy Andretti Autosport)

Andy Brown brought another element of engineering to Target Chip Ganassi, recalled Dan Wheldon. (Author's collection)

Andy Brown brought another element of engineering to Target Chip Ganassi, recalled Dan Wheldon. (Author's collection)

managed Kraco team with driver Michael Andretti and an English-born race engineer in Peter Gibbons. In 1988 Porsche engines were first fitted to a March and Belli became chief development engineer for the 89P and 90P versions. The latter was designed to be an all-carbon fibre car. However, following a series of accidents, CART introduced a rule stating that the bottom of any car had to be made of aluminium honeycomb or sheet aluminium for the three years which would end in 1990. March thought it would take advantage of the ending of this rule and so designed the carbon-fibre car, which, as Belli recalls "was banned in the January." Converting it back to an aluminium honeycomb floor was something of a nightmare. "There was so much shape to it that it was almost impossible to do, so it spent most of its life with a massive weight penalty ... and then Porsche pulled out of the series."

Belli then spent a number of years in Formula One working with Les Mactaggart, who was to become IRL technical director. He returned to the Speedway in 1995 with Forsythe Racing and driver Teo Fabi, with whom he had worked on the 89P. That was the year that Penske failed to qualify. "They were pitted next to us and it was interesting to watch them ... struggle. It was not something that you had come to expect but it showed that everyone is human." In 1998 he found himself at the Speedway again with the Pagan Racing team and Roberto Guerrero.

At then end of 1998, Belli moved permanently to the US to work again with Barry Green. That meant his next visit to the IMS was 2002, "the year that Paul Tracy 'won' the Indianapolis 500!" Belli, the team's technical director, is in no doubt that, whatever the eventual result, Tracy "clearly" had taken the lead prior to the yellow lights coming out on the last lap. "We had independent people do a full analysis based on the timing of the cameras and all the information that was available, and when the yellow lights came on he was in front of Helio Castroneves." Officialdom thought differently. In 2002 the now Andretti Green team moved full-time into the IRL with Belli engineering new boy Dan Wheldon for the month of May. Typically, Belli no longer race-engineers cars, unless there is a need to fill in, his current role being more of an overseer.

Not far from AGR's Zionsville Road base is the headquarters of Target Chip Ganassi Racing and another trio of Brits. One of these is Andy Brown, whose Indianapolis roots go back to 1984 when he started at March. His main priority for his first three years there was the Formula 3000 programme but there were times when it would be "all hands to the pumps" to work on the Indy cars. "I can look at the uprights on the 1986 car and say 'I drew them.'"

Time spent on the Leyton House Formula One project meant that Brown then moved away from Indy cars for a while. By 1991 he was with Brabham "and getting terribly fed up with Formula One." He decided to set up his own Formula Three team and was looking around for premises. Alan Mertens, who describes Brown as "a genius" and

who had been his boss at March, had taken over the March premises in Bicester for Galmer and said he could run the team out of there. As recounted elsewhere in this book, the F3 project did not happen but Brown ended up as assistant technical director for Galmer, and thus involved in its 1992 Indy 500 victory. "I guess I was a travelling library on the day," Brown says. "I had been involved in the design side of the car as assistant technical director in England and not the running of the team."

When manufacture was stopped and the team decided to run Lolas for 1993, Brown again flew to Indy for the race "... and ended up being coerced into running the fuel programme for Kevin Cogan's car, although my main function was again as a travelling aero library." Such a role was not enough for Brown, and he found himself also assisting

Bruce McCaw's team which was running a year-old Galmer. From this association grew PacWest Racing with Mertens and Brown involved, the latter as chief race engineer. "I came here for two years, fifteen years ago," he reflected.

The original idea was also to be a manufacturer but for the 1994 season Lolas were purchased. Brown engineered Dominic Dobson's car at a not particularly successful 500, while Mertens looked after Scott Sharp's. Danny Sullivan came on board for 1995 but he was towards the end of his career. Thus, the team turned towards another colleague of Brown's from Leyton House days, Mauricio Gugelmin. "It was an ex-Formula One club." The result was a much more successful 500 with the Brazilian leading the most laps but his car developed "a huge push" when it was put on softer tyres for the run to the flag. "I wasn't initially interested in oval racing," recalled Brown. "There were only two corners, how much could there be to it? You soon learn! When you get it wrong it is spectacular."

The 'split' meant that he now missed a few Indy 500s. However, Champ Car was travelling further and further afield and, in his eyes, becoming more like the Formula One he had chosen to leave. Thus, for 1999, he accepted an offer to join Panther Racing as technical director. "It seemed like a strange move to some of my colleagues but the draw of getting back to the 500 was very strong.

"Although Panther had had a difficult first season in the IRL, it seemed to me that it had all the ingredients in place to be successful. It was certainly very close to Chevrolet, which funded wind tunnel testing at the ARC tunnel in Indianapolis. Brown had been involved in the initial setting up of this, with Adrian Reynard and Bruce McCaw being amongst its founding fathers. "It was interesting to go back as a customer."

In 1999 Brown thought that the team had a decent chance to win the 500 – driver Scott Goodyear was running third in his G-Force when the crank broke – but the year after, following some bad accidents for Goodyear, "... we were just droning around making up the numbers. When you get into these kind of situations, you ask is it me? Is it the engineering of the car?" Various drivers were tested, with Sam Hornish proving the most impressive. Brown did three 500s with the American and also engineered him to two IRL championships.

With the big names starting to come over from Champ Car, the decision was taken to run two cars and Brown stepped back from engineering to expand the team (one of the drivers for 2004 was to be Englishman Mark Taylor). Although Chevrolet was giving plenty of support, he felt that a bigger engineering effort ought to be made in house.

The year 2005 was one of the most enjoyable for Brown at Indianapolis. Chevrolet wanted Panther to enter a third car. Team owner John Barnes did not want to take on an extra person to engineer the car, so Brown was asked to perform this role for former 500 winner Buddy Lazier. "I enjoyed working with Buddy immensely. I kept asking myself when is this guy going to complain about something. If I don't know if anything is wrong, I can't fix it. We put together a one-off crew just to do the event, and it was great to do as well as we did," said Brown.

However, Chevrolet and sponsor Pennzoil both pulled out of Panther, and Barnes, who was unfortunately ill at the time, gave Brown a list of people to dismiss. "It was soul destroying. These were friends."

Brown was to move on to Target Chip Ganassi Racing where he became a lead race engineer. "My contract still says 'Lead Engineer, Grade Three.'" Fellow Brits Ben Bowlby and Julian Robertson were already in place at Ganassi, overlooking the whole operation and the IRL cars respectively. Dan Wheldon had just joined the team. Panther had run him for a couple of races in 2002, and Brown was interested in returning to race engineering following his experience with Lazier. He therefore took on the role with Wheldon, and the pair quickly gelled, winning their first race together at Homestead.

Wheldon reflected that he perhaps did not have the time at Target Chip Ganassi to develop the same close bond that he had enjoyed with Eddie Jones. However, there is no doubting his admiration. "Andy Brown definitely brought another element of engineering to Ganassi," says Wheldon, who he also engineered in 2007. "When I went there they were coming off a lean period. They have great engineers there but the addition of Andy and his attention to detail was very impressive. It is not to say that other engineers aren't but he is incredibly intelligent. He is detail orientated. You work in a different way to that with Eddie Jones because Andy has not driven but he perhaps uses the laws of physics more. Two very different relationships but two incredibly talented engineers. You would be hard pressed not to put them as two of the best in the paddock."

For 2008 Brown stepped back from race engineering, travelling less and with more of a research and development roll, primarily on the aerodynamics of the IRL cars. However, he was to continue performing that role at the 500, engineering Alex Lloyd. Ganassi and Bobby Rahal had decided to jointly enter a car for the young Manxman and "... who was the spare race engineer? It was just like 2005 all over again." A year later and he and Lloyd were reunited for a second run at the 500.

Brown reflected on his time at the Speedway: "If Indy teaches you one thing, it is patience. Just wait and it will come to you."

His two British colleagues at Target Chip Ganassi, Ben Bowlby and Julian Robertson, are more likely to be found at the team's Woodland Drive base than at the Speedway itself. Bowlby runs the team's advanced engineering group; a team of six, which has been involved in NASCAR and Grand-Am racing, as well as the IRL. His road to Indianapolis was via Lola where he became chief designer. In 1996 he moved on to Lola's Champ Car programme from Formula 3000, ultimately becoming one of those responsible for Lola's turn around in fortunes in North America. Champ Car was by then the only competitive series in which the company was still involved. The split had by now occurred, and so this work did not concern the Indianapolis race. However, Bowlby also worked on a possible IRL car but eventually learnt that the League was not going to grant Lola one of its manufacturer 'slots.' Still, because of his work on US open wheelers, Chip Ganassi made Bowlby an offer to move to the US and work for his team. "Like many Champ Car designers before me, I got sucked into America."

GARY NEAL

Gary Neal is another English refugee from Formula One, having been with McLaren for nine years. In the last of these, he engineered Michael Andretti, with whom he built up a good relationship. He accompanied the American to Chip Ganassi's team when he returned to the US after his sole season in F1. "We won our first race, it was a great start to my career with Ganassi."

"When I first visited Indy it seemed like a small but neat city and I was determined to live there," recalled Neal, helping to explain the move.

He joined the Ganassi team when it was in its infancy and saw it grow into what he now describes as a "powerhouse." Initially he engineered Andretti, and then, for a number of seasons, Jimmy Vasser. Neal was running the test team when Juan Pablo Montoya scored Ganassi's first victory in the 500. After seven years he left the team, got out of racing for a while, but then moved to Dreyer & Reinbold, which he saw as being similar to Ganassi in its early days. "I had been there and done it with Ganassi. Now I want to do the same with another team," said Neal.

In between leaving Lola and moving to Ganassi, he worked alongside the Panoz G-Force staff, many of who were "Lola refugees." Contractually he was unable to join the Target-backed team for six months, but by working with G-Force he was able to bring himself up to speed with the IRL. Bowlby helped with the aero package of the new IRL car for 2003, which Ganassi used to win the championship. "We had a good advantage by understanding the car inside out and knowing how to use it."

Bowlby was also involved in the updating of the Panoz G-Force for 2004, flying back to the UK to assist Simon Marshall, who had been his right-hand man at Lola, and Nick Alcock in the Imperial College wind tunnel. Once again, the march was stolen on Dallara thanks to the underbody solutions that G-Force introduced. In the States, Bowlby was to be involved in another, but far from conventional, tunnel. Originally Ganassi himself had found "a hole in the ground" tunnel near Pittsburgh, but this was not long enough. Then, in September 2003, he discovered one in Laurel Hill, Pennsylvania – half full of road making material. "It was very crude, simply a sealed, one mile long tunnel."

"One of the first things that was developed in the tunnel was the G-Force 2004 airbox," said Bowlby. Dallara had come up with an airbox solution "... that we felt wasn't going to be allowed, so we hadn't investigated it." Bowlby admits that G-Force did not think that there was potentially as much to gain as was to become apparent. Dallara had done a great job with the new airbox but G-Force managed to respond very quickly. "If we had gone the CFD route, or via a scale model wind tunnel, I don't think that we would have got it sorted out in time (there was a one month window before spec freeze). When we had gone to the first IRL open test of 2004 we were something like six miles an hour off the pace. The redeveloped airbox meant that the car was fully competitive," remembered Bowlby. However, the new Honda engine had come on strong, which ensured that, by the time of the Indy 500, Ganassi's Toyota engines "got smoked." The team struggled with a massive horsepower deficit but proof of the benefit of the aero work on the G-Force was shown by Rahal-Letterman's win at the 500, albeit with a Honda engine.

Towards the end of 2009 all the talk in Indianapolis was of a

The DeltaWing project thrust Ganassi's Ben Bowlby into the limelight at the start of 2010. (Courtesy Ben Bowlby collection)

"radical" new design that Bowlby was working on for Indy. Much had already been said about what would replace the Dallara-Hondas in 2012. Bowlby admitted that he had been working on a design for around nine months, and that an announcement might be made shortly. Then, early in February, his DeltaWing concept (see chapter twenty-nine) was unveiled at the Chicago Auto Show. It clearly indicated that whatever the future of the Indianapolis 500, the British will still have a hand in it.

The other member of Ganassi's British trio, Julian Robertson, is a former Team Lotus designer who recalled that, during his time there, Indy car entrant Dick Simon had been talking to the 1965 500 winning company, "... but that fizzled out." However, Simon was looking to sign a group of engineers, and in 1992 Robertson flew to Indianapolis to join his operation and has "... been here ever since." David Cripps and another Brit, former Formula Three driver John Bright, were already working with Simon at this time. When Nigel Mansell joined the Newman Haas team, the Dick Simon Brits took delight in pointing out how Bright had beaten him in F3; "One of our engineers is quicker than your driver!" Robertson's first two 500s saw him engineering Raul Boesel. Simon would habitually run a large number of cars for the race. "It was a good place to work – it was all action."

In 1993 Robertson joined Target Chip Ganassi, then the first

Julian Robertson has been with Target Chip Ganassi since 1993. (Courtesy Target Chip Ganassi Racing /Getty Images)

customer for Indy car Reynards. Michael Andretti had just returned from Formula One and Robertson engineered him for his first 500 with the team. A year later he was responsible for Jimmy Vasser. On the team's post-split return to Indy he continued to run the American. In 2001, Chip Ganassi was originally going to enter just Vasser and Tony Stewart in the 500, his two regular Champ Car drivers Bruno Junqueira and Nicolas Minassien being considered too inexperienced for the 500. Following first qualifying Ganassi changed his mind, and Robertson was called upon to engineer Junqueira into the race. After many years of engineering Vasser, Robertson moved on to Kenny Brack for the 2002 500, and then Scott Dixon for the next two years, before Ryan Briscoe in 2005. After that Robertson stopped engineering specific cars and took on a more overall role.

Third of the Indianapolis-based Indy car teams to employ more than one British engineer is Panther Racing. The year 2008 was team manager Chris Mower's first time working at the Indianapolis 500, but certainly not the first time he has been to the Speedway. Mower had worked his way through Formula Three, Formula 3000, and Formula One (like his father with Team Lotus) before returning to F3000 to set up Nordic Racing with his father Derek. With the latter seeking to retire, Mower Junior looked towards the US and, in late 2002, joined the then Champ Car team, Indianapolis-based Conquest Racing. The announcement of the 'unification' between Champ Car and the IRL, thus bringing Conquest to the 500, was significant to Mower. In the 1970s and 1980s his father had regularly engineered in the race, initially commuting with Team Lotus and then staying with Vel's Parnelli Jones, and then Fletcher Racing. This meant Chris was no stranger to the city, having lived there for about sixteen years from the age of two.

The family would move from Phoenix in time for the May, staying for a few months because of the number of races then on the east coast. Mower would go to the track with his father in the morning and then "... do my own thing," not seeing him again until the end of the day. "When I was a kid it was just like any other track, just a lot bigger." He and his mates, boys such as Al Unser Jr, Robby Unser, and Tim Cindric, who would go on the become president of Penske Racing, would cycle around getting into mischief, and even into some of the suites thanks to being known by the security guards. "Then the race was not our highlight. In those days you could have the run of the place, even without a pass. The only place we were not allowed was the pit lane," said Mower.

That first year back Mower's team was working with rookie drivers. The one benefit of this was that the pressure was not on in the same way that it would be for a front-running team. At the end of the season Mower moved to Panther. In the month's leading up to the 2009 race he could see that it would be different with this team. "We have the opportunity to get results," he said.

David Cripps arrived in Indianapolis in 1990 and "... had no intentions of staying." He had been with endurance sports car manufacturer Spice Engineering, and then with Williams. Impatient to make his way in the sport, he was convinced by John Biddlecombe – later to be one of the founders of G-Force – to join the new Onyx F1 team. "It was a disaster!" On paper it seemed a good step, moving out from what he saw as a back room at Williams. In retrospect, perhaps he should have stayed there a few more years ... As the Onyx team rapidly "fell to pieces," so nearby, and expanding, Benetton put out a blanket offer to the staff. It was suggested, though, that Cripps considered Indy Car, and he was given a pamphlet about the teams. He was in his office at Onyx about to fire off some applications, when the phone rang. It was Dick Simon asking how soon he could get to Indianapolis. Three or four weeks later Cripps flew to watch a race but initially decided that the team was not for him. "I was hoping that one of the top teams would take me but Dick was very persistent. I decided it was not as if I was to make Indy Cars a permanent career move, so why not accept?"

Cripps was impressed by his first race with the team, at the

Chris Mower started early at Indianapolis. (Courtesy Chris Mower collection)

Goodyear and Jacques Villenueve, who had run the Brazilian down after a two-lap penalty. Five laps later, in one of the biggest brain fades in Indy history, Goodyear anticipated a return to green and shot past the pace car before it had returned to the pits. With Goodyear disqualified and Villeneuve having the momentum, Fittipaldi finished in second place. Cripps still muses on how Walker Racing could have won that year. The following year he was with the Della Penna team, another rookie, Richie Hearn, and what he believes to be another near miss. The American driver finished in third place, seven seconds down on the winner and the last to complete the full 200 laps.

Cripps' recent career has been with Panther Racing, which he joined in 2003. For two years he engineered Tomas Scheckter. Then engineer and driver took a gamble and transferred to Tony George's Vision team, although Cripps returned to Panther in 2008.

The experience of the Ganassi, AGR, Panther Indianapolis-based octet is proof of the depth of British involvement still apparent at the Speedway. And they are not alone, another Indy-based team, Dreyer and Reinbold, has a British team manager in Gary Neal, while out of town teams, such as Penske and Newman Haas Lanigan, will also come to the track with one or more Brits. For the 2009 500, Britain contributed five engineers in

Michigan Superspeedway. A few weeks later he was involved in a test at Indianapolis. Now he was being attracted by the thought of the 500, and accepted when Simon offered him full-time employment. "My first 500 was 1991; it was quite an experience, I was hooked." A chance meeting at Rick Rising-Moore's Union Jack pub resulted the following year in his marrying an American girl, Joy, who had travelled to Indianapolis on business. "It was good racing then. You genuinely felt that you were in with a chance, even if you were with a lesser team."

Cripps never did go back to Formula One but worked for a succession of Indy car teams including Dick Simon Racing, Walker Racing, Della Penna Motorsports, Kelley Racing, Bradley Motorsports, and Mo Nunn Racing. The 1997 500, the first of the IRL's own formula was the only one that has missed in all this. "Missing the 500 was not an option for me, so that was when I went to an IRL team, Kelly Racing. I could not see how Champ Car was going to survive without the Indy 500."

In 1995 Cripps had engineered rookie Christian Fittipaldi for Walker Racing. "For a little while it looked as if we might win that race. Christian was having a torrid time. The underwing stays had broken and the underwing was cracking and degrading. Losing downforce, he was getting slower and slower and basically just wanted to pack it in. He didn't realise at the time that he was near the front!" With fifteen laps left, Fittipaldi was in third place; behind Scott

By 2009 Mower, who, as a lad, had played at the Speedway, was team manager for Panther Racing. (Author's collection)

BRIAN LISLES

Formula One engineer Brian Lisles had married Julie, a girl from the southern States. For a while she had followed him to Europe but hankered after a return to America. Therefore, Lisles decided that the time had come to leave Tyrrell and seek employment in his wife's country. Designer John Barnard said he had heard Carl Haas was looking for a race engineer. In late 1988 the pair met "... and did a deal. By default, I was about to do the Indy 500."

His first visit to the Speedway was in 1989. In those days the 500 was all consuming. If the team was based in Indianapolis that was fine, but Newman Haas was located in Chicago and that meant a hotel, day in, day out. Lisles admitted that, to an American, the Indy 500 can be something special, but "to me it was just another race … and a pain in the butt." It is quickly obvious that he does not share the enthusiasm for the race that some of his compatriots have developed. "It's like an extended Le Mans. It defines your season; it unbalances everything. If you are doing a championship, every race should be of the same stature. Maybe if I had won it, and it had put a handful of gold in my pocket, I might think about it differently." The days of the split when the Champ Cars were absent from the Speedway were fine for Lisles.

In his early days with Newman Haas, the team was running the two Andrettis, Mario and Michael, "who could qualify with their eyes closed and only four cylinders running." However, the sheer amount of time available at the track meant that there was still plenty of work to do in seeking out the ideal setup. For Lisles, it was far too much of an effort for just the one race. "It all goes slowly. There's a strange Einsteinian time warp there. At every other race everything has to be immediately."

Lisles had absolutely no experience of ovals when he first arrived in the US but he was lucky that he was working with Mario Andretti, who "... just loved the place. He would run every day that he could," said Lisles. The challenge of Indianapolis is as much mental as it is anything, and having Andretti to work with was ideal as he was able to explain so much to the Englishman. Michael too, was an extremely fine oval racer, although probably not so fond of the place, and was able to impart much to Lisles.

When it returned to Indianapolis, the now Newman/Haas/Lanigan team was described as one of the "transition teams." It was as if it was having to start again, although Lisles said that the challenges were basically the same. In its Champ Car days, despite never winning at Indianapolis, Newman Haas had been the dominant force. Indeed, during the split years it won the last four consecutive championships, making eight titles in total. One of the reasons for this strength was, wrote British-born journalist Gordon Kirby, the meticulous Lisles.

Brown, Cripps, Jones, McDonald, and Beresford, while Harrow's Mike Cole was jack man for Justin Wilson, and Clive Howell, Bernie King, and Brian Lisles were up in the spotters' galleries. Even non-qualifier Stanton Barrett would have had an English mechanic, Tony Von Dongen, working on his inside front.

The meticulous Brian Lisles has been a major force at Newman Haas Lanigan. (Author's collection)

Dan Wheldon had good cause to be delighted with his crew in 2009. A camouflaged David Cripps was equally pleased. (Courtesy Panther Racing)

23

SCOTTISH HERITAGE – DARIO FRANCHITTI

"It was very British, wasn't it, winning the Indy 500 in the pouring rain."

Compare and contrast. Take first the victor's press conference following the 2009 Long Beach Grand Prix. Winner Dario Franchitti is obviously a contented man. He has done what he is paid to do. In only the second race of the season, and following an aborted foray into NASCAR the year before, the Scot is obviously 'back.' Job well done. Then, fast rewind to just under two years previously, and the winner's press conference after the Indianapolis 500. This is something very different, and not just because his hair is considerably shorter. Franchitti appears less like a race car driver and more like a small boy who has just been given a magnificent toy ... and who can blame him?

The 2007 Indianapolis 500 finished in a downpour with Dario gingerly guiding his Dallara-Honda past the chequered flag in first place. It was a strange race that year. He had qualified on the outside of the front row in his Andretti Green Racing Dallara, a car resplendent in orange and black Canadian Club livery. It had appeared perfect for the whole of the second week of practice, and Franchitti and his engineer, fellow Brit Allen McDonald, were feeling confident. "We may not have been one of the fancied runners but we knew that we could do it." Then, on the Wednesday before the race, Franchitti's father, George, hit a hole-in-one on the difficult seventh of the Indianapolis Motor Speedway's own golf course. Everything seemed to be going well, perhaps too well.

When the race started Franchitti's car "was junk," thanks to a mistake in the setting of the right front shock absorber. The car just wanted to go to the wall. "It's understeering like a pig," he said over the radio. The team worked on this during the pitstops while the Scot made what adjustments he could from the cockpit. By about lap seventy, they had got the car back in balance and Franchitti was up to third and then second. On the fifty-seventh lap team manager and strategist John Anderson had radioed over that rain was thought to be an hour away. With the race closing in on half distance, Franchitti almost glided past Sam Hornish for the lead. However, for most of the leaders a green flag pit stop was imminent, and Franchitti was the first in. Team-mate Tony Kanaan, out of sequence with the front-runners, resumed his place up front. With rain fast approaching and the possibility that enough laps would have been run for the race to be called, Franchitti was back to sixteenth, thanks to his stop. More wrecks and another round of stops brought him back up to fifth.

With 112 laps completed, and with Kanaan now at the head, the rain

THE BRITISH AT INDIANAPOLIS

Brits to the fore again; Franchitti
leads Wheldon in 2007.
(Courtesy Indianapolis Motor Speedway)

Buddy Rice (15) may have had the pole in 2004
but he shared the front row with the Brits,
Dan Wheldon (26) and Dario Franchitti (27).
(Courtesy Indianapolis Motor Speedway)

The stops eventually fell Franchitti's way.
(Courtesy Indianapolis Motor Speedway)

really came down. Out came the red flags and to many it seemed that
the Brazilian at last had his name on the Borg Warner Trophy. The rain
was expected to last another forty minutes plus, and then it would take
around two and half hours for the track to be dried out.

To have thought that the race was over would, though, have been
to dismiss the sheer determination of the Indianapolis Motor Speedway
operation. Out came the driers, round went the support vehicles and
as the afternoon seemed to be drawing to a close, the opportunity was
seized to try and finish the race.

Almost immediately, a cut tyre forced Franchitti to pit, putting
him back to fourteenth place. With a car he reckoned to now be the

Very British, winning in the rain. (Courtesy Indianapolis Motor Speedway)

equal of Kanaan's, he then carved his way back to seventh. On lap 137 the leaders pitted and Franchitti, his cut tyre having put him out of sequence, moved to the front. Eight laps later he, too, was back in the pits for a routine stop. It was now an all-out sprint with rain predicted to return in about thirty minutes. Then Marty Roth hit the wall, and the subsequent yellows became the make or break moment of the race. The cards again fell in Franchitti's favour as others ahead of him pitted. He would not be headed again.

The rain clouds were rolling in from the southwest as another incident again brought out the yellows. Franchitti had enough fuel for eighteen more laps as the green flags flew once more. Then came Marco Andretti's and Dan Wheldon's crash on the back straight, and that effectively was that. It now looked as if a monsoon had struck out on the track. High up on the gantry the chequered flag was waved

alongside the yellow as Franchitti splashed his way towards the start line with Scott Dixon riding shotgun to his rear and slightly to the left. The fans huddled towards the rear of the adjacent grandstand where they could keep dry, leaving a few hardy souls at the front to wave their arms in salutation. Franchitti's film star wife, Ashley Judd, appeared very wet and very happy.

Much has been made of how the rain may have handed Dario the win, but that is to ignore the way in which he carved his way back through the field once his cut tyre had been changed. "The rain was welcome because it made the win a sure thing, but my feeling had been that, if the race had run its full distance, it would have come down to a fight between Tony [Kanaan] and I," said Franchitti.

Recalled Allen McDonald, "A lot of people still see that victory as fortunate because of when the rain fell, but Dario's drive from the back

The chequered flag waves with the yellow, while a few hardy souls stay out in the rain to greet Franchitti as he heads for the line. (Author's collection)

of the field was truly phenomenal. He absolutely deserved the win."

There is, though, the story of AGR's secret weapon, which helped take some of the guesswork out of the weather conditions. One of the team's partners, XM Satellite Radio, gave it exclusive access to accurate, real-time weather data, delivered straight to its trackside computers. While others relied on local weather forecasts, AGR received a constant stream of data that was overlaid on a GPS map and could be viewed in a variety of formats. Current and approaching weather measurements could then be studied, enabling the team to formulate race strategy. As Franchitti recalled, "The one comment that sticks in my mind was John Anderson saying on the radio, 'the rain's eight blocks away.'"

Anderson had called the Indy 500 for 2005 winner Dan Wheldon, but the rain-devastated 2007 event was something different, and "Ando" was able to react accordingly with the team's unique advantage. Franchitti recalled that Anderson "... also had his mates calling him from places like Brownsburg" with weather updates. Even Franchitti's spotter had a call from his wife to tell him that it was raining on the Georgetown Road just outside the Speedway. "It was very British, wasn't it ..." said McDonald, "... winning the Indy 500 in the pouring rain?"

As Franchitti crossed the line, the first thought he had was of his friend Greg Moore, who had been killed at Fontana in 1999. "I just wished he had been there to see it. Then it crossed my mind that I would have probably have finished second had he been there. It was then that I realised I had just followed in Jimmy Clark's footsteps. It took a lot of pressure off me because I had won one of my big goals. Winning the Indy Car series later in the year was very important because you have to prove yourself in a number of disciplines, but the 500 overshadows the whole season."

There is no doubting that Franchitti has a

Franchitti, delighted at the winner's press conference to have emulated Jim Clark. (Author's collection)

Bosch drives home another Indy 500 Win

Dario Franchitti
celebrates after winning the 91st Indianapolis 500.

BOSCH
Invented for life

As Champion produced a poster to celebrate George Robson's win in 1946, so did rival sparkplug manufacturer Bosch with Franchitti in 2007. (Courtesy Bosch)

crash. As when he had narrowly missed out on the Champ Car title the day his good friend Greg Moore had been killed, so this put any success in motor racing into perspective. "After that there seemed nothing worth celebrating." With the preparation that then became necessary for Franchitti's move to NASCAR taking over, it may be only on his return in 2009 that it sunk in that he had won the Indianapolis 500. The smile on the face that year certainly indicated that this was so.

Dario first went to the Speedway in 1997 to watch a practice session – he was driving for Carl Hogan's Mercedes-Benz-powered team in Champ Car at the time, which had a shop in Indianapolis' Gasoline Alley. "I was blown away by the size of the place. I remember watching the cars coming out of Turn Four. They would appear as a little speck and then very quickly they would be gone. From certain angles the turns at this track look very big but from others you can see what they are, ninety degree corners. I was taken aback by that."

It was in 2002 that Franchitti's then CART drive, Team Green, reappeared at the Speedway. It would be another year before, reorganised as Andretti Green Racing, it committed itself to a full Indy Car season. One cold day in April the Scot and team-mate Paul Tracy tested at the Speedway, the former's first time on the track. "We were running wide open and flat, and I was thinking, 'OK, what's the difficulty here?'" Come the month of May it was warmer and windy. Then it was, "This is the most difficult track I have ever driven in my life ... and I still have that opinion."

Franchitti remembers that first year as "terrible." In the previous two years Champ Car regulars had won the 500 without necessarily committing to the Indy Racing League season. Team Green was still a Champ Car team and "We were treated like outsiders first of all. It was not a very friendly atmosphere." At the time, the team was also changing from a Reynard to a Lola in Champ Car. Thus, not only was he having to learn the Speedway but Franchitti had to keep jumping on a team plane and flying to Mid Ohio to test the Lola. "I had no days off during the entire month." The team did not really understand the IRL cars that year and "We had really shit motors. There were Chevys and there were Chevys, and we blew our best motor before qualifying. "Despite all this, Franchitti ran reasonably well for the first half of the race before experiencing a flat tyre and losing a lap. There was also controversy over the finish. Team-mate Tracy actually received the chequered flag in first place having taken Helio Castroneves with one lap to go. However, at that point an accident had caused the yellow lights to come on. Tracy thought he had passed before the caution, the stewards said he had not and the Brazilian was given the race. "Paul got robbed, so my first impressions were not good," said Franchitti.

However, he believes that it was during the course of the 2002 race "... that I first began to understand what people were going on about." Despite what had happened, he was looking forward to the next year. He already had an idea that he would be part of the new Andretti Green team that was being formed and that it would be competing in the IRL. Honda was also entering the championship and Franchitti already had an excellent relationship with the Japanese manufacturer.

sense of heritage. He is all too aware that just two Scots have won the Indy 500 and that the other one is Jim Clark. Photos of his fellow countryman are to be seen in Dario's motorhome, while he also has a collection of Clark memorabilia. Franchitti had been aware of Clark's achievements but it was not until a dinner in Edinburgh in 1993 to mark the twenty-fifth anniversary of his passing that he truly understood the legacy. Jackie Stewart invited Dario, who found himself sitting next to a group, including one of Clark's biographers, Eric Dymock. "They began telling stories." From then on he started learning more about the Lotus star. A present of prints showing Clark started what was to become a collection. His wife Ashley mentioned the Scottish connection in an interview just as her husband crossed the finishing line in 2007. That got the American press pack going.

Ask Franchitti what it was like to win the Indy 500 and he admits that he still has not come up with a good answer. "It's everything, it's up with Le Mans, the Monaco, GP, Daytona 500 – the biggest races in the world. You get a massive feeling and a sense of achievement. In the press conference I was really in shock. There had been times in the past when I had been in a position to win and it had gone away. The shock lasted for months!"

It is probable that as he concentrated on, narrowly, taking the Indy Car Series that year, it still had not sunk in to Franchitti that he had won the 500. Perhaps it might have after he swept past an out of fuel Scott Dixon to win the championship at the end of the season, but about then occurred the tragic death of fellow Scottish motorsport icon, former World Rally Champion Colin McRae, in a helicopter

Franchitti announced he was back in IndyCar by winning the 2009 Long Beach Grand Prix. (Author's collection)

In the April, Franchitti broke his back in a motorbike accident just three weeks prior to the activities at Indianapolis. The medical profession had said he would have no problem being fit enough to race by then ... that was until he arrived in Indiana and was seen by Terry Trammell. "He said, 'no way!'" Thus, Franchitti had to miss the 2003 race. "It was really horrible to see someone else in my car." (Robby Gordon qualified it on the front row.)

Returning in 2004, Franchitti also put his Dallara onto the front row of the grid, having found the month easier than during his debut year. "No May is easy here, but it was an OK month this time." There was one point during the middle of the race that the lead shuffled between fellow Brits Wheldon and Franchitti and a couple of others, but eventually he was to finish fourteenth; last of those to complete the 180 laps, at which point the race was stopped due to rain.

2005 was the year that Franchitti genuinely thought he could win. He qualified in sixth place and for the race reckoned that he had "a really good car." During the early part of the race, he and AGR team-mate Tony Kanaan were passing the lead back and forth in

Fast on the track but not during the pit stops was the story for Franchitti's 2009 Indy 500. (Author's collection)

company with Sam Hornish. "I felt really good." Unfortunately a bad pit stop put him back in the pack – something that was to occur again in 2009. On one of the last restarts he did find himself "... right up against the gearbox" of eventual winner Dan Wheldon. "I reckoned that, being that close, I would be able to draft him and pass into Turn One." The pair were on the outside, with Sebastian Bourdais, who was being lapped, on the inside. Then Bourdais "... just drove me into the wall. He told me that he didn't see me, and that his spotter did not tell him that I was there, but that really did not matter. At that point I thought he had just cost me the 500. I was happy that Dan had won because he did a pretty good job but I was gutted for myself," said Franchitti. Sixth place was just not good enough for the Scot on what

he knew was the fortieth anniversary of Jimmy Clark's win. The fact that compatriot Jackie Stewart was present probably did not help his feelings.

The following year was "a disaster." "We weren't fast all month and only qualified midfield. Seventh place was the final result. "As a team we did not have fast enough cars." Recalled his engineer Allen McDonald, "We had a really bad race and really struggled to get speed."

Kim Green, AGR joint team owner until the end of 2009, reckoned that, as Franchitti had been with Team Green and then AGR from 1998, he "... was like a member of the family. My brother [Barry] and I saw this driver, who worshipped Jimmy Clark, grow up from a young road

Franchitti makes the sparks fly entering Turn Two. (Author's collection)

racer to become a great technical and oval driver. It was good that the circumstances played out to give him an Indy 500 win. I am not sure that when he first when to Indy he had the right respect for the place but most drivers after their first year come away with respect. It's not really an oval; it's like a fast road course. It's a rectangle with not a lot of banking in the corners and that is why a lot of great road racing drivers have adapted well to it."

Green reckoned that what put Franchitti in a position to win the Indianapolis 500 was the tough decision he made in 1997 to leave Mercedes-Benz for whom he had been a junior driver. (In addition to Champ Car he had driven for the German car manufacturer in the International Touring Car Championship, forerunner to the Deutsche Tourenwagen Masters.) At that point he left Carl Hogan, "... became a Honda family member," and moved to Team Green.

At the end of 2007 Franchitti left AGR as it had become and took himself off to NASCAR with Chip Ganassi's operation. The season did not start well with the Scot having to miss a number of races early in the year due to a fractured ankle. By the time the Sprint Cup teams had arrived at Indianapolis for the Brickyard 400 – NASCAR's day at the Speedway – Ganassi had disbanded the Scot's number 40 team due to

a lack of sponsorship funds. Indianapolis has hosted a NASCAR race since 1994, but this was the nearest that any Brit has ever come to driving in it.

Chip Ganassi kept faith with Franchitti and brought him back to Indy cars for 2009 as a replacement for fellow Brit Dan Wheldon. That he was home was quickly shown by the Long Beach victory. On his return to the 500 he showed an aggressive streak, particularly on the restarts, powering past pole sitter and eventual winner Helio Castroneves into Turn One, having qualified in third place. He led for sixty laps and by midway it looked as if the question was to be which of the two Ganassi drivers, he or Scott Dixon, would win his second 500. However, on the 134th lap, a miscommunication caused Franchitti to leave his pit before the fuel hose was disconnected from his car. It was a particularly galling mistake and he was back in the pack. "The Target guys are normally fantastic on pit lane," he said after the race. "They do a great job. But one mistake, unfortunately, is very, very costly. The Target car was pretty bloody good today (but) when you get too far back in the pack like we did with that problem with the pit stop, it's tough to get back to the front again. When I managed to take the lead and was running away, I had a big smile on my face, I can assure you. That

JONNY KANE

In 2000 former British Formula Three champion, Ulsterman Jonny Kane, was in his second year racing in Indy Lights for Team Kool Green and living in Indianapolis. (Dario Franchitti was one of that team's Champ Car drivers then.) "We lived on Georgetown Road, which runs parallel to the start/finish straight. We were exactly four miles from Turn One." Kane and a party of mechanics from Team Green went to watch the 500 that year. "It was interesting to see Champ Car people going to an IRL event because there was still a lot of friction between the two."

This was the first year that some of the Champ Car teams had decided to also run in the 500 and Kane was able to watch his former team-mate from Formula Vauxhall days, Juan Pablo Montoya, win the race. "We were very much Champ Car orientated, so those we wanted to do well differed from who the fans around us wanted to win. It was a bit like being at a soccer match and being in the wrong enclosure with the wrong shirt on."

"It was a race that I has always wanted to go and watch. Living there at the time, it made sense to see what it was all about. There was a fairly amazing atmosphere. The first thing that struck you was the number of people there. Just getting to the track was a major drama. You end up parking your car in someone's garden, give them your car keys and wonder whether it will still be there when you return. However, we were able to park in a friend of a friend's garden. We all had our cool boxes with our sandwiches and beer."

Kane and his mates still had quite a walk to the track despite having arrived at about 6.30am. "On the way there I noticed these huge bones in the road. They were like human thighbones. A hundred or so yards up the road I saw this huge saying 'Jumbo Turkey Legs.' These things were like something out of 'The Flintstones.' We get fairly big turkeys at Christmas time back in Britain but they are nothing like these!" For the Brit, everything about the Indianapolis 500 is larger than life back home. "Then we got in at about 7.00am and everyone was on the beer already. It was a great event. I really enjoyed it."

In Kane's day there was no Freedom 100 so, although he raced on a number of ovals such as Fontana, Michigan, Homestead, and Milwaukee, he never competed at the Brickyard. Despite having been Indy Lights Rookie of the Year in 1999, he returned to Europe after his two years in the series, becoming a leading sports car driver.

Jonny Kane eventually became a fine endurance racer, finishing second for Lola in the LMP2 class at the 2009 Le Mans 24-hours. A year later he went one better in the Strakka Racing HPD.
(Author's collection)

was cool. But, it was a tough deal. It was tough in traffic. When we got back in the pack, it was really difficult. But that's the Speedway."

The way he had taken the lead, and then held it for well over a quarter of the race, had shown that, despite a year's hiatus, Dario Franchitti still had the potential to become the first Brit to win the Indy 500 twice. This was underlined at Homestead in the final race of the season. As his championship rivals Dixon and Ryan Briscoe frenetically burnt up fuel, so he followed them, staying on the same lap and sweeping into the lead in the closing laps as the pair pitted to take both the race and his second IndyCar championship. "He's a quality driver," summed up Target Chip Ganassi engineer Julian Robertson. "You know when you meet one."

24

THE ROCKINGHAM FIND – DARREN MANNING

"I think I'm an underdog kind of guy."

In theory, the Rockingham, Northamptonshire track should have been the British route to the Indianapolis and Daytona 500s. In practice, only one driver can be said to have benefited in this way, making Darren Manning unique in the post-war history of the British at Indianapolis. "That's what got me the drives in Indy Car," he observed.

By the late 1990s Knaresborough-born Manning was a winner in Formula Three, with victories at the Macau Grand Prix as well as in the British Grand Prix support race, and a test driver for BAR. In seeking out a direction for his future he was talking to Champ Cars teams "... but we were always getting the same vibes – no oval experience."

With the Formula One testing not looking as if it would lead to a race drive and the money having dried up after two seasons in Formula 3000, Manning was glancing further afield. For the first time in the UK since the war, an oval racing series was on offer in the UK. The new Rockingham track on the outskirts of Corby was already running a domestic championship using former ASA cars from the US, maybe a lot slower than a full-blown NASCAR but, to European eyes, looking like the same thing. ASCAR, as it was to be called, had attracted some big names for its second year such as Jason Plato, Kelvin Burt, and Frenchman Nicolas Minassian, who had already raced at the Indianapolis for Target Chip Ganassi. "This could be a way of getting some experience on an oval, albeit a stock car," Manning recalled thinking.

The Rockingham management was keen for Manning to become involved. He reacted by saying that he was interested in ASCAR if it

could help him get a drive in the track's Champ Car race. The 1.5-mile oval – Britain's first since Brooklands – had originally been built to attract the Champ Car series. In its first year, the Rockingham 500 (that is kilometres, not miles) was initially beset with problems. For three days it looked as if it just was not going to happen. Rain had caused water to seep through the track – 'weepers' became an 'in' word. When the race did start it was late and the distance shortened to 140 laps. Despite what appeared to be the one grove nature of the track,

A Yorkshireman abroad – Darren Manning at Indianapolis. (Author's collection)

ASCAR could have been the starting line for Brits wanting to break into US oval racing. Only Manning (centre front row) made it to Indianapolis. (Courtesy Kingpin Media)

The launch of Team St George fittingly took place at Brooklands. In the foreground is John Cobb's Napier-Railton, which twice won the Surrey track's own '500,' the BRDC 500. (Author's collection)

38,000 spectators saw a frantic duel between Gil de Ferran and Kenny Brack. The latter took the lead with less than two laps to go only to hand it back to de Ferran in the last corner of the race. Dario Franchitti, who finished ninth, was the only British driver that day.

From Manning's approach came the idea of Team St George, an English team that could help promote the race itself for the next year. Brooklands was used as the venue to launch this initiative, in which ASCAR regular entrant RML (Ray Mallock Ltd) would run a Lola-Cosworth owned by Champ Car team, Dale Coyne. Nobody would have been surprised if this inexperienced operation had failed in front of the might of the Champ Car regulars. In the event it performed admirably, with Manning even leading for a total of eighteen laps before finishing ninth. If the air jacks had not have failed on the last pit stop he might even have finished in the top four. "I was even side-by-side with Dario (Franchitti) for a while." (The Scot went on to win – his first victory on an oval track.)

"I believe that my performance then directly contributed to my getting a full-time Champ Car ride," recalled the Yorkshireman. "That led to an Indy car ride which then led to my getting to

Manning's performance in the Rockingham 500 was sufficient for him to earn a drive in CART. (Courtesy Kingpin Media)

Indianapolis debut in 2004 with Target Chip Ganassi. (Courtesy Indianapolis Motor Speedway)

Indianapolis. It opened all the doors." He took the opportunity to talk to the Champ Car teams again, travelling to the States on a number of occasions, including to Indianapolis. ASCAR had served its purpose.

A deal was now done with Scottish-born team owner Derrick Walker for 2003. In what was to be his only full Champ Car season,

Manning finished ninth overall with his best place a second at Surfers Paradise. He already had a deal with Patrick Racing to stay in Champ Car the following year, but as the season progressed he also started talking to Target Chip Ganassi Racing about an IRL drive. However, this opportunity was given to the more experienced Tony Renna. That

2007 was the first of Manning's two years with A J Foyt's team. (Author's collection)

October Renna was killed testing at Indianapolis and Manning was offered the drive. "It was a championship winning team, backed by Toyota with a big sponsor. I jumped at it."

Manning admits to have been "a bit out at sea" at Homestead, his first race for the team, but still finished sixth. At Phoenix he went one place better, and then one better again at Motagi. Then came Indianapolis. "We always knew that our qualifying pace wasn't too good but we thought our race pace could be alright. I got up to third and then stalled at a pit stop." Sam Hornish had done likewise, and the pair found themselves having to charge back from the back of the field. "We were passing Greg Ray. I had gone to the high side in front of Sam into Turn Four. Sam was going up the inside, Greg slid up into me, hit my wheel and spun me. He then collected Hornish and the three of us went barrelling into the polystyrene attenuator at the end of the pit wall. The remains of three cars made their way down the pit lane, scattering mechanics. It was an accident that Englishman Alex Lloyd was to replicate on his own in 2008.

By 2005, the team had such a deficit with the now uncompetitive Toyota engine "... that we were just terrible. We trimmed it out so much and had so little downforce that I actually ended up parking my G-Force." After ten races of that season, Manning points out that he was ahead of his team-mates Scott Dixon and Ryan Briscoe in the championship but the team was having a torrid time. He is still not sure of Chip Ganassi's reasoning but he was replaced by Jaques Lazier for the remaining oval races of the season. The change from Toyota to Honda engines transformed Target Chip Ganassi the following year with Manning forced to watch from the side lines as Dixon and his new team-mate, Englishman Dan Wheldon, took second and fourth in the championship. "Why couldn't you have done that with me!" thought Manning.

Manning's parents, Pete and Val, were present that second year with Ganassi and making use of their son's new motorhome while he was on Target appearance duty the night before the 500. At 10.00pm Manning and Dixon, who was parked next to him, returned to find his parents had returned to their hotel with the keys and that he was locked out. Thomas Scheckter came out of his motorhome in his pyjamas to see what was happening. It led to the strange sight of Dixon and Scheckter trying to force Manning through the trash can opening the night before the big race.

Manning stayed in Indianapolis, where he had made his home, until after the 2006 Indianapolis, but then, unable to find a drive, decided to return to the UK and forge a career elsewhere. Fortuitously, his house did not sell and he received a call from Larry Foyt, son of four times Indy 500 winner A J. As a former member of one of the top Toyota teams, Manning had helped out Foyt's smaller budget but then similarly powered operation. "I think he respected that and when it came for them to upgrade his operation my name was on the list. I was a friend of the team and they knew that I would work well with them."

Thus, for 2007 the Yorkshireman found himself back in the IRL but with one of the smaller teams. He professes to being happier in this kind of environment having experienced front-running operations with BAR and Ganassi. "I think I'm an underdog kind of guy."

With Ganassi, the Indianapolis 500 "... was just another day. It was very job like. It was very professional, very black and white. I'm not saying that it was not professional with A J but it was very seat of the pants and what he works for. He is all about May. I like the history of motorsport and A J is history. It was nice to get to know the race a bit better through him. At Ganassi it was just another race. OK, it was the biggest one but with A J it had a meaning. It has got more history that you can ever imagine. We weren't expected to win but it was special in a different way driving for him."

In his first year with it the team struggled a little at Indianapolis. Running out of fuel did not help. However, in 2008 it had what Manning remembers as "... a very quick car. We had a good month with a new car. They had spent a lot of time preparing it for the race. This is what the big teams were doing and we realised we had to as well, and it paid off."

KEITH WIGGINS

Keith Wiggins had risen through the engineering ranks before founding Pacific Racing in 1984. The highly successful team won championships in Formula Ford, Formula Ford 2000, Formula Three, and Formula 3000 before moving into Formula One for 1994. Grand Prix racing proved an altogether different challenge, and after two seasons the team returned to F3000.

Having participated in F1, Wiggins found that F3000 was now doing nothing for him. At the time, Lola was in receivership; an opportunity, he thought, for his friend Martin Birrane to acquire this famous name. This Birrane did, and Wiggins joined him, in 1998, as vice president for America. The country was new to him. "In all my time in F1 we did not race there." Nevertheless, he and his new wife moved to Indianapolis. The deal was that he should spend two years there helping Lola to get its sales back. Getting to know the team owners instead of running his own operation was, he felt, a much-needed break. He moved back to Britain at the start of 1999 as VP of sales and marketing while retaining his role with the American market.

Through Scottish engineer Tom Brown, Wiggins became acquainted with Champ Car entrant Tony Bettenhausen Jr, whose team was backed by the Herdez brewery organisation. At the time of the season's first test, Bettenhausen was killed in a plane crash and Wiggins was asked if he could take over the running of the operation. He agreed to but only as consultant. Within six months of having returned to England, he and his family were back in the same Indianapolis apartment. Through what he calls "a series of adventures," Wiggins ended up owning the Gasoline Alley-based team.

It was when Herdez ceased sponsorship in 2005 that he actually took over what is still, nevertheless, called HVM (Herdez Viva Mexico). One of his drivers was Englishman Dan Clarke who, despite being a rookie, put his car on pole at the Road America Champ Car race in 2006. The team was struggling when Paul Stoddart bought into it in 2007, the result being that, until he left it the following year, it was known as Team Minardi US, after the Australian's former F1 team. "When Champ Car ceased at the start of 2008, Paul thought that we would be crazy to go on, so I dusted off the HVM name and took up the challenge by myself." The team contested its first Indianapolis 500 in 2008 with E J Viso driving. The following year, Viso was joined by Nelson Philippe for the 500 as HVM became a two-car team. At one point there had been a possibility that Wiggins might also run an Englishman, Dillon Battistini, but the funding could not be put together in time. Nevertheless, at the start of 2010 there was still a possibility that the 2007 Freedom 100 winner could yet drive with HVM for that year's 500.

"We spent our time in Champ Car saying that the Indianapolis 500's not a big deal so who cares, but then when you walk into the arena on the day of the race you just think 'bloody hell, this is impressive,'" said Wiggins.

Two Brits during a reception held by the UK's Motorsports Industry Association at the Indiana Governor's Mansion; Wiggins and the IRL's Roger Bailey. (Author's collection)

Manning was disappointed not to qualify on the first day but a conservative run the next weekend saw him in fourteenth place, one better than the year before. In the race he was running in a comfortable sixth place. "This is great, I thought. We were trying to hang around until the last pit stop and then go racing, and yet we were in the top six." Then a front wing was knocked off on one of the pit stops and he dropped back to twenty-fourth before working his way back to ninth. "It needed to be longer than 500 miles." He puts his hand up for the pit lane incident. "We were in a funny pit stall. Alex Lloyd, who was out by that stage, would have been in front of us and then there was a big gap before Buddy Rice. Generally, you just go when the car has been dropped. Larry Foyt, who was on the radio was, though, shouting

Nelson Philippe drove for Keith Wiggins at Indianapolis in 2009. (Author's collection)

'no, no, no' but, because I had a clear run in front of me I made my mind up to filter in. If Alex had been in front of me I wouldn't have gone." Unfortunately, Rice was cutting in early to make his stop, an understandable move given the space between them. In doing so he clipped Manning's wing end plate, taking part of it off. The team decided to replace this, hoping to be able to make up the time lost but it was a race punctuated by too many yellows and there just was not time enough. "But, twenty-ninth to ninth, it was my best Indy." A J Foyt reckoned but for that incident, Manning would have finished in the top five that year.

Manning parted company with Foyt at the end of 2008. Faced without a regular drive in the IRL, he accepted a seat from Dreyer and Reinbold for the St Petersburg and Long Beach races that started the next season, bringing some experience to a team that at the time comprised just the one rookie, fellow Englishman Mike Conway. Others less talented were able to bring sponsorship to the team for the next race of the season, the Indy 500, and so Manning, having helped it on its way for 2009 found himself without a drive for the big one. Hopeful, he was seen in the paddock during the month of May talking to people but nothing was arranged.

BRITAIN'S OWN 500

For a brief period between the wars, Britain had its own '500,' the Brooklands-based, British Racing Drivers Club (BRDC) 500. Like so much that happened at the Surrey track, this was a handicap affair. Using the outer circuit, the race ran from 1929 to 1937, becoming the fastest long-distance race in the world.

The nature of the race was so that it could be won by such as the 4.5-litre Bentley of Jack Barclay and Frank Clement in 1929, or the little orange Austin Seven of SCH 'Sammy' Davis and the Earl of March the following year. Despite this, and perhaps fittingly, the fastest car ever to compete at Brooklands, John Cobb's 24-litre Napier Railton, twice won the event. In 1937, in an attempt to cut down both expenses and the number of retirements, the BRDC reduced the length of the race from 500 miles to 500 kilometres. Partnered by Olivier Bertram, Cobb, a future Land Speed Record holder, rumbled round that outer edge of the banking, all four wheels sometimes clear of the concrete, at an average of 121.28mph. It was not until 1949 that an Indianapolis 500 was won at a faster speed, and that by only 0.05mph and from a rolling start.

Another twice victor was the mercurial winner of Tourist Trophies on two, three, and four wheels, Freddie Dixon with his 2-litre Rileys. Such was the unforgiving nature of the track that two drivers were usually required to win, but on a couple of occasions a solo run sufficed, one of these being Dixon's first 500 victory.

BRDC 500 winners
1929 Jack Barclay/Frank Clement (Bentley)
1930 SCH 'Sammy' Davis/The Earl of March (Austin)
1931 Jack Dunfee/Cyril Paul (Bentley)
1932 Tommy Horton/Jack Bartlett (MG)
1933 Eddie Hall (MG)
1934 Freddie Dixon (Riley)
1935 John Cobb/Tim Rose-Richards (Napier-Railton)
1936 Freddie Dixon/Charles Martin (Riley)
1937 John Cobb/Oliver Bertram (Napier-Railton)

In 1935, furrier John Cobb took the BRDC 500 with Tim Rose-Richards. Two years later he teamed up with Oliver Bertram to again win the shortened race. In both cases he used the mighty Napier-Railton that had initially been built with a view to breaking the World 24-hour record. (Author's collection)

25

ROGER BAILEY AND THE FREEDOM 100

"For us, it's the greatest race of the year."

Sitting in his office just across the road from the Speedway, British Racing Drivers Club member Roger Bailey exudes an enthusiasm that belies his fifty years in motor racing. This former mechanic and engine builder with a fund of stories has a position of influence running the Indy Lights programme that can potentially place drivers – some of them fellow Brits – on the road to the Indy 500 itself.

Bailey's North America odyssey arguably dates back to the end of 1969. Grand Prix driver Chris Amon declared to Bailey, then the New Zealander's engineer, that he was leaving Ferrari to go to March Engineering. Bailey visited the March headquarters in Bicester with Amon "... but there was something about the place that did not appeal to me after Maranello, so I decided to take a year off."

A few weeks later, Bailey was asked to help build the Tony Southgate-designed BRM P154 Can-Am cars, and thus moved to a small flat in Bourne that he shared with a number of others, including Bruce McIntosh who had been involved with the BRP Indy car. Once the cars had been finished, he was asked if he would like to help run them. "America did not appeal to me at the time but I thought, what am I going to do anyway?" That move to work in Can-Am led to him joining McLaren Engines in Detroit for 1971. This meant Bailey was going to help build its Offenhauser engines for Indy. "I had only been there for a little while before I was told that I had to go down to Indianapolis to work with a Herb Porter. I set off early in the morning not really knowing where Indianapolis was in relation to Detroit. I eventually got there, drove in and headed for garage number sixty-nine. I asked for

Mr Porter and heard a voice from the back of the garage say 'We start at 8.00am around here!'" At the end of the day Porter took Bailey to his hotel. "And Mr Porter liked to drink, it was a long night. I won't go into the details, but that was my first day at Indianapolis ...

Roger Bailey (left) reminisces with Adrian Reynard. (Author's collection)

205

The next two months saw Bailey working as the engine builder for the McLaren M16s. For some years he stayed with McLaren at Detroit, primarily building the Indy engines but also working on the big Chevrolet V8s for Can-Am. In 1974 he returned to the UK to start a boat business, only to find that fuel was rationed and VAT had been put on luxury goods. It was not the best of ideas. In 1976 McLaren's Teddy Mayer asked if he was ready to return to the States. A deal had been done with BMW to run in the IMSA touring car series, and there was a need for a team manager. For three years he ran this out of the engine shop in Detroit. In 1980 IMSA's John Bishop offered Bailey the post of technical director for said sports car racing organising body. He had only been married for a month, and now he and his wife were on their way to Connecticut.

He kept that post for five years, during which he renewed his acquaintance with March founder Robin Herd. The latter needed somebody to sell cars in North America, Bishop did not mind if Bailey moonlighted "... and so I ended up working for IMSA during the day and selling March Indy cars in the evenings." His future colleague at the Indy Racing League, Les Mactaggart, was then production manager for March, building the cars in Bicester.

"We had a couple of good years. In 1985 we sold over forty Indy cars." However, March was now building sports racing cars. This came to Bishop's attention. "It was alright while I was selling Indy cars but selling sports cars was a conflict of interest. These were the products that I was writing the rules for!" By then, though, March was talking to Pat Patrick about starting an American version of Formula 3000. "That sounds like an interesting project, I thought." Thus, at the end of 1985 Bailey quit IMSA and returned to Detroit. Buick agreed to provide 3.5-litre V6 engines, which were installed in twenty March 85Gs, the F3000 car designed by Ralph Bellamy. This became the original American Racing Series car. The series ran through to 1990 when, with a change of tyre supplier from Goodyear to Firestone, it became Firestone Indy Lights. Although the series did not yet run at Indianapolis, the Speedway was prepared to licence the Indy name to it. In 1993 Lola took over as the car manufacturer, with Bailey and Patrick selling the series to CART four years later.

Having signed a clause agreeing not to work in any competitive environment, Bailey stayed with the series, increasingly disenchanted with its managers. In 2001, in the course of an interview with the *Milwaukee Sentinel* he voiced his sentiments. The owners of CART, upset by this, requested his resignation. That, though, would have meant no unemployment benefit. He refused, CART declined to sack him, and for some months he sat in his office with little to do.

The break-up between CART and IRL had happened by this time and Tony George and Brian Barnhart were looking to start their own equivalent of Indy Lights. In the November Bailey's five-year contract was over and he travelled to Indianapolis to start the IRL Indy Pro Series – using Infiniti engines – which had its first race at Kansas early in 2002. Firestone was soon to become involved and the Indy Pro title was eventually dropped in favour of Firestone Indy Lights, the name of Bailey's former series. "We've effectively had four different names for the same series."

Indy Pro initially struggled against its rival, the Toyota Atlantic championship, which had history on its side, and also the fact that not everybody wanted to race on ovals. Atlantics ran at the Long Beach Grand Prix, and the newer series needed an event of equal, if not greater, prestige to combat this. The logical thing was to race at the Brickyard. "It would be difficult to find somebody who would not want to race there. We gave even those who would never get into an Indy car the opportunity to race at Indianapolis."

Thus, the Freedom 100 was born in 2003. For the first two years the forty-lap race was held during practice for the Indianapolis 500. However, in 2005 it was moved to what is traditionally known as Carb Day, the Friday before the 500. "Now we have tremendous crowds and tremendous racing," stated Bailey. "For us, it's the greatest race of the year," said 2009/2010 Indy Lights contestant Pippa Mann. Such is the nature of the Speedway that there is an almost surreal appearance to the race. Looking out from the infield at the empty grandstands it appears that nobody is interested in the field of scrapping Dallaras, despite the prestigious nature of the race. The appearance is deceptive. Around 80-100,000 people could be watching from the inside of the track. It is only two days later that the grandstands will fill up for the 500 itself. Bailey compares the Freedom 100 crowd to at least that for the MotoGP. With the annual pit stop competition and a concert, the Friday Carb Day has become part of a weekend festival.

British successes in the various series that have led up to the Indy Lights include Steve Robertson's CART Indy Lights championship in 1994, Mark Taylor's title in the 2003 IRL Infiniti Pro Series, and championships for Jay Howard and Alex Lloyd in 2006 and 2007 respectively, the two years that it was run as the IRL Indy Pro Series. Taylor, Howard, and Lloyd all got their chance to run in the Indy Racing League.

The fact that Indy Lights now includes Indianapolis in its schedule has meant further opportunity for British success at the Brickyard. Taylor came third in the Freedom 100 in 2003, Howard went one place better in 2006, but the first Englishman to win it was Lloyd in 2007 (see chapter twenty-seven). The Manxman also took victory in the Indy Pro supporting race for the Indianapolis Formula One Grand Prix in 2006, with Howard and another Brit Scott Mansell finishing further down the field.

Lloyd dominated the Freedom 100 in 2007, pulling out a lead on restart after restart as the field of twenty-four identical Dallaras droned round the vast spaces of the Speedway. In the F1-backing road race he finished second. A year later Dillon Battistini from Ewell, Surrey – not the only Brit to carry an Italian name in this story – ensured that the Freedom 100 title stayed in England.

"There's a definite mystique about the place; there's so much history there," said Battistini, who in 2007 had won the Asian Formula Three championship. "It feels very special, It's so much difference from other tracks." For Battistini who, unlike Lloyd, won the Freedom 100 but not the Indy Lights championship, it was like winning the FA Cup in soccer as opposed to the League. "The track is large, the speeds are high and it is intimidating."

Battistini came to Indy inexperienced in the ways of ovals after driving that year for Panther Racing. It was only his third such race.

Dillon Battistini (car number 15) battles with James Davison at the start of the 2008 Freedom 100. The Panther Racing Brit was rarely to be headed. (Author's collection)

At the end of 2007, when he had been in the US to take a Champ Car test with Indianapolis-based Minardi US, he had taken the opportunity to have a look at the Speedway. "It was almost like holy ground." At the time he was aiming for Champ Car, unaware that the series would not exist the following year. Little did he think that within a few months he would have won a race at Indianapolis, "... definitely the biggest one of my career."

Battistini took pole for the 2008 Freedom 100, his only one of the season. Carb Day that year brought rain, causing the race to be postponed for twenty-four hours. That meant a smaller crowd but it was something Battistini did not notice, "I was so zoned in." The delay, he recalled, "... was really hard. We did not know that the race had been called off so we were on standby for hours. When you are psyched up to run a race it is mentally draining." A rumour had been going the rounds that it was going to happen later in the day. "When they eventually announced the race would take place on the Saturday I was pleased because by then I was mentally exhausted."

By the time the race started Battistini was relieved just to be getting on with it. "I felt that I was on top of my game that day." While other drivers were fighting for every inch of ground, he was finding that he knew when to back off and set up the next overtaking manoeuvre. When anyone passed him he was able to strike back. "I felt that I was probably going to win as long as I didn't throw it away."

At the winner's press conference the thirty-year old Battistini

appeared almost stunned. "It meant everything to win that race; it is so good for your CV." His photo went up large on the outside wall of the Pagoda next to that of Lewis Hamilton. There was now hope that he would land a full Indy car drive for the next season; this came close but not quite close enough. However, at the start of 2010 efforts – ultimately unsuccessful – were still being made to put together sufficient funding for him to drive for Keith Wiggins HVM team in the 500.

There was to be no hat trick of British Freedom 100 victories. Having entered one Brit in 2008, Panther Racing had two for the following year. With Dan Wheldon also driving the team's IRL car, it was an all-English line-up for the Indianapolis-based team. Pre-season testing at Homestead indicated that the pair, Martin Plowman and Pippa Mann, from European Formula Three and World Series by Renault respectively, might be among the front-runners. Plowman and Mann had known each other since their teenage years. "He has been like my annoying kid brother," said Mann, somewhat prophetically. Quite how "annoying" he could be was yet to be seen. "They seem like brother and sister," added Panther's PR Mike Kitchel. "It's quite entertaining."

Plowman and Mann were not the only Brits in the race that year. After a last minute call from Team PBIR, 2006 Indy Pro champion Jay Howard was back following a brief foray into the IRL the previous year with Roth Racing that had not included the 500. Northern Ireland's Alistair Jackson was also in the line-up, although Stefan Wilson,

The cap says it all for Dillon Battistini at the winner's press conference. (Author's collection)

the start took him aback and he narrowly avoided a few near misses. During around the second and third laps he had some loose moments where the car nearly stepped away from him. In-car changes were made to improve the balance, and Plowman started to feel that he was getting into a rhythm. Then, going into Turn One on lap seven, the car snapped loose, and "... the next thing I knew was that I was bracing myself, thinking 'shit, this is going to hurt.'" The wall was the only place that he was going. "It seemed like my head had exploded." Spotter Pancho Carter observed that the accident "... was just one of those things."

Meanwhile team-mate Mann was "... just cruising around, saving my tyres. It was too early in the race to be playing games." She had a new car for the Freedom 100 and had been shaking it down during official testing. The car was oversteering "... which made my first experience of Indianapolis a little too interesting for my liking." By the time of qualifying the car had been sorted and the team chose to run it in race rather than qualifying trim. "For the first six laps of the race it was just fantastic," she recalled.

From her position behind Plowman she reckoned that he had turned in from the middle of the track. The Indy Lights cars were topping at about 195mph and as Plowman was to say the next day, "If you miss your turning point by a fraction, the consequences are huge."

Seeing his back end break away, Mann had a split second to decide which way to dive. She probably made the correct choice as,

present to watch brother Justin in the 500, was sitting this one out as his season only included the road courses.

"The first time you come to this place you are just blown away by the size of it," said Plowman. "Anybody who does not respect it will probably be bitten hard. Going into Turn One it is as if you are staring the wall in the face. The track gives you the biggest adrenalin rush that you can image." He admits that it took him about eight or nine laps of his initial test before he was anywhere near flat out. Plowman adds that, "Practice was the most white-knuckle ride that I have ever had in a race car. However, my first qualifying lap felt as perfect as it could be. It felt like the car was floating."

For the young driver the highlight of race day morning was signing autographs for a group of disabled fans. He held out his hand to shake that of a little girl with Downs Syndrome and instead "... she ran at me and gave me the biggest hug."

Plowman was not sure that he had the optimum balance for the beginning of the race. The start would be difficult but he hoped that the balance would come to the car later. He admits that the aggression of his fellow competitors at

Martin Plowman, early in the 2009 season at Long Beach. (Author's collection)

Pippa Mann, not just the only British lady to have raced at the Indianapolis Motor Speedway but also, in 2010, the first female of any nation to win a pole at the track. (Courtesy Indianapolis Motor Speedway)

going on the high side, she did just manage to miss him. However, in doing so she clipped her tyres on the wall. "Better one wrecked Panther car and one with bent suspension than two in a big heap," she remarked. In a second both Panther's Brits were out. British pride was sustained by Jay Howard who, despite having been offered the drive at the last minute, moved up into fourth place during the final laps.

Plowman and Mann experienced tough rookie years in Indy Lights, but both planned to be back for the 2010 Freedom 100, although in different teams; Plowman with AFS Racing, Mann with Sam Schmidt Motorsports.

Having won in 2008 with a Brit, Panther entered two the following year. However, with just one incident, Plowman (15) and Mann (16) became the first to drop out. Jay Howard (37) was the best British driver that year. (Author's collection)

Former British A1GP driver James Winslow also signed to run with Schmidt, while it was announced that Stefan Wilson would contest the full championship for Bryan Herta Autosport. With Lloyd and Howard likely to line up in the 500 for Dale Coyne and Sarah Fisher Racing respectively, and Battistini a possible for HVM, what might be described as Roger Bailey's protégés remained an important part of the British at Indianapolis story.

Charlie Kimball finds himself sandwiched by the British with Howard ahead and Mann following. (Author's collection)

DERRICK WALKER

At the end of the 2009, the Indianapolis-based team run by ex-patriot Scot Derrick Walker announced that it would be expanding its Indy Lights programme from two to three cars for 2010 and was still looking to make an eventual Indy Car comeback. The team had been running Brit Stefan Wilson on the road courses round of the Indy Lights series and had hoped to continue its relationship with Justin's younger brother.

Walker, a former chief mechanic at Brabham, joined Penske back in 1976, becoming Poole-based Penske Car's general manager and then moving to the US to become Penske's vice president of racing. He formed Walker Racing in 1990, having purchased the assets of Porsche's short-lived Indy factory team. Walker Racing has made history at Indianapolis on more than one occasion. Driving one of Walker's cars, Willy T Ribbs became the first African-American to qualify for the 500 in 1991, while nine years later Sarah Fisher became the youngest woman to start the race. In 1992 Scott Goodyear lost the 500 by a scant 0.043 seconds, at the time the closest finish to an Indy 500. In 2005 Walker joined forces with Australian businessman Craig Gore to form Team Australia, initially to run in Champ Car. Following 'unification' the team had one start in the Indy 500 with Will Power driving before being disbanded. Walker Racing continued the following season with Wilson in Indy Lights.

Derrick Walker's eponymous team made history in 1992 when it lost the 500 by a mere 0.043 seconds. (Courtesy Indianapolis Motor Speedway)

Following a brief foray into IndyCar racing with Marty Roth's team, Jay Howard returned to Indy Lights for 2009, his reward being a 2010 drive back in the top level with Sarah Fisher Racing. (Author's collection)

26

GRAND PRIX VICTORY – LEWIS HAMILTON

"... I instantly felt at home."

Dillon Battistini's win in the 2008 Freedom 100 had a certain significance: it was the fourth consecutive open-wheel race at the Indianapolis Motor Speedway to have been won by a British driver. Fellow Englishman Alex Lloyd had come first in the corresponding event the year before, while Scot Dario Franchitti had won the 500 itself a couple of days after Lloyd's victory. The third of the four wins had, though, been in a type of racing that had been divorced from Indianapolis throughout the Twentieth Century; a road course Formula One event. The other man in that running streak was McLaren driver Lewis Hamilton, who, in under a year and a half, would become F1's youngest ever World Champion.

The Indianapolis 500 had been the US round of the World Championship for the first decade of the latter's existence ... not that anybody noticed. Only Alberto Ascari of the Grand Prix regulars ever qualified for the 500 during this period. Nevertheless, Indy results are included in the Championship tables of the 1950s with, for example, Jimmy Bryan classified as thirteenth with eight points in 1958 – the first year that the World Championship was won by a Briton, Mike Hawthorn. Ironically, as the 500 was replaced in the Championship by a US Grand Prix, initially at Sebring and then Watkins Glen, so Grand Prix drivers began taking an interest in the Speedway. It is an irrelevant fact that Graham Hill would have climbed up the Championship table from fifth to third in 1966, had the 500 still counted for points, with Jim Clark following him from sixth to fourth.

Grand Prix drivers have raced in the 500 but, until the early years of this century, F1 and Indianapolis have had very little to do with

Two Brits – Hamilton and Battistini – on the Bombardier Pagoda wall; a site reserved for winners. (Courtesy Richard Dencer)

each other. The IMS is billed as 'The Racing Capital of the World' but, despite the introduction of a 400-mile NASCAR race to its calendar, this title had a hollow ring outside of North America. Then president and CEO Tony George was determined to bring Grand Prix racing to Indianapolis and thus justify the track's sobriquet. A winding road

The Pagoda provides a familiar backdrop but it's a Formula One car in the foreground; Justin Wilson's Jaguar. (Courtesy Indianapolis Motor Speedway)

course was built inside the oval and in 2000 a round of the Formula One-only World Championship was held at the Speedway. It was not an easy sell. "Formula One is not perceived in the same way here as around the world, in Europe and Asia," said George. "It's a tough dynamic."

British drivers David Coulthard and World Champion-to-be Jenson Button entered all the races until they came to an end after Hamilton's win in 2007, Coulthard's third in 2002 being the next best result. Eddie Irvine (twice), Johnny Herbert, Allan McNish, Justin Wilson, and Anthony Davidson also competed in the event. Wilson was to return to the Speedway as an Indy car driver in 2008. Herbert also tried to qualify for the Indianapolis 500 in 2002, two years after he ran in the GP there. Driving for Duesenberg Brothers Racing, he never made the grid and left the track to race an Audi R8 in a clashing sports car race at Sears Point.

The US Grand Prix ran into trouble in 2005 when practice indicated that the Michelin tyres provided were unsafe for the race. Just six, Bridgestone-shod, cars started. However, George does not blame everything on the one debacle, other factors intervened to bring an end to the race. The final GP, 2007, was one, though, at which to wave the Union flag – an early success in the story that was to take Lewis Hamilton to the world crown the following year.

Despite being in his rookie season, the twenty-two-year old Hamilton arrived at Indianapolis leading the championship on the back of his first GP win – Canada – the week before. The beginning of the week saw the Englishman in New York unnoticed, except by a few European tourists – the US can be like that about Formula One drivers. It was then on to Washington and a delayed flight that saw him arrive for his first look at Indianapolis on the Thursday morning.

Hamilton was under pressure as his team-mate, two-time World

Justin Wilson's first appearance at Indianapolis was in the 2003 US Grand Prix, running as high as third at one point. The Formula One cars have now left the Brickyard, but the Englishman was back in 2008. (Courtesy Indianapolis Motor Speedway)

Champion Fernando Alonso, was just then starting to complain that McLaren was giving him preferential treatment. Despite that, Hamilton seemed not to be phased. Making his debut at the track, and with the team not having found an optimal setup prior to qualifying, Hamilton still claimed pole position. He recalled the British flags that flew around the track then.

The practice had begun on the Friday morning. The session had been running for some time before Hamilton appeared on the track. At that point Jarno Trulli and Toyota had the best time on the board. Trulli was no slouch, particularly at Indy. In short, he sets a good benchmark. And Hamilton blew it away on his first flying lap.

"Not many people were paying attention in the press room," recalled British journalist Matt Youson, "But of those that were, most nodded in appreciation. In the age

Turning right at the Speedway. Lewis Hamilton on his way to victory in the 2007 Grand Prix. (Courtesy Indianapolis Motor Speedway)

Hamilton left the Indianapolis Motor Speedway leading the World Championship, despite this being his rookie year. (Courtesy Indianapolis Motor Speedway)

of simulators, it wasn't exactly a blind run, but to go out on a track that he'd never previously visited, and instantly go quickly suggested ... good things." Eventually Hamilton finished the session third fastest, but it was that initial run the stuck in Youson's mind. Alonso stayed in front for the next two practice sessions, but when the times started to matter Hamilton sneaked ahead, qualifying on pole with just over a tenth of a second to spare.

A clean start in the race saw Hamilton off into the lead. Alonso tried to go around the outside, Hamilton covered it. The Spaniard then moved inside, trying to go the long way around at Turn Two; he could not make it stick, Hamilton had the better line and stayed in front by a couple of metres. Alonso was right behind, though, gaining on the straight whatever the Brit was pulling out through the infield.

This was still very early on in Hamilton's F1 career and he certainly was not widely regarded as Alonso's equal. The assumption was that the latter qualified with more fuel on board. He had, but not much more. Hamilton stopped on lap twenty-one, Alonso one lap later, McLaren was impeccable with both men and the order was maintained. Alonso sometimes dropped off a couple of seconds, but closed the gap to half a second whenever backmarkers appeared.

At one point after those initial pit stops, the Spaniard took the opportunity presented by a back marker and was right on Hamilton's tail. He got alongside out of the last corner (which would be the first turn in any other race at Indianapolis) and the two McLarens were neck-and-neck going down the main straight, but Hamilton already had one Grand Prix victory under his belt and he was not about to lose this one. Moving to the inside and braking late he kept Alonso behind, but for a few corners it was, as he recalled, "tough." That was the first time all season the pair had raced wheel-to-wheel, and Hamilton had survived the examination.

The pair then held position through the second round of pit stops and Alonso seemed to lose heart after that and backed off. Towards the end, Hamilton pulled away and controlled the race, keeping happy the many British fans in the 100,000 plus crowd. He remembered those last fifteen laps in the heat as "draining."

The result at Indy was a turning point in the year. Hamilton had been leading the championship since the beginning of May, but there was never any belief that he got the drive with McLaren as anything other than Alonso's understudy. That changed at Indy, where he matched, and beat the double and reigning world champion in a

scrupulously fair fight. Indianapolis was the first time the pair went absolutely head-to-head. For Hamilton to come out on top laid down a huge marker. And after that the game was different.

The Englishman left Indianapolis with a ten point lead in the World Championship and a memory of the support that he had received there. What happened to that lead is well recorded. Suffice to say that he was to fail to become the first ever driver to win the Championship in his first Grand Prix season by a solitary point. The title was to come the following season but by then the Formula One cars had left Indianapolis. Tony George wanted them to return, but admitted that what he felt he could offer to retain the event and what F1 supremo Bernie Ecclestone wanted differed by US$10 million. Without a title sponsor, the Grand Prix was not going to return to the Brickyard, at least not for the foreseeable future.

Two years, one world championship, and a gigantic leap into the superstar stratosphere later, Hamilton had no problem recalling his triumph at what was, still then, the most recent United States Grand Prix. "It sticks in the mind most because it was my second win in two weekends. Actually, it was my second win ever in Formula One, so it was a pretty important time in my career and an unforgettable experience."

The most endearing thing about Hamilton as an F1 rookie was the obvious pleasure he took in being there and doing it. He smiled all the time. Did he recall seeing the P1 board after his first flying lap of Friday morning practice? Had he found that sort of speed through endless, intensive hours in the simulator? "No, I can just do that." He said it very earnestly, then realising that perhaps it sounded a touch too

MATT YOUSON

The advent of the Indy Racing League saw a falling off in interest from the British press in the 500, which has arguably continued to this day. However, the situation was very different when the Formula One circus came to town, bringing with it its own press corps. Matt Youson, then of The Red Bulletin, was one of its number.

"I've never been to the Indy 500, but watching it on television the thing which always takes a while to get over is the way they go around the track 'the wrong way,'" observed Youson. "Having spent most of this decade attending Indianapolis as an F1 writer, it seems natural to me that Turn One is really Turn Thirteen, and the cars should run clockwise!

"Indy was a favourite venue for the travelling F1 circus. The team facilities inside and behind the garages are superb. The media centre is second to none, and the organisation is precise. All the usual niggles that upset the equilibrium, particularly at a flyaway race, just weren't there at the Brickyard. The town itself is always very welcoming. Apparently, when F1 is in town more is spent per capita than would be the case during the other big events. "Y'all drink a lot more wine," concluded one bartender by way of explanation. Certainly all the way from the Slippery Noodle on Meridian Street to Rock Bottom on West Washington, F1 tended to let its collective hair down.

"At the track itself there was a little bit of an edge. The famous yard of bricks tended to inhibit traction for whoever was unlucky enough to be just behind them. Over the years quite a few drivers asked if they could be removed and replaced with asphalt.

"My memories of the 2007 United States Grand Prix are still sharp, though it was the build up, rather than the race itself, which was most distinctive. As a nation America really doesn't 'get' F1 but Indianapolis is different: Indy treated F1 much better than F1 treated Indy. Mainstream America might dismiss the series but had you gone into any bar, shopping mall, or restaurant in Downtown Indy you would have been be engulfed in knowledgeable and articulate banter. And in 2007 the name bubbling all over the conversation was 'Hamilton.'

"The timing really couldn't have been better. Lewis had taken his first pole position and his maiden F1 victory a few days earlier. He came to Indy with his lead in the championship enhanced and serious voices, albeit still in the minority, were just starting to think that maybe a rookie could win the World Championship. Indianapolis bought into it wholesale. Precocious talent always finds a welcoming embrace, but Hamilton had looks, charm, and an endearing English accent, too."

The race was a little milestone for Youson. After forty-five Grands Prix "bumming around" in the paddock and pit lane with team accreditation, he was finally credentialed as a bona fide journalist and summoned to the media centre to pick up a permanent media pass. "The guy behind the desk noted my accent and jumped to entirely the wrong conclusion: 'They've sent you out here to cover Hamilton, I guess?' I explained I'd been around the block a few times already – but I imagine there were plenty of UK media outlets who, after Montreal, did decide to despatch their sports editor to Indianapolis, mostly to find out if Lewis Hamilton was the real deal." As Youson observed, "They would not leave disappointed."

serious a toothy grin appeared. "Well, sometimes I can, and sometimes I can't. But I've always found it easy to learn a circuit."

Moving forward to qualifying, putting his McLaren-Mercedes on pole was, he recalled, no great shakes. "At that stage in the season I had a really, really good car. The first and third sectors of the circuit are not very difficult. The middle sector is more complicated, and I'd had to work hard at that. But with a really good car, getting on pole wasn't so hard."

Hamilton split race day itself into two distinct memories. "The first is that the crowd were absolutely mega. I had some great fans out in the grandstands; lots of British flags being waved but I also felt a lot of support from the Americans in the crowd. They seemed to take to me and I had fantastic support all weekend. I'd go so far as to say I instantly felt at home.

"The second thing is that I had a great, great battle with Fernando. He was right there with me for a lot of the race, and a few times right up my backside. The moment where Tonio (Liuzzi) slowed me down a touch meant things got really close for a little bit! But looking back I can't really remember that much about it! But I do remember it was close, and I felt I really had to work incredibly hard to win the race."

Vitantonio Liuzzi takes Matt Youson around the Speedway's Grand Prix course. Liuzzi briefly slowed Hamilton during the race, while Youson interviewed him afterwards. (Courtesy Matt Youson collection)

27

PINK LLOYD – ALEX LLOYD

"It was a heck of an achievement ..."

Alex Lloyd talked about a "buzz" that has only happened to him three times in his career. Two of these were his first win in karts and his first victory, again in a kart, in a British Championship round. The third was crossing the winning line at Indianapolis. Lloyd, Manchester born but a Manxman, is one of that select band of Brits who have won at the Brickyard.

Lloyd's victory, an impressive one, came in the 2007 Indy Pro Series Freedom 100 – just part of a championship winning year that put him on the road to the 500 itself. It should also be pointed out that Lloyd's win in the Freedom 100 was, in fact, his second at the Speedway (a feat Dario Franchitti was to copy in 2010). The year before he had come first in the IPS race that had been on the same card as the US Grand Prix and which used the stadium's road course. It made him then the only Brit to have won twice at the Indianapolis Motor Speedway, as well as the first driver to come home first on both its road and oval courses.

Five minutes before he had to go out to the grid for the road course race he had still been on a drip in the medical centre. Problems with his left ear had been causing dizziness. Someone else had taken the car out to the grid and, at the last moment, Lloyd was allowed to grab his helmet and rush out for the start "... feeling as if I was about to throw up." Problems also with the car meant it was what Lloyd recalled "a strange race" but when Graham Rahal made a mistake towards the end he was able to slip into the lead and his first win in the IPS. It was, though, "... for whatever reason, nothing like winning the Freedom 100 the following year."

Alex Lloyd talks to the press on media day prior to his first 500.
(Author's collection)

Having won every round of the 2007 IPS coming up to Indianapolis, Lloyd was favourite not only to win but also to put himself in the record books. "It would be a nice thing to have, a piece of history," he mused.

In winning the Freedom 100, Lloyd became the first Englishman to score two victories at the Indianapolis Motor Speedway. (Author's collection)

Lloyd had come to Indianapolis, via a variety of European single-seater series, including the 2003 Formula Renault UK championship in which he had finished second to Lewis Hamilton, being given the BRDC McLaren Autosport Young Driver of the Year award for his pains. By 2006 he was racing in the then Indy Pro Series and living in Indianapolis, marrying his English wife, Sam, ten minutes from the Speedway in the April – the day after his first open test there. Their first daughter, Ava, was born in Indianapolis the next October. After a part season with AFS Racing, which started after the Freedom 100, Lloyd signed with Sam Schmidt Motorsports for the following year. He was to qualify on the front row of the grid for every race he contested, winning eight rounds and the championship.

His first laps of the Speedway oval were not, though, in an IPS car. Far from it, they were at the wheel of Mario Andretti's 1967 pole

winning Hawk. The car needed a shake down prior to it being driven by Andretti in a celebratory parade. The IPS drivers were at the track that day and Roger Bailey was asked if he could recommend one with the 1969 winner's stature. Lloyd duly obliged.

Come the Freedom 100 itself he looked unstoppable. Despite failing to win the pole, he went round the outside of Turn One into the lead, and was never headed again. Every time the yellow lights came on the field bunched up and every time they went green, Lloyd opened up a gap again. "For the first time in my entire life it all went to plan."

At the end of 2007 Lloyd was signed up by Target Chip Ganassi for an Indy Car drive. Prior to the merger between the Indy Racing League and Champ Car, he had seven races lined up. However, the merger actually hurt his plans "... and the deal went away." With the additional car count brought about by the merger, it had no longer

Ganassi car. However, a deal was done whereby, for budgetary reasons, Ganassi collaborated with Bobby Rahal. The car was to be used as a one-off promotion by Ganassi sponsor Target to launch the Wi-Fit product and, basically, Lloyd and engineer, fellow Englishman Andy Brown, were loaned out to Rahal. Most of the car was built at Ganassi's before it was shipped to Rahal's operation. It was engineered out of the Rahal garage with Brown as the only Ganassi employee "... feeling a bit like the round peg in the square hole." Brown underlines the fact that the Rahal people were very supportive but feels that there were still things that both sides were holding back from each other. "Sometimes when you put one person's good ideas with another's, the result is not a good idea at all!"

Initially, though, all went well and Lloyd was full of optimism. "Had I known what I know now I would have been more concerned. Indianapolis in an Indy car is so different from in an Indy Lights. I had never driven an Indy car before other than a day or two's testing on a road course."

Lloyd was quickest in the rookie phase, feeling comfortable even if everything was so different. Former double winner Arie Luyendyk was coaching the young Englishman, telling him the line take. "There is no room to make errors at Indy. If you turn in half a car's width too late you are in the wall. It's not like other tracks where you can try high and low lines. I didn't have the experience of what the car should feel like so I was having to learn a tremendous amount while not making any mistakes and trying to get the car up to speed. The was a lot of information I was having to take on board but we were still going very quickly."

Conventional testing now commenced and the team was gradually removing wing in preparation for qualifying. "Everything felt very good and we were in the top ten. We came to 'Fast Friday' and we were going really well. Indeed, at one point Lloyd was fifth fastest. At this point it all went wrong.

"I have to say that we got a bit carried away, trying to go faster too early," said Andy Brown. "I'll admit that I made a mistake on the setup as we were trimming the car out. I mistakenly put down that we should

Lloyd follows Jaime Camara during practice in 2008. (Author's collection)

been important for the League to help put a drive together for him. Indianapolis, though, was still on the cards.

There was never any intention that his entry for the race should be a one-off, but by the April there was still no sponsor for a third

Lloyd's wild ride down the pit lane has just come to an end. (Author's collection)

add front wing instead of taking it out. What happened was totally not Alex's fault, but a driver with more experience would have said that it did not feel right and parked it. The car did perform a bit of a wiggle coming out of Turn Four, the lap before he had his accident."

"I was going into Turn One ..." recalled Lloyd, "... when I realised something was not quite right and I smacked into the wall very hard. [Lloyd's head went through about 180g during the impact.] From that moment the month changed dramatically for us."

Suffering from neck pain, Lloyd was hospitalised for a couple of days while the badly damaged car was repaired; never an ideal situation. When he did get back into it, having missed the first day of qualifying, he was still not feeling right. The car never seemed as good as it had done prior to the crash, and his speeds dropped massively. "From being competitive in the top ten we were barely scraping into the top twenty. We just could not figure what was wrong. Something

did not feel right and I did not have enough experience of driving an Indy car to say what was wrong."

After the accident, a combination of trying to over-compensate for what had happened plus the very cold weather meant that the team was not able to string together a satisfactory run. "The wind was always howling and so that was moving the car around," said Brown. His colleagues at Target Chip Ganassi confirmed this but their drivers, Wheldon and Dixon, were able to compensate for it, thanks to their far greater experience. Lloyd did not really know what the car should feel like in these conditions, and so the team never really evolved a good race setup. "It was probably the worst year that a rookie could have chosen to take on the Indy 500 because the weather was atrocious," he said.

Lloyd qualified nineteenth. This was much further down the pack than the two regular Ganassi drivers, and thus Brown felt that the

His 2008 race over, Lloyd glances back down the pit lane to see just how far he has spun. (Author's collection)

he could see where he was going and, through sheer luck "threaded the needle" between the attenuator and the pit wall. When he did hit the wall it was a glancing blow and nowhere near as bad as Lloyd had envisaged. "I lucked into that." The accident still looked spectacular as the Dallara continued to spin down the pit lane, bouncing of the wall but, thankfully, nobody working in the lane was hurt. As he came to a stop, Lloyd felt that "I had dodged a bullet."

It was a bittersweet month for Lloyd but Brown had been impressed. "I'd love another crack at Indy with Alex," said Brown over the next winter. "I have a supreme belief in his ability." He was to get his chance.

The following year Lloyd was still on Ganassi's books but with no sponsor to ensure a series drive. However, a deal was done with HER Energy Drink that enabled him to enter the Indy 500 with a joint effort, rather like the previous season but with Sam Schmidt Motorsports this time providing the partner for Ganassi. Brown was again part of he package. Right from the start Lloyd was the centre of attraction. The problem, if that is what it was, was the sponsor HER (Healthy Energy Revitaliser) was an energy drink marketed at women ... and its colour scheme was pink. That meant not only a pink car but also a pink suit and helmet. You have to give Lloyd his due, he saw the positive side of this and soon he was being referred to as "Pink Lloyd" after the band, Pink Floyd. As if that was not enough to ensure the column inches, his

team had to run him with more downforce than was being used on Dixon and Wheldon's cars. However, the rain light bracket that had been added that year to slow the cars down made the rear wing very inefficient. "When you added downforce, you added quite a lot of drag. That meant he had too much drag to pass people."

Lloyd was still not happy with the car as race day loomed. "Deep down I did not feel that our troubles were going to go away." And thus it proved. Very quickly, especially from the second stint onwards, he realised that he was struggling just to hold on to the car. At the first pit stop, someone, Lloyd reckoned it was fellow Brit Darren Manning, hit his rear wheel and the car had to be repositioned. "Whether that did any damage it is difficult to say but we were really hanging on. What should have been the most enjoyable experience quickly became a day I wanted to end. Every lap I felt I would be in the wall soon."

The team kept lowering his Dallara at each pit stop to get more grip and eventually went too far and the car bottomed out in Turn Four. This bounced it to the right and on into the wall. The bottoming out was only something that was noticed on the data later. To Lloyd it felt as if the car had simply stopped turning. The car grazed the wall, fishtailed and he felt that he might have held on to it. "Then it just snapped." The car was now facing the opposite way down the track and, in Lloyd's mind heading toward the attenuator of the pit wall. "If I hit this it is going to be really, really bad." The car then swung round so that

Pink Lloyd. (Author's collection)

Lloyd passes the pits during the final Friday practice session in 2009. (Courtesy Tim Wagstaff)

wife Sam was due to give birth at about the time of the race. At one point the due date was about a week later, then it was put about that Sam might deliver that very day, although she breezed through the pits during the week as if nothing was about to happen. Initially, this was a 'wind-up' but then it seemed that the baby might, indeed arrive a week early. Sam told pit lane reporters that she was having contractions every five minutes during the race. Indeed, she was having them on the Saturday night, although she did not tell her husband. After the race the couple went to the hospital and stayed there until about 2.00pm the next morning when it was decided that the contractions had been a false alarm, probably brought on by the stress of the race. In the event, the supportive Sam was still appearing in public at the Victory Banquet, baby Bethany having the decency not to put her father under too much pressure by arriving on June 2.

Speaking in the months prior to the 2009 race, Lloyd reckoned his situation to be similar to that of the previous year. He had competed in only three races in 2008 and it would be a whole twelve months between oval races. "We are definitely making it tough for ourselves. It is like being thrown in at the deep end with a mildly heavy weight, which is not quite pulling you down but is stopping you from swimming."

Impressively, Lloyd qualified on the first day, in eleventh position. Dario Franchitti recalled that he had felt his own car was good and told Andy Brown to use the same settings for Lloyd's car. "We seemed to be quick when we needed to be quick," said Lloyd. "I felt pretty confident going into the race."

However, come the day, the young Englishman had to pit early on to have his rain light fixed, putting him a lap down. He returned to the track with the lead pack and then proved himself more than capable of staying with it. "It showed what he and the car could do," said Brown.

"What happened ..." admitted the engineer, "... was a moment's carelessness by one of the guys who assembled the car." It had been

EMMA DAVIES-DIXON

Sally Stokes had been forced to watch her then boyfriend, Jim Clark, win the Indianapolis 500 from the grandstands. In 1965 women were not allowed in the garage area, let alone the pits. By 2008 all that had changed, and the pits were where Scott Dixon's English wife, Emma, wanted to be. "I had a suite pass, but I was almost too scared to leave the pits where I could see the crew and hear Scott's voice. I did go up to the suite on a couple of occasions during the race, but I would be there for about two seconds before I snuck back down."

The month had, she said, been "weird." There seemed an inevitability about the result. "After Scott had got the pole it felt like the win was always going to happen." On the morning of the 500 she made him his traditional race day breakfast of pancakes – "... the English version, not the American!" Her husband left the motor home at about 9.00am to attend to various duties, and she tidied up before he returned and they walked to the track together. "I try and give him a pep talk and probably make him more nervous." When Dixon was summoned to the stage to be introduced to the fans, Emma headed for the grid. "Even though I am a Brit through and through I have to admit that Americans know how to put on a sporting event."

For Emma the 2008 race could not have been better. "We had the big win that year and it was such a British affair. I had seven people over from the UK, including one of my sisters, Rhea, and my mum. After the race, I was crying, running down the pit lane to the winner's circle in my six-inch wedge heels – I don't know what I was doing that morning when I got ready. I was shaking with three laps to go. Scott always looks out for me and I got to him straightaway. I made my exit as I knew the milk was coming and I didn't want my hair to get wet!" Emma points out that she never has to struggle to greet her husband straight after a race. "They (the Speedway officials) really encourage the family to be part of the win.

"The days that followed were a whirlwind. That evening, we went to a nightclub but Scott was so tired. The next minute we were getting up ready to attend the morning photography session. Then were whisked off to New York for a media tour. Every network you name, Scott was on it."

The sporting life was nothing new to Emma for she is an athlete in her own right, and was the leading lady 800 metres runner in Great Britain for three years. She has competed in two Commonwealth Games as well as the World Juniors. Husband and wife train together and Emma believes that they have the same mental attitude towards competition, something that not all wives might share. "I think I am harder on Scott than the average girlfriend."

Emma had first met Dixon not long before the 2006 500. The New Zealander was in London on business and did not know anybody. A mutual friend rang Emma and asked if she and some friends could take him out for the evening. "It was nothing romantic, I was dating someone at the time but my friends left us early noticing that we had really clicked. We spent the next two days hanging out together and starting dating about a month later." Emma flew out to Indianapolis to watch practice that year, although she was unable to stay for the race. However, "I got a taste." In the August she moved to the US to be with Scott, and in 2008 they were married.

The following year's 500 must have been a worrying time for at least three of the drivers in the race. A trio of wives were pregnant and two of those were British. Alex and Sam Lloyd's baby was due at any time, leading to various rumours about when and just what the father would do if the child should appear on race day. For the Dixons the timing was less crucial, and in July their daughter Poppy was born.

Emma Davies-Dixon poses with husband Scott the morning after his victory.
(Author's collection)

noticed in practice by Dario Franchitti that Lloyd's rain light, which should also come on when the yellow is thrown, was not working. It was returned to Target Chip Ganassi Racing for repair, and then it seems that when it was fixed back onto the car the bolts were not done up. As Brown observed, it was to show just what a team sport motor racing is. An entire month's work was to be ruined by a moment's carelessness.

"The main reason for running him in the third car was to give him experience and he certainly got an education in something," said Brown. "He was, at least, able to see what it was like running with the leaders." Lloyd, though, was able to get that lap back and then found himself running further down the pack on the road "... which is a different ball game," observed the engineer. "You look at the steering

A lap down following his early pit stop, Lloyd proved he could run with the leaders. Eventual winner Helio Catroneves appears to be trying to intimidate him with a flying tear-off visor. (Author's collection)

and throttle traces and it is all arms, elbows, and doing a tap dance with your right foot."

Brown sums up: "He didn't give up, the team didn't give up, and he did very well. It was a heck of an achievement to get the lap back." The result was thirteenth place, not bad at all when one considers that the errant light had put him to back of the field.

Sam Lloyd (centre) almost stole the headlines by having contractions while husband Alex (left) was out on track contesting the 2009 Indy 500. A year on and the Lloyds were back at the Speedway with their now two daughters, Ava and Bethany. The livery of Lloyd's Dale Coyne car celebrated the 100th anniversary of the Boy Scouts of America. (Courtesy Indianapolis Motor Speedway)

28

ON TWO WHEELS

"I said that it would have been all right as long as [the bricks] had been repointed."

The first races round the Indianapolis track were not for cars but for motorcycles. Some said these contests, which took place in 1909, were a fiasco, others a qualified success. Whatever, it is pretty certain that no British were involved and it would be almost a century before the motorcycle brigade was to return. When it did so the entry was international. Ninety-nine years after that first meeting British motorbike racers took to the Indianapolis track, albeit one very different from that first event.

The loss of the Formula One Grand Prix was a blow to Tony George's ambition of making Indianapolis "the racing capital of the world." However, the addition in September 2008 of a round of the MotoGP World Championship certainly underlined the fact that the track was no longer a once a year race wonder. The intervention of Hurricane Ike was to cast a shadow on the event but the signs were all there that it could become a regular fixture on the Indianapolis calendar.

The appalling conditions that first year caused the 250cc race to be cancelled but four British riders did get the chance to compete on the programme, including the reigning Superbike champion, James Toseland, who had now moved up to MotoGP.

In the 125cc race fifteen-year old Quedgeley-born schoolboy rookie Scott Redding was in fourth place when the red flag was shown on lap seventeen. Just one tour earlier he had been third – a podium place – but a missed gear on the main straight dropped him back a spot. Starting from ninth on the grid, the Aprilia rider, who some weeks before had won the 125cc British GP, had stormed up to second on

the opening lap before settling down to a steady third. Fellow Brit and Aprilia rider, Oxfordshire's Bradley Smith finished eighth after a sluggish start, while the third English teenager and one of the smallest riders on the grid, Danny Webb, came in fifteenth having qualified fourth.

In the main event Britain had just one contestant, Toseland. The days when Britain provided many of the leading runners in the top motorcycle Grand Prix class are long gone but in 2008 twice Superbike World Champion – not to mention talented piano player – Toseland succumbed to the lure of MotoGP. Twenty-seven-years old at the time of his Indianapolis debut, the Yorkshireman was looking to a spot in the top ten of the championship at that stage, but a disastrous choice of tyres damaged his chances. It was certainly an eventful week for the Tech 3 Yamaha rider, which started, as do such things, in Las Vegas.

Toseland flew out to Nevada on the Saturday evening a week before the race to help launch the new Yamaha R1 superbike. "The Sunday was just a rehearsal day for a pool party at the Mirage Hotel. Yamaha has 1500 dealers in North America so there were 3000 guests there. Everywhere you looked there was a Yamaha T-shirt. We all rode out to fireworks on R1s. The show was just spectacular. Afterwards we went to the Circ de Soleil. It was the one with the Beatles theme so I felt quite at home. I also sat there waiting for a heart throb of mine, Cher, but she cancelled at the last minute through illness."

Yamaha may be known for its motorcycles but its largest industry is the music sector for which it manufactures everything from pianos to French horns, and when it comes to pianos Toseland is able to show

James Toseland had twice won the World Superbike Championship before moving into MotoGP.
(Author's collection)

Toseland played piano with the Indianapolis Symphony Orchestra the week of the first MotoGP there. (Courtesy Indianapolis Motor Speedway)

that his talents are not just confined to 'bike racing. His own band, 'Crash,' is a class act, mainly performing classic 1980s American rock from such as Guns and Roses, Bryan Adams, Bon Jovi, U2, and ACDC. On the Tuesday, Yamaha had booked Toseland and his band to perform an outdoor concert at the Mirage. "It was a really good gig. They seemed to know all the songs." The next morning he flew to Indianapolis to get on with the serious business of 'bike racing.

Not quite so. On the Thursday he had barely taken his leathers and helmet out of their crate before he was on a stage in the paddock playing 'Walk in Memphis,' 'Mustang Sally,' a couple of his own songs, and 'In the Mood,' the first song that he had learnt on the piano, with the Indianapolis Symphony Orchestra. "We had no rehearsal, we didn't even know what we were playing but it went down well." The proceedings went to a charity known as Riders for Health, which buys motorcycles for medics in Africa, enabling them to travel to remote places.

"We have all heard about the Indy 500 and I was looking forward to just seeing the track. It's the biggest seated arena we perform in. What also excited me was that it would be a new track for everybody. It promised to be a great weekend but, unfortunately, it was the same weekend as Hurricane Ike."

Toseland was, at last, out on the track itself on the Friday. He had previously raced at the Lausitzring, which is also an oval track with an infield. Toseland compared the two, "It was similar to the EuroSpeedway, just on a bigger scale." Toseland reckoned the track designers to have "... done a pretty good job on the layout. There is only so much you can do when designing a track within a restricted area.

"It was interesting to look at the yard of bricks and think that the whole track was made up of that. One of the officials asked how would I have liked to have raced on the bricks. I said that it would have been alright as long as they had been repointed."

The riders' first session out on track lasted an hour and a half rather than the normal hour, as

Toseland at Indianapolis in 2008, although, with the weather appearing fine, it must be assumed that this was not the race itself.
(Courtesy Indianapolis Motor Speedway)

the circuit was unknown to everyone. The weather was appalling with continuous rain. Indeed, it was so bad that the riders boycotted the last ten minutes of the second session. "We couldn't see Turn One, it was just a lake."

"The build up was going so horribly wrong," said his young compatriot in the 125cc race, Bradley Smith.

Toseland described what faced the riders that day. "The first turn was obviously covered in new asphalt. That was OK but the drainage was terrible. There were two sections, comprising three or four corners, of this new surface. When it rained, Turn One did not drain at all. There was such a massive puddle, which decided whether we were or were not racing. In the dry it was fine. It was a third gear, over 100mph

entry, followed by a tight Turn Two and Three, and then a first gear hairpin. Then you accelerated up to fourth gear before going 'inland' from the Indy track and a second gear left-hander, and then back onto new asphalt ... and more water. There was, without exaggeration, twice as much grip on the old surface as the new one. You almost had to have two riding styles. You could push so hard on the old and then slam the brakes on and just try to get past the new. This made it difficult to set the bike up. The suspension had to be so stiff to cope with the braking and acceleration forces on the old asphalt but then you wanted it soft to find some grip for the new.

"Then we went down the back straight, which was parallel to the start and finish. The corners were very similar on both sides of

All the riders, including Toseland, struggled to keep their bikes upright on the straights in 2008. (Courtesy Indianapolis Motor Speedway)

the track; left, right, left, right, chicane. The last corner was a really tight left-hander just inside Turn One of the 500 oval. The only way it was separated from the old track was a metal curve that acted like a chock. This was good for us as it was almost like a berm in moto-cross. If that had not been there we could have used a lot more of the track but then we would have had the wall on the outside!" said Toseland. Bradley Smith who, despite being only seventeen at the time, had already enjoyed a career in moto-cross, recalled that the first thing he noticed as he walked the track was these temporary metal curves, which were bolted into the surface of the track. "If you ran out of road you just had to jump over them and carry on using the Indy car track to rejoin when you could."

The forecast for the Saturday was more of the same but it turned out to be a pleasant day. Toseland recalled that predictions for race day varied, "... some said we would be lucky, others not. On the Sunday morning we woke up and it wasn't too bad. It was still dry for the warm-up but the closer it got to the race the darker it got overhead. Just before we started to race the rain really came down with gusts of 70 to 80mph."

About half an hour before the race, when the riders were thinking about getting suited and booted up, the wind was gusting unbelievably. The 250cc race, which was supposed to have started before the MotoGP, was stopped because of the rain and the wind ... which the crowd did not appreciate. "I was looking out of a window having a cup of tea and thinking this is not going to happen. The canopies on the pit lane were being blown down. That shows you just how strong the wind was." Just before the race the wind died down and the rain stopped. Now it was just like a normal, grey, wet race day. Toseland went out on the warm-up lap "... and everything seemed good." With the rain clouds certain to return, he chose a softer Michelin tyre.

Toseland was tenth on the grid but made a good start to move up to seventh, feeling that he was slightly gaining on the leading pack. However, it refused to rain again for a good fifteen laps and the old, grippy asphalt started to rip up Toseland's tyres. "As it was drying out so I was going backwards. Then, with about ten laps to go, the hurricane really hit. I was leaning at an angle down the straights to compensate for the wind. On one lap the wind would be from the left, the next it would be from the right. There were all kinds of debris flying about the track. I was going into Turn One dodging coke cans and dustbin liners. I thought 'what the hell are we doing out here' and just as I thought that the red flag came out with seven laps to go." Thanks to

the problems that he had encountered, the frustrated Toseland had dropped all the way back from seventh to eighteenth. Television reporter Suzy Perry warned him not to take off his leathers yet because there was talk of still running an eight-lap dash. "I looked out of the garage and asked where was this taking place, in Spain? It just wasn't possible."

Toseland voiced his sympathy for the Speedway at having to experience such conditions for its first MotoGP. "Other than the weather and the drainage, everything else – the track, the organisers, and the fans – were all fantastic."

He intended flying back to the UK on the Sunday evening. At first a ten-minute delay was announced for his flight. Then the plane arrived, the passengers disembarked, and the flight was called off. The official reason was a technical fault but, given the weather conditions, Toseland admired the fact that the plane had even got to Indianapolis. Stranded, he went first to a sushi bar with Perry, and then on to a party hosted by one of his sponsors, Red Bull. The next morning, fearing that he might get stuck with his connection flight, he cadged a lift to Chicago with some of the BBC crew. At about 5.00pm he eventually flew out from Chicago for the UK.

A year later Toseland was back and, in considerably better conditions, finished sixth, equalling his career best. It was felt that the result had boosted England's only MotoGP rider's chances of remaining in the series. However, at the end of the season he was replaced in the Tech 3 team by Ben Spies, returning to World Superbikes on the Yamaha vacated by Spies.

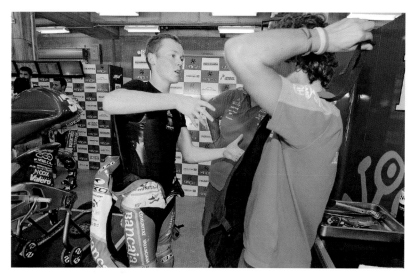

Bradley Smith makes a point in his garage at Indianapolis. (Courtesy Bradley Smith collection)

There was greater success for the British in the 125cc race that year with young Bradley Smith finishing second on his Aprilia, a scant 0.12 seconds behind the winner. The 18-year old Bancaja Aspar Team rider described Indianapolis as one his favourite races of the season. Added to the helpfulness and friendly nature of the people involved, there was a small matter of the US being an English-speaking country. The MotoGP event does not attract anywhere near a full crowd, and Smith mused on what it must be like to see the stadium full. "It looks empty with just 70,000 to 80,000 people." Nevertheless, on his first visit in 2008, Smith was struck by how different the Speedway was to the majority of tracks visited by the 125cc World Championship.

Smith, who was 125cc World Championship rookie of the year in 2006, appreciated that fact that, in 2008, the 125cc riders were the first ever to practice on the new track. He noted that it was something of a "bitza" circuit that did not flow, nothing like any other that he raced on during the season, "... but not bad." Ironically, the new

"The commentators were going ballistic" as Bradley Smith fought for the lead in the 2009 125cc race. (Courtesy Bradley Smith collection)

surface was flooding and slippery, whilst the old was giving the best wet grip he had experienced all season. During the dry Saturday qualifying the riders had about ten laps to discover which rubber to use. Smith admits he was caught napping and finished way back, one of his worst qualifying performances of the year – it left him concerned for the race. His start was reasonable, but he was knocked onto the grass on the second corner, falling to near the rear of the field. He charged through the field, setting fastest laps, and was up to eighth when the race was cut short. Such was his progress through the field that he believes a podium was a possibility had it gone full distance.

That first year Smith also managed a round of golf, part of a charity event, on the Speedway's own course. He was teamed with former Grand Prix star, his mentor, Randy Mamola, plus British 125cc compatriots, Scott Redding and Danny Webb.

For 2009 Smith decided to motor down to Indianapolis from Chicago on the Wednesday, and was disappointed to discover that there was nothing to see on the long drive. Unlike the previous year, there was only one, slightly longer Friday practice session. With more rubber on the track it was in a much better condition. He felt good with the bike from day one. In each sector during qualifying he was often the quickest, but could not get the speed in the last section to set a fastest time, and finished fifth overall. On the Saturday evening the team went to the downtown Hard Rock Café. The atmosphere was electrifying and the parking appalling. It was, thought Smith, definitely worth going downtown to experience the night before a race, although this was probably not a good idea for those competing the following day.

Having already won two races earlier in the season, Smith felt that he could make it three at Indianapolis. Five riders, of which Smith was one, pulled away from the rest of the field. The nature of the track was such that, closely bunched though the group was, passing was proving difficult. On the last lap Smith slipstreamed down the main straight and went

Smith's father, Allan, came across this group of visiting Brits who were obviously delighted by the podium place. (Courtesy Allan Smith)

The chequered flag is waved for Smith's second place. (Courtesy Bradley Smith collection)

GUY SMITH

The Indianapolis 500 has been run most years since 1911, with usually thirty-three cars on the grid. Yet, in all that time, no driver with the surname Smith has ever qualified for the race. In some cases it has not been for want of trying.

Yorkshireman Guy Smith, who in 2003 was to be in the winning Bentley at Le Mans, was one such. Much of Smith's latter career has been spent racing in the US, most recently in the American Le Mans Series. He first went there to try his luck in Indy Lights, finishing his first year second in the championship. In 2003 he also spent a half season in Champ Car having replaced the inexperienced Nelson Philippe in the Rocketsports Racing team.

In 2000, Smith was driving a Reynard sports car for the Johansson Matthews team partly owned by former Grand Prix driver and Indianapolis veteran Stefan Johansson. The Swede knew that he was still intent on racing single-seaters and possibly Indy cars. "Stefan, being the wheeler-dealer that he is, was speaking to March founder Robin Herd." Herd wanted to bring the March name back to Indianapolis and ultimately become a constructor again. Some, what Smith now refers to as "so-called backers," were going to fund the project.

Johansson was going to be team manager for the programme and it was he who put Smith's name forward to drive in the 500. A fairly unknown team, Sinden Racing, was to run the car. The idea was that Jeff Sinden should run a Dallara that year, with a new March chassis appearing, phoenix-like, the following year.

Sinden Racing was based in Gasoline Alley almost opposite the Johansson Matthews workshop. Smith was able to spend time there, having his seat fitting and getting ready for his rookie test. A first instalment of $50,000 had been promised but this had not arrived on the due date. "That was the first sign that things were a bit 'iffy.'" Every day Smith and Sinden would jump into the latter's truck and drive to the bank. Despite promises to Herd from the 'investors,' no money seemed to be appearing. The rookie test loomed and Sinden decided that he would run the car for that whatever. "Just don't crash it."

"I turned up at the Speedway. It's just an awesome place, a bit like Le Mans," recalled Smith. "When you drive into these kind of places they give you butterflies. It is something that Silverstone just can't do. It is so special." He had already driven a number of the short ovals in Indy Lights and really enjoyed them "... but Indy, which is not strictly an oval, was something else."

Al Unser Sr oversaw Smith's test as he built up speed. "We had lots of wing on it so it was very easy. I got to the point where I had done about 215mph. I had by now passed my rookie test and everything was going well. Jeff Sinden suggested that we take some downforce off, start trimming the car, and see what speed we could do. I was flat out all the way round and got up to about 218mph before coming in to make an adjustment." At this point a valve train failure brought a halt to the proceedings.

It was by now, though, increasingly obvious that the 'investors' were not going to provide the money promised. "It was going to be fantastic, an exciting project – March has a great history – but unfortunately it never happened," recalled Smith. To date, no Smith, British or otherwise, has started the Indy 500.

around the outside into Turn One for second place. The commentators were "going ballistic." On the last lap he set a new lap record but a slight mistake on the final bend meant not enough speed to catch the leader. For his second place, to his delight, he was given a trophy that featured one of the original bricks from the Brickyard. The previous year's British podium man, Scott Redding, who was suffering from an ankle injury, retired in the race, while Danny Webb came home eleventh. Smith's performance had shown that there was the potential for British racers to win at Indianapolis on two wheels as well as four, and it came as no surprise to find that he was one of the favourites for the 125cc championship as the 2010 season loomed.

No Smith has ever started the Indianapolis 500, although Guy Smith took his rookie test. In 2003 he did win another of the world's classics, the Le Mans 24-hours. (Author's collection)

29

THE RECORD-BREAKERS

"That was really fast."

It was 3.33pm on 'Bump Day' for the 2009 Indianapolis 500. Indy Car Series chief operating officer Brian Barnhart gave the traditional handshake to the next driver due out on the track, Mike Conway from Bromley, England. In the tenseness of the moment, its significance to the story of the British at Indianapolis was probably going unnoticed.

Rookie Conway had qualified fairly comfortably for the race the previous day, having crashed hard during one of the earlier qualifying sessions. ("I had hit my head and they asked me in the medical centre what day it was. The month of May is so long at Indianapolis that I would not have been able to answer even if I hadn't had the accident.") However, it was cooler the next day and conditions at the track had improved considerably. Of the three drivers who had not made the grid, two were good enough to improve on their times to 'bump' the slowest of the qualifiers. They, in turn, would be forced out onto the track again; they too would improve and, so, one by one, the slower drivers found themselves 'on the bubble.' Eventually, the session would end and somebody was going to get caught out.

Brian Barnhart gives final words of advice, as Mike Conway is about to set off on Bump Day.
(Author's collection)

The Fab Four, (left-to-right) Darren Manning, Mark Taylor, Dan Wheldon, and Dario Franchitti, walk the 'Abbey Road' bricks. IMS director of photography Ron McQueeney had fun trying to capture the iconic Beatles image. Several times the quartet walked past but only a single frame had one of them – Manning – out of step. (Courtesy Indianapolis Motor Speedway)

Conway's Dreyer and Reinbold team was not going to be that one. Team-mate Milka Duno had already run at around three mph faster than the previous day, so the team withdrew Conway's Saturday time and wisely, long before it was necessary, sent him out again. If he could again make the grid a record would be broken – five Britons, the highest number ever, would have qualified for the Indianapolis 500.

Barnhart sent him on his way, observing that he had done a good, clean, consistent run the previous day and advising him to do the same again with no heroics. What was the pressure like? "I was busting for the toilet, so I was trying not to think too much about going to the loo as I went out." The first lap looked good – 221.799mph, the next three were slightly slower but enough for an average of 221.417mph. With what he described as a fairly conservative car, Conway was back in the field, twenty-seventh on the grid and more Brits than ever were about to start the race. It could so easily have been more. Darren Manning had 'subbed' for Dreyer and Reinbold earlier in the season, and was seen, complete with helmet, in the paddock hoping to find a drive that could help him improve on his ninth place of the year before. The previous year's Freedom 100 winner, Dillon Battistini, was also in deep negotiation with a potential sponsor and with HVM Racing right up to the last minute.

"Yesterday I didn't know what time I had to achieve, today I was sure of what time I had to do," said Conway. "We knew we would be quicker because it was cooler. I just had to get in the right frame of mind. You still have to go out there and do it each time. I really pushed it on that first lap. We put up a good number, and then I was just trying to keep it consistent. I was getting more comfortable with the car every run. The car felt good underneath me. It was still a bit windy through Turn One. I had to keep it flat and consistent. Hopefully we'd done enough to be safely in the field."

During the winner's press conference in 2007 an English journalist, having listened to a spate of comments from the locals with regard to Dario Franchitti's Scottish heritage, decided to redress the balance with a question that reminded him that he came from Great Britain. "People keep telling me that," said the patriotic Scot with a smile. "Did he ..." asked the scribe, "... think that, following his and Dan Wheldon's wins in the 500 added to Alex Lloyd's victory in the Freedom 100 two days before, more British drivers would be attracted to race at Indianapolis?" Franchitti agreed that this might be the case.

Whether it was due to the above influence or not, but by 2009, a record number of British drivers were on the grid for the 500. Excluding the two winners, the first of the new generation of Brits had arrived in 2004, with Mark Taylor making his only appearance and Darren Manning the first of his four to date. The IRL celebrated the occasion with a photo of the four British drivers that year walking on a pedestrian crossing, re-enacting the famous photo of the Beatles outside the Abbey Road recording studios. (In September 1964, the Merseyside group had performed at the Indiana State Fair, staying at the Speedway Motel adjacent to the track. The Speedway's director of photography, Ron McQueeney, also recalled meeting George Harrison at the Long Beach Grand Prix in the early 1990s. The former Beatle expressed a desire to photograph the Indy 500 and McQueeney offered to put him on his staff with a fake name tag so that no one would know he was there. Harrison thought about it but decided that it would be too much of a pain if someone recognised him.)

In 2003 Taylor had run away with what was then known as the Menards Infiniti Pro Series, the feeder championship that was to become Indy Lights. The word "annihilation" was used as he won seven of the twelve events. On two of the oval tracks he led every lap from pole, while at Chicagoland he was engaged in a battle for the lead that changed seventeen times. He only managed third in the Freedom 100 at Indianapolis, though, his first defeat of the year.

Taylor, who was driving for the Panther Racing team that

Mark Taylor made his sole Indianapolis appearance in 2004. (Courtesy Indianapolis Motor Speedway)

season, had proved adept at this level, having come from the British Formula Three championship the previous year in which he had gained a pole, one victory, and seventh in the standings. Prior to that, he had been European Formula Ford champion. Perhaps his drive with Panther flattered to deceive for he was unable to maintain his progress when he moved up to the Indy Racing League in 2004 to drive a Dallara-Chevrolet for Team Menard. He was involved in accidents in five of his six starts with the team, including Indianapolis where he crashed on lap sixty-two. He was subsequently dropped by Menard, finishing the rest of the season with Access Motorsports. Failing to secure a drive for 2005, he returned to England. By contrast, Darren Manning, as recorded earlier, was in Indianapolis to stay.

It was to be another four years before any more new Brits came

along and, like London buses, there were two of them. Franchitti was having his 'year out' with NASCAR but 'old hands' Wheldon and Manning were joined by former Grand Prix driver Justin Wilson and by the previous year's Freedom 100 victor, Alex Lloyd.

The 2001 Formula 3000 champion Wilson had raced at Indianapolis before when he came eighth in the 2003 US Grand Prix for Jaguar. "That was strange. You came to this famous place that was all about high speed and great tradition. Yet we were going round on a track that was fairly pathetic. You felt like a bit of a fraud. Thus, I really liked coming back in 2008 and going out in the right direction on the proper track. It just felt right. I enjoyed it from the moment that I got there. It was very relaxed and friendly compared to Formula One. It had the openness of club racing and yet all the seriousness of a professional series."

Wilson's Formula One career had ended and he had moved into the Champ Car series, initially with Conquest Racing and then with RuSport. During his four years in the series he was placed third in the championship and then twice the runner-up with a total of four wins. At the end of 2007 Wilson took over the Newman Haas Lanigan drive of four times champion Sebastian Bourdais and looked likely to inherit the Frenchman's mantle. However, it was not to be. Over the winter the so-called merger took place between the IRL and Champ Car and, from being the favourite, Newman Haas Lanigan found itself one of the disadvantaged 'transitional' teams. "It all happened so fast that we were on the back foot from the start. By the time we got to Indianapolis the former Champ Car teams were doing whatever they could to keep going."

At Newman Haas Lanigan there was tragedy when Londoner Davey Evans, an old school mechanic with the team, was savagely kicked in the head during an altercation in an Indianapolis bar and died shortly afterwards. The coroner's office stated that a stroke had been induced by the stress of the fight. Evans had originally worked at Lola before moving to the US in 1970 to join the then Lola distributor Carl Haas. When Haas and Paul Newman started their Indy car team the knowledgeable Evans became a permanent fixture. Following his death, the team was in a sombre mood as Wilson took his rookie test. "It was a difficult time for everybody."

Towards the start of the race itself, Wilson was on a different pit stop strategy from most of the field. Not stopping when most did under a yellow flag, he was at one point running as high a second. There was nothing particularly clever in this strategy, just a late call to stop that came as Wilson was already past the start of the pit wall. "I knew it was not going to last long." The only, and probably forlorn, hope was that he might get lucky with a pit stop that put him on the same cycle as everyone else, and yet kept him near the front. He was pleased to find that, although the Newman Haas Lanigan Dallara was not as quick as the Ganassi cars that were looking the likeliest winners, Wilson was able to hold his own. "I enjoyed that part of the race."

On lap 133 he felt the back of his car lighten up so came off the throttle. "It just slowly came around and the next thing I know I'm going backwards. I tried to keep it out of the wall, but it just ran out of real estate."

For 2009 Wilson moved to the Dale Coyne team, which had no way near the equipment and resources of NHL. Prior to the Indy 500 he felt that the team was making progress, proving this later in the season by winning a road race at Watkins Glen – the first ever championship victory for Coyne as either a driver or entrant, despite a history that went back to 1984. There

'I'm lovin' it.' Justin Wilson made his 500 debut in 2008. (Courtesy Indianapolis Motor Speedway)

was also a marked improvement in performance from the time that the team arrived at Indianapolis to qualifying day. "It was really cool to see," said the tall Wilson.

The race itself proved to be something of a disappointment. Wilson had been running midfield when, during a pit stop, he performed a half spin in front of his box and stalled. He worked his way back up the field to tenth before losing eleven places in another single pit stop. With forty laps remaining, he hit the wall for the second year running, his car sliding round the south chute to come to a stop on the exit to Turn Two. "The car started to turn towards the wall and I tried to get it back down but couldn't save it."

Wilson's younger brother Stefan accompanied him to the Indy 500 that year but did not compete in the Freedom 100. Although he had a package to race in Indy Lights with Walker Racing, it did not include the ovals. He mused on the possibility of two English brothers in the same team for a future 500. "Now that would be really cool."

Justin appears not to hanker after Formula One. "I want to enjoy my racing and that is what Indy Cars do for me, enable me to enjoy my racing. That's a bigger deal." He is also very aware of the British influence on the series that has now become his home. "One in ten people in the paddock seem to be of UK origin, even our truckie Mike (Cole)."

In February 2010 it was announced that Wilson was leaving Dale Coyne to join Dreyer & Reinbold Racing, thus creating a two man English line-up at the Indianapolis-based team ... which neatly brings us back to the newest Brit in the 2009 500. Dennis Reinbold had been impressed by a test that Mike Conway had with Panther at Infinion Raceway in 2008 and was looking for a driver who could perform on the road courses. Once signed by Dreyer & Reinbold, Conway had

In 2009 Wilson was regarded as one of the best Indy cars drivers not then with a top team. (Author's collection)

tested at Homestead – where he delighted Reinbold – and run a race at Kansas, otherwise Indianapolis would have been his first laps on an oval. Actually, his first were on foot, running in a mini-Marathon around the track. He recalled that he came "500th and something" but there were around 35,000 contestants. His time of 1h 29min just achieved his aim of a sub 1 hour 30min run.

After the Homestead test, which saw him fastest rookie, Dreyer & Reinbold team manager and fellow Englishman Gary Neal had described Conway as "... a driver who is going to surprise many people. He is so calm and in control. He is very much like Ayrton Senna when he got out of the car, never out of breath and never excited." (Neal had worked with McLaren during Senna's time with the team.)

Conway quickly became comfortable during his Indianapolis rookie orientation laps. Engineer Larry Curry recalled that after his first fifteen circuits averaging around 190mph he returned to the pits, observing, "That was really fast!" As he got quicker so he then felt he was actually going slower, but, as Curry pointed out to him, his brain was adjusting to the speed. It is Curry's belief that road racers adapt to ovals far quicker than vice versa.

The following day was rained off and people told Conway that this was what he must expect from the month of May. He kept looking at the empty grandstands, realising that they would be nearly full come race day. He was living in his home in Carmel to the north of the city and, on race day, he found it "pretty cool" to have a police escort to the Speedway. Come the driver introductions to the fans Conway really started to realise what this race was all about. Not only were many of his family present but also his manager, former Grand Prix and Champ Car driver Mark Blundell, whose time in the latter series coincided with the 'split,' thus meaning that he had never driven in the 500 himself.

With eight minutes to go before he had to

You can't stop 'ere, sir. Wilson's run in 2009 came to an end on the exit to Turn Two. (Author's collection)

Wilson took his Z-Line Furniture sponsorship with him to Dreyer & Reinbold for 2010, and continued to show how competitive he was on the road circuits. Here, he leads a couple of Penske entries on his way to second place in the Long Beach Grand Prix (Author's collection).

get in the car, Conway realised that he did not have a water tube in his helmet. Luckily, the team had a spare piece; it fitted better than the old tube. At the beginning of the race he just wanted to ensure that he finished. Halfway, and climbing through the field, he began to think that he could have "a good result." Now he wanted to do more than just finish. If you had asked Conway five years previously if he would have wanted to race on ovals he would have answered with a resounding no. Now he confessed to really enjoying the discipline.

As the race drew to a close, Conway was in tenth position with his nearest challenger for rookie of the year, the far more experienced Canadian Alex Tagliani, three cars back. The team was not sure about the fuel situation and thought that others were about to pit, so Conway was called in to ensure enough ethanol to the finish. Apart from Ryan Briscoe who was, anyway, out of sequence, and Conway's two team-mates, nobody else pitted. Caught out, Conway finished a disappointing

Mike Conway (24) in the pack for the start of his first 500. (Author's collection)

At one point Conway looked to be in the running for the 2009 Rookie of the Year award. (Courtesy Tim Wagstaff)

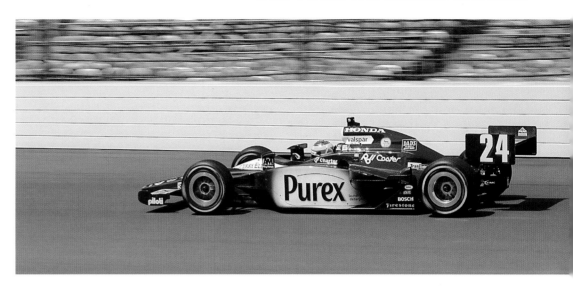

eighteenth as a result. He had certainly proved himself, though. At one point just before half-distance, he set a lap time that was the fastest for quite a while and, ultimately, second quickest of the day. It was Franchitti who eventually beat him to the fastest lap. The British may not have won in 2009 but, with the two fastest laps, Wheldon's second overall and the fact that Franchitti led the most laps, they had again made their mark.

On being reminded of his comment at the 2007 winner's press conference that his win might attract more British drivers to Indianapolis, Franchitti said, "Are we here now? I hope so, there is such a rich seam of British talent about."

By the end of the season the signs were there that there might even be more Brits at the 2010 Indianapolis 500 than the record-breaking five of the previous year. Franchitti, Wheldon, Wilson, and Conway all seemed established. Alex Lloyd, freed from his Ganassi contract, had run his second race of the year, having joined Newman Haas Lanigan for the final IndyCar Series round at Homestead where

The opening rounds of the 2010 IZOD IndyCar Series saw five Brits amongst the regular entries. Mike Conway (seen here) had been joined in the Dreyer & Reinbold team by Justin Wilson. Alex Lloyd had moved to Dale Coyne, while Dario Franchitti and Dan Wheldon remained with Ganassi and Panther respectively. Jay Howard joined their ranks at Kansas, all six on the entry list for the Indianapolis 500 when it was announced in late April. (Author's collection)

Beatle George Harrison (right) would have liked a photographer's pass for the Indy 500. Ron McQueeney (centre) would have been happy to oblige. Here they socialise with Emerson Fittipaldi. (Courtesy Dan R Boyd)

THE DELTAWING

Indianapolis had been abuzz in early February 2010 and it had had nothing to do with its Colts team getting to the National Football League Super Bowl. British designer Ben Bowlby's much-anticipated and futuristic design for the next Indy car was to be unveiled at the Chicago Auto Show. The philosophy behind the DeltaWing, as it was known, was to reduce the amount of power required to produce 235mph laps times and therefore the amount of fuel needed, in line with road car modern trends.

Rumours that the DeltaWing might look something like Craig Breedlove's land speed record breaker Spirit of America proved correct, although FIA regulations ensured that it did have two front wheels – any less and it would have been classified as a motorcycle. Those front wheels, though, were incredibly close together and tucked well into the bodywork. Bowlby pointed out that 54 per cent of the drag of the current Indy cars was the exposed rotating wheels. "Enclosing them creates a sports car, which is not the identity wanted. The breakthrough was that the vehicle dynamics are very robust if you go for a narrow track with a much more rearwards weight distribution and widely-spaced rear wheels."

The differential featured full torque vectoring active technology with drive control of gain for balance adjustment. The steering lock was the same as any conventional car, making it perfectly suitable for somewhere like Long Beach.

Lap speeds of 235mph were being predicted, using half the horsepower and improving fuel economy by 100 per cent over the current Indy Dallara. The ultra narrow front track design saved weight, while the fairings for the front wheels both reduced drag down to below 0.24 CD – about 40 per cent of the current car – and prevented wheels from interlocking. The delta plan view shape also provided undisturbed airflow to the downforce generating ground effect underbody venturi located beneath the car's centre of gravity. This was just ahead of the widely-spaced rear wheels. The resemblance to Spirit of America was enhanced by a high rear fin. This replaced the conventional inverted rear aerofoil in order to broaden the yaw stability envelope without inducing drag on the straights. Eighty per cent of the downforce acted on the rear of the car.

It was predicted that, if it won IRL approval, a prototype would be on the track by August 2010. It was intended that this would be powered by a 2.0-litre 4-cylinder turbo-charged engine, which along with the transmission would be a non-stressed member of the chassis structural design. "The car has been designed with an engine cradle that can accommodate and incredibly wide variety of engine configurations and capacities," said Bowlby. He believed that it would need to produce around 300hp to attain performance targets. "With this kind of performance, why would you want a V8?" asked Panther Racing's John Barnes. It was hoped that the project would encourage multiple engine suppliers.

A cost of just $600,000 with engine was being predicted, so it was perhaps not surprising that the team owners were said to be fully behind the project. DeltaWing did not see itself as a manufacturer, although it would be responsible for the production of the prototype. Bowlby said that he would be happy for a manufacturer such as Lola to be involved as a sub-contractor. "We don't intend becoming a racing car constructor." However, he was to be disappointed when, in mid-July, the IRL rejected Bowlby's proposal in favour of a Dallara-built chassis.

he had underlined his undoubted ability after a misjudged first turn. A planned 2010 season with NHL did not materialise when his sponsorship deal fell through. However, he became a last minute addition to the opening round at Sao Paulo driving for Dale Coyne. At the end of 2009, Sarah Fisher Racing announced that it had signed Jay Howard for a number of races, including the 500. Then, in the February, KV Racing tested Oxford-born Formula One development driver, James Rossiter. With Battistini apparently a possible for, at least, the oval races and Manning still in the wings, it looked as if the British influence could be greater than ever during the hundredth anniversary of the first Brit ever to race there.

British designer Ben Bowlby's revolutionary vision of the future IndyCar. (Courtesy DeltaWing)

HUNDREDTH YEAR EPILOGUE

The hundredth anniversary of Hughie Hughes' first appearance at the Indianapolis Motor Speedway saw the most dramatic 500 of all for the British, arguably surpassing even the 1966 race: Dario Franchitti became the first Brit ever to win the event twice; there were four Brits in the top seven, with a podium lock out before a protest dropped one of them back from third to fourth; three Brits led the 500 at some stage, one of whom was involved in a horrendous accident just before the end; while another Brit became the first lady to take the pole for the Freedom 100, indeed for any race at the IMS. To add to all that, the Rookie of the Year's team principal was British. (And, for those that were interested, former Indianapolis Grand Prix winner Lewis Hamilton came first in the Turkish Grand Prix the same day as the 500, with fellow Brit Jenson Button in second.)

The 2010 proceedings almost began with a record number of Brits making what was to be the hottest Indy 500 on record. It was close, so very close. Six of them took part in the new, two-day only qualifications for the race, while it was announced that a seventh, A1 GP champion Adam Carroll from Northern Ireland, had signed with Andretti Autosport for later in the IZOD IndyCar Series season. With the clock ticking all six were in the field, but newcomer Jay Howard

Car owner Sarah Fisher wishes Jay Howard well during the 2010 qualification weekend. Despite the messages of goodwill written on his helmet, the Englishman was caught out by the drama of Bump Day's final minutes. (Courtesy Indianapolis Motor Speedway)

was 'on the bubble,' despite having been quickest in the morning's general practice session. Driving for Sarah Fisher Racing, Howard had also been fastest during the Rookie Orientation Programme but now, faced with being 'bumped,' he withdrew his time, added a little more front wing to combat understeer, and took to the track again, only to post a slower average speed. Such are the draconian rules of Indy 'Bump Day' that meant he was out of the next week's race, ironically replaced by a driver who had not been as quick. The gamble had been even more dramatic than Mike Conway's the year before but this time it had failed. "I didn't think this would happen," he reflected, but it did, making him the first Brit to be permanently bumped from an Indy 500 grid.

Of the five that remained, Dario Franchitti, Justin Wilson, and Conway had all qualified the day before, the Scot in what now seemed his usual third place. The new rules meant that only the first twenty-four made the grid on the Saturday. Alex Lloyd quickly ensured that he joined their number by being second fastest of the Sunday qualifiers.

Between qualifying and the race, came the Freedom 100 and, although the field of Indy Lights cars was smaller than normal, four of them, a quarter of the field, were British. There was also the matter of a 10-lap iRacing computer simulation race with three of the 500 starters competing against 'drivers' around the world. Two of the trio were British, with Wilson finishing but Conway being eliminated in a 'crash.' It was an unfortunate omen.

Up until this point Sam Schmidt Motorsports' Pippa Mann had not been having a particularly successful season. However, on Thursday May 27, 2010 in practice for the Indy Lights race, she became the first female pole winner in the history of the Indianapolis Motor Speedway. During the morning practice the team worked on how the car would run in traffic, in the afternoon, as the weather became hot, so it went to work on its speed. "I knew I had a fantastic car in traffic, but I was quicker than I thought I would be in clean air," she observed. "I have a car that I can drive inside, I have a car I can drive outside, I have a car that likes the dirty air, I have a car that likes to be out front."

Come the race, Mann made a poor start and was in the middle of the pack heading into Turn One on the third lap when Jeff Simmons spun and took her out. She exonerated the American reckoning that he had been pushed hard down by her Indianapolis nemesis, Martin Plowman.

Behind Mann, Dan Clarke was competing at Indianapolis for the first time, her former team-mate Plowman was back to see if he could get a lot further than in 2009, while Stefan Wilson was making his oval debut. None of these three Britons was to bring the trophy back to the UK, being placed fourth, fifth, and seventh respectively, the younger Wilson finishing in the same place his brother Justin would be in the forthcoming Sunday's 500. Clarke really enjoyed what he described as "one hairy race," Plowman stormed into second place at the start but fell back as his car developed a push, while Wilson was pleased with a seventh considering his rookie status. The same day, Dario Franchitti topped the speed charts during final practice for the 500, another omen perhaps.

As usual there was no racing at the Speedway on the Saturday, but to the north west of the city American Conor Daly took his third victory in a row when the Star Mazda Championship cars visited O'Reilly Raceway Park for the traditional 'Night Before the 500' meeting. The relevance was that Daly is the son of Irish Indy 500 veteran Derek.

Come the Sunday Franchitti again proved himself the fastest man on the track, although this time over the full 500 miles. He hit the front within the opening turns of the race, and from then on dominated the proceedings leading five times for a total of 155 laps, including the vital last eight. At times he was as much as ten seconds ahead of the field, and only fell back due to strategy vagaries. Fellow Brits Conway and Wilson also hit the front, the former from laps 163 to 177, the latter taking over from him until lap 188. Earlier in the race Graham Rahal put Wheldon onto the grass at over 220mph, receiving a penalty for his misdemeanour. Unlike his fellow Brits, Dan never saw the lead but steadily made his way through the field as he had done the previous year.

The race leaders pitted on lap 163 in the hope that they could make it to the finish but from then until almost the end there were no cautions and fuel consumption became an increasing problem.

With just twenty laps to go there were several drivers gambling on alternate strategies as Wilson was in the lead with Franchitti back in fifth. Then the Englishman was forced to pit for fuel, others did the same, and on lap 192 fellow Brit Franchitti returned to the lead he was to retain until the end.

During the final stint Wheldon continued to move up the field, passing both Tomas Scheckter and Marco Andretti, while several others who were out of sequence had to dive into the pits. With five laps remaining he trailed only Franchitti, and Tony Kanaan and then the Brazilian, too, had to pit for fuel, leaving the two Brits at the head of the field and heading for a repeat of 1966.

Franchitti was obviously saving fuel. With just over a lap to go there were a couple of backmarkers between him and Wheldon. Such was the leader's reduced pace that the tail-enders unlapped themselves in Turn Three, leaving the Englishman to see the Scot ahead. The gap narrowed rapidly. Panther team manager Chris Mower admits that his man was also on an economy run but believed that the Target Chip Ganassi car was in a worse position. Whereas in the closing laps of the previous year Wheldon was more in danger of losing his second place than taking the lead, now Mower thought there could be a chance of victory.

Then Mike Conway, who had looked set for a top ten finish, and Ryan Hunter-Reay became entangled in the frightening crash in Turn Three, which catapulted the former into the air. Whether or not Wheldon could have run down Franchitti became academic. As Hunter-Reay, low on fuel, slowed down, so Conway made contact, his Dallara being launched into the catch fencing before being ripped in half, the cockpit section coming to rest upside down on the track. Conway, who waved to the crowd as he was taken from his car, went to the Methodist Hospital where he had surgery to repair fractures to his lower left leg. He also had a soft tissue injury to his leg and a compression fracture of one of his thoracic vertebrae, resulting in his being out of racing for some months.

Some of the non–specialist British media predictably dwelt more on Mike Conway's horrific crash than on Dario Franchitti's historic second win.
(Courtesy Indianapolis Motor Speedway)

As in 2007, Franchitti led past the chequered flag under caution. That previous time, although he had deserved his victory, there were others who were often quicker during the race. In 2010, he had been the dominant driver and even Mower admitted that had Wheldon passed him on that last lap, it would have been a victory of strategy over pace. The yellow lights, though, ensured that this was never put to the test and Franchitti became the first Brit ever to win America's greatest race twice. For the second year running, Wheldon both started in eighteenth position and finished in second.

"Up until ten laps to go, I was pretty relaxed. Then all hell broke loose with fuel savings and all. I just needed to know what the other guys were doing. If they were saving more than me, they were doing

something special here," reported the winner who earned a purse of $2.75 million. "He's the consummate professional," observed his team boss, Chip Ganassi.

Wheldon wistfully admitted that he was perhaps more disciplined than he had been in the past. In the final three laps the team was "... getting on my butt about saving fuel." He mused that a younger Wheldon might have ignored them, taken more notice of his spotter than the pits, and tried to run Franchitti down when he saw that he was slowing.

Impressively, Alex Lloyd advanced twenty-two positions in a relentless march to fourth place. "I figured out a way of how I could save fuel and still get good runs on people at the end. I was lifting a lot

Same scene as 2007, except that the rain has been replaced by hot, dry conditions and there is an Englishman behind the Scot. (Courtesy Indianapolis Motor Speedway)

going into turns one and three, saving the fuel, but then keeping it hammered through the exit of one, exit of two, and saving through three and four, to get a good run out. It meant I could jump some spots while saving fuel. That was really the key for us.

"The boys did a great job in the pits. We said beforehand we know that we've got a good car. We know that where we qualified wasn't where we deserved to be based on speed. So we figured we'll keep digging, we'll keep working, we'll be patient and the race will come to us, and it did. This is maybe even better than we could have dreamed of," said Lloyd after the race. He had originally been classified in third place, but Marco Andretti successfully protested that he (and two others) had passed him under the final yellow and the young Manxman was relegated to fourth, still a great result for the unfancied Dale Coyne team. Lloyd had undergone a frustrating time since his Indy Lights championship but the 2010 500 was, as he stated, "... a great day. It was even better when it was a Brit sweep of the podium but still first, second, fourth, and seventh isn't a bad day for the Brits!"

Justin Wilson, who was to auction off his race day helmet for charity, finished seventh. The team knew towards the end that it was ten laps short on fuel. The key, reckoned Wilson, was to push as hard as possible, stretch the field out and be able to stop in a good position. Asked about leading, it was, he replied "Nice to have a taste of that." Unlike many of the other front-runners, he was not having to conserve fuel towards the end, leading to another 'what if' the last lap yellows had not come out.

Simona de Silvestro took the Rookie of the Year award driving for Briton Keith Wiggins HVM team, while, perhaps little noticed back in twentieth position, following a pit stop

Alex Lloyd put the tribulations of 2008 and 2009 behind him to finish an impressive fourth. (Courtesy Indianapolis Motor Speedway)

Japanese driver Takuma Sato's helmet celebrates the history of the British at Indianapolis, bringing together 1965 and 2010. (Courtesy Lotus)

A very British hug. Franchitti and Wheldon congratulate each other as the Scot's actress wife, Ashley Judd, stands by with a Caledonian flag. (Courtesy Indianapolis Motor Speedway)

penalty, was a Japanese driver in an Italian car that honoured the British at Indianapolis. Lotus had been assisting in the aerodynamic and suspension development of Takuma Sato's KV Racing car and had been funding work in Dallara's Varano de'Melegari wind tunnel. "Lotus Engineering and Motorsport has been looking into areas such as how to reduce friction levels at oval circuits and improve the overall control and stability of the car at street and road circuits," reported Lotus director of motorsport Claudio Berro. The advent of a new IndyCar formula for 2011 begged the question, would Lotus return to the Brickyard as something more than just a team partner? Berro was cautious, but perhaps teasing, in his reply; "The advent of new regulations always offers new challenges and potentially new opportunities. The potential to start on an even playing field could be an interesting proposition. It is true to say that we are keeping a close eye on the situation and, depending on the nature of the new rules and the future direction of the sport, this could prove to be a catalyst to change the way we approach the [IndyCar] Series."

"I've missed you." Franchitti is reunited with the Borg Warner Trophy; the first British driver to acheive this. (Courtesy Indianapolis Motor Speedway)

Sato's helmet, the colour scheme of which was the work of Lotus designer Jason Fowler,

ONE FRIDAY EVENING IN SUMMER

Jim Clark's historic 1965 500 winning Lotus 38/1 was consigned to the Henry Ford Museum in Greenfield Village, Michigan in the late 1960s. There it deteriorated into a sorry state before Ford realised just what it owned and sent it to Classic Team Lotus – run by Colin Chapman's son, Clive – back in the UK for restoration. The result did this iconic car justice at last.

The restored car ran for the first time in public at the 2010 Goodwood Festival of Speed, driven by Sir Jackie Stewart (in a dark blue helmet in tribute to his friend Clark) and Lord March. As the evening shadows lengthened on the Friday, Charles March drove the car down to the start line. Two gentlemen in immaculate black shirts made their way to the trackside fence in the hospitality area. They were two of the slow talking, fast moving Wood brothers, Leonard and Delano, who had help make that 1965 victory possible. They had not seen the car since that day 45 years earlier when the British had first set their stamp on the Indianapolis 500.

There to see Lotus 38/1 for the first time in 45 years, Leonard (left) and Delano Wood. (Author's collection)

paid tribute to Jim Clark's 1965 victory with an image of his Lotus 38, while his car brought the iconic and patriotic green Lotus livery back to the Speedway. There was no doubting that the British had become part of the very fabric of the Indianapolis 500.

The Friday evening of the 2010 Goodwood Festival of Speed, and Charles March sets off up the hill in the 1965 Indianapolis 500 winning Lotus. (Author's collection)

APPENDIX 1

British citizens and British-born drivers who have practiced for or raced in the Indianapolis 500

ROBERT ARBUTHNOT
1946 Lagonda   DNQ

HENRY BANKS*
1936	Miller	Alternate
1937	Viglioni	Relieved Ronney Householder
1938	Miller	21st
1939	Cheesman	DNQ
	Weil	Relieved Billy DeVore
1940	Cheesman	Incomplete qualification attempt
	Alfa Romeo	Relieved Chet Miller
1946	Snowberger	27
1947	Miller	24
1948	Miller	DNQ
1949	Miller	Bumped
1950	Maserati	25 (Relieved by Fred Agabashian)
1951	Lesovsky	6
1952	Lesovsky	19
1953	Hopkins	Incomplete qualification attempt
1954	Hopkins	DNQ

JUSTIN BELL
1996 Lola   DNQ

LESLIE BROOKE
1947 ERA   DNQ

JIM CLARK
1963	Lotus	2 (Rookie of the Year)
1964	Lotus	24 (Pole)
1965	Lotus	1
1966	Lotus	2
1967	Lotus	31

MIKE CONWAY
| 2009 | Dallara | 18 |
| 2010 | Dallara | 19 |

JIM CRAWFORD
1984	Theodore	Incomplete qualification attempt
1985	Lola	16
1986	March	29
1987	March	Wrecked in qualifying
1988	Lola	6
1989	Lola	19
1990	Lola	15

1991	Lola	26
1992	Lola	25
1993	Lola	24
1994	Lola	DNQ
1995	Lola	DNQ

JOHN DUFF**
1926 Elcar   9

ERNEST ELDRIDGE
| 1926 | Eldridge | 19 (relieved by Herschell McKee) |
| | Eldridge | Relieved Hawkes |

JACK FAIRMAN
1962	Kimberley Special	DNQ
	Concannon Choice Car	DNQ
	Connaught	DNQ

DARIO FRANCHITTI
2002	Dallara	19
2004	Dallara	14
2005	Dallara	6
2006	Dallara	7

2007	Dallara	1
2009	Dallara	7
2010	Dallara	1

W DOUGLAS HAWKES

1922	Bentley	13
1926	Eldridge	14 (relieved by Eldridge)

JOHNNY HERBERT

2002	Dallara	DNQ

GRAHAM HILL

1963	Thompson	Wrecked in practice
1966	Lola	1
1967	Lotus	32
1968	Lotus	19
1969	Lotus	DNQ

DAVID HOBBS

1971	Lola	20
1973	Eagle	11
1974	McLaren	5
1976	McLaren	29

JAY HOWARD

2010	Dallara	DNQ

HUGHIE HUGHES

1911	Mercer	12
1912	Mercer	3
1913	Keeton	Relieved Bob Burman
1914	Rayfield	DNQ
1915	FRP	DNQ
	Maxwell	Relieved Billy Carson

RUPERT KEEGAN

1986	March	DNQ

ALEX LLOYD

2008	Dallara	25
2009	Dallara	13
2010	Dallara	4

DARREN MANNING

2004	Panoz	
	G-Force	25
2005	Panoz	
	G-Force	29
2007	Dallara	20
2008	Dallara	9

NIGEL MANSELL

1993	Lola	3 (Rookie of the Year)
1994	Lola	22

ALFRED MOSS

1924	Barber-Warnock	16
1925	Miller	Relieved Herb Jones

DARIO RESTA[†]

1915	Peugeot	2
1916	Peugeot	1
1923	Packard	14 (Relieved by two drivers)

GEORGE ROBSON*

1939	W-A Rotary	DNQ
	Litz	Alternate
	Blume	Relieved Harry McGuinn
1940	Miller	23
1941	Greenfield SS	DNQ
	Weil	25
	Adams	Relieved Tommy Hinnershitz
1946	Adams	1

(Note Canadian born brother Hal Robson 1946, 25; 1947, 20; 1948, 15; and 1949 and 1950 DNQ)

JOHN SCALES

1920	Gregoire	DNQ

MIKE SPENCE

1968	Lotus	Wrecked in practice, died

JACKIE STEWART

1966	Lola	6 (Rookie of the Year)
1967	Lola	18

MARK TAYLOR

2004	Dallara	30

NOEL VAN RAALTE

1915	Sunbeam	10

JEFF WARD*

1995	Lola	DNQ
1997	G-Force	3 (Rookie of the Year)

1998	G-Force	13
1999	Dallara	2
2000	G-Force	4
2001	G-Force	24
2002	G-Force	9
2005	Dallara	27

DAN WHELDON

2003	Dallara	19
2004	Dallara	3
2005	Dallara	1
2006	Dallara	4
2007	Dallara	22
2008	Dallara	12
2009	Dallara	2
2010	Dallara	2

JUSTIN WILSON

2008	Dallara	27
2009	Dallara	23
2010	Dallara	7

COUNT LOUIS ZBOROWSKI

1923	Bugatti	20

Republic of Ireland

DEREK DALY

1983	March	19
1984	Lola	27
1985	Lola	12
1986	March	DNQ
1987	March	15
1988	Lola	29
1989	Lola	15

MICHAEL ROE

1985	Lola	DNQ

* Born in the UK but moved to North America and became a US citizen.
** Born in China of Canadian parents, lived most of adult life in England.
[†] Born in Italy but moved to England as a child and became a British citizen.

DNQ Did not qualify

APPENDIX 2

British-built chassis that have raced in the Indianapolis 500
(Total qualified plus wins)

SUNBEAM
1913 (1), 1914 (2), 1915 (2), 1916 (1), 1921 (3*)

BENTLEY
1922 (1)

COOPER
1961 (1)

LOTUS
1963 (2), 1964 (3), 1965 (5, win), 1966 (4), 1967 (3), 1968 (3), 1969 (1)

FERGUSON
1964 (1), 1965 (1)

BRABHAM
1964 (1), 1965 (1), 1966 (1), 1968 (2), 1969 (3), 1970 (2), 1971 (2), 1972 (2)

LOLA
1965 (2), 1966 (3, win), 1967 (3), 1968 (1), 1969 (3), 1970 (1), 1971 (2), 1972 (3), 1978 (1, win), 1979 (2), 1980 (3), 1983 (2), 1984 (2), 1985 (6), 1986 (8), 1987 (5), 1988 (18), 1989 (24), 1990 (21, win), 1991 (28), 1992 (27), 1993 (28), 1994 (20), 1995 (18), 1996 (21)

BRP
1965 (2), 1966 (1), 1967 (1)

MCLAREN
1970 (2), 1971 (4), 1972 (5, win), 1973 (7), 1974 (6, win), 1975 (7), 1976 (6, win), 1977 (7), 1978 (8), 1979 (4), 1980 (3), 1981 (3)

PENSKE
1978 (3), 1979 (9, win), 1980 (12), 1981 (13, win), 1982 (3), 1983 (5), 1986 (1), 1988 (3, win), 1989 (5, win), 1990 (8), 1991 (3, win), 1992 (3), 1993 (4, win), 1994 (6, win)

CHAPARRAL
1979 (1), 1980 (1, win), 1981 (1), 1982 (1)

MARCH
1981 (3), 1982 (17), 1983 (18, win), 1984 (29, win), 1985 (23, win), 1986 (24, win), 1987 (28, win), 1988 (12), 1989 (4), 1990 (4)

GALMER
1992 (2, win), 1993 (1)

REYNARD
1994 (7), 1995 (15, win), 1996 (12, win)

G-FORCE**
1997 (14, win), 1998 (13), 1999 (10), 2000 (18, win), 2001 (13), 2002 (10)

* One of these cars was branded a Talbot Darracq.
** G-Force's UK base was closed in September 2002. In early 2003 a few carbon tubs were manufactured in the UK by SPA Design but these were shipped to the US where final assembly took place. From then on, all tub production and car assembly took place in the US.

APPENDIX 3

British engine manufacturers that have raced in the Indianapolis 500 (Total qualified plus wins)

SUNBEAM
6-cylinder	6.1-litre	1913 (1)
6-cylinder	4.5-litre	1914 (2), 1915 (1)
4-cylinder	4.4-litre	1915 (2)
6-cylinder	4.9-litre	1916 (1),
8-cylinder	3-litre	1921 (3)

BENTLEY
4-cylinder	3-litre	1922 (1)

COOPER-CLIMAX
4-cylinder	2.75-litre	1961 (1)

COSWORTH
DFX AND DFS
8-cylinder	2.65-litre t/c	1976 (1), 1977 (4), 1978 (11, win), 1979 (20, win), 1980 (24, win), 1981 (29, win), 1982 (29, win), 1983 (32 win), 1984 (30, win), 1985 (30, win), 1986 (29, win), 1987 (22, win), 1988 (20), 1989 (14), 1990 (5), 1991 (5)

XB
8-cylinder	2.65-litre t/c	1992 (4), 1993 (12), 1994 (18), 1995 (23, win), 1996 (24, win)

JUDD*
8-cylinder	2.65-litre t/c	1987 (2), 1988 (2), 1989 (5), 1990 (3), 1991(4)

ILMOR
8-cylinder**	2.65-litre t/c	1986 (1), 1987 (6), 1988 (7, win), 1989 (7, win), 1990 (10, win), 1991 (12, win), 1992 (17, win), 1993 (14, win), 1994 (7), 1995 (5), 1996 (1)
8-cylinder[+]	3.4-litre	1994 (3, win)
8-cylinder[++]	3.5-litre	2003 (9, win),
8-cylinder[++]	3.0-litre	2004 (11), 2005 (14), 2006 (33, win), 2007 (33, win),
8-cylinder[++]	3.5-litre (ethanol)	2008 (33, win), 2009 (33, win), 2010 (33, win)

* Including branded Brabham/Honda
** Including branded Chevrolet and Mercedes-Benz
[+] Branded Mercedes-Benz
[++] Branded Honda

APPENDIX 4

Race appearances by British drivers and riders at the Indianapolis Motor Speedway other than in the Indianapolis 500

1910
SEPTEMBER MEETING

Five-lap handicap Hughie Hughes	Parry	6th
Two lap scratch race Hughie Hughes	Parry	8
Five-lap handicap Hughie Hughes	Parry	5

1916
HARVEST RACING CLASSIC

20-mile race Hughie Hughes	Hoskins Special	3
50-mile race Hughie Hughes	Hoskins Special	2
100-mile race Hughie Hughes	Hoskins Special	2

2000
US GRAND PRIX

David Coulthard	McLaren	5
Eddie Irvine	Jaguar	7
Johnny Herbert	Jaguar	11
Jenson Button	Williams	Ret

2001
US GRAND PRIX

David Coulthard	McLaren	7
Jenson Button	Benetton	10
Eddie Irvine	Jaguar	14

2002
US GRAND PRIX

David Coulthard	McLaren	3
Jenson Button	Renault	8
Eddie Irvine	Jaguar	10
Allan McNish	Toyota	15

2003
US GRAND PRIX

Justin Wilson	Jaguar	8
David Coulthard	McLaren	Ret
Jenson Button	BAR	Ret

FREEDOM 100

Mark Taylor	Dallara	3

2004
US GRAND PRIX

David Coulthard	McLaren	7
Jenson Button	BAR	Ret

2006
US GRAND PRIX

David Coulthard	Red Bull	7
Jenson Button	Honda	Ret

THE BRITISH AT INDIANAPOLIS

FREEDOM 100

Jay Howard	Dallara	2
Alex Lloyd	Dallara	5

INDY PRO SERIES IMS ROAD RACE

Alex Lloyd	Dallara	1
Scott Mansell	Dallara	14
Jay Howard	Dallara	18

2007

US GRAND PRIX

Lewis Hamilton	McLaren	1
Anthony Davidson	Super Aguri	11
Jenson Button	Honda	12
David Coulthard	Red Bull	Ret

FREEDOM 100

Alex Lloyd	Dallara	1

INDY PRO SERIES IMS ROAD RACE

Alex Lloyd	Dallara	2

2008

FREEDOM 100

Dillon Battistini	Dallara	1

INDIANAPOLIS MOTORCYCLE GRAND PRIX
MotoGP

James Toseland	Yamaha	18

125cc race

Scott Redding	Aprilia	4
Bradley Smith	Aprilia	8
Danny Webb	Aprilia	15

2009

FREEDOM 100

Jay Howard	Dallara	4
Ali Jackson	Dallara	19
Pippa Mann	Dallara	21
Martin Plowman	Dallara	22

INDIANAPOLIS MOTORCYCLE GRAND PRIX
MotoGP

James Toseland	Yamaha	6

125cc race

Bradley Smith	Aprilia	2
Danny Webb	Aprilia	11
Scott Redding	Aprilia	Ret

2010

FREEDOM 100

Dan Clarke	Dallara	4
Martin Plowman	Dallara	5
Stefan Wilson	Dallara	7
Pippa Mann	Dallara	16 (pole)

INDEX

Northeast American Sports Car Races

1950-1959

Terry O'Neil

Hardback • 25x25cm • £100 • 432 pages • 475 photographs • ISBN: 978-1-845842-54-3

This unique, hugely comprehensive book examines the emergence of sports car racing in Northeast America between 1950 and 1959. It was a defining era for the nascent sport, whose evolution was neither easy nor uneventful for drivers, clubs or track owners – the politics, intrigue and tragedy that came to characterise the period are covered here in fascinating detail. Also features extensive results tables for almost every event of the time.

LOTUS 49

THE STORY OF A LEGEND
BY MICHAEL OLIVER

In association with the Ford Motor Company Limited

FOREWORD BY KEITH DUCKWORTH OBE

Hardback • 25x20.7cm • £50 • 256 pages • 300 photographs
• ISBN: 978-1-904788-01-0

The Lotus 49 was one of the most evocative and successful Formula One cars of its era, and the first to use the Cosworth DFV V8 engine. Here is the definitive story, from inception to the fate of the cars today. Includes a racing record and individual chassis histories. A highly acclaimed book.

– 4th Edition with Revised Chassis Record –

LOLA
T70
THE RACING HISTORY & INDIVIDUAL CHASSIS RECORD

The definitive racing and development history of one of Britain's most important sports racing cars. Includes international competition history and completely revised individual chassis histories of the T70, T160 and T165.

Hardback • 25x20.7cm • £45 • 192 pages • 200 photographs
• ISBN: 978-1-845841-89-8

For information on any Veloce book, call 0044 (0)1305 260068, email info@veloce.co.uk, or visit us on the web at
www.veloce.co.uk / www.velocebooks.com • Prices subject to change • P&P extra